Needs
Assessment

THEORY AND METHODS

Needs Assessment

THEORY AND METHODS

EDITED BY
Donald E. Johnson
Larry R. Meiller
Lorna Clancy Miller
Gene F. Summers

IOWA STATE UNIVERSITY PRESS ⏻ AMES

Composed by Iowa State University Press from disks provided by the volume editors
Printed in the United States of America

First edition, 1987

Library of Congress Cataloging-in-Publication Data

Needs assessment.

Bibliography: p.
Includes index.
1. Needs assessment.   2. Needs assessment — Political aspects.   3. Needs assessment — United States.   I. Johnson, Donald E.
HN29.N43   1987   302.3   87–16972
ISBN 0–8138–0241–5

Contents

v

Foreword

THIS BOOK ADDRESSES one of the thorniest
questions about the democratic process. How can every citizen be given a
chance to participate in decision making? In small and simply structured
groups the issue of how individuals make themselves heard is not pressing.
Communicating with those who manage the public's affairs is relatively
easy. But most late twentieth-century political systems are neither small nor
simple. Broadly speaking, they fall into one of two categories: either they
are already modern, industrialized, and technologically sophisticated, or
they are struggling to become so. In both cases, there is likely to be little
communication between the citizenry and the political and economic elites
directly responsible for making and implementing public policy.

To be sure, there have always been and will continue to be political
movements that question the need for controlling elites of any kind. Most
revolutions, including the American Revolution, have been fueled by the
idea that government should be by as well as for the people. Similarly, the
recurring call for increased citizen participation by all the people at least
some of the time is based on the notion that increased political activity
means diminished government control (Barber 1984).

But revolutionary fervor dies down after a time, and in modern complex societies even greatly increased citizen participation can never eliminate or even significantly reduce the institutions and bureaucracies that
characterize their governments. German sociologist Robert Michels made
the point early in this century. In his seminal book, *Political Parties,* he laid
down what has come to be the major political argument against Rousseau's
concept of direct popular democracy. He "argued that the malfunctioning
of existing democracy, in particular the domination by the leadership over
the society and popular organizations, was not primarily a phenomenon
which resulted from a low level of social and economic development, inadequate education, or capitalist control of the opinion-forming media and
other power resources, but rather was characteristic of any complex social
system" (Lipset 1962). Michels formulated the "iron law of oligarchy,"
which stated first that nation states cannot function without large institutions and second that large institutions cannot function without being dom-

vii

inated by the few who hold positions at the top. To be sure, there are advantages to this arrangement. The general public saves time and energy while its collective affairs are handled by officials who presumably have the requisite expertise. But that brings us back to the problem of how ordinary people can make themselves heard and participate in decision making.

Those in the business of needs assessment address precisely the issues of community integration, self-help, and empowerment. As noted in Chapter 3, needs assessment serves as the means by which these goals are achieved. This does not mean, of course, that soliciting people with regard to their needs, wants, and wishes is without its own problems. In fact, concerns that bedevil even the best-intentioned efforts to get individuals and groups to speak on their own behalf attest to the fine line between being caring and being patronizing.

Consider these hard questions: Who is doing the assessing? How can assessors get respondents to articulate their own agenda instead of merely responding to agendas set for them? And do those practicing needs assessment have a responsibility to concern themselves with getting needs addressed as well as expressed?

It should be said at the outset that to collect data there must be funding. Thus assessment of needs demands legwork and demands that some private or public agency put up the cash to secure the information. By definition, then, most needs assessment projects are backed by individuals or groups in positions of power. To really understand any given needs assessment project, therefore, we must find out whose idea it was in the first place, why it was deemed necessary or desirable, and how it was decided to invest human and material resources into getting this particular population to express itself. Obviously, the range of information uncovered in an investigation of this kind will be quite wide. The motivations for undertaking needs assessment programs undoubtedly include the extremes — on the one hand, a genuine interest in finding out so as to respond and, on the other, the attempt to legitimize decisions that have already been made by others.

The problem of how needs assessors can get target populations to voice their real concerns inevitably prompts the questions of why needs assessment programs are necessary in the first place. In a democracy, at least, citizens should surely be able to articulate their needs without special efforts. What are we really saying then when we say needs assessment? We are admitting that in some cases people will be able to express themselves only when we undertake a program of inquiry devised specifically for that purpose. At the same time, we know that those with resources such as education, money, and organizational skills are usually quite capable of making themselves heard. At the least, they are more able to do so than those without these advantages. In general, then, needs assessment projects are designed to uncover the preferences of those who are for one reason or another unwilling or unable to speak up on their own. But there is a problem here: this is precisely the population that is generally the least well equipped to recognize and articulate what it lacks—even when directly asked.

Gaventa (1980) explores this problem. He asks what it is about certain situations of social deprivation that prevents issues from arising, grievances from being voiced, or interests from being recognized. "Why, in an oppressed community where one might intuitively expect upheaval, does one instead find, or appear to find, quiescence?"

Taking his cue from the work of Freire (1970) in Latin America, Gaventa concludes that for groups to develop a political consciousness they must have some opportunity for political participation, "for nonparticipation serves to preclude 'conscientization'." This suggests, in short, that if needs assessors are interested in uncovering citizens' genuine concerns (rather than in merely getting them to respond to agendas already framed by others) they must first ascertain that these particular individuals have had the political experience that will have enabled them to develop a political consciousness.

Finally, there is the issue of whether those conducting needs assessment programs ought to concern themselves with follow-up. Having stimulated people to express their needs, does the investigator have a moral and political responsibility to see to it, at least insofar as possible, that these needs are addressed? In short, is it enough simply to collect and interpret data?

I would argue that needs assessment studies should not be undertaken without some commitment to obtaining the resources necessary to address the deficiencies that such studies are likely to reveal. In general, needs assessment programs are conducted with at least some foreknowledge of what they will reveal. The virtues of expanding on that early information seem to be purely academic unless the additional data is used to some practical political end. In that sense, it behooves people in the business of needs assessment to assume leadership roles. Having uncovered what is required, they are on some level at least responsible for generating the political support necessary to furnish it.

This book can only begin to grapple with some of these tough issues. Its singular virtue is that it does in fact provide both sociopolitical context and methodological information. In short, the chapters that follow are intended for those with a special interest in needs assessment and for those with a more general commitment to a responsive society.

BARBARA KELLERMAN

Political and social contexts of needs assessment

CHAPTER 1

Democratic governance

GENE F. SUMMERS

CITIZEN PARTICIPATION in decision making is the essence of needs assessment. It concerns grass roots democracy and the importance of people being free and able to express their views on matters that affect their lives, families, and communities. Needs assessment is a social institution that integrates ideas from political theories of democracy with practices flowing from the mainstream of social science research. In the broadest sense, citizens participate in community and societal activities in many ways: as consumers, as members of voluntary civic groups, through religious organizations, and in electoral politics. However, throughout this book, citizen participation denotes the involvement of people in political decision making outside the electoral process. We are concerned with the citizen-government relationship, particularly citizen interactions with the administrative apparatus of government.

This chapter sets forth briefly the rich theoretical heritage of needs assessment. Democratic governance principles are discussed to make clear the continuing tension between populist, elitist, and Marxist conceptions of the proper role of citizens in relation to government, followed by a discussion of the recent history of pressures for greater citizen participation in the United States and in developing nations.

Principles. Needs assessment is far more than a matter of choosing techniques for gathering information about citizens' preferences or discovering failures in the delivery of public services. It is a special case of citizen participation, and participation issues are essentially questions of value.

3

Needs assessment is an emergent social institution; an organized behavior with underlying beliefs, values, and assumptions.

The meaning and importance of participation comes from political philosophy, a body of theories and values that define basic purposes in society, the nature of human existence, and the proper relationship between citizens and government. What people do has little meaning without these normative beliefs, which provide substance and direction to behavior. Thus our discussion of needs assessment must begin with a consideration of the goals of participation in a democracy. Three schools of thought are most relevant to needs assessment in contemporary society. Populism, elitism, and Marxism all incorporate conceptions of democracy with utopian objectives for the ultimate relationship between citizens and government. It is from these value-laden issues that the emerging institution of needs assessment gains meaning and substance.

In the United States we are taught that citizens have a right to be heard and to expect that elected leaders and other officials will be responsive. Government should be "of the people, by the people, for the people." Every citizen is held to be equal in "the eyes of the law." In short, democracy is the heart of our ideology and we believe it is the supreme form of governance.

We are also taught that our nation's leaders must have authority to exercise control. Laws are enacted to ensure order and stability in society and citizens must obey them. Bureaucrats are permitted to draft regulations and administrative procedures to execute the laws efficiently, and these administrative rules have the effect of law.

Obviously, exercising the authority of the state limits individual freedom and liberty. There is an inevitable tension between the principles of democratic governance and statist values and between individual freedom and collective security, equality, and efficiency. The history of every democracy is a record of conflict and compromise between the ideals of democracy and statist values.

In reviewing populism, elitism, and Marxism, an impression may be inadvertently conveyed that they are totally different and unique objects with sharply delineated boundaries, much like three beach balls floating in a swimming pool. They are not. A more accurate image of their distinctiveness would be one portraying the swimming pool moments after red, blue, and yellow dyes had been dumped into it at dispersed locations. While the centers of the dye sources remain quite distinct, a great variety of colors are found at the places where they begin to blend and mix. To describe the pool as containing red, blue, and yellow dyes is accurate, but it is an oversimplification and is a distortion of the kaleidoscopic reality. Our brief review follows the more extensive work of Bennis et al. (1969) and Kasperson and Breitbart (1974).

POPULISM. In reviewing citizen participation and democratic theory, Rosenbaum (1978) notes that political equality and popular sovereignty are the two central principles of democratic practice that emphasize direct and extensive citizen participation in government. Both ideas have a very ancient origin, at least as old as the political theory of Aristotle and the Greek city states. The early architects of democracy based their arguments largely on philosophical premises and derived prescriptions for democratic practice through the use of logic. But with the emergence of social sciences, and especially since World War II, there has been considerable empirical research to support the theory.

Political equality is the essential condition of democratic practice. All citizens must have an equal opportunity to exert influence through political activity if they choose to do so. To comply with the principle does not mean all people must exert equal influence, only that everyone be included. A review of democratic governance theories reveals three arguments for the correctness of this idea. First, since interests and values are personal and subjective, it is essential that each citizen make his or her own choices. No one person can speak fully and accurately for another. Second, political activity is the only way to ensure that personal values and interests are not disregarded, either inadvertently or intentionally. Third, only through individual political activity can citizens become fully aware of their responsibility to society, gain confidence in themselves as citizens, and achieve self-realization.

The essence of the principle of popular sovereignty is that democratic government is self-government. Government is a creation of the citizenry and responds to people's needs and wishes, nothing more and nothing less. Often it is also the principle motivating citizen demands for government reform.

There are two basic arguments for the correctness of the principle of popular sovereignty. In the first place, it is the most effective defense of liberty and freedom. By limiting government to those activities that are responsive to citizens' needs and wishes, individual freedom is maximized. The second argument is that the right to govern can only derive from citizens' feelings of voluntary participation and satisfaction that their interests are being served by government. Rule by force and coercion is inevitably short-lived. The right to rule must be secured and that requires responsiveness to the needs and wishes of the governed.

According to populists, public policies should be determined only by reference to citizens' values, preferences, and priorities. Only by active participation in formulating the rules shaping society can individuals be truly free. This view presumes a very high regard for the notion that human beings can be improved, even to the utopian ideal of perfection. Collective action should not be allowed to pursue short-term material goals at the expense of the ultimate end of individual freedom through increased competence.

Given the commitment to self-realization, it is natural that education is a central concern to the populists. But education takes on a special character because it is presumed that citizens are active, creative, and motivated learners rather than passive and reactive. Citizen-students are seen as capable of contributing to the educational process as co-actors with teachers. The teacher-student relationship is seen as a partnership aimed at improving individual competence for active participation in civic affairs. There is much evidence in social science research to support the belief that education plays a powerful role in fostering active participation.

ELITISM. The elitist theorists divide the citizenry into two groups. The elites are those who possess a commitment to the rules of the game; high levels of knowledge; and superior skills of analysis, bargaining, and manipulation. The masses are seen as having little interest beyond satisfaction of their immediate hedonistic desires and having little information or ability. Much of contemporary political science begins with this presumption and develops a theory of democracy emphasizing the important role of the elite, while relegating the masses to a limited spectator role. Democracy is essentially a peaceful competition among the elite. The route to societal improvement is the creation of a more enlightened and skilled leadership of influentials and opinion leaders.

Almond and Verba (1965: 478) argue that leadership requires passivity among followers: "If elites are to be powerful and make authoritative decisions, then the involvement, activity, and influence of the ordinary man must be limited. The ordinary citizen must turn power over to the elites and let them rule. The need for elite power requires that ordinary citizens be relatively passive, uninvolved, and deferential to elites."

The role of the masses in decision making is indirect. Periodically, they are allowed to express their acceptance or rejection of ruling elites through elections. Wilson (1962: 343) argues this is better than increased citizen participation. "Far from increasing public participation in the choice of candidates and issues, democracy is best served by reducing and simplifying those choices to a single elemental choice—that of principal elective official."

The arguments against greater involvement of the masses reveal an essential commitment to statist values: stability, efficiency, and authority of the state. Elitists argue that increased participation leads to greater instability. By overloading the political system with irresponsible demands for services and subsidies for various special-interest groups, government is made less stable. Also, greater participation encourages single-issue politics, which undermines continuity of officeholders and their ability to develop an appreciation for the system that best services the collective welfare. It is also argued that increased participation raises expectations. When they are not fulfilled, and they cannot all be met in a pluralist society, discontent and dissatisfaction increase and threaten stability.

Elitists argue that greater participation decreases government efficiency. Time and money are wasted in sharing information to gain informed citizen participation when elected officials or hired professionals could have made a reasonable decision at a fraction of the cost. Many decisions require technical knowledge or understanding of complex matters that are beyond the competence of most citizens, and therefore citizen participation would seriously threaten efficiency.

Finally, elitists argue that increased citizen participation undermines or at least threatens the authority of state officials who have been properly elected or appointed. It is the duty of state officials to make decisions, and it is the obligation of citizens to accept that decision making as a right of their office. Widespread citizen participation curtails creativity among bureaucrats and officeholders, who fear judicial challenges. Thus judicial review, which can be demanded by individuals or small groups, provides an effective veto power to vocal and aggressive minorities who thereby thwart the will of the majority. Faced with such threats to their authority, public officials resort to making decisions that will provide a minimally acceptable outcome to all groups. Ultimately, citizen participation erodes the authority of the electoral process, since legislative bodies and elected officials are bypassed and administrators are left to contend directly with citizen demands and challenges. The core institutions of representative democracy are made less powerful through increased citizen participation.

MARXISM. Citizen participation is crucial in Marxism, but in a way that is strikingly different from populist and elitist theories. In Marxist theory the most meaningful citizen participation is in the struggle between classes, especially between capitalists and workers. Since the apparatuses of civil society are controlled by the capitalist class, any participation in them is seen as having limited value. It furthermore thwarts or delays the time when workers realize their real interests. It clouds their perception that true freedom can only be achieved through class awareness and by rewriting the rules of society.

Much of Marx's writing with regard to citizen participation is a critique of capitalist democracy. Marx is less clear on the nature of citizen participation or the role of citizens in the utopian socialist democracy. It is clear that he envisioned a society in which the state had disappeared, private property had been abolished, classes no longer existed, and therefore politics in the form of class struggle was unnecessary. It is also clear that he envisioned a communistic society having "universal participation" as a central practice, but the exact means of such participation was never specified.

For Marx, social justice and the supremacy of humanness were the ultimate measures of things. He was, above all, a humanist who believed that full development required productivity, health, and purposive participation. His criticism of capitalist society was prompted by his belief that the capitalist system caused workers to become alienated from their work, their community, and their fellow beings. Therefore, one can observe that Marx, especially in his early writing, shared with the populists a dedication to the idea of improving humankind. His concern was to free people and allow them to develop fully, very much like the populists. But his strategy for achieving that goal was radically different from populist theorists such as Aristotle, Rousseau, or J. S. Mill, who proposed a strategy involving greater and more competent participation in civil society.

There have been many attempts at socialist democracies based on Marx's theory. In practice, the populist ideology gives way to an elitist structure in which the workers' party and its central planning committee assume a leadership position closely resembling that prescribed by elitist theorists. The chief difference is that the party becomes a surrogate for the state. The "dictatorship of the proletariat" is nonetheless a dictatorship.

Against this brief background of populist, elitist, and Marxist conceptions of the proper role of citizens in relation to government, let us turn to the recent history of pressures for greater citizen participation in the United States. In the U.S. experience the tensions have been almost entirely between the ideals of populists and elitists.

Needs assessment in the United States. The recent surge of interest in citizen participation and needs assessment in the United States was born on the heels of World War II when the U.S. Congress passed the Administrative Procedures Act in 1946. Since then, the processes of government decision making have been profoundly altered. Virtually every ensuing major congressional act mandates active citizen participation in administrative policymaking and program evaluation. State and local governments have widely adopted the practice of encouraging greater citizen participation. Even though most public administrators and bureaucrats have accepted this practice, there are doubts about its legitimacy, appropriateness, and utility. What is its role in a democractic state? How much is enough?

The history of the United States has seen a steady broadening of the practice of the political equality and popular sovereignty that are so central to populist theory. The legal enfranchisement of nonproperty owners, blacks, women, the young, and the poor has been fought for in the pursuit of greater political equality. Direct election of U.S. senators, popular election of more local political officeholders, introduction of the citizen initiative and the referendum, and the recall petition have removed some of the initial restraints on the exercise of popular sovereignty. Yet each accomplishment involved severe opposition, and invariably the elitist values of statism were central to the opposing arguments. It was claimed that enactment of such legislation would lead to instability, inefficiency, or the undermining of the authority of state officials.

In the postwar era, the battleground shifted from constitutional revisions to administrative and bureaucratic decision making. The growth of public bureaucracies and the enormous discretionary power of public administrators and bureaucrats beyond the legislative process were increasingly perceived as intolerable. Americans were becoming better educated and informed, more affluent, and more organized, although much of their organizing behavior was outside the traditional political parties. There was a keen sense that some citizen groups were being systematically excluded and ignored, an affront to the principle of political equality. Moreover, there were widespread encounters with administrative arrogance. People working in public bureaucracies often seemed unresponsive, insensitive, and unaccountable to the citizenry; the principle of popular sovereignty was being undermined by administrative rulemaking. Thus, while there was clear evidence that democratic practice was coming close to the principles of democratic theory, in certain respects there was also a growing frustration.

Research into the causes of social movements, revolutions, and less drastic forms of citizen protest against government clearly indicates that, when trust is lost, people demand more input. What might account for the frustration and lack of trust in government actions that became apparent in the United States shortly after World War II? There are several reasons, some with origins in the changing structure of American society and others attributable to altered expectations of the people.

CHANGING STRUCTURE OF SOCIETY. At one time, the United States was 95 percent rural and agriculture was the single most important occupational pursuit. Since then, the nation has passed through its version of the Industrial Revolution to the present postindustrial society. The specific examples of change are beyond retelling, but patterns are discernible in the gradually shifting kaleidoscope of institutions. A fundamental restructuring of the basic institutions has been a common experience of all industrialized nations and has been largely responsible for the surge of democratic impulses in the midtwentieth century.

Within almost any community today there is less homogeneity among citizens, at least in their source of livelihood. Differentiation in the division of labor has increased the number and diversity of occupations. Similarly, new industries have emerged to produce a wider variety of goods and services. Some old industries have disappeared, but differentiation has generated more that are quite specialized. One of the most significant consequences of this gradual process has been the greater diversity of economic interests among citizens. We have shifted from a nation of small towns, where nearly everyone's livelihood was enmeshed with agriculture, to a mosaic of occupationally and industrially complex urban centers. Even rural areas and communities are more differentiated.

With greater economic differentiation and specialization came increased interdependence. Products became more complex and manufacturing firms began relying on other companies to supply needed machinery and equipment; component parts for assembly; and legal, accounting, and marketing services. Efforts to increase economic productivity through technological innovations resulted in the emergence of a class of professional workers. It also created the need for a vastly expanded office industry, an army of clerical and managerial workers to keep track of the daily activities and plan for the future supply of inputs and access to markets. More coordination became an obvious need.

Centralized decision making in all institutions has been the predictable response to coordination problems. Perhaps the initial movement was in economic institutions, where technology was introduced to increase efficiency and productivity. Usually, this meant more capital was required to run existing businesses or to start new ones. The corporate structure of business organization emerged and evolved to the multinational and transnational business organizations of today. But the same concerns for coordination, greater efficiency, and increased productivity spread to all societal institutions, including government. Rational, calculated, long-range plans for organizational operation were deemed essential, and the modern-day giant bureaucracies grew from these conditions.

With increased specialization in virtually all areas of work and the centralization of decision making in basic institutions, localities became less meaningful as the focus of social organization and decision making. In business, fewer establishments were locally owned, and management decisions were more sensitive to the corporate balance sheet than to the well-being of communities where the stores, factories, and offices were located. In education, consolidation of local schools may have improved organizational efficiency and state boards may have created better long-range plans for equality of educational opportunities, but local preferences were not always considered. In government, expanding state and federal roles in securing political equality and enhancing the commonwealth also meant a decreasing autonomy of local authority.

In a very real sense the traditional means by which citizens were able to voice political preferences were dead or dying at the end of World War II. Decision making had slipped away from the "locals" in critical interest areas. Locality was no longer the primary basis of social organization. Resource allocation decisions were being made by people unknown to the citizenry and perceived by them as callous and unfamiliar with local conditions. The values of statism — efficiency, stability, and authority — seemed to dominate decision making in virtually all realms of life. The surge of interest in democratic principles was a reaction to these omnipresent and oppressive conditions.

ALTERED PUBLIC EXPECTATIONS. Structural changes alone seldom explain public behavior. They provide circumstances in which new behaviors can emerge, but creative action also requires a mental or emotional arousal of the citizenry. This may be the awakening of hope for the achievement of long-held goals in the new environment. It may be a perception of threat to existing values, or it may be the emergence of new values, goals, and expectations. The complexity of society is such that no single explanation of change ever seems entirely adequate. However, there are at least three major sources of altered public expectations that contribute to an understanding of the demand for greater citizen input into political decision making.

World War II propaganda surely altered the value premises of a generation of Americans. For nearly 10 years the public was bombarded with the ideology of democracy in print, on radio and the movie screen, in speeches by political and religious leaders, in schools, and in personal conversation. America was at war, and supreme personal sacrifices were demanded of all citizens. The emotional fervor of those years is impossible to convey adequately. But there is no question that a vast majority of Americans internalized the correctness of these messages and were prepared to defend them at great cost.

In a related development, World War II also directly affected the later citizen participation movement. During the war a great deal of research was undertaken by the emerging social scientists, especially social psychologists. The architects of the war movement understood the value of studying small-group dynamics, attitude formation and change, social structure, and personality. These research efforts gave inspired democratic ideologists an array of scientific instruments to gauge public opinion, sort out various special-interest groups, and organize effective citizen action groups.

Mass media brought the world into America's living room. Events and human conditions from the most remote reaches of the world became regular features of the six o'clock news. The exposure was not limited to the social or educationally elite; the poorest of families had television. The precise impacts of television on the viewers are not understood fully, but awareness of conditions beyond one's personal ambience offers an increased consciousness of kind. A political rally in Selma, Alabama, can attract donations and participants from all across the nation. The family of an infant needing a kidney transplant in Middleton, Wisconsin, can expect thousands of letters, telephone calls, and personal visits offering expressions of concern. Injustices inflicted in Detroit, New York, or some small village in northern Montana can ignite public reaction nationwide. Citizens have learned that their concerns are shared by people in other places, and an emotional bond is aroused that can be stimulated and manipulated to support broadly based citizen action efforts.

Thus the surge of democratic values fundamental to the citizen participation movement and needs assessment has its source in structural changes and altered public expectations. The mechanisms of democracy have not kept pace with changes in the organization of society and the public will. Therefore, the emerging instruments of citizen participation and needs assessment are seen accurately as trial solutions to the continuing tension between the principles of democractic governance and the key criteria of statism.

Needs assessment in international development. By the 1950s the industrially advanced nations had expanded their development efforts and had launched nation-building experiments worldwide. In these experiments one can more clearly see the perspectives of populism, elitism, and Marxism. International development projects sponsored by the U.S. government and private organizations drew ideological assumptions from elitists and populists, while Marxist ideology dominated the international development projects of the Soviet Union and Eastern Bloc nations. The struggle was centered on the differing views of how best to achieve desired goals.

United States–based international development projects continue to be dominated by the assumptions of the elitist model and in this context are known as the technical assistance approaches to development. In such projects a change is introduced by an agent (external to the target), who believes it will improve the person, organization, community, or nation and is in line with the self-interest of the target. Because people are assumed to be rational, it is also believed that they will adopt the proposed change if it can be rationally justified and can be shown by the external change agent that they will gain by the proposal.

Perhaps the fundamental article of faith in this approach is the belief that ignorance, superstition, and incorrect information are the chief foes of improvements in the human condition. Scientific research will expand the knowledge base and education will free humans from ignorance and superstition. When confronted with an unmet need, it is presumed that basic scientific research can and will discover the causal factors involved and that a solution can be engineered. When the solution has been discovered by applied scientists, people in the target nation, community, or organization will follow their rational self-interest and adopt the revealed solution to their problem.

This development approach also implies certain conditions about the provider-recipient relationship. First, someone decides that the recipient needs assistance. Usually this is the provider or the project sponsor; seldom is it the recipient. Second, the provider knows something superior to the recipient's knowledge. Third, a social and political climate exists in which a provider-recipient relationship can be established.

The elitist ideology and its technical assistance approach to international development generally has led to the belief that problems restraining the human condition are primarily biological or physical, not cultural, social, political, economic, or demographic. Thus application of biological and physical sciences is believed to offer the greatest hope. Since social sciences are relative newcomers to the academy of sciences and decision making in international development organizations is still dominated by physical and biological scientists, technical assistance continues to be the preferred approach.

A great many achievements have been made as a result of the technical assistance approach. This is particularly true where the root problem is indeed biological or physical. Improvements in health and nutritional sciences have profoundly affected human welfare over the past 100 years.

Without denying the value of the technical assistance approach, protagonists of the populist and Marxist perspectives argue against its universality and exclusive superiority. Criticism centers largely on the locus of control in the development process. Who decides there is a problem in need of solution and the best course of action? Who decides on the availability of resources? Critics argue that the answers to these and other questions are always the same in the elitist-derived technical assistance approach—it is the external agent, who may be an absentee landlord, a national ministry, church missionary, foreign capitalist, or foreign government.

Marxists and populists believe that most people want to control their own lives. They share the elitist view of humans as rational beings, capable of learning and guided by self-interest. They also accept science as a valid method in the search for truth, empirically verifiable knowledge. They disagree sharply with the elitists as to who should control. They also disagree with each other.

The basic premise of Marxist-derived international development is that barriers to improvements in the human condition are determined by the predominant manner in which people are organized for production purposes. While the precise form of these relations will vary, there is always a ruling class in capitalist societies controlling the means of production—land and other natural resources, capital, and knowledge. Because of the power of the ruling class, their ideology pervades the centers of education, religion, and government. All who work in and for these institutions are tools of the power elite. Exploitation of productive workers is the basis of power held by the ruling class. The elite will occasionally accommodate minor demands, creating an illusion of reform, while in fact retaining their power. Thus a radical reconstitution of the ruling class is the only hope the proletarian class has of successfully bringing in the changes they desire. Only through a revolutionary social movement can the dispossessed proletarian class replace the ruling elite.

The basis of contemporary revolutionary movements lies in a proletarian class consciousness. Thus worker mobilization is the first task of Marxists. When the oppressed are made aware of the true source of their discomfort and misfortune, they can be mobilized to challenge the power elite. It is not necessary for all workers to be mobilized; some may play a supportive role. The objective of the movement is to seize control of production and replace existing managers with members of the proletarian class who will establish a nonexploitive system of social relations. Strategies for gaining control range from electing a favorable government to violent military action. But in all cases the ultimate goal is to replace the ruling elite.

The establishment of a socialist state is presented to people in developing nations as the best strategy for accelerating economic growth and thereby the process of improving human conditions. Marxists often express the opinion that a state-controlled economy can mobilize available resources more easily and quickly than western capitalist democracies. But populist critics argue that the Marxist approach leads to violations of human rights and the establishment of dictatorships. The ruling capitalist elite is merely replaced by another ruling elite, the self-appointed leaders of the revolutionary movement.

Populist-based development places great emphasis on political equality and popular sovereignty as the means by which citizens control their own lives. In this view, a primary function of the state is to guarantee every citizen's right to freedom of expression. While these concepts are ancient in the history of democratic theory and are crucial to modern liberalism, contemporary statements of the populist ideology derive major support from behavioral and social sciences. Thus, when contrasted with elitist ideology, one finds a subterranean clash between physical and biological scientists on the one hand and social and behavioral scientists on the other.

What is perhaps most distinctive about populist-based development is the emphasis placed on the individual citizen; it is client centered. All people are believed to be inherently active in searching for need satisfaction. Their behavior is purposive, and experiences in their daily lives are continually and consciously evaluated in regard to their utility in need satisfaction. People learn from their experiences and evolve workable systems of beliefs, values, and behaviors. Thus their experiential learning is a method of truth seeking and reality testing not unlike the scientists' experimentation. Preserving citizens' rights to engage in experimentation and to incorporate what is learned into everyday living is the ultimate guarantee of freedom and civilization.

While there are many variations on the populist ideology when translated into development approaches, all emphasize the client system and the necessity of active client involvement in working out programs of change. The change agent must learn to work in partnership with the client, who actively participates in defining the problem, considering alternative solutions, assessing availability of resources, and choosing a course of action. The problem is not assumed a priori to be one that can or must be solved by more technical knowledge, although that possibility is not ruled out. Indigent knowledge is treated as having equal value with scientific knowledge and the possibility is maintained that a workable solution to the problem may be a combination of the two. Moreover, the methods and concepts of the social and behavioral sciences, as well as those of physical and biological sciences, are accepted as resources for the client and change agent.

There appears to be rising interest in the potential benefits of greater citizen participation and needs assessment in developing nations. One can only speculate about the reasons for the recent interest. Perhaps it is because the donors of funds come from industrially advanced nations where bureaucrats and officials have become more sensitive to democratic governance principles and the validity of social science concepts and methods. It is also possible that leaders and citizens of developing nations who have studied abroad are less willing to accept passively the decisions of external change agents. There are also many examples of failures of elitist- and Marxist-based development projects that are known to donor organizations and potential recipients in developing nations. And one cannot overlook the possibility that the ruling elites of developing and developed nations see increased citizen participation and needs assessment as a compromise that will make peasant and urban proletarian mobilization more difficult for Marxist-based development efforts.

Whatever the reasons, advocates of client-oriented international development approaches are experiencing more receptivity to their ideas. Until recently, development efforts were "top-down" and emphasized local adoption of technologies created by applying scientific research knowledge. Indigent knowledge was ignored. Many development agencies are now attempting to incorporate more participation by locals — villagers and field staff. They also are incorporating more social and behavioral science concepts and methods at the project design phase. While this may be cause for optimism by advocates of populist-based development, it also poses a major challenge. Many needs assessment techniques used in developed nations may be of little use in developing nations where educational levels are low, resources are scarce, there is no history of democratic participation, and populations are extremely diverse culturally and linguistically.

Approaches to needs assessment. Citizen participation is the active involvement of citizens outside the electoral process in making decisions affecting their lives. This fundamental concept of democracy has a long history; and while the demand for more public input increases, the motives are not always altruistic. Within government there has been a concern for mobilizing public support. Bureaucrats have been quick to recognize that members of citizen committees and advisory groups can be co-opted and transformed into advocates for their programs. In many instances, government-sponsored citizen committees, public hearings, and forums have become transparently ritualistic and self-serving. Then too, many citizen special-interest groups have distorted the concept of citizen participation to further narrow causes not in the general public interest. These instances may be more the exception than the rule. The fact is that most people today want a greater voice in decision making.

Needs assessment has been primarily a component of citizen involvement intended to gather information about relevant publics. Generally, this means bureaucrats systematically use scientific research tools to get a picture of the people to be affected by the execution of government decisions. The same information gathering methods are also used to solicit public response for new programs and to set priorities among alternatives.

Within the practice of needs assessment there are two fundamentally divergent approaches: the social indicators approach and the self-report approach. Users of the social indicators approach assume that the needs of people are known and the task is to measure how well they are being fulfilled. Discrepancies between accepted performance standards in a system and observed performance are used to infer unmet or partially met needs. It is further presumed that performance indicators can be found that do not require direct citizen questioning; these are objective social indicators of system performance. Thus statistics such as percent unemployed, proportion of households below poverty level income, rate of infant mortality, and hospital beds per 1000 population are understood to be objective indicators of how well a community or society is performing its task of meeting citizens' needs.

The self-report approach assumes citizens understand their needs but that the needs may not be known to decision makers. The task for users of this approach is to assist citizens in articulating felt needs. There are a wide variety of information gathering techniques available that originate in social science research. Some of the techniques were developed in the course of small-group research, others in the analysis of large, formal, and complex organizations. Still others were developed initially to study the public opinions of large populations. The array of techniques available offers considerable choice to users, and a key consideration is the nature of the public whose articulation of needs is to be assisted.

Citizen-initiated action groups seldom devote much effort to needs assessment. Instead, their very existence presumes the presence of special interests held by participants in the initial organizing efforts. They know their needs, and the task of the action group is mainly to express them in a politically effective manner. This means generating political power by any means available. The information gathering stage in which perceived or felt needs are assessed is a minor element in the overall activity of these groups. However, since the techniques of needs assessment used by citizen-initiated action groups are the same as for involvement efforts of government officials, they need not be treated separately.

CRITERIA FOR CHOOSING TECHNIQUES. The array of techniques for gathering information from relevant publics is extremely large. Faced with many choices, one must have criteria for selecting an appropriate tool. One must ask, What function or functions of citizen participation are to be served by the needs assessment? There are at least four possible answers. First, the goal may be informational, giving information to or gathering information from the public. Needs assessment almost always involves this goal, but it need not be limited to this function. The needs assessment effort also may be intended to serve the interactional function of getting citizens and officials working together. Or it may serve to assure that public views are being heard, even when the public is divided. This is the maintenance function. Finally, the effort may be needed to meet legal requirements, as in the case when local government agencies apply for senior government grants. Ignoring this legal or ritualistic function risks rejection of funds for failure to comply with regulations.

A second fundamental question is, Where in the decision-making process does the needs assessment fit? This relationship is a question of timing. For our purposes let us identify six steps: (1) defining the problem, (2) gathering information, (3) developing alternative solutions, (4) evaluating alternatives, (5) choosing a course of action, and (6) action. While many needs assessment efforts are intended to assist in defining the problem, they have a much greater range of utility. The choice of techniques should depend upon the final planning decisions.

A third fundamental question is, Will the results accurately reflect the public studied? This is especially crucial, but it is not as simple a question as may first appear. One must first decide on what constitutes the relevant public and then select a technique that will provide representative information; that choice involves considerable technical knowledge of sampling theory and design. The fact that the relevant public often shifts as one moves through the decision-making process compounds the problem.

A fourth question is, What is the cost in time and money? Here one must also consider the agency sponsoring the needs assessment and the public whose needs are to be articulated. It is assumed that cost in time and money are to be kept to the minimum without jeopardizing other goals.

The final choice of techniques for needs assessment must flow from a consideration of all four of these criterion dimensions. Trade-offs often become necessary, but they should be made from an enlightened position. To make wise choices, it is necessary for decision makers to be aware of alternative approaches and techniques and to understand when each is an appropriate choice. Unfortunately, that is all too often not the case. Indeed, this book is dedicated to the primary objective of increasing that capacity.

Summary. The ideals of democracy are difficult to achieve. Building a responsive government of, by, and for the people is equally as great a challenge to the most technologically advanced nations as to the least developed societies. How can every person be given a chance to participate in decision making? Is this possible in very large nations such as the United States?

The editors and authors of this book believe it is possible for all people to have a voice in public decision making. To create such a responsive society, it will be necessary to use a variety of methods. Electoral politics is one means by which people may be heard. Unfortunately, it is not sufficient by itself.

Needs assessment is another means of citizen participation. By using the tools of social scientists, it is possible to help groups, communities, and even entire nations express their real concerns more accurately. Of course, doing so does not guarantee all concerns will be addressed. It does mean that all groups, no matter how different their views may be, have an opportunity to influence decisions affecting their lives. In a pluralistic society, making sure all groups are heard is an essential condition for building a responsive society.

CHAPTER 2

Strategy
for needs
assessments

DARYL HOBBS

IN DOING A NEEDS ASSESSMENT, no consideration can be more important than a clear specification of the purpose it is intended to accomplish. Purpose is the principal criterion in choosing from among the wide range of procedures other chapters describe.

We emphasize here that the purpose of a needs assessment is very often political; therefore, whom the information is intended to inform/influence should have an important bearing on what information is collected, from whom, and how.

The context of needs assessment. The practice of doing formal needs assessments has only recently come into widespread use. To be sure, people have always had needs, and there can be little doubt that they have always expressed them, especially to those close to them in family or community who they perceive can help satisfy their needs. The need for people to express needs and organize their behavior to satisfy them is fundamental to human existence. But the contemporary idea of formal needs goes beyond individuals' informal expression and dependence on each other for their satisfaction.

The emergent use of needs assessments is largely traceable to fundamental changes in the society and how it goes about providing for certain needs of its members. As the society has become more differentiated, supplying some of the resources and services to meet human needs has increasingly become the business of government at all levels—local, state, and federal. The enlarged role of government is at least partially attributable to an emergent liberal ideology that seeks to achieve some reallocation of resources within an existing societal framework. This ideology is further predicated on an assumption that the society is pluralistic, but differences exist among sectors in their capacity to have their needs taken into account and/or acted upon. Implicit is the idea that those who have needs are often not in possession or control of the resources necessary to satisfy them. Were it otherwise, individuals, families, groups, or communities presumably would apply available resources to satisfy their needs.

An advanced industrial society also generates new forms of public needs—often addressed to collective rather than specific individual or family needs. These might be described generally as infrastructural, including such public services and facilities as hospitals, streets, water systems, libraries, swimming pools, soil conservation, and vocational training schools. A distinguishing feature of infrastructural needs is that communities or other political jurisdictions provide the frame of reference for need rather than individuals or families. It thus becomes appropriate to speak not only of individual and family needs but of community, county, state, or regional needs as well.

The mechanism society has depended on most for response to unmet needs is the specially created agency. These are typically organized to provide for some specific type of need. Thus there are employment agencies, health agencies, recreational agencies, and the like. Since there are numerous kinds of individual, group, and community needs, numerous agencies have been created. A differentiated society tends to produce even more differentiation.

Although society has generally adapted to the idea of services being provided more often by public agencies than by family and neighborhood, most such agencies are of relatively recent origin. The New Deal of 50 years ago and its supporting ideology extensively expanded the number of agencies and their role in delivering services. Since then there has been a steady growth, with another boom period coming during the 1960s emphasis on the Great Society, War on Poverty, and similar programs.

CONSUMERS AND PROVIDERS. Vesting greater control and responsibility for satisfying human needs in the hands of bureaucratically organized agencies does more than reflect a more active role of society. It also drastically alters the relationship between those having needs and those allocating resources pertinent to satisfying those needs. It introduces roles—those with needs become "consumers" or "clients"; the service/resource agencies become "providers."

Inherent in this distinction is that consumers and providers become socially and organizationally separated and distant; their relationship becomes formalized. Clearly, the consumer and provider roles are different, but their interests and motivations may be either congruent or at odds. Their relationship may be fully cooperative (shared interests such as schools and parents collaborating to produce evidence of a need for more support for public education) or adversarial (such as consumers contending an agency is ineffectively allocating resources to meet needs it is charged with serving). Also, contrary to interpersonal needs-satisfying relationships, the role of consumers and providers are seldom reversed or reciprocated; consumers continue to be consumers, and providers continue to be providers. As a part of their role, consumers have a responsibility to supply information about their needs, usually on a form or questionnaire; providers have a responsibility to respond rationally (i.e., fairly, responsibly) to the information supplied.

The providers' need for information as a basis for making resource allocation decisions has contributed much to energizing the idea of needs assessment. It is a general expectation that bureaucracies operate on universal criteria—anyone demonstrating a need is served, within resource limitations—and that they seek and use data, or information, as a basis for rationalizing their actions. There must be some defensible criteria for making allocation decisions; although from a political economy perspective, criteria other than the greatest needs often influence agency allocations. These other criteria may include tradition, a standard formula based on population or some other easily measured quantity, political efforts of interest groups, or an effort to curry the favor of some segment of a population. But a concomitant value of the liberal ideology is that credible information about the kind and distribution of needs should guide allocation decisions. Both agencies and consumers have therefore increasingly turned to enlisting social science research methods in their efforts to assess and document needs for administrative and program purposes.

NEEDS ASSESSMENTS AND CHANGE. Recognizing that agencies attach credibility to certain formally gathered information, groups of consumers have begun to add formal needs assessments to their repertoire of tactics for instigating change. When used by a consumer group in an effort to influence the political process and modify agency allocations, a needs assessment becomes part of a strategy of sociopolitical change.

Assessing (e.g., determining, measuring) needs is usually done with the idea that a demonstration of unmet needs of some part of a population has a probability of producing a response by some agency having the capacity, responsibility, and/or resources to respond. This linkage of the idea of needs assessment with the expectation of response also places needs assessment in a broad family of developmental change techniques.

As important as agencies have become in the process of providing for various individual and community needs, the agencies themselves operate within a political context. In a sense they lie between consumers and the political bodies who establish the programs and allocate resources to the agencies.

The needs any agency is organized to address are ones that have typically surfaced through a political process. Therefore, consumers having needs may address them to an agency or, as likely, to a legislative or executive level having broader powers. Consequently, another context for needs assessments involves the political process and questions of social policy (whether at a local, state, or national level). As suggested by Kerr (1984: 9), "With the 'Great Society' legislation . . . federal agencies, ill-prepared to take on public responsibility in matters that had been local and private issues, almost overnight needed to know much more than they already knew in order to make nonarbitrary decisions about social policy." This triggered a rapid growth in research and data gathering intended to inform social policy including, as Kerr suggests, involvement of "special interest groups, who, in a forensic spirit, seek to find 'supporting evidence' for their policy preferences."

Formulating a strategy. Most of the remainder of this chapter is devoted to the idea of needs assessments as producing supporting evidence. The term "supporting" clearly implies that needs assessments are done with a political, policy, or program purpose in mind. There is a preference or a point of view that the organizers of a needs assessment, whether a special-interest group (consumers) or a provider agency, think will be advanced more effectively if documented with evidence. Similarly, the term "evidence" connotes more than just the production of information. As Kerr suggests, evidence takes on a forensic quality. It implies information that is organized and presented with the intent of proving a case. It implies as well a circumstance involving competing interests, claims, and needs – a circumstance in which interests and needs that are backed by the strongest evidence will likely receive the greatest attention.

But we have used "evidence" in quotes because not all information is perceived as evidence by those it is intended to inform or influence. Information, such as might be collected by a needs assessment, must be transformed into evidence. The facts do not always speak for themselves. Producing evidence involves consideration of the purpose to be achieved, to whom the evidence is presented, and how it is produced. It involves an organized strategy. Not just any needs assessment exercise will suffice if the goal is to produce change or influence a political process.

Effectively linking method with purpose to produce evidence is the crux of a needs assessment strategy. Regardless of how carefully done and methodologically sound an effort may be, its value is limited if it fails to influence policy and/or allocation decisions, either changing or rationalizing them. Therefore, the features of a strategy that we will emphasize stress the interrelationship between how a needs assessment is done and what it is intended to accomplish. Methods should be chosen to optimize the chances of fulfilling the purpose.

We consider key features of a needs assessment strategy as including:

1. Who is the assessment attempting to inform, influence, or persuade? This is important because organizations, policymakers, leaders, and the like can be expected to differ in their perception of evidence.

2. What purpose is the needs assessment intended to accomplish? We will suggest that, in addition to administrative and political purposes, some kinds of needs assessments may be useful for improving group or community processes.

3. Whose needs are to be assessed? The evidence produced will depend in part on who supplies the information. Certain methods tend to attract more response from some groups than others.

4. What questions are asked? There are certain traditional categories we use to describe needs, such as health care and education, but actual needs may not neatly fit those categories. An effective needs assessment strategy will devote attention to creative questions — questions that depart from traditional categories in search of what people feel rather than what may be socially acceptable.

5. What resources are available to do a needs assessment, including time and organization as well as funds and expertise?

Each of these features will be discussed in some detail.

WHO IS THE NEEDS ASSESSMENT INTENDED TO INFORM/INFLUENCE? Virtually any needs assessment effort will produce information (although those that are well done produce more valid and reliable information than those that are poorly done), but there are important differences between information and evidence. For information to become evidence, it must be perceived as valid, credible, and/or compelling by those it is intended to inform or persuade; it must be something to which they pay attention. Not all data or information are equal in their potential to influence or educate different people, organizations, or sectors of a population.

Gerlach and Hine (1973) suggest that different thought systems have different "rules of evidence" and/or "rules of logic" as tests for whether or not a given bit of data is believed and convincing. By using thought systems, the authors include different cultures, but also different populations, occupations, and/or organizations within a particular culture. What is regarded as evidence, therefore, can be expected to differ among people, based on their experience, education, sociopolitical location, and so forth. A carefully done, random-sample survey of a population might be regarded as evidence by a bureaucratic agency and therefore something to which they pay attention; whereas a politician might be more persuaded by two dozen handwritten letters from constituents. Thus, before questions are devised and methods chosen, the organizers of a needs assessment should determine whom the results will most influence if the purpose is to be accomplished. Various ways are discussed below in which planning for a needs assessment can increase the prospects of producing evidence.

Incorporate into the process the people the assessment is intended to inform or influence. There are numerous forms of potential participation. Those whose actions will be essential to achieving the ultimate purpose can be asked to contribute ideas for questions, offer suggestions on design, make resource contributions, or even cosponsor a needs assessment. Generally, people are more likely to perceive the results of a needs assessment as evidence if they have contributed to its design and development. They become part owners of the information and are more likely to take the results seriously, even if the results contradict their conventional wisdom. This kind of involvement of decision makers can be relatively easy to attain at a community level, especially by seeking the input of city officials and organization leaders. The opposite side of this suggestion is that well-designed and inclusive needs assessments can and often do present challenges to the views of leaders and decision makers. When those controlling resources are challenged or potentially threatened by the data and they have not been involved, they are likely to look for reasons to discount or discredit the information produced.

Build a coalition of sponsorship for a needs assessment. Often views of decision makers on whether information is evidence depends on who has produced and is presenting it. The sources of information often have as much to do with its perceived credibility as various qualities of the information itself. Decision makers are especially likely to be skeptical of information produced by special interests who are seeking an increase in their resources. The information, regardless of how valid, may be perceived as self-serving and thus be discounted. A strategy for overcoming that perception is to broaden the base of sponsorship. If, for example, public schools are undertaking a needs assessment with the idea of producing evidence in support of increased state aid to education, they may be well advised to attempt to gain cosponsorship of parents, teachers, unions, and other public interest organizations. The association of various groups who are perceived as representing the public interest can contribute to the results being accepted as evidence.

Provide impartial and expert technical assistance. Yet another way of increasing the chances of needs assessment data being perceived as evidence is to seek the involvement of impartial organizations having relevant expertise or technical assistance capabilities. Such organizations might include state or local colleges and universities and some technical assistance agencies of government. Association of such sources of expertise with the information a needs assessment produces can be expected to improve its perceived credibility.

Use of intraorganizational or agency needs assessments. For the above reasons, needs assessments undertaken by an organization or agency for its own administrative purposes seldom fail to meet the criteria for becoming evidence. Those who design, develop, and carry out such an assessment usually pay attention to the results, even if it is not well done. Because credibility and validity are often built into such intraorganizational assessments, there is an inclination to heed the results whether the assessment is well done or not. Poorly done or limited assessments can and usually do produce misleading results and therefore may lead to resource allocations that are out of step with needs. We suggest, therefore, that from time to time resource allocating agencies, which depend on their own methods for needs assessments, subject their procedures to external review and/or broadened input to ensure that they are producing valid information. Valid information may fail to be perceived as evidence by those it is intended to influence. But the reciprocal can also be true. Invalid information produced by an in-house effort may be treated as evidence anyway.

Use of methodologically sound procedures. Regardless of the purpose and whom a needs assessment is intended to inform/influence, the strategy should produce valid information. Information that does not meet this test can be more easily discredited by those who are looking for reasons to ignore it and can be misleading if taken seriously. Consequently, in addition to the measures discussed above, needs assessments should have as an overriding objective the production of valid and reliable information. As chapters in Sections 2 and 3 emphasize, there are a variety of methods and techniques to choose in producing valid and reliable information.

How the information is presented. Who presents the information from a needs assessment and how it is presented also contribute to whether it is perceived as evidence. Consideration of characteristics and style of those to be informed/influenced is important. For some decision makers, a detailed written report with statistical documentation may increase the prospects of the information being perceived as evidence, while for others a few well-chosen words from a credible person may be more convincing. A detailed written report with documentation should be one product of a needs assessment, but the strategy question is whether that is the form in which the information should be presented to those whose decisions it is intended to influence.

WHAT PURPOSE IS INTENDED? The strategy for a needs assessment should clearly specify not only who it is intended to inform/influence but also the intended outcome, as a basis for making an informed choice of how the assessment will be done. There is a piece of folk wisdom that cautions, "If you don't know where you are going, any road will get you there."

A clear statement of the purpose — what the organizers hope to accomplish — is pertinent to determining whether to even undertake a needs assessment. An assessment that is sufficiently well designed and implemented to produce supporting evidence requires a planned and sustained commitment of resources. The expected outcome should be weighed against the amount of effort involved. Prospective sponsors should base their decision to proceed on an evaluation of the effectiveness and appropriateness of a needs assessment for accomplishing their purpose. A well-done assessment begins with a considered judgment to do one and a sound rationale for why it is being done.

For discussion we have grouped the purpose of a needs assessment into two broad categories: program/resource allocation administration and attempts to produce sociopolitical change.

Administrative purposes. Separation of the world of service delivery into consumers and providers has produced a need for providers to have information as a basis for planning and resource allocation. Consequently, assessments of consumer needs, in varying degrees of elaborateness, have become standard operating procedure for many agencies and organizations. We refer to these generally as administrative uses, which include those that follow.

Rationalization of the status quo. Although we have stressed a linkage between needs assessment and change, a frequent (perhaps the most frequent) use of assessments is to rationalize agency allocation decisions. Needs assessment data can help produce criteria that determine who is eligible for benefits and can also help justify providers' existence by producing evidence that they are effective in satisfying the needs they are mandated to serve. Consequently, it is not unusual for a provider organization to do a needs assessment with the idea of demonstrating that it is doing its job. Although it is unlikely that a group of consumers would undertake an assessment to demonstrate that needs were being met, it is common for consumers to collaborate with providers. Collaboration may occur if a provider, on whom many consumers depend, is threatened with program reduction or even elimination. Programs and agencies are often exposed to such threats. When that occurs, providers typically turn to data collection from among their clients to obtain evidence that their existence is essential. When existence of a provider program is threatened, retention of the status quo can become a common interest of the agency and those it serves.

Program evaluation. Even in the absence of consumer dissatisfaction, providers may initiate a needs assessment to evaluate their general effectiveness or the effectiveness of some innovative procedure with which they are experimenting. A provider may use a needs assessment to determine whether its resources or services are reaching those for whom they are intended. Frequently, such program evaluations are required of provider agencies by those who allocate resources to them. In those cases evaluation tends to be routine and a standard part of administrative practice. For the most part, program evaluation use of needs assessments is initiated by providers for their own purposes. There are, however, occasions where evaluation is initiated by whoever (typically some level of government) is responsible for funding the provider. Such evaluational use of needs assessments may be routine and/or administrative, or it may be a part of a consumer political strategy to produce change. Dissatisfied consumers may go over the heads of a provider agency and make a political appeal for external evaluation of an agency's procedures and effectiveness. Thus program evaluation uses of needs assessments are usually administrative but may be a part of a political strategy oriented toward change.

Program planning and development. Some provider organizations have a broad mandate to serve and are in repeated need of information to determine public needs and how they can best be served. Being able to demonstrate that the provider is aware of and is addressing important needs is a way of preserving the mandate. Such organizations may include churches, university extension/adult education programs, and state and area agencies on aging. Even organizations such as school boards and city governments often turn to surveys and other methods of obtaining client feedback as a source of ideas for programs and initiatives. Typically, a needs assessment used as a basis for program planning enables a provider organization to establish priorities for allocation of its resources.

Sociopolitical change. The use of needs assessments as a sociopolitical change tactic was implied in the earlier discussion of whom it is intended to inform/influence. The frame of reference of that discussion centered on the use of needs assessments to produce evidence in support of some change.

Change-oriented assessments are usually initiated by consumers. Consumers, more often than providers, can be expected to be dissatisfied with the status quo. A major option at their disposal to produce change is to bring pressure to bear through the political process. Evidence that a provider is not fulfilling its charged responsibilities can be an effective form of pressure.

There are generally three kinds of change that consumer organizers of a needs assessment may be attempting to produce: (1) a modification in who is served by existing resources, (2) an overall increase in resources addressed to a particular need, and/or (3) an allocation of resources to address previously unserved needs. Assuming that existing allocation is based on information (evidence of need) and certain politically established priorities, success in achieving change is likely to be linked with producing new evidence of needs and/or influencing the political process. For either case, the burden of proof is likely to be borne by those attempting to produce change.

As part of their strategy, the instigators of change must be concerned with the rationale for the existing allocation of resources. If the existing allocation is based on some past needs assessments, to what extent were those assessments flawed in the questions asked, the format for asking them, or who was asked? A needs assessment intended to produce new and/or more politically useful evidence should be particularly sensitive to methods and the source of information.

In general, new evidence is likely to be produced by broadening the base of who is included in a needs assessment, by seeking responses to different questions, or by employing different techniques to obtain responses. These features of a strategy will be discussed in following sections.

Generally, needs assessments intended to produce sociopolitical change will be initiated by consumers, who usually face a more difficult task than providers because they are attempting to produce change and must exert more effort to obtain the necessary resources. Providers usually do needs assessment as part of their regular activity and are able to call on the resources of an agency for expertise, staff time, and the like. Conversely, consumers usually must devote effort to enlisting and organizing volunteers and other resources. Also, as we have noted, attempts to produce change frequently encounter resistance and skepticism. Consequently, consumer-initiated needs assessments oriented toward producing change must generally be more concerned with the quality of the evidence they produce and matters of organization and strategy than those initiated by providers for administrative purposes.

We turn next to consideration of the importance of doing needs assessments that are inclusive of all segments of a population, especially the underserved and often less assertive elements.

WHOSE NEEDS ARE TO BE ASSESSED? As a variation on the purpose of producing sociopolitical change, a needs assessment may be a highly suitable method for broadening the base of views incorporated into policy/resource allocation decisions. Some segments of any population are typically more assertive and active than others. Consequently, needs assessment methods that depend on consumers taking some initiative, such as attending public hearings, are likely to produce a distorted or certainly a limited view of public needs and preferences. If a full range of consumer (and potential consumer) views is to be incorporated, it is usually essential that the sponsors of a needs assessment take the initiative to seek out all segments of a population, using methods most likely to produce valid responses.

Needs assessments can be effective in addressing imperfections in articulation of needs (desires, aspirations) by part or all of a population. An absence of comprehensive and equal consideration may be attributed to part of a population that is not aware of the organizations or agencies to which they should direct their expressions of need, of ineffectiveness in expressing needs, or of political or agency unresponsiveness. Whatever the cause, these may be indications that the existing political process is not producing information sufficient for equitable allocation decisions.

Needs assessments are done in a political context in which there may be vested interests in more effective expression of need or, conversely, in suppressing such expression. Obviously, organizations differ in their commitment to democratic processes. Some resource allocating organizations may be seeking to improve their responsiveness to needs, whereas others may respond less enthusiastically to information about unmet needs. In either case, evidence of unmet needs has the potential for evoking a response — either rationalizing (or denying) their existence or attempting to provide for them — from politicians or from the responsible provider agency. Therefore, a strategy that attempts to broaden the base of inclusion in a needs assessment can be instrumental in producing change.

If previously unrepresented segments of a population are incorporated into a needs assessment effort, new evidence will probably be produced and, insofar as it is credible, at least create a potential for change. Some outcomes that can occur as a result of broadening the base of inclusion in a needs assessment may include the following:

1. The production of evidence of contradictions or conflict, often by seeking the views of those seldom heard. Here a community or a provider

may discover much less consensus than leaders or administrators may assume.

2. A change may occur in the cognitive structure of providers and/or leadership. The views of problems and needs held by community or organizational leaders often occur as a result of conversations limited to those they see most often. Leaders tend to talk to and reinforce each other. A community or organizational leader can therefore come to have a view of reality that is out of step with the majority of consumers. A broad-based needs assessment can bring to the attention of those leaders or administrators views that contradict their conventional wisdom. Changed perceptions of leaders can be productive of modified policy initiatives.

3. The articulation skills of the underrepresented may be enhanced. A rationalization for why some segments of a population may be underrepresented or underserved by resources and services is that they do not, or are not in a position to, adequately express their needs on their own terms. Where that is the case, needs assessment techniques can be employed that are less dependent on verbal skills and articulation.

4. Segments of a population may be politicized. A needs assessment undertaken to incorporate some politically inactive segment of a population can open the door for their becoming more active participants in efforts to enhance their resources or to access them. People whose views are seldom solicited may respond enthusiastically to being taken into account.

5. Evidence of additional underserved segments may be discovered. This, of course, is the ostensible purpose for undertaking most needs assessment efforts.

Existing methods of assessment may systematically fail to reach all relevant segments of a population and therefore continue to underestimate the extent and distribution of certain needs and policy preferences. Some segments of a population can be disenfranchised in numerous ways. Broadening the base of inclusion in a needs assessment can contribute in two ways to producing sociopolitical change: through producing new evidence and through the potential of a needs assessment to mobilize certain segments of a population.

Different methods have differing capabilities of eliciting meaningful responses from populations. A self-administered questionnaire may be a valid method of obtaining views from some groups, whereas small-group discussion methods may produce more valid information from others. Whatever method(s) is chosen should not, a priori, preclude the prospect of valid expressions of need being attained from all segments of a population.

WHAT QUESTIONS ARE ASKED? As a result of the pattern of creation of specialized providers charged with meeting specific needs, needs often come to be thought of in certain programmatically (administratively) defined categories (e.g., health care needs, nutritional needs, transportation needs, farm credit needs). Because of these administrative boundaries between different categories, both providers and consumers may fall into the pattern of adopting a frame of reference of needs that fit into the existing provider categories. A result is that efforts, bound by the provider frame of reference, often end up reifying the prevailing categories. Continuing to ask the same questions of the same people frequently produces the same answers.

Change in what needs are identified (new evidence) therefore can occur as a result of seeking answers to new questions or seeking questions that transcend traditional provider categories. In general, consumer groups undertaking needs assessments are less constrained in the questions they may ask than are providers who are expected to respect the boundaries of other providers.

Often new perspectives on consumer needs and problems can be achieved by asking open-ended questions, ones that do not presume the existence of already institutionalized solutions. By using questions that step outside existing provider categories, it may be found, for example, that the greatest health problems of the rural elderly may have less to do with doctors and hospitals than with transportation, home care, nutrition, adequate heating, or even loneliness. Whether these other factors are discovered in a needs assessment will very likely depend on what questions are asked, who is doing the assessment, and the circumstances under which it is done.

There are ways of producing questions that transcend existing provider categories. One method is to precede the development of a needs assessment instrument with numerous informal interviews with people who represent various needs (e.g., poor, low-income elderly, single parents). In such interviews the emphasis should be on conversation and listening carefully for different expressions of need. Similarly, informal small-group discussions among those presumed to have certain needs may produce different perspectives. Any number of techniques may suffice. The important strategy issue is that the sponsors of a needs assessment take the perspective of consumers rather than a priori adopting the perspective of the presumed needs and the solutions reflected in existing provider programs. If a needs assessment produces "new" evidence, it will be the result of seeking responses to some "new" questions.

WHAT RESOURCES ARE AVAILABLE? In these days of widespread use of political polls, market surveys, standardized tests, and other commercial uses of social science methods, it is possible for consumers and communities to conclude that such methods are beyond their reach in cost and/or expertise. But that need not be the case. The capability for doing a valid needs assessment is within reach of most communities or even organizations. To be sure, good assessments can be costly, but not necessarily in funds. The time and commitment of volunteers, resources of community-based organizations, access to data processing, publicity, and expertise of publicly supported specialists are all prospectively available at relatively little direct cost. Obtaining the commitment of such resources, however, takes time and initiative of the needs assessment sponsors.

The availability of resources should be considered in conjunction with the other features of the overall strategy we have outlined here. Sponsors must balance producing valid and credible evidence against a realistic appraisal of the amount of time and expertise necessary to employ different methods. We will not attempt to enumerate various methods of assessing needs and the specific resource requirements associated with each. Because there are so many unique features of any needs assessment, we suggest that prospective organizers attempt to obtain the services of someone knowledgeable about questions of design and method. Often such qualified persons can be found within a community or may be available from a local college or state university. Such expertise is likely to pay the biggest dividends if consulted early in the planning process.

Before leaving the question of resources, we reiterate a point made earlier. Depending on committed volunteers and supportive organizations is not only a way of accomplishing a valid needs assessment at relatively little cost, but there are other potential benefits as well. Generally, people who have contributed their time and ideas also exhibit greater interest in the results and the prospective courses of action they may imply. Thus organizing to do a needs assessment can pay dividends, not only in the evidence produced but also in building a base of cooperation and collaboration, which can be important to achieving the objectives the results suggest.

Summary. The purpose for doing a needs assessment is to produce information. But if the information is to contribute to achieving the intended purpose, it must be perceived as evidence by those whose actions or decisions it is hoped to reinforce or change.

The consideration of producing evidence becomes all the more important in the context of what is being called an information age. Information is being produced at an accelerating rate. But a greater supply of information does not necessarily mean that it is all heeded. In effect, information must compete for attention. That is where a strategy for doing a needs assessment becomes important. A strategy should combine technical considerations with purpose to produce information that will be taken into account. This strategy is summarized in Table 2.1.

TABLE 2.1. Strategy for needs assessment

Who is the needs assessment intended to inform/influence?
   Incorporate those to be influenced in the process
   Build a coalition of sponsorship
   Seek impartial and expert technical assistance
   Include intraagency needs assessments
   Use methodologically sound procedures
   Understand how information is presented
What purpose is intended?
   Administrative purposes
     Rationalization of status quo
     Program evaluation
     Program planning/development
   Sociopolitical change
     Modification in who is served
     Increasing resource commitment
     Meeting previously unmet needs
Whose needs are to be assessed?
   Produce evidence of contradictions
   Change cognitions of leaders
   Enhance articulation skills
   Politicize segments of population
   Produce evidence of underserved
What questions are asked?
What resources are available?

CHAPTER 3

Approaches and models of community intervention

JACK ROTHMAN ● LARRY M. GANT

CANADIAN HUMORIST Stephen Leacock wrote of the young man who "flung himself upon his horse and rode madly off in all directions." This singular behavior may be attributed in part to youthful exuberance. It can also be described as a failure of assessment, since the young man had not decided what his needs and wants were, or at least had not put them in any order of priority. Assessment is a method for helping decide which direction to take.

Community practice can be described as a process of problem solving. It requires the design of strategies or directions for resolving critical social problems. Community organization in social work is often defined as a practice "method." In this sense it entails a series of logically interlinked steps that produce an intended outcome or achieve a desired goal, namely, the prevention or amelioration of substantive community problems. Additionally, community organization may be directed at "process" rather than "task" goals, that is, improving community relationships, attitudes, and collaborative problem-solving capabilities. One of the earliest steps is assessment, and that will be the focus of attention here.

Assessment. Assessment as a function has received heightened attention, partly in response to demands by the public and legislative officials for greater accountability in the provision of human services. Segments of the public have demanded that human services be delivered in a manner relevant to experienced needs. Legislative and government officials have focused attention on fiscal responsibility and cost effectiveness. Developments in evaluation research have also made professionals increasingly attentive to precise goals and measurable outcomes. As a result, pressures have been placed on agencies and professionals to be more clear, explicit and rigorous in justifying their service patterns.

An early step in any problem-solving activity is the analysis or diagnosis of the problem being confronted. One is tempted to say that assessment is the first step in this process, but this is not necessarily so. There are ordinarily precursors to assessment, what Brager and Specht (1973:89) have referred to as "preorganizing." Precursor activities may initially entail identifying and organizing a constituency or action system with which to work. The constituency then can become the medium through which assessment takes place.

Assessment entails gathering pertinent evidence and drawing inferences from that evidence about the nature of a given problem and actions and resources needed to deal with it. This process can involve an analysis at two different levels: the core problem in substantive terms and the solution environment surrounding the problem. A variety of questions needs to be asked about the core problem, with the following issues most salient:

1. Who composes the population requiring attention and who constitutes the primary beneficiaries of the change effort? What are their social, economic, political, and demographic characteristics?

2. What is the nature of the problem in terms of type (economic, psychological, organizational), scope (how many people are affected), and degree (how severe is the difficulty)?

3. How did the problem start and how has it changed over time? This may entail the development of a theory or theories. For example, chronic unemployment might be related to structural factors like racism. A case of child neglect could stem from the inadequacies of individuals or from chance events in nature (maternal incapacity because of stroke).

Defining needs. The formation of the problem influences the approaches selected for conceptualizing the needs. Just as there are different theories of the problem, different concepts of need also exist. Bradshaw (1972) has suggested a number of alternative concepts of need as defined among planners and researchers. All are appropriate under the proper conditions.

A *normative need* is said to exist when a standard of service or of living is established and certain people are found to fall short of enjoying that desirable standard. This standard (such as the number of hospital beds for a given population) is most often set by experts, professional bodies, or government bureaus.

Comparative need is not based on a set standard but rather on the relative position or condition of a group when measured against some other group. The disparity existing between two groups is the criterion applied to determine the existence and extent of the need (e.g., comparing the quality of housing in low- and middle-income communities).

Felt need is the need perceived by individuals experiencing the problem. It may be equated with want and is phenomenological in character.

Expressed need is a felt need that is articulated as a demand. It is a need put into action in the form of asking for service, protesting, signing a petition, and so forth.

Analyzing a problem and conceptualizing a need can be a fairly technical and solitary activity carried out in an office surrounded by computer printouts and area maps. However, it can also be conducted on a collaborative basis in neighborhood clubs and meeting halls, with the professional and the constituency taking joint responsibility as partners. Often planning models of community practice employ the former and organizing or community development models, the latter.

Approaches to needs assessment. Horton's comprehensive investigation into the types of needs assessment (cited in Meenaghan et al. 1982) yields six approaches widely used in conducting needs assessment research: (1) general population survey, (2) target population survey, (3) service provider survey, (4) key informant survey, (5) review of social indicators, and (6) review of administrative and managerial records. These techniques can be grouped under the two more general categories of social surveys (approaches 1–4) and secondary analysis (approaches 5–6).

SOCIAL SURVEYS. Survey approaches are often employed when no currently existing appropriate base of information exists. Such surveys often stimulate interaction among community residents or between residents and a survey team.

General population survey. In the general population survey a selected crosscutting sample of community members is interviewed or is requested to complete a questionnaire. Information can be obtained by addressing community members' description of problems, identification of special needs of individuals, actual and potential use of community services, and satisfaction with services provided. A major strength of general population surveys is the ease of adapting existing survey instruments for use in a given community or among selected respondents. Another strong point is that, if properly applied, there can be a high level of statistical generalizability and validity to the assessment. However, general population surveys tend to be expensive and require considerable staff time and effort. Frequently they necessitate particular technical skills (e.g., sampling, questionnaire construction and validation, data processing) that are not readily available. Consultants often must be engaged and compensated for their assistance.

Target population survey. Target population surveys are smaller, more focused, and generally concerned with a specified population at risk within the community. They can sometimes provide more in-depth information than general surveys. If the target population is a population currently being served, much data regarding effects of current services, access and barriers to service delivery, and the like can be easily obtained.

Target surveys share some of the strengths of the general survey (i.e., ease in adapting existing instruments); however, they are likewise often expensive and time consuming. Skills assumed in executing a target population survey are the same as those required to perform a more general one. It should be recognized that the methods for selecting a specific subgroup of individuals from the larger population (i.e., stratifying the sample) introduces a sample bias, minimizing the extent to which findings about the group at risk are generalizable to the entire community.

Service provider survey. In addition to assessing community opinions regarding services or agencies, it is often useful to gather data from the service personnel of community agencies. Staff perceptions of unmet needs and barriers to service may provide other rich sources of information. Providers can illuminate objectives and contexts of service delivery as seen from a professional perspective. Service provider surveys can be conducted by using or expanding on existing data collection procedures within agencies and hence may involve only moderate costs. Results, while potentially valid, are not generalizable to other community populations. Care is required on the part of the data collector to recognize evidence of cultural or class bias in response patterns. Also, the bureaucratic needs of service organizations (rather than service needs of agency clients) may be reflected in the findings.

Key informant survey. Persons questioned using key informant surveys are recognized leaders or representatives within the community. Such key informants may be formal leaders such as agency board members, elected officials, or ministers. However, informal leaders should also be contacted. These are grass roots individuals, whom people seek out for advice or assistance even though they hold no formal positions. Surveys of key informants can provide insight into what community problems may emerge as issues of public record and who is likely to support or oppose proposed changes. While the results of this type of survey are not generalizable, they are valid in their own terms, since they indicate what community leaders believe. Existing survey protocols may be adapted to this type of inquiry, and administration of such surveys typically requires small outlays of time and money because a relatively small sample is required. However, some caveats are in order, including surveyor awareness of personal and political biases of informants and realization that even the most widely known and respected community leaders represent only some, not all, of the constituents of any given community.

SECONDARY ANALYSIS OF DATA. Secondary analysis of data refers to the study of community-related information that has been previously collected, tabulated, and organized in a coherent printed manner. Inspection of such data can be useful in identifying key social problems and agency responses (or nonresponses) to them. Secondary analysis may also be useful in specifying contexts in which social problems co-occur. Meenaghan et al. (1982) indicated several ways to maximize the effectiveness of secondary analysis, with the following most critical: the social data should be as current, reliable, and valid as possible; and the information gathered should be directly related to the focal issues and objectives being addressed, not used simply because it is available.

Relevance as well as access is a critical consideration. Among the advantages of this approach are the relative ease of use (since many methods and strategies of secondary analysis are readily available), easy access to information sources, and the low cost of performing analyses. However, secondary analysis is primarily a descriptive technique, since such a total needs assessment may not necessarily be derived from it. If possible, secondary data analysis should be combined with other approaches. Also, given its descriptive nature, secondary analyses are usually not generalizable to other contexts. Since the data normally precede the study conceptualization and design, there may not be a perfect fit between issues raised and available data.

Social indicators. A large volume of statistical data exists on a variety of subjects: economic and income levels, spending patterns, occupational status, job satisfaction, adjustment of children in school, community solidarity, and fear of crime. These statistics are accumulated, synthesized, and published on a regular basis by government bureaus, research institutes, universities, and professional organizations.

The advantages of social indicators are clear. Techniques of analysis are well developed, data bases are extensive and comprehensive, and access to such information is relatively straightforward. Social indicators are indirect, albeit potentially potent, indices of needs.

Review of managerial and administrative records. With review of managerial and administrative records, information regarding client characteristics, services provided, services needed but unavailable, and referrals across agencies and organizations can be obtained. An intimate picture of service patterns can be easily constructed. There are, however, barriers to accessing this type of information for those who are not housed within an agency system. Furthermore, given that most agency records are prepared in-house, data collection formats are likely to differ significantly across agencies, making comparative analysis difficult.

Models of community intervention.
We posit a relationship between needs assessment approaches and community intervention modalities. Because of the intellectual and value stance inherent in the models, there is within each a tendency to favor some needs assessment approaches over others.

Three models of community organization have been identified by Rothman (1974): locality development, social planning, and social action. As discussed below, the models differ in their underlying perspectives, assumptions, ideologies, targets, strategies, and tactics used. Not all intervention situations are characterized by utilization of a distinctive model. Many situations have mixed or sequenced intervention patterns. Nevertheless, for analytic purposes it is useful to construct ideal types and to recognize tendencies in strategies of community action.

LOCALITY DEVELOPMENT. Locality (or community) development has been characterized as "citizens from all walks of life learning new skills and engaging in a cooperative self-help process to achieve a wide variety of community improvements. It implies a condition of limited resources and effort to increase and expand such resources for mutual benefit" (Cox et al. 1970). The solution to community problems requires active involvement of local people in appropriate organizational and community activities. Underlying the problem perception/solution set implicit in locality development are four assumptions:

1. Locality development suggests that grass roots or "bottom-up" organization is critical.

2. It suggests that broad participation of residents in decision-making spheres of community life is not only desirable but necessary.

3. The community needs to be reconstructed as a meaningful integration of various community member perspectives and competencies, that is, a "union of meaningful social and moral relationships" (Spergel 1977). This implies fraternal attitudes and cooperative relationships among citizens.

4. There must be an effort to bring about an increase in individual efficacy, confidence, and self-esteem as well as collaborative problem-solving, community-based structures. Self-help projects are an important means of accomplishing this.

SOCIAL PLANNING. Social planning consists of the selection of ends and means for changing social arrangements and implementing actions to reach desired ends (Perlman 1977). The social planning approach focuses on programs to address the social needs of community members for new, better, or expanded social services. The emphasis is on substantive problems (task goals) such as health, delinquency, or housing rather than on changing attitudes and social relationships (process goals) as in the case of locality development. While locality development sees action growing from a process of community dialogue, social planning emphasizes use of factual data for giving programmatic direction. Thus planning is viewed "as a rational-technical skill, requiring special training and often a professional jargon emphasizing neutrality, the facts, and the public interest" (Cox et al. 1970).

In keeping with this perspective, there are some processes that have been identified in the literature as comprising the essential framework of planning: (1) problem identification, (2) delineating causal elements of the problem, (3) formulating strategies in response to the problem, (4) weighing the efficacy of different strategies based on available inter- and intra-agency resources, (5) developing a program implementation design, (6) implementing the program, and (7) evaluating program effectiveness.

Given this framework, there is a particular problem perception/solution set implicit in the social planning model. The problem is conceptualized as having rational, identifiable (and often quantifiable) causes. The issue of concern, seen as a substantive community problem, can be articulated by means of analytical methods. Likewise, formulating a solution is a rational, factually based task. Implementation of the solution is rigorously monitored and evaluated. Assumptions of such a problem perception/solution set are: (1) highly qualified, technical, and experienced professionals are involved in this process (i.e., frequently a "top-down" approach); (2)

the problem and solution are analytically perceived through empirical means; and (3) community members are seen as consumers of potential services.

SOCIAL ACTION. A prime goal of social action is the redistribution of power and resources in the community. Community problems are seen as a function of an oppressive, hostile, and/or dysfunctional social system. Institutional behavior affects deprived community members in a disproportionately negative fashion. Problem resolution comes about through organizing the disenfranchised around clear crystallized issues and confronting the alleged source of the problem (oppressive institutions and power holders). This approach involves identifying some community members as victims, identifying community agencies and institutions as seats of oppressive power, and making redistribution of power relations a key objective.

Relating needs assessment to community intervention modes.

As indicated above, the locality development model assumes a strong emphasis on community involvement and self-help. United Nations publications on community development have emphasized the importance of "gathering knowledge about . . . the community . . . ; stimulating the community to realize that it has problems and helping people to discuss as well as seek the most pressing problems . . . ; fostering community self-confidence in respect to decision making; and assisting community groups to recognize and work toward increasing their capacities for self-help" (cited by Spergel 1977).

Needs assessment approaches that stimulate local responsibility and involvement will receive priority consideration by locality developers. Techniques that include direct engagement with the population and draw local people into the process of problem analysis are particularly pertinent. For this reason, all the surveys included in the first category of assessment have relevance, especially those that include a cross section of citizens. Thus the general population survey has much appeal. It allows for contact with many residents, asks their opinions about local situations, stimulates them to think about problems, and generally can initiate a process of collaborative work. In addition to yielding data, the survey process allows for the identification of articulate individuals who can be moved toward leadership positions at later stages. It prepares the groundwork for inviting respondents to take part in the interpretation of findings. It foments a climate of awareness and personal identification with issues, which provides a good basis for asking people to join into action programs that grow out of the needs assessment effort.

The key informant approach is also highly applicable to community development. It requires the identification of both formal and informal community leaders, an activity that is critical in the locality development process under any circumstances. The assessment provides for structured contact with these leaders and offers an unintrusive vehicle for gaining access to them. As with the general population, the assessment stage establishes the groundwork for later involvement of leaders in the action stages of intervention.

The survey of service providers is of less interest to locality developers. Providers are often seen as encompassing too narrow a group of professionals and bureaucratic representatives to be given high emphasis. The target population survey would, however, be of interest in that it allows for firsthand learning of how members of the community who have special needs are experiencing their problems. Such individuals could then be drawn into self-help projects.

The prime goal of social planning is solution of substantive community problems. Factual information about the problem must be obtained as well as information assessing the availabilities and strengths of current agency resources. Needs assessment is an integral empirical component in social planning. To this end, all assessment techniques could be of some use in collecting information pertinent to the task. However, the techniques involving hard facts and emphasizing service provision would be most compatible with social planning. Thus secondary analysis approaches utilizing existing data, especially social indicators and reviews of administrative records and agency resources, are highly appropriate. Also, the survey of social providers would have some appeal in allowing planners to obtain perspectives of professionals and experts on problematic situations. This is an extension of informal methods that planners frequently use anyway in attempting to understand such situations.

For social actionists, needs assessment is less a technique for information gathering than for organizational mobilization. The social actionist comes to the situation with a developed analysis and problem identification. Certain individuals are at a disadvantage because those with greater power are exploiting or disregarding them. The task is to mobilize the powerless so that resources and decision-making authority can be more equitably dispersed. Needs are defined and appraised in relation to their utility as issues around which to organize a constituency. Information serves as a weapon rather than a planning aid. Needs assessment approaches that lead to that end are heavily drawn upon. In addition, social actionists typically have few resources along the lines of funds, expertise, or staff. For this reason, use of social indicators is a prime tool. Such information is readily available in libraries, news stories, and free government reports. One can take the oppressors' own published information and use it against them. The social actionist will also lean toward grass roots neighborhood surveys, either of the general population in particular deprived neighborhoods or of target populations. Such surveys provide a means for making contact with the population, discovering who are the most dissatisfied or action-oriented in the area, and laying the groundwork for citizen mobilization. Neighborhood surveys in this mode of intervention are conducted on a nontechnical, informal, low-cost basis.

Summary. The main points of this discussion are summarized in Table 3.1. While we suggest an association between needs assessment approaches and intervention models, this presentation does not imply that certain assessment techniques must and are exclusively used within given community organization models. Clearly, depending on the type of information required, any assessment technique might and should be used with any of the three models. Further, since many community intervention undertakings have mixed rather than unitary intervention modalities, a mixture of needs assessment approaches accordingly will exist in many projects. We have hypothesized that, on the whole, some assessment techniques are more prototypical of a given community organization model than others. This position is subject to and should be given empirical testing. By revealing the biases that we suggest exist, practitioners favoring certain assessment techniques might become open to more varied applications and thus to more informed, multifaceted bases for decisions concerning planning of strategic interventions.

TABLE 3.1.   **Prototypical needs assessment approaches used in various models of community intervention**

| | Models of community intervention | | |
Approaches	Locality development	Social planning	Social action
Social surveys			
General population survey	X		X
Target population survey	X		X
Service provider survey		X	
Key informant survey	X		
Secondary analysis			
Review of social indicators		X	X
Review of administrative and managerial records		X	

CHAPTER 4

Social and political process:
The Minnesota hazardous waste case

LUTHER P. GERLACH ● LARRY R. MEILLER

CLASHES OVER ENVIRONMENTAL ISSUES have captured headlines and have, in the process, produced a number of interesting glimpses into needs appraisal and the processes of mobilization and debate. Technological and political orders seek to develop and deploy new technology efficiently and economically and to manage such development comprehensively and systematically. However, people mobilize from the grass roots to challenge these efforts as threats to their interests and principles. Although it is an injustice to the complexity of the situation, we will refer to this phenomenon as the interaction of established orders and mobilizations.

For example, hazardous waste improperly managed in the environment—contaminating water, soil, and air—is increasingly recognized as a serious threat to the public welfare. Places where this has happened—Love Canal (Gibbs 1982), Times Beach, Spring Valley—become synonyms for disaster. When it appeared that officials in the Environmental Protection Agency were lax, or worse, in tackling the hazardous waste problem, they became political liabilities to those who appointed them and easy targets for investigation by journalists and legislators. A survey of 250 environmental groups in Minnesota indicates that hazardous waste is considered by these organizations as an environmental problem second only to acid rain in significance.

We have come to expect that federal, state, and local government bodies will protect us from the threat of hazardous wastes and compensate us for damages from past exposure. It seems in the broad public interest to establish legislation to clean up existing waste dumps and to manage and process new wastes so they are reduced and the residue disposed of using the most advanced technology.

However, while people want the protection of such legislation, they often do not want its consequences. For example, most of us do not like the idea of having waste processing facilities sited in our neighborhoods or having to accept the regulations, inconveniences, and costs necessary to reduce everyone's contribution to the waste problem.

In response, some legislatures have required that the process of finding technical solutions to the waste management problem be accompanied by a process of involving, learning from, and educating the people. The subsequent interaction has often been marked by controversy. It produces a transactional process, one dimension of which is a lively debate about needs as well as risks and benefits. We can call this "needs appraisal" to distinguish it from more formal needs assessment procedures, often mandated as part of official, formal decision making. Yet we note that needs appraisal includes and builds around this more formal effort.

In Minnesota the state legislature established a nine-person Waste Management Board (WMB) with a staff of technical, public relations, and information specialists to develop and conduct technical and participatory processes to find solutions to the state's hazardous waste situation. This process resulted in serious tensions among various public and private interests, particularly concerning the rights and duties in the environmental resources area. What has transpired to date in Minnesota provides an interesting glimpse into the interaction between established orders and mobilizations, the transactional process that develops through it, the needs appraisal that is part of it, and the sociocultural changes that follow. This chapter will review what has been learned in this case and compare findings from it with those from other cases.

Actor groups and tensions in the participatory process. Tensions or conficts over resource issues develop quickly and can be initiated by virtually any or all of the groups involved in the participatory process. The tensions created are often viewed within the context of public interests as opposed to private interests or rights. Generally speaking, tensions occur and are variously identified as being (1) top-down or bottom-up, (2) centralized or decentralized, and (3) micro or macro.

A number of groups and individuals participate, and all may initiate or respond to these tensions in the participatory process. However, there are two groups that might be considered the major contenders. The first consists of the proponents of a resource development or management project or of technological deployment. They represent the established order. The second group consists of the challengers, resisters, or protestors of such development and deployment. These people are mobilized at the proverbial grass roots level, sometimes evolving into a full-fledged movement. They may come from any sector of society. Two major types can be identified within this group—ordinary people fighting initially for specific self-interest and more professionalized challengers of established order, including staff members of watchdog organizations. In addition to these major groups, several other participants can be identified.

One contending group consists of elected and appointed government officials charged with managing or regulating actual or anticipated controversy between the major contenders. Another is made up of lawyers and legal specialists who work for the contenders and regulators. A third consists of media people and institutions that amplify the process and sometimes help to shape it. A fourth is composed of consultants—experts in the subjects being contested or in managing the contest. They work for any of the other groups and/or give expert testimony at hearings. The fifth group may be termed the broader public; this group seems to be a target for communication from many of the above and the audience for the drama, but its role is diffuse.

All these groups became embroiled in controversy in the 1970s over the siting and construction of a high-voltage ±400-kv DC power line across west-central Minnesota. Thousands of Minnesotans carried their fight against the line, and the rural electric cooperative associations building it, through years of public meetings and hearings and into the litigation. Many engaged in civil disobedience as a last-ditch means of resistance, and at least a few engaged in or tacitly supported sabotage of the lines. During all this, the resisters came to identify as enemies the state government bodies that one by one became involved in the controversy:

1. The Minnesota Energy Agency, which determined through hearings that the line was needed.
2. The Environmental Quality Board (EQB), which conducted the public process required to determine a route for the line and to grant the line builders a construction permit.

3. The Minnesota and federal courts, which heard the many different cases brought by resisters to stop the line and by the rural electric co-ops to stop the resisters.

4. Three Minnesota state governors, who sought to mediate or resolve the dispute but who eventually felt compelled to call upon law enforcement agencies — first local sheriffs, then state police, and finally the FBI — to control conflict emanating from both resisters and builders.

5. The Minnesota state legislature, which had to face quite conflicting demands for resolution from resisters, co-ops, and other interest groups worried about how this jeopardized their interests and the welfare of the state.

During the process, the rural electric co-ops also came to see as foes any who seemed to sympathize with the resisters or even to question the co-op policy. Eventually the line was built, at times under the guard of state police. It is being maintained under the watchful eye of the FBI. People under and around the line across west-central Minnesota continue to regard it as something forced upon them. To date, 16 towers carrying the line have been brought down by sabotage, the latest occurring long after authorities said that people should have learned to live with the line.

This power line case is perhaps the biggest horror story told in Minnesota government and industry circles of what can go wrong when people do not accept a facility. And while the above is an extreme case, it clearly reflects the root causes for tensions, which are features of all types of society. Tensions may occur for several reasons. In the power line case one can see the classic situation of public interests versus private interests or rights. Summers commented in depth on this area in Chapter 1.

One may also view this confict (and many others) as a case of global and ecosystem interdependence versus independence, self-actualization, and self-reliance. These themes are put forward separately by the different social movements as being needed for survival and/or evolution. In such situations, attempts to reduce tension and close the gap between levels often leads to more tension with those resisting technocratic management.

The power line case was examined by the Minnesota legislative committee, that worked to design the Waste Management Act of 1980. The committee wished to draw lessons it could apply to avoid such dangerous conflict in siting facilities and developing regulations to manage hazardous wastes. Members of this committee and the WMB came to share the perception that protest by citizens was a function of the way the decision-making process was conducted. The behavior of decision makers and the process for making decisions affecting private and local interests was considered to be at least as important as the decisions made. It seems likely that the process of siting the high-voltage power line across west-central Minnesota was flawed in the procedures used and behavior displayed by the rural electric cooperative associations and their lawyers as well as the EQB and staff conducting the siting process. Critics would add that the power line case was made worse by the ways some protesters, outsiders, lawyers for the protesters, and media reporters exploited the issue.

In response to the problems, the WMB focused on developing and implementing extensive public participation in determining waste management site facilities; handling of hazardous wastes, recycling what could be put to new productive use; and disposing of the processing residue. Under advice from a legislative commission on waste management and from the legislators who authored the Waste Management Act, the entire state was designated as a search area for these sites. This not only seemed the most socially equitable way to proceed but the best way to motivate people throughout the state to attend meetings the WMB planned to hold as part of its search. Working with citizens thus aroused, the WMB would then proceed over four years to eliminate unsuitable areas and increasingly narrow the search until the best were determined.

The WMB effort was an attempt to reduce tension among contenders and represents three basic and positive responses to established orders of tension management:

1. Involving citizens in decision making and indeed in defining needs and subjects for decision, including incentives and compensation.

2. Communicating the facts and concepts to facilitate participation and close gaps where differences exist.

3. Exploring third-party mediation, including the so-called science courts, when conflict still persists and there is an impasse.

Such positive response characteristically takes place in public meetings and hearings in which there are important official assessments of need. Indeed, an important finding in such hearings is whether there is or is not an officially determined need for the project or facility. If need is determined, the official decision-making process moves forward to questions of siting or implementation.

Negative responses may also be used by established orders, essentially to control, challenge, or restore order lost through the controversy or to seek to prevent such loss of control. These responses include:

1. Ignoring complaints, stonewalling.

2. Seeking to lower citizen expectations as to what they can or should say in the matter or to discourage hopes of better solutions than those

conventionally proposed; urging them to recognize that they have to give to get.

3. Using covert methods of control, collecting intelligence information about protest, and applying dirty tricks.

4. Applying overt force ranging from legal action to arrest and crowd control.

It should be noted that in some situations the positive responses cited earlier are used to legitimate the negative responses. In that sense the terms "positive" and "negative" may be somewhat misleading.

Process design. As the WMB began operations, it became apparent that it could have trouble in meeting its objectives, especially in controlling conflict. As the WMB narrowed site candidates to a few, it increasingly found people around the final sites mobilizing to resist. The mobilization took the form of protest not unlike that of the power line protesters. In addition, some local governments sought to "zone out" the waste management facility. They did not accept the legitimacy of powers given the WMB by the Waste Management Act to override local government restrictions and to exercise the right of eminent domain to secure use of the land needed for the facility. It was also thought that use of police would be necessary to enforce taking the land and controlling resistance to surveying, soil testing, and construction.

Many people surmised, however, that the WMB would be much more likely than the rural electric cooperatives to claim legitimacy for its actions and support from the media, local government, and the public. The WMB staff reasoned it would be able to refer to its long and careful public participation process. It was felt that any attempt at siting had to include a very active program of public participation to have any chance of gaining broad support for its actions.

An attempt at stimulating active participation is considered noble, good, and necessary by most people. However, active participation of major contenders in this type of process can frustrate the basic positive and negative measures described earlier. In general, participation results in three basic actions:

1. It increases mobilization of resister groups.

2. It increases expectations of success of ordinary participants and hence alienation when expectations are not met.

3. It frustrates the quest for the systemically and technologically most efficient and rational solutions — or seems to. Furthermore, if participation

is accomplished only after basic scientific, technological, political, and economic groundwork is laid, resistance is legitimated because citizens were asked to "rubber stamp" an accomplished fact. But if participation is encouraged so very early that it includes involvement in deliberating these basics, resistance is legitimated on grounds that established order does not know what it is doing and wants to make people "guinea pigs."

In its 1980 report on the siting of controversial facilities, a task force of the Citizens League of Minneapolis, a nonprofit public policy study group, indicated that a major factor affecting siting outcomes was, indeed, satisfaction with the participatory process of site selection. It observed that in cases where major problems developed, both those proposing and those opposing the siting of facilities found the process to be defective and disturbing. Many did not have "confidence in the legitimacy of the decisions, regardless of outcomes."

The report indicated variation in the extent to which facility siting has been resisted in Minnesota. For example, from 1970 to 1977 only four of nine solid waste landfill sitings met with resistance; from 1974 to 1975 three major power lines were significantly resisted, while three were not; and from 1974 to 1979 four major power plants met with resistance, while one did not. The Citizens League report suggests that the level of resistance might be affected by variations in the siting process. It was felt that sensitivity to citizen concerns and openness to citizen input and involvement made a difference in some outcomes. Regardless of the outcome, there are a number of generalizations that can be made about the communication process that may result from these efforts:

1. Facts are disputed with equal strength and certainty or uncertainty by people on all sides, including qualified experts. People share in a realization of uncertainty, which can increase anxiety about risks and need fulfillment.

2. Facts are often confused with values, but the distinction is not made.

3. Needs as well as risks and benefits are presented as real entities, objectively determined, but are likely to be heavily filtered and selected by unstated cultural premises.

4. Mediation is put into effect with hope of success only when there is an impasse. But by the time impasse is recognized by both sides, each is alienated. This means that a mobilization has likely become a movement and has developed an organization that is segmentary and polycentric. Therefore, while it can come together to resist effectively, it cannot do so to sign an agreement. The signers are branded Uncle Toms, or worse.

5. Force increases risks, which commit protesters and also helps delegitimate the established order. It can produce a legacy of distrust and puts the democratic principle at risk.

6. Lowering of expectations may curb protest from the outset, but it also threatens the drive of the cultural system, generally delegitimating it.

7. Ignoring or stonewalling can be overcome eventually, but it may be a very successful strategy, more so than is sometimes accepted.

8. Covert countering eventually becomes overt and produces suspicions that linger and contaminate other processes.

In spite of such limitations these measures are used and, of these, participation and communication become major tools. Participation and communication are probably becoming increasingly effective as more is learned about them through experience and research. Development of more objective measures of needs assessment will probably help in such use. But in any event, the action and interaction of the major contenders and the supporting contributors produce a real process that we can call transactional.

In 1980 a public participation consultant organization prepared, under contract to the Minnesota state planning agency, a plan of action for public education and participation in the establishment of a hazardous waste management system in Minnesota. This consultant offered a two-way communication process with all interested audiences, to build and maintain credibility for the board and for the process and decisions made. Some consultants are more cautious in what they feel process can accomplish. For example, an author of a workbook on how to conduct the public involvement process admits that "involving citizens will not always guarantee success." His main theme, however, is that ignoring such involvement will "guarantee failure of the project." He warns that citizens now find it "very easy to stop a project" once they turn against it (Bleiker 1978).

The most common faults in process include not showing openness or candor to citizens; losing temper under fire; not being well prepared, accurate, or honest; and not taking citizens and their complaints seriously. Other problems include being too legalistic, overemphasizing the reports of scientific and technical experts while downplaying information from ordinary citizens, and not being flexible enough to do such things as modifying the order in which subjects are considered. Other faults include not involving citizens early enough in the siting process and seeming to pay too much heed to powerful economic and political interests at the expense of ordinary citizens.

A legislative analyst indicated that the "prevailing or traditional way of making siting decisions across the country" has been to use a combination of "the rational, comprehensive planning process and the ministerial deci-sion-making process." Agencies using this combination deduce what to do from abstract propositions. They apply science, technology, logic, and an orderly sequence of plan; decide policy; and then use due process and "other legally correct methods," including mandated citizen participation, to implement policy. This process seems to be very reasonable and to "pro-duce technically sound, legally defensible and officially fair decisions" (Todd 1980). Increasingly, however, the analyst notes, it fails to gain accept-ance from the public.

While the waste management and siting process does not ignore these administratively and scientifically correct approaches, it "superimposes upon them . . . a quasi-legislative and political process which not only ac-cepts conflict as necessary, productive, and inevitable but goes so far as to create conflict, to promote the development of interest groups which will conflict with each other, and enlarge the scope of the controversy" (Todd 1980).

The authors of the Waste Management Act urged the WMB to deliber-ately create controversies over policies and to encourage debate about everything before deciding. The board could thus give people a lot to ne-gotiate about. One can argue whether this is a creative way of promoting active public participation or is simply a way of preparing to make the best of a conflict situation that cannot be avoided. It could also be a method to promote citizens fighting each other instead of the WMB.

It appears that the authors of the legislation and the WMB and staff recognized that such interest-group action and interaction was inevitable but could be made to work for instead of against the project. Under this theory the various interest groups compete. They debate the expanding controversies and will thus have a lot to negotiate about. The interest groups are called "artificial constituencies," since they are composed of people who come together because of the issues and controversies generated in the waste management process. The process is designed to put them into competition instead of uniting them in opposition. In the Minnesota situa-tion, the WMB wanted to become a referee among competing interests, helping to achieve an acceptable negotiated settlement. It also attempted to insulate state government from becoming involved as a contestant. Then elected and appointed officials could contribute to this process as referees. It is assumed that the interest groups would compete to have the facility put in a community other than their own—a kind of reverse of traditional competition to secure new industry.

From all this it can be concluded that the process was designed to control conflict by managing both the organization and the subject of par-ticipation. It is presumed that people would organize and protest, but that the organizational development of protest would be interrupted. Debate would occur, but the WMB would control this play of ideas. Organization and debate would be expected to produce demands that could be negotiated but would protect rather than jeopardize the mission to manage hazardous wastes. In short, the WMB would build organization and ideas, debate, and negotiation that revolve around the established order and its mission.

Organizational management. A first step in organizing such an effort is to get people to attend meetings and become involved in ways that will lead to negotiations, contributions, and agreements.

In the Minnesota case, the WMB knew that one of the big complaints against the power line sitings was that citizens were not involved in the process early enough. Early citizen involvement, however, can be difficult to achieve. The average person will often not take the time from an otherwise busy schedule unless the issue personally affects him or her. Research shows that few citizens will become involved and stay involved in organized efforts to deliberate public policy matters. Those who do become known as career citizen representatives. Some move from this to elected or paid positions in the citizen involvement or environmental specialist field. From the beginning the WMB sought to work with a much larger and more representative cross section of the population.

To achieve broad involvement, the WMB felt it should promote the potential threat of putting the hazardous waste management facilities, particularly the disposal facilities, in any neighborhood in the state. By declaring the whole state a search area, the WMB not only advertised its stand for openness and fairness but potentially threatened everyone.

One factor that can affect participation is the mode by which people hear about a meeting and its purpose and the methods used to promote attendance. To get representative turnouts at meetings, it is necessary to use more than official announcements in local newspapers. Accordingly, the WMB encouraged local news media to cover the subject in news reports, feature stories, and editorials. It also contacted local government and voluntary associations to help in its communication. Research indicates that this still is not enough. People turn out in large numbers when many activities coincide; when the media reports make people both aware and angry; when the local associations—through newsletters, meetings, or calls—join in making people worried and angry and urge them to attend and demonstrate their discontent; and (especially) when angry and worried people have contacted neighbors, friends, relatives, and co-workers or collared people at shopping centers, churches, or other meeting places and told them to come out. When enough of this face-to-face recruiting coincides with a media and newsletter blitz, communities start buzzing about the issue. This approach usually results in angry crowds.

Another problem is that people do not regularly attend meetings and persist in their involvement. Aside from pressure upon their time, people may gain confidence in the process or, on the other hand, begin to feel there is really nothing they can do to change outcomes. It could be that, following their initial display of anger to warn, they feel it is best simply to wait and see what will happen. The implication is that people will again come out, angrily and in large numbers, if the process eventually selects their neighborhoods as finalist candidates. In at least three cases in Minnesota, inital meetings in the community were poorly attended, but later meetings were crowded with people eager to display anger. In at least two of these cases, people's interest grew dramatically when they learned their areas remained as candidate sites.

All this frustrates efforts to build a kind of standing set of citizens who would progress, along with the established order, step by step through the siting process, sharing in a growth of knowledge and buying into the process with each of many small negotiated settlements. At any meeting throughout the process there are likely to be people present who demand basic information about the project, which was covered in the earliest meetings. At any meeting there are new people who raise old questions that were thought to have been resolved. Whether this is a natural result of meeting dynamics or a ploy to upset the meetings, it not only troubles the established order but bothers participants who have attended all along and want to keep moving forward. It may lead to citizen withdrawal from the process and contribute to cynicism about citizen sincerity. In sum, social and cultural factors external to the process of hazardous waste facility siting prevent the established order from exercising the kind of control of process that would facilitate its mission.

One factor that importantly affects the manner meetings are conducted is the way citizens organize their participation. Leaders of grass roots groups may also seek to make the most of the energy latent in citizen action by directing or controlling it in some way. They know there are times when it is useful for crowds to display an apparently uncontrollable anger and even to have some persons threaten violence. It is a warning of how bad things can get.

In both the Minnesota waste management issue and the power line case, citizens gathered locally to plan their overall strategy and determine tactics of presentation at siting meetings. According to their interests and capabilities, members of the groups were assigned to gather specific types of information and/or present their information in testimony before the officials. Groups that demonstrated good skills in this at the public meetings and hearings inspired others to the same approach. It would appear that people are learning more about how to participate effectively. People who have been involved in these kinds of events since the 1960s and 1970s say that they see an evolution of capability, a growth in citizen skills to match the growth in the capability of those conducting the participation process. It is to be remembered that many of the same people, who at any one time might be active in a grass roots citizens group challenging policy and decision making from some agency, board, or corporation, will on other occasions be some of those in authority, provoking challenge. Thus the conduct of the meetings and hearings in the waste management process owes as much to the action and design and capabilities of participating citizens as it does to the established order. It seems that while the established order can set the framework within which any meeting is conducted, it cannot alone determine its shape.

The WMB had trouble producing and shaping the desired artificial constituencies. People did their own organizing, often building on and around networks established previously for other purposes. To begin with, the constituencies were only partly a function of the threat of waste management facility siting. As the case progressed, interests also broadened, partly through the efforts of protest groups to be more things to more people and to take charge of the meetings both organizationally and conceptually. The WMB had difficulty in following the organizer's injunction to have these groups conflict and compete against each other while the board acted as a kind of third-party referee.

At the beginning and the end of the seven years of protest over the power line, there was noticeable division among some communities organized to fight it—first as each sought to build local resistance efforts and then as each sought to explain what finally happened and to find scapegoats. But for about six years of the conflict, farmers and rural townspeople across west-central Minnesota devoted much of their ideological and organizational efforts to persuade people everywhere to resist the line and build coalitions among various resister groups that formed. Indeed, some eventually became like missionaries as they traveled to all parts of Minnesota and into the Dakotas to spread the word and motivate people to action against the construction of other power lines, power plants, and other big projects. It is not surprising that after they knew they had lost their particular struggle, some worked hard to rouse people against WMB efforts. It had become a symbol of what they had been fighting.

While there were efforts to build large and lasting coalitions to resist the WMB quest for sites, alliances were not as strong and effective as those that wove together the various groups of power line protesters. Some of this attempted coalition building was lead by people who have become known as career activists and community organizers. They drew upon tested organizational skills and used established citizen lobby networks and newsletters. They were able to bring representatives of a number of siting resister groups together to talk about forming a statewide front, the Hazardous Waste Opposition Coalition, to fight the WMB and change the waste management legislation. While participants agreed to this in principle, they were unable to bind their various local members to the pact. Attempts to establish a permanent, statewide coalition of waste facility resister groups were unsuccessful.

On the other hand, at least some group members, whose areas were dropped as candidates, volunteered to help those still in the process, at least by sharing knowledge. For example, the leader of one successful resister organization in central Minnesota volunteered to help other groups with information and ideas. He and some others in his organization assisted close neighbors in building a parallel organization and using parallel tactics to show why their area in the Minnesota River valley was not suitable as a site for hazardous waste disposal deep in crystalline rock. In this latter effort, as in at least one other in northern Minnesota, organizations of Native Americans became involved as allies to fight siting on the premise that it polluted sacred ground and threatened traditional (Dakota and Chippewa) religious practice.

The WMB was not successful in overcoming the problem of stimulating people to come to meetings without generating angry crowds. It also did not really try to control groups by pitting them against each other and probably could not, had it tried.

Protesters were able to build some effective organizations, but not all communities were equally effective. Effectiveness seemed to relate to the presence of preexisting organizational experience and networks. By example and direct assistance, successful organizations helped others become effective. While groups helped each other with information and showed reluctance to fight against each other, protesters found it difficult to build and maintain large coalitions.

Organizing citizen action or controlling such organizational development in this waste management process is not an end in itself. It is a means to obtain and present information and ideas to influence the opinions of decision makers and gain public and media support. The architects of the process referred to it as producing a debate.

Debates about trade-offs. In the trade-off a kind of large sociocultural futures debate takes place, a debate about continuity and change, about what has transpired and what future directions should be taken. The debate has elements in it of a drama, a giant play in which people perform certain defined roles. It is in such debate that, among other things, a kind of informal "needs appraisal" develops, to be distinguished from formal needs assessment.

The parties in this kind of debate differ over the main subject matter to be discussed, that is, over the levels at which debate is to take place. Established orders want to hold debate on the level of discussion to trade-offs, based on the premise that the project is needed but what can be negotiated is distribution of risks and benefits associated with risk acceptance. With this, established orders will work out compensation and incentive approaches, increasingly touted as "answers."

Authorities use the trade-off approach directly or indirectly in their interactions with the public. It is built into the decision structure and legitimates it. Authorities seek to justify the assessments or impacts they impose on citizens as a trade-off for the benefits. In cases of protest, opponents bridle at the suggestion that they are gaining anything they need or want. As such, they do not see why they should give up anything in exchange, be it taxes, access to their property, or the acceptance of a change in their community. They come to feel that even by talking trade-offs they are acknowledging that the project is needed and they have a duty to help meet this need. Accepting this, they must then talk compromise rather than simply saying "no project." A public relations officer of one of the rural electric co-ops began a talk to citizens by saying, "I know that you don't like to hear about trade-offs, but . . . " Citizens grumbled agreement.

Citizens have found some advantage in talking trade-offs, since discussion enlarges the scope of the controversy to cover more that exists within the conventional framework. A case of drainage ditch repair in a northeastern suburb of Minneapolis illustrates this very well. The owner of a trailer court petitioned the local watershed board to repair an old drainage ditch, arguing that repair (dredging, removing tree roots and other obstructions) was needed to remove runoff from rains and snowmelt sufficiently to prevent flooding in the trailer court. The watershed board decided that this repair would benefit all the property owners whose lands were drained by the ditch and so held a meeting to discuss landowner assessments. Some who came were farmers specializing in the growing of sod, and they were in favor of water level control. But most who attended were owners of small-acreage hobby farms or residences. They were afraid that improving drainage would jeopardize the wetlands environment, which they liked, and pave the way for more housing and trailer court development, which they dreaded. The protesting citizens balked at talking about the need to achieve balance and compromise among competing interests. Eventually the project was subjected to an environmental impact assessment, as demanded by the citizens. The engineering consultant who made the assessment wrote that there were five options in this project, each of which had costs and benefits, that is, trade-offs: (1) thoroughly cleaning all 8.2 miles of the ditch, (2) partially cleaning the ditch, (3) building ponds to handle flooding, (4) obtaining flood control easements and, (5) doing nothing. The protesters were unwilling to agree that the last option, doing nothing, would also impose costs on them, such as lowered land values. They regarded the environmental impact assessment as a way of stopping the project, if only for a time, rather than a way to improve consideration of trade-offs. They warned that the project would have negative consequences well beyond anything brought into the assessment. Proponents of the project felt that the protesters were being unreasonable and selfish.

Debates on alternatives. Challengers/resisters want to escape the debate about trade-offs, regarding it as a trap in which they must accept too many established-order assumptions and objectives. They seek to move to a level of debate over alternatives, over other ways of meeting the same needs, but avoiding risks as they see them.

When power line protesters said they did not want to accept the risks of a high-voltage transmission line in their neighborhoods, they were labeled selfish by those who claimed the line was needed to carry energy to power modern technology, including the farming technology used by protesters. One response of the protesting farmers and their allies was to say there were technological alternatives to the power line, which would provide as much energy in better, safer, more efficient ways. The alternatives they proposed included running the line along highway or railway easements or putting it underground or under rivers. Protesters also suggested and indeed actively promoted the kinds of alternatives touted as small, soft-path, and solar renewable. In this they were joined by people who advocated such a shift as an end in itself.

Finally, a few protesters not only proposed but actively experimented with the technology of broadcasting electricity without wires, using the ideas of electrical genius Nikola Tesla. Their experiment served as a symbolic statement of their claim that they, not the power company, were willing to explore high-technology solutions to the nation's energy problems.

It is probably fair to say that the rural electric co-ops did not take any of these alternatives seriously and were not prepared to debate them realistically, even in terms of their costs and benefits relative to overhead lines.

The co-ops, like other energy utilities, went to siting hearings with the technology already determined through conventional models and projections (Maeder 1976).

Protesters, sometimes the same ones who criticized the WMB for an apparent technological uncertainty, called for the WMB to consider technological alternatives to landfill siting. Some angered the WMB chair by indicating that the organization was reluctant to consider alternatives. The chair indicated quite the opposite—that the WMB followed through on suggestions by studying them carefully, sometimes with a task force.

One major technological alternative, which some protesters proposed and which was studied by the WMB task force, was above-ground storage of waste, where it could be more easily monitored than if disposed of in landfills. Further, the subject of hazardous waste would be kept in the public eye and mind as a problem yet to be resolved.

The WMB charged some of its staff to carefully assess the feasibility of above-ground storage. They found that the trade-offs did not favor it and also that the proposals for recycling were not much different from their own or those they thought would be forthcoming from their consultants.

In early 1983 the WMB decided to turn to a major alternative to landfill siting—namely, to the disposal of hazardous waste residues in repositories to be built in structures excavated very deep in one of the deposits of crystalline bedrock found at various places in Minnesota (Foresite, vol. 3, p. 13, 1978). It was a technology being considered nationally and internationally to dispose of high-level nuclear wastes (Rebuffoni 1983). Apparently this alternative was suggested to the WMB because by 1982 the WMB siting process had produced only four sites acceptable as final candidates. Of these four, two were considered suitable as a site for a temporary above-ground storage facility only.

The WMB committed approximately $1 million to investigate the crystalline bedrock option, feeling that this effort would enable it to increase the number of finalist candidate sites and that the option might in fact be significantly superior to the landfill mode. Hence it decided to reopen the process, leading to a recommendation for six final candidate sites for disposal in bedrock. This required the WMB, with legislative approval, to extend the process for an additional two years. It also meant that the WMB had to go back to a few regions found by the earlier process to be unsuitable for landfill siting (often because of the risks of water quality) and now to consider them for bedrock disposal.

While this met the WMB promise to pursue alternatives, it contradicted the promise to citizens that once their area was dropped they were out of it. Some felt the reopening of the search in their region was vindictive. An organization was reconstituted to fight the new siting, and people living in or near the targeted bedrock deposits were picked to be its new leaders. They sought through legal action to stop the WMB on the grounds that it was now violating the criteria for site selection that it had developed with citizen input during the first meetings (when landfill technology was assumed).

Debates about principles and root causes. Discussion about principles and root causes shifts debate from alternatives to cultural principles or, more precisely, to the subject of sociocultural change. Challengers argued that according to some basic or changing principles the whole subject must be reconstituted and that the assessment of needs was wrong at the root, based on wrong cultural premises. Two major sets of principles are argued, often by different people among the challengers (different segments with different ideologies) but sometimes by the same people at different times.

One set of principles has to do with what is claimed to be fundamental cultural varieties—core truths that have been ignored by those advocating the contested project. There is an expressed need to return to basics. The other set has to do with the premise that we have come to a time of fundamental cultural change, of paradigm shift, as we evolve to some new level of adaptation. These are new basic needs, but some so fundamental that if they are not changed, society risks survival. Protestors argue that even if it can be shown that there is a need for the project to deal with ongoing problems, such as disposing of wastes, helping people escape drug addiction, or preventing pregnancy out of wedlock, this should not be done in ways that perpetuate the root cause of the problem by helping people adjust to it.

Findings from case studies of hazardous waste siting, energy facility siting, new-right challenge of secular humanism, and more show that established orders tend to accept the agenda of challengers; debate moves to alternatives and principles, particularly those concerned with orientation to future change. For example, citizens have argued that the best way to control wastes is to get at their root causes, rather than to dispose of them after they are generated. If industry, government, and people know that a technology is in place to take care of these wastes, they will have no incentive to reduce or stop generating them.

This kind of argument is heard in many cases ranging from energy production to abortion and sex or drug information programs. People resisting energy facility siting will say that if the facility is built to meet projected needs for electric energy, there will be no incentive for conservation and eventual transformation to less wasteful life-styles. Instead, increased energy use will be promoted to pay for the facilities (Meadows et al. 1976). People resisting operation of abortion clinics or the drug or sex information programs say that making these available to teenagers actually encourages the unwary to experiment in premarital sex or drug use, allows the experimenters to escape the consequences of their transgressions, positively reinforces immoral behavior, and may even be part of a humanist conspiracy to control America (LaHayle 1980).

The WMB explained that uncontrolled dumping already existed, and sites in which hazardous waste is improperly stored must be identified and cleaned. WMB members indicated that no matter how much society strikes at the source of the problem, industry will probably always generate some wastes that will require safe repository. According to a WMB report (Hirigoyen and Johnson 1983) control of wastes through measures that internalize costs was endorsed by a broad range of contributors from industry and public-interest groups. They disagreed on how, why, and when specific costs or burdens should be distributed among consumers, taxpayers, industry, and government as incentives or disincentives to change behavior (Hirigoyen and Johnson 1983:13).

At local meetings across the state, held by the WMB or protest groups, people often argued that the price mechanism could not be relied upon to curb waste generation and improper disposal. It was felt that state agencies should develop powerful regulations to monitor and control waste generators before pushing ahead with siting facilities. The WMB responded that it had a nontraditional approach on siting, that it wanted to involve citizens even before it had this technical information assembled. By promoting early involvement, the WMB has achieved its one purpose of getting citizens to demand that it gather technical information and have the power to force compliance for requests for such information.

The WMB proved to be quite adaptable in allowing propositions from actual or potential proponents to be encompassed within its own framework, concepts, and policy explorations. This generally stands in contrast to the ways other established orders dealing with other concerns have opposed or ridiculed ideas from their grass roots opponents (even though they may later not only accept these as legitimate but propose them as their own.)

Expanding the issue. In many instances a debate about one issue becomes a platform on which people promote debate about others. This type of loading, both symbolic and substantive, often becomes a feature of debates about energy development and hazardous waste disposal.

Energy facility siting controversies provided a kind of stage on which people could attack or defend not only the facility but the whole western industrial way of life. Energy facilities, especially nuclear, become symbolically significant in this larger debate. People load other concerns and issues onto them (Breach 1978).

To their proponents they stand for progress, for the advance of technology to solve social, economic, and political problems (Hoyle and Hoyle 1980). They have also come to stand for conservative political and religious positions (Williams 1980). To opponents, they stand for failure, for technology as a deadly and runaway master that dominates people or requires immense security systems, which jeopardize personal freedoms (Myshaw 1977; Jungck 1979).

Small-scale energy technologies are examined as a way of decentralizing energy production, distribution, and decision making (Craig and Levine 1981). Some advocates of these techologies also argue the virtues of political and economic decentralization generally (Stoiken 1976–1983). Attempts to site larger fossil, hydroelectric, or nuclear facilities in rural or politically sensitive areas become the focus for debates about protecting these areas and the life-styles of their residents from exploitation and domination by urban-industrial culture.

In places where political minorities are active in rights movements, energy development projects can become the focus for debates about the oppression of these minorities and the need for their political and cultural liberation. For example, some Native Americans and their supporters fight energy development in the Black Hills of South Dakota as part of the whole American Indian movement struggle.

As has been learned, the need for growth was pragmatically used to defend energy development projects, while the limits to growth and the sufficiency ethic were used with alternatives to challenge such projects. However, the growth debate certainly had a powerful life of its own, which was nourished by controversy about energy development.

The future of energy development and the debate about it has been of major concern to analysts at the International Institute of Applied Systems Analysis, Laxenburg, Austria. Two in particular (Thompson 1980; Caputa, pers. comm., 1981) have been struck by the way positions in energy development controversies reflect basic preexisting social (structural) and cultural (worldview) orientations of the holders. Energy controversies are used to state these more basic orientations and to seek adherents to them.

In Minnesota the debate over the management of hazardous waste and the siting of waste management facilities has not provided a forum for discussion of more than the ostensible issue. The WMB was prepared to encourage a much broader debate as it called upon people to join in developing a comprehensive waste management plan. Perhaps it was because the WMB was primed for debate that it did not have to do so. The WMB and staff were ready to deal with broad concerns, in part to develop a comprehensive waste management plan. Yet it is unlikely that they would want such enlargment to escape their control. As noted, the WMB did not want to have the siting process taken over by what have been termed "career protesters," who could carry on the power line dispute endlessly or attack government and mainstream society with radical political theory. It also seems that some WMB people were worried that proponents of above-ground waste management technology might use the case to make money selling this technology or to gain influence as the professional watchdog of the WMB. But their reluctance to allow the case to be used by others in these ways would not itself prevent such loading. The main barrier could be that waste and its management is simply not as rich or manipulatable a symbolic platform as energy. Perhaps the major social concerns and issues of the present do not fit the waste platform.

A main concern seems to be to improve the economy by increasing worker and industry productivity and encouraging labor and management to cooperate rather than conflict. Another is to improve the quality of education, especially to prepare people for a high-technology future. Perhaps it is the established order that can best use the waste management issue to talk up its concerns. It is possible that the researchers will examine cases of managing hazardous wastes to learn more about how social and cultural barriers to cooperation for productivity can be removed and how high technology can be advanced.

Research may enable us to learn more about how to conduct a successful siting process involving the public, but perhaps it will reveal more striking evidence that process cannot change public resistance into acceptance. This could persuade some that government should not devote time and resources to involve the public in siting nuclear waste repositories. This could lead some to argue that government must simply resolve to find sites in spite of resistance and not spend time trying to gain acceptance through process. During the last years of the Carter administration there was considerable pressure for as well as against the establishment of a Federal Mobilization Board and "fast-track" procedures to facilitate and speed up the siting and construction of critical energy production and distribution facilities. Opponents of this were sure a fast track meant that public involvement in this would be greatly curtailed. What will the hazardous waste management facility siting process teach?

Summary. The Minnesota waste siting controversy has yet to face all tests of project suitability and acceptability, yet others are already turning to this case for lessons they think it teaches. Learning what can usefully and reliably be transferred to other cases would seem to call for the major efforts of a nonpartisan research team working independently of any of the parties involved, but with their cooperation. The team would need to use techniques of observation, interview, document and media survey, and perhaps application of a questionnaire. With these they would examine the action of the WMB and other government organizations as they become directly concerned with this issue; the action of citizens and their interest groups across the state before, during, and after winnowing has included or dropped their area as a site; and the interaction of these parties.

To be sure, the WMB has contracted with public relations consultants to help it design and conduct aspects of its process. But this does not qualify as being independent, nonpartisan, and scholarly research. It is not sufficient as a means to consider and seek answers to test the proposition underlying the siting process.

The WMB entered its project with some guiding hypotheses about how to proceed and what to expect. It talked about testing the ability and willingness of people and organizations across our society to join the search and has considered the project to be a challenge for everyone. It appears to have conducted the search openly, energetically, and adaptively; shifting to avoid pitfalls; branching out to learn more. But it also seems that there has been no systematic evaluation of these guiding hypotheses as they are put to the test across the states. When the process is completed, even the basic premises and approach underlying it will remain as much a matter of personal preference, speculation, and philosophy as they are now. If people use these in the future, it will necessarily be with about the same uncertainties held by the designers and practitioners of this hazardous waste management facility siting process. What could have been taught has not been learned.

CHAPTER 5

Role of mass communication

C. N. OLIEN ● P. J. TICHENOR ● G. A. DONOHUE

SOCIETAL ASSESSMENT OF NEEDS is an exercise in social power. Whenever a community or state builds a new health clinic, joins two or more school districts, or opposes a plan from the agencies of distant government to build a local disposal site for hazardous waste, the needs for those actions are defined by groups that dominate the power and influence structure, either within the community or beyond the control of the community (Donohue 1974). If the definition of needs occurs in an atmosphere of conflict, that conflict will be a result of challenges to or uncertainties about power of relevant groups (Coleman 1957; Dahrendorf 1959; Donohue et al. 1973). The needs of American blacks in the 1960s and 1970s were accommodated largely because the civil rights movement was seen as a threat to social stability and therefore challenging to control by the existing elites. The accommodations that occurred had the primary consequences of maintaining the existing power relationships, rather than necessarily meeting needs for reform as defined by the black community. Similarly, the farm action groups of the past century (including the Farm Bureau, Farmers Union, National Farmers Organization, and American Agriculture Movement) are often credited with creating a number of programs for alleviating rural distress. By and large, these were accommodations that may have satisfied some of the short-run concerns of the activist groups but were at the same time maintaining a pattern of government assumption of risks and minimal guarantees that shored up agriculture in much the same fashion as government has shored up such supercorporations as Chrysler and Lockheed (Gross and Donohue 1970).

Since stability is a prime concern of power structures, an expression of need will meet resistance if satisfying it appears to have destabilizing consequences. If the Civilian Conservation Corps erosion control projects of the 1930s had been seen as providing competition with the business and industrial sector, they would not have been viable ideas for public investment. When the city of Brainerd, Minnesota, resists state-mandated fluoridation of its water in the interest of maintaining local control of vital services, this community is clearly viewed as deviant and therefore a threat to established agencies for control of health practices. One outcome of such a threat may be measures to co-opt the protesting subgroup. Brainerd's deviance may be tolerated or accommodated so as to reduce the possibility that this community and others with similar views will defect and embrace an extremist philosophy. Acquiescing to certain demands of labor unions and ethnic minority groups (both within the United States and in other countries) is considered a necessary trade-off for co-opting the loyalty of these groups to prevent them from "going communist" or otherwise destabilizing the system.

Mass communication and social needs. It is generally assumed that communitywide participation in any collective decision such as identification of needs requires maximal dissemination of information and that mass media such as newspapers and television are basic to this process. The extent to which media accomplish this dissemination, as well as social consequences of how they disseminate information on public issues, has been a subject of public criticism and research. A synthesis of research findings should shed some light on how mass media influence the definition of needs in communities with varying structures and conditions of community conflict.

One of the historically pervasive views of the media is that they function as a Fourth Estate, which has the power to independently perform a surveillance and judgmental function about events and relationships in society (Hocking 1947; Hachten 1963; Rucker 1968; Cater 1969). In its extreme form, this view would assign to the media the capacity to independently define needs for the system as a whole. Support for First Amendment protection of freedom of the press is frequently justified as essential for maintaining such an independent status and the corrective ability that it implies for identifying social wrongs and, thereby, needs for change.

The underlying notion of an autonomous press is taken as a given by both media advocates and critics but is evaluated in far different ways because of the different interests involved. One major reason for journalists embracing the Fourth Estate interpretation is its potential for legitimizing their operations and protecting them from criticism. The critics generally represent groups who see certain kinds of media reporting as contrary to their interests, leading these groups to charge that media are "too big for their britches," "out of control," and need to be made less autonomous. The latter view finds popular support, as when the White House criticizes coverage of the Vietnam conflict, petroleum executives assail a "60 Minutes" TV program that raises questions about oil companies, or the U.S. Department of Defense prohibits coverage of the invasion of Grenada.

There is a well-established research tradition on the agenda setting role of media (McCombs and Shaw 1972; Shaw and McCombs 1977; Weaver et al. 1981). The theoretical rationale is attributed to such earlier analyses as (1) Lippmann's (1922) reference to the authority over imagination of photographs, the movies, and the press; (2) Cohen's (1963) claim that the press "is stunningly successful in telling its readers what to think *about*;" and (3) Lang and Lang's (1966) conclusion that the media "are constantly presenting objects suggesting what individuals in the mass should think about, know about, have feelings about." These analyses present strong associations between media coverage of issues and public rating of the importance of those issues.

The assumption of the independent power of media is stated succinctly in a monograph by Weaver et al. (1981: 4, 207): "In its most radical form, this idea of agenda-setting amounts to an assertion that over time the priorities of the press become the priorities of the public." Priorities implies definition of needs. The same monograph further explicates the power implications by asserting it is "no exaggeration to say that the media can make or break presidential hopefuls."

While the strength of correlations between media and public agendas may vary with community, medium, and issue, there is little question that public perceptions may be influenced by media presentations (McLeod et al. 1974; Palmgreen and Clarke 1977; Katz 1980; DeFleur and Dennis 1981; McQuail 1983). Agenda setting research is considered by many scholars as solid empirical refutation of the conclusions of the late 1950s and early 1960s that media have only limited effects on perceptions held by the public (Klapper 1960).

The role of media in the agenda setting literature assumes media primacy and rarely addresses the question of how the media agenda itself is set and by whom (Westley 1976). The question is whether the media are indeed independent agents having the capacity to initiate such public agendas. Structurally, media are not a Fourth Estate but rather are highly integrated within the existing system and subject to its constraints. The agendas that media report are primarily those of the power groups, including the conflict relations among them. Thus media are part of the acceleration and deceleration processes in development of controversies but have neither the primary function nor the capacity to initiate the definitions of social needs that give rise to social action. Media are instruments of information control and are thus vital to social control according to the primary values and powers of the system (Donohue et al. 1973). Information in newspapers and televised reports may draw attention to an issue, reinforce the status of authoritative sources, contribute to increased membership of an emerging group, or withdraw legitimacy from a group by labeling it deviant. Media decisions are largely responsive to and supportive of the power centers of society, particularly those in government and business. This point was argued in the Commission on Freedom of the Press report (1947), and research evidence supporting this conclusion was reported by Breed (1958) and more recently by a number of investigations, including Olien et al. (1968), Paletz et al. (1971), Sigal (1973), Molotch and Lester (1975), Curran (1978), Schudson (1978), Tuchman (1978), Gans (1979), Lemert and Larkin (1979), Fishman (1980), Gitlin (1980), Morley (1981), and Shepherd (1981).

Research findings. A synthesis of research findings, in the form of a series of generalizations, will provide a summary and perspective on current thinking about the role of the media in social definition of needs.

REPORTS OF CONFLICT. *Conflicts in needs definitions are more likely to be reported by media in pluralistic structures than by media in less pluralistic structures.* Conflict and consensus approaches may be seen as alternative modes for definitions of needs (Dahrendorf 1959; Donohue et al. 1978). Consensus may result from an acceptance of the authority of leadership in determining needs without extensive participation of groups outside the leadership structure. Leadership groups usually interpret silence from the community at large as support for the leaders' definition of what the community needs.

Social conflict, while generally viewed as a disruptive condition, has a variety of positive functions such as stimulation of communication, articulation of old ideals or generation of new ones, and strengthening cohesion of one or more participating groups (Simmel 1955; Coser 1967). Rather than being disruptive, conflict may be seen as a sign of vitality that may lead to a clarification of needs in the community. Conflict is more likely to occur as a routine process in structures that are more pluralistic, emanating from the greater number and diversity of potential sources of organized power. The metropolitan community, with its array of employment opportunities, political and government agencies, educational centers, and religious organizations experiences more conflict as a normal course. The formal relationships among the agencies and interest groups incorporate a set of mechanisms for accommodating the conflicts while minimizing the disruption of the basic power relationships within the system (Donohue et al. 1973).

Newspapers and broadcast stations are constrained by structural conditions the same as other groups. In small, more homogeneous communities the media tend to avoid reporting conflict that would threaten the power structure, which operates as an oligarchy via a consensus mode of decision making. Conflict, when it is reported in small communities, is usually about relationships with external organizations and agencies. Local consensus is preserved if not strengthened by struggles with attempted control from outside.

In the more pluralistic community, media reporting of conflict is more frequent and routine, since conflict is inherent in such a structure and communication about the needs, positions, and actions of the different groups is necessary for the system to function. Given the complexity of the system, communication on an interpersonal, face-to-face basis is not as adequate as it is in the small, more homogeneous community. The pluralistic structure of the large metropolitan center requires an extensive network of accommodative mechanisms and formal communications, of which the newspapers and broadcast stations are a vital part. Conflict reporting routinely abounds in such a structure, as when a newspaper reports debates among such groups as government units, labor and management groups, environmental groups and industrial firms, renters and apartment owners, and antipornography groups and city councils. In fulfilling these social control functions, media reflect and reinforce the basic processes of their communities. The small-town weekly reflects a small-town outlook, while the urban daily reflects an urban outlook and legitimizes the leadership roles and the conflict processes that are characteristic of pluralistic communities. A content analysis of Minnesota newspapers in 1965 and 1979 indicated that among newspapers that are locally owned dailies reported more conflict in local government than did weeklies. Dailies are published in communities that are more pluralistic. Except for metropolitan suburbs, weeklies are more likely to be published in communities that are more homogeneous (Donohue et al. 1973). The structural control of media definitions of needs is clear when small-town interests clash with those of a large urban center that dominates the region in which the small town is located. Weekly papers in small towns near the Boundary Waters Canoe Area (BWCA) of northeastern Minnesota mirrored the local view on multiple use of the area, which would include mining and logging as benefits to local economic growth. Dailies in Duluth and the Twin Cities were more likely to draw attention to and support a view favoring restrictions on motorized transportation (access by snowmobiles and boats to the BWCA) as well as restrictions on mining and logging in the wilderness area.

MEDIA PERCEIVED AS HELPFUL. *More established agencies and powerful groups tend to perceive mass media as more helpful to their organizations than do leaders of less established groups.* Mass media tend to reflect the outlook of dominant power centers. In an extensive case study of a city council in North Carolina, Paletz et al. (1971) found that newspaper reporting consistently supported local government authority when challenges occurred from citizen groups. This support occurred in the greater frequency and selection of attributions to city council and government agency members, as contrasted with citizen groups, and in styles of reporting that gave the council or agency proceedings a more rational and methodical appearance than might be perceived by an outsider attending the sessions. Molotch and Lester (1975) found that newspaper coverage of a major oil spill was heavily dominated by events concerning large corporations and federal agencies, and Sigal (1973) found that nearly 60 percent of the sources of the *New York Times* and *Washington Post* for national and international news could be classified as routine contacts with legislative bodies or government agencies. It should be pointed out that much of this contact is a result of the purposive control of agendas by these agencies and therefore not by the press. Similarly, Lemert and Larkin (1979) found that nearly half the individuals who succeeded in having their letters to the editor published were active in four or more community activities. By comparison, less than a fifth of those whose letters were rejected and a tenth of those who did not write to the editor at all were active at that level in the community. Also, the newspaper appeared to reinforce existing power interests by restricting letters to discussion of issues rather than organizational strategy. A newspaper policy that prohibits this "mobilizing information," as Lemert and Larkin term it, on the editorial page removes one type of organizational tactic from groups seeking to increase their power base.

This is not to say that media operate in a deliberate, conscious, and diabolical fashion, as W. R. Hearst, Joseph Pulitzer, and Rupert Murdoch have been accused of doing, but the consequences of media actions for exercise of power are the same. In actuality, reporters, editors, and other members of the media, like any other occupational group, are socialized in the context of the existing system and subject to all of its pressures. Since socialization tends to be accompanied by favorable perceptions of the member group, it follows that leadership groups that generally receive favorable treatment from the media recognize it as such and reciprocate by rewarding the media for their efforts.

Several bodies of data from Minnesota research support the conclusion that leaders of more established groups are more likely than leaders of less established groups to see the media as more helpful to their causes. These include a 1978 study of leaders quoted in the media about local issues in two communities, a similar study of sources quoted in local issues in four communities in 1980, and a study in 1979 of sources quoted about the American Agriculture Movement (AAM) (Table 5.1) (Olien et al. 1981).

Compared with the "other" groups, such as citizen and student groups, the "officials" or "officials and business groups" were more likely to see none of the media as harmful in two of the three studies, and in each study were less likely to see one or more media as harmful. In addition, in each study there is a greater tendency among the "officials" than among the "others" to view the media as neither helpful nor harmful. This latter finding by itself suggests that among groups seeking to increase their power through the media, its role is more sharply defined as either positive or negative. While some of the more established groups, from their power position, can afford to view the media in a relatively detached way, such is not the case for the less established groups.

The most relevant media for these leader groups differ somewhat in the three studies. In the 1978 two-community study, the principal media were a regional daily and a small-town rural weekly, whereas the key media in the AAM study included Twin Cities newspapers and television; the national television networks; Washington, D.C., newspapers; and regional dailies and weeklies. In the 1980 study the media included the daily papers of St. Paul and Red Wing, weeklies in suburban Cottage Grove and rural Zumbrota, and the television and radio stations of the local communities and the Twin Cities metro area.

Taken together, the findings summarized in Table 5.1 illustrate how news media are seen as supportive by groups that are dominant in the social system. In the 1978 study the local media are perceived as more supportive by the local power groups than by citizen groups that were often challenging established agencies. In the AAM study, following the "tractorcade" event, the national media are perceived as more supportive of the established agricultural groups than of the AAM challenge. In the small towns of southwestern Minnesota, AAM had established itself as a group dealing with a problem of general concern to the region. The organization was generally reported in local media in a way reflecting farmer needs, and this reporting was seen as positive by AAM. The rural weekly newspapers were instrumental organizational resources for the AAM, much as weekly

TABLE 5.1. Evaluations of helpfulness or harmfulness of media in three studies in Minnesota

Newspaper and/or broadcast media	1978 two-community study[a]		1979 AAM study[b]		1980 four-community study[c]			
	Officials (%)	Citizens (%)	Officials (%)	AAM members (%)	Officials, business (%)	Citizens, students (%)	Total officials (%)	Total other (%)
	(n:29)	(n:6)	(n:11)	(n:28)	(n:53)	(n:22)	(n:93)	(n:56)
Helpful, neither harmful	72	20	64	21	55	59	61	36
Neither helpful nor harmful	17	0	18	4	22	9	20	5
One or both harmful	10	80	18	75	23	32	18	59

[a] "Officials" refers to elected and appointed persons in government and educational agencies.

[b] "Officials" refers to appointed heads of state and federal agricultural agencies and heads of older, established farm organizations. AAM refers to members and leaders of the American Agriculture Movement, a new and militant organization at the time of the study.

[c] "Officials, business" refers to news sources who are elected or appointed officials in government, business owners or managers, or consultants to government or utilities.

papers in another area were instrumental for groups that organized in opposition to high-voltage power lines brought into west-central Minnesota by external utility cooperatives. Newspapers in the Twin Cities and Washington, D.C., however, structure their reporting from the perspective of the needs of the dominant power groups statewide and nationwide rather than according to the parochial needs of any local-interest group. This difference does not occur out of a lack of sophistication on the part of the weekly but is a reflection of local power and what a local community may be opposed to, whereas the metro media are a reflection of urban needs.

The 1980 study differs from the other two in that the citizen and student leaders are slightly more likely than the "officials, business" groups to see the media as helpful. In contrast with the other two studies, the less established leaders see harm from the media in less than half the cases. The 6 citizen leaders in the 1978 study and the 28 AAM members were mounting more direct challenges to authority than was the case in the 1980 study in which several local controversies involved interaction among groups over relatively routine civic matters. One of these was a student challenge to recently appointed administrators of an energy training center concerning the handling of a new educational curriculum. While these students achieved a considerable amount of newspaper coverage, they were challenging specific administrators but not the primary leadership group in the community. Surveys of the general population indicated that this was seen as a low-intensity issue, however intense the student activity itself may have been. It might be likened to the familiar situation in which public criticism of a football or basketball coach occurs as a ritual that leaves the basic structure intact even though it may lead to censure or dismissal of a particular specialist from whom the primary leadership structure can maintain a comfortable distance.

Given that media tend to support the need definitions of dominant groups and that their support is recognized by those groups, one might wonder why the media occasionally come under such sharp attack by established leaders. Vice President Agnew's criticism in the late 1960s, the criticisms by officials of the petroleum industry for alleged media unfairness in environmental reporting, and the widespread hostility toward the media that surfaced in the 1983 Grenada invasion might lead to questioning the conclusions stated here. It must be remembered that while media reflect the need definitions of dominant power groups, they also reflect power relationships. If there is a confrontation between dominant power groups, the media will reflect it. If there is a power vacuum or outright confusion about who has power, media will reflect that confusion, as has occurred frequently in reporting of the Mideast crisis and earlier in the Vietnam war era. Several writers have pointed out that media reporting initially was supportive of the need for a U.S. military effort in Vietnam and that questions about that war appeared in the media when it became increasingly clear that the war could not be won militarily and when a number of powerful political groups in the United States challenged the official U.S. position in that war. There were, correspondingly, several challenges by opposition political groups to the idea of a U.S. invasion of Grenada. By mounting that invasion as it did, the U.S. government in effect bypassed those challenging groups and went "straight to the people" for legitimation, using a tactic well known in politics. In such a situation the media, having reflected the previous challenges to the act in question, became the convenient scapegoat, since attack on them was less costly politically than it would have been to challenge the national loyalty of the political opposition itself. Furthermore, it should be noted that in most international crises, the domestic conflict reported by the media has been at the center of political interaction and not at the political extremes. U.S. media are as quick as media in any system to apply the labels of "vandalism" or "terrorism" to acts that are considered nonlegitimate by the dominant power groups. When such labels are used, the implication is that the needs of the sponsoring groups are not recognized within the system. Finally, it should be noted that recurring criticism of the media is itself a control action (Dreier 1983). A U.S. president may gain popular support by raising in a press conference the question of "whose side the media were on" in the Vietnam war, thereby placing pressure on those media to demonstrate their national loyalty.

The media function largely to maintain the existing balances of power. When media appear to be acting on behalf of an underdog, one will find that the rationale provided for such a position is couched in terms of primary system values at one extreme or in terms of political expediency at the other. Apparent controversy between the media and a particular administration of a business or government power center is basically a reflection of the power struggle among societal groups during periods of transition and instability.

INFLUENCE OF EXTERNAL AGENCIES. *Leaders in more pluralistic structures are more likely to perceive influence of external agencies in determination of community needs than are leaders in more homogeneous structures.* Increasing differentiation and pluralism have generally led to greater centralization of control. For any particular community this means increased dependence upon agencies outside the community for government, business and financial, educational, legal, and religious activity. Evidence relevant to this generalization comes from a 1980 study of leaders in 10 small communities of southwestern and northeastern Minnesota (Table 5.2) (Donohue et al. 1985). The southwest is a less pluralistic region in which businesses have been traditionally initiated as family enterprises, whereas the northeast is a more pluralistic region with a tradition of investment from external agencies, as occurred in lumbering, mining, taconite processing, and paper milling. The southwest has less ethnic diversity, more dependence on agriculture, and fewer linkages with external sources of control compared with the northeast. Also, compared with the northeast, the southwest ranks higher on an index of traditional family organization and lower on a socioeconomic status index based primarily on proportion of poverty households, income, and education.

Leaders in this study were identified by reputational techniques, which are especially appropriate for small community analysis. A characteristic of a consensus structure is that the sources of influence are widely known and acknowledged. In a more pluralistic community, the specialization is such that leaders in one sector may be unknown by leaders in others; thus the reputational approach may be questioned in that setting.

The southwestern leaders were generally more likely to name local government, business, human services, and citizens as influencing need than were the northeastern leaders. Similarly, the northeastern leaders were more likely than southwestern leaders to name nonlocal groups as influencing needs. At first blush, it may appear that one finding in Table 5.2 is not

TABLE 5.2. Leader perceptions of local and external determination of need for development projects in more and less pluralistic structures

Leader perception	Southwest (less pluralistic) (%)	Northeast (more pluralistic) (%)
	(n:79)	(n:76)
Needs determined by:		
Local government	48	54
Local business	73	54
Local human services	54	46
Local citizens	56	45
Average local need influence score[a]	3.36	2.83
Nonlocal citizens	0	4
Nonlocal government	29	51
Nonlocal business	10	43
Nonlocal human services	4	8
Average nonlocal need influence score[b]	0.63	1.37

[a]This score is derived from a question asked for each of three local development projects that the respondent had identified: What person, group, or groups were involved in determining this need? Responses were coded in six categories, including the four listed here plus local media and local other. The score is the sum of categories mentioned across the three projects. The scores ranged from 0 to 7, with an overall mean of 3.1 and a standard deviation of 1.53.

[b]Computation of this score was based on the same question employed for local score as above. In this case, the distribution is slightly skewed, with 39 percent of the leaders mentioning no nonlocal groups at all. The mean is 0.99 and the standard deviation is 1.02.

supportive of the generalization, in that northeastern leaders were slightly more likely than southwestern leaders (54 vs. 48 percent) to name local government as influential. It should be pointed out that in the northeast, leaders were more likely to name government sources of any type than were southwestern leaders, and the proportion of influential government agencies that are nonlocal is much higher in the northeast than in the southwest. Since greater dependence upon government for coordination of developmental efforts is a characteristic of more diverse systems, this finding is consistent with the structural model.

One of the most striking outcomes of the study is that local groups in both areas are seen as more influential than nonlocal groups. Even when a community is dealing with increasingly diverse and complex external control centers, local commercial and political bodies remain important for dealing with those external centers. This finding is particularly important for people engaged in developmental activities in local communities. While power may be shifting to regional and national metropolitan centers, the rural community continues to be a strong force that provides an identity and power base from which local groups define their collective needs.

DETERMINING COMMUNITY NEEDS. *Community leaders generally perceive media as having a secondary rather than a primary role in determination of community needs.* Among the earliest data relevant to this generalization are those reported by Edelstein and Schulz (1964) from a study of Grangeville, a small, homogeneous, rural community having a typical consensus-based decision structure. More than half the 46 leaders in this community believed that the weekly newspaper "should publicize controversies only when others have discussed them," and only a third thought the newspaper should take the initiative in publicizing controversies. Furthermore, the leaders' perceptions of the newspaper's performance were very much in line with their prescriptions. The secondary role of the media in defining needs, while reflecting the need definitions of established sources, is implicit in Tuchman's (1978) report that in all her observations of reporters and editors she had "never heard them challenge the right of an elected or appointed official to make news."

Gieber and Johnson (1961) referred to a journalistic tendency to treat politicians' statements as those of a total community, for example, "the city is trying to balance its budget." Molotch and Lester (1975) refer to news creation as "accomplished according to the occasioned event needs of those with access to the media." In their later study of the Santa Barbara oil spill, these investigators found that this accident became a national controversy primarily because a local elite developed an alternative conception of the problem based on its own interests. This conception was reflected in the

Santa Barbara media but not in the national media where views of federal and oil company officials held sway. There are several bodies of evidence that media support elite definitions of need through direct interaction with those elites. A group at Northwestern University concluded from a study that media exposure affected agendas of leaders and the general public. The same researchers found that policy changes, however, were connected more to active collaboration between journalists and public officials than to change in public opinion, which is often inferred from media content by leaders rather than measured directly (Cook et al. 1983).

Further evidence that community leaders perceive media as having a secondary rather than primary role in need definition is available in the 1980 study of leaders interviewed in 10 small Minnesota communities (Table 5.3) (Donohue et al. 1985). First, leaders were asked in an open-end format to name the agencies that determined the need for specific local development projects. The local newspaper was mentioned in response to that question by fewer than 5 percent of the leaders. Next, leaders were asked specifically whether the local newspaper did or did not "play a part in determining the need." For each project, half or slightly more indicated that the newspaper "did play a part" (Table 5.3). When asked how this part was played, the leaders' responses most frequently fit the "informing" category, with "editorializing" second, for each of the projects. In no more than 15 percent of the cases for any one project did the leaders indicate that "identifying" needs was the role of the local newspaper. They infrequently

TABLE 5.3. Leader perception of media role in determination of need for development projects in 10 communities

Leader perception	First project (%)	Second project (%)	Third project (%)
	(n:155)	(n:155)	(n:155)
Percent saying:			
Local newspaper did play a part in determining this need	54	50	50
Local newspaper did not play a part in determining this need	36	43	36
Don't know	7	5	7
No response	3	2	7
Total	100	100	100
If newspaper did play a part, played it by:[a]	(n:84)	(n:77)	(n:78)
Informing	75	61	81
Editorializing	41	38	45
Identifying	10	14	15
Editor's own action	14	10	4
Newspaper doing study	7	6	4

[a]These percentages do not add to 100 because of multiple responses. Percentage is based on number saying newspaper "played a part."

mentioned the media as primary agencies in need determination, and the supporting role that they see is generally one of reporting. It should be pointed out that these are small, outlying communities. In more complex communities the media would be expected to have an even greater and more complex linkage role in the process of definition of needs.

ROLE IN CONTROVERSIES. *Mass media tend to play an accelerating role in controversies rather than an initiating role.* To say that the media infrequently initiate controversies is not to conclude that they are without a major role in development of conflict. Given the greater access to media by groups with more power and legitimate status and given the centrality of information control in the interest of social control, one would expect media strategies to be basic to any major power contest.

As an information resource for power, media coverage is sought by newly emerging groups wishing to take their message to the larger public for legitimation and eventual political action. These groups often find irony in the fact that they require media attention to achieve social power but must first possess a modicum of power before they will be recognized by the media. Lacking such power, an emerging social movement may find the media initially reflecting the hostile reactions of the dominant groups in society, as occurred in the women's movement (Tuchman 1978) and the campus protests (Gitlin 1980). Coverage tends to bestow increasing legitimacy on a movement as it attains visibility. Media affect a controversy, become part of that controversy, and are affected by it in a reciprocal process. Similarly, when conditions change and a protest group's power is contained or diminished by other sources, media will reflect delegitimization and may become part of a process of deceleration. Such a process, according to Gitlin, seems to have occurred in media attention to the Students for a Democratic Society movement of the late 1960s and early 1970s.

The media acceleration role is illustrated by the controversy over a high-voltage power line in Minnesota from 1974 to 1978. As noted in Chapter 4, two regional utility cooperatives sought to establish a 400-kv DC line from a generating plant in North Dakota across west-central Minnesota, connecting with a substation near Minneapolis. Along the line a number of groups organized to protest on the grounds that the manner in which the line route was selected was being carried out over the objections of local communities and property owners by outside groups that had not demonstrated need for the electricity in the first place. Opposition was eventually highly organized and intense, and the groups claimed repeatedly that the line was environmentally destructive, a hindrance to agriculture, and hazardous to human beings and livestock. The groups pressed their arguments in several hearings organized by a state agency to resolve the issue and eventually in court. All of the hearing and court outcomes, however, were in favor of the line and it was eventually constructed, indicating where the power to define needs rested. Electric power and social power were consolidated in the same centers.

The initial coverage of the controversy was primarily in small-town weekly papers and a few regional dailies along the proposed route. In the typical community the proposed project was first reported in the local weekly following a meeting of the county board where utility representatives stated the plan for the line and their claims of benefits for the local area. Subsequent editions of the newspaper contained, in sequence, letters to the editor from individuals objecting to the line, announcements of meetings of newly formed opposition groups, and follow-up stories about organizational activities of these groups and their intended actions. When the state-organized corridor hearings were held in 1975, coverage increased in regional and metropolitan daily papers. When a permit for construction was issued in spring 1976, hostile demonstrations occurred in line route areas around utility work sites. At that point, television camera coverage began and increased through winter 1978, when the line was eventually constructed amidst intense media strategies that included organized picketing and a variety of other techniques. Media strategies, therefore, were basic to carrying out the controversy.

From summer 1975 through winter 1978 an analysis was conducted on the power line reporting of a weekly paper in an affected rural community, a metropolitan daily newspaper, and two metropolitan television stations. Interviews among general population samples were conducted in the rural community and in a metro suburban community on the power line route at four times—early fall 1975, winter 1976, spring 1977, and late winter and early spring 1978 (Table 5.4).

The findings in Table 5.4 are consistent with the conclusion that the media had an accelerating role in the power line controversy, when considered alongside the previous point that the media coverage itself depended primarily on organized activity. In this controversy there is a clear progression in coverage from one medium to another. Weekly coverage peaked early, as the controversy became a statewide issue covered by daily newspapers and eventually television. Weekly coverage even during the final intense stage did not exceed the level of winter 1976. Daily reports in 1978 (22.0) were more than double the 1977 rate, while TV visual reports (12.5) in 1978 were more than four times as frequent as the previous year (3.0).

Perception of conflictiveness was measured by asking whether the respondent considered the topic a "touchy subject around here." Survey findings indicate that through spring 1977 the increasing public perceptions of conflictiveness and importance were parallel to the increase in media cov-

TABLE 5.4.   Volume of media coverage of power line controversy and perception of the
issue over time in two communities

	Fall 1975	Winter 1976	Spring 1977	Winter/ Spring 1978
Media coverage				
Average monthly number of:[a]				
Rural weekly newspaper reports	2.4	5.6	2.6	5.0
Metro daily newspaper reports	1.0	1.4	9.0	22.0
Metro TV visual reports	0.0	0.0	3.0	12.5
Percent perceiving issue as:[b]	(%)	(%)	(%)	(%)
Touchy subject in suburban area	20	36	64	54
Very important in suburban area	19	33	47	45
Touchy subject in rural area	42	48	79	75
Very important in rural area	31	35	67	69

[a]For each of the three media reports, the average is for a five-month period, including the
two months preceding the survey, the two months after, and the month when the survey was
conducted.
[b]In each area the specific months of the surveys were: fall (September), 1975; winter
(February), 1976; spring (March and April), 1977; and winter/spring (March), 1978. Sample
sizes for the successive surveys were 140, 91, 200, and 139 in the suburban area and 136, 111,
167, and 120 in the rural area. In each area the first two interviews were conducted in homes,
and the second two were by telephone.

erage. In the suburban area the proportion perceiving a "touchy subject"
increased from 20 percent in 1975 to 64 percent in 1977, then dropped back
to 54 percent as the controversy wound down; in the rural area the change
was from 42 percent in 1975 to 79 percent in 1977 and then a slight decline
to 75 percent in 1978.

Ratings of importance followed a similar progression, except that in
the rural area the proportion perceiving the issue as "very important" increased slightly in the final interviews. It should also be noted that at each
time, proportions perceiving the issues as "touchy" and "very important"
were higher in the rural than the suburban area. This difference is expected,
since such a controversy tends to totally consume public attention in a
homogeneous community, whereas controversy is common in the more
pluralistic suburban area and the power line debate was one of many such
issues.

Just as media may be part of an acceleration process, they may take
part in deceleration. The slight drop-off in proportion perceiving the issue
as conflictive in 1978 may reflect the fact that, intense as the confrontations
were at this point, the struggle was seen as a lost cause and one that needed
to be resolved one way or another. The media coverage reinforced this "lost
cause" definition by repeatedly reporting a state supreme court decision
favoring line construction and eventually referring to several acts against
the line as "vandalism." At that point the conflict itself became the story
and the fundamental issue became the restoration of social order.

INTENSITY OF CONFLICT. *The higher the intensity of conflict about an issue in a community, the greater the awareness of specific components of the issue.* The consequences of conflict for stimulation of attention have been identified in a number of studies (Donohue et al. 1975; Tichenor et al. 1980). Conflict is a basic condition for generating increases in media coverage, and audience attention will be drawn to the same conflict.

Additional analyses of the power line study data suggest that awareness of an issue will grow as the issue becomes increasingly perceived as immersed in intense controversy (Table 5.5). For purposes of comparison, this table repeats from Table 5.4 the progression of perceptions of the issue as a "touchy subject." Respondents were asked what they had seen or heard about the issue, and their responses were scored according to whether they contained accurate knowledge.

In both the rural and suburban areas, the percent having any accurate knowledge is higher in the final wave of interviews than in any previous one. However, the percentages do not vary with the proportion perceiving the topic as conflictive. In both areas there is a slight drop in knowledge from the first to the second waves of interviews; in the rural area there is a substantial drop (64 to 56 percent) between the second and third interviews, then a sharp rise in the fourth. In the suburban area the percent having

TABLE 5.5. Perceptions of conflict, accurate knowledge, and knowledge gap over time in power line issue in two communities

Perception	Fall 1975 (%)	Winter 1976 (%)	Winter 1977 (%)	Winter 1978 (%)
	(n:140)	(n:91)	(n:200)	(n:139)
Suburban area				
Perceiving issue as touchy subject	20	36	64	54
Having any accurate knowledge	46	44	68	70
Knowing opposition groups	7	12	45	...
Hearing effects on human health				
Opposition perspective	9	10	19	...
Neutral or power association perspective	9	3	15	...
Agreeing that electricity is one of the greatest				
needs	59	31	68	...
Correlation, education × knowledge	−0.09	0.03	0.17	0.22
Rural area	(n:136)	(n:111)	(n:167)	(n:120)
Perceiving issue as touchy subject	42	48	79	75
Having any accurate knowledge	67	64	56	72
Knowing opposition groups	23	20	38	...
Hearing effects on human health				
Opposition perspective	12	18	36	...
Neutral or power association perspective	9	5	17	...
Agreeing that electricity is one of the greatest				
needs	49	49	66	...
Correlation, education × knowledge	0.02	−0.10	0.002	0.12

accurate knowledge was high in both the third and fourth waves.

The dip in knowledge in the rural area while intensity of conflict was increasing may reflect the changes in stages of the controversy and some confusion of the issues in that community. Knowledge in the rural community shows the sharpest drop in winter 1977, following a summer and fall during which the controversy had shifted from a bureaucratic confrontation phase, which had drawn attention to the technical problems, to an informal confrontation stage, which emphasized interaction among contesting groups. The underlying issue was shifting from technical consequences and safety to emphasis on the fundamental question of fairness in loss of property through eminent domain procedures, thereby giving the issue a different complexion.

It should also be pointed out that many of the protest organizations originally defined the issue as urban exploitation of rural areas. As the controversy entered the informal confrontation stage in summer and fall 1976, it became apparent that there was much urban support for the protest groups, which subsequently dropped the antiurban slogans and concentrated on the more universal question of the fairness of eminent domain procedures in this case. This meant that by early 1977 the issue was taking on a different complexion, particularly in the rural areas. The antiurban theme had been prominent in 1975 when there was minimal metro media coverage, which suggests that the issue was presented in a more crystallized fashion throughout the controversy in the suburbs. In the rural area, however, the shift in issues meant reinforming the public, which for large segments may have meant starting over in following the news about the controversy.

A study of the audience responses in 1975 and early 1976, particularly in the rural areas, was dominated initially by such technical factors as location and characteristics of the line, its effect on farming, and the question of potential hazards to human health. As the controversy shifted to a new phase, the media reports were increasingly devoted to conflict over eminent domain and the confrontations along the construction route. This shift may have produced a greater degree of confusion in the rural area than in the suburbs, where neither the antiurban theme nor the technical facts were as much of a factor initially in either media or interpersonal communication.

The power line data also make it possible to examine the consequences of conflict for the magnitude of knowledge gaps between more educated and less educated groups. In any community some groups have capacities, values, and behavior patterns that are more conducive to change than others; these characteristics are reinforced by agencies that distribute services and resources differentially. Typically, those with organized capacities for change are more likely to acquire the distributed services and undergo even more change. This differential process applies to information as well as any other resource, so that more highly educated groups typically benefit more from an increased flow of media publicity than less educated groups (Donohue et al. 1973). The consequence is that existing elites tend to be maintained through possession of greater levels of knowledge upon which they can act in their own interests. Such differentials and their social control consequences have been noted frequently in the literature (Werner 1975; Neuman 1976; Shingi and Mody 1976; Suominen 1976; Ettema and Kline 1977; Genova and Greenberg 1979; Dervin 1980; Katz 1980).

The knowledge gap hypothesis may not hold for all situations. In a previous analysis of knowledge about issues in 19 Minnesota communities, the knowledge gap between education segments was lower in communities where there were heavier media inputs and a higher level of system conflict. As a stimulating condition, conflict increases the likelihood that interest groups will take an active role and inform their membership through means that include mass media. The more intense the conflict, the more the situation highlights the values that are universal to the community and therefore to all groups, high or low in education. The power line issue drew attention to the question of whether the eminent domain principle should be employed to take private property from individuals and local communities without their having an effective voice in the decision. Such a question of individual rights and community prerogatives tends to transcend interest group identities, including groups that differ on education. In effect, the most persuasive argument the rural protesters had in reaching urban residents was the appeal that can be expressed as, "If they can do this to us, they can do it to you."

Since the power line was an intense social conflict engaging such basic values, one might expect knowledge gaps to narrow between more educated and less educated groups. Such appears to be the case (Table 5.5). The correlations between education and possession of accurate knowledge are low and statistically nonsignificant at all four times in the rural area, where intensity was the highest and the structure is the most homogeneous. In the suburban area, the knowledge gap correlations are significant in 1977 and 1978, but not in the earlier waves, and appear to increase in a way that parallels the media publicity more than the change in perceived conflictiveness. These knowledge gap findings as a whole seem to reflect the differences in pluralism between the rural and suburban areas. Previous studies have demonstrated that high homogeneity is accompanied by lower knowledge gaps (Tichenor et al. 1980). Also, although the correlations are low, it should be noted that in both areas the knowledge gaps are highest in the final wave when the coverage was high but the controversy was winding down. As suggested above, this was a point when, quite literally, it was "all over but the shouting." When such a situation occurs, groups with lower levels of education have the most to lose and indeed will lose the most in knowledge as a basis of social power.

DEFINITION OF ISSUES. *The greater the degree of pluralism in a community, the greater the similarity between leaders and the general public in their definitions of issues.* Leaders in a community are in a position of structural marginality. They are links in the networks between the local community and the larger society, as Vidich and Bensman (1958) observed. In this linkage role, leaders must be responsive to the external control centers such as government and business headquarters at the state or national level as well as to the concerns of the local community. With one foot in the local community and one foot in the larger society, leaders may confront questions of identification when they accept and act on need definitions. An example might be property tax breaks by external corporations who are being sought to build local factories or retail outlets. A consequence is that awareness of and responsiveness to purely local needs may vary according to the degree of pluralism of the structure and the consequences for local organization that this pluralism implies.

One of the less obvious characteristics of consensus structures is that leader marginality is especially likely to lead to mistaken perceptions of what other members of the community think about local problems and needs. A consensual system does not necessarily operate on the basis of full participation or full knowledge about what everybody else thinks and believes. The leadership oligarchy itself is well known and typically makes decisions according to tradition without its authority to do so being questioned. In such a process, passivity and silence are often indicators of acquiescence based upon lack of an organized basis for offering an alternative proposal or need definition. Such passivity may be interpreted by leaders, however, as active support for what is being done. Indeed, passivity by any clientele body when action occurs has the functional consequences of reinforcing the status of the leadership groups taking that action.

Discrepancies between leader and local group definitions may become apparent when passivity is shed and there are fundamental changes in grass roots organization that lead toward challenges of the existing power structure. Particularly in small, homogeneous communities the established power elite may be surprised or even offended when a citizen group organizes and expresses a need that the dominant groups have not recognized in the past. If a city council member ridicules a senior citizen group's request for late-night bus service, that ridicule and the associated expression of prejudice may reflect a lack of awareness and appreciation of the needs of a group that has little power and has not been heard from in the past (Paletz et al. 1971).

Such surfacing of public awareness that leaders are out of touch may mark a shift from a consensus to a conflict mode, which implies a challenge to existing power allocations. A coal-fired electrical generating plant was proposed in a southern Minnesota community in 1974, with the state and the power utilities justifying this construction as necessary for meeting state electric power needs. They also made the argument that construction would bring economic benefits to the host county and region. Ordinarily, the local leadership group would act upon these externally introduced criteria on the assumption that the local community would concur with whatever the leaders decided. In this particular case the county board initially favored the construction and later expressed genuine surprise when a group of local farmers organized media strategies that dramatized their angry confrontation with the board over its earlier action. The generating plant in this case was not built. Less than two years later, boards in several counties at first appeared to have difficulty assessing local opposition to the high-voltage power line. Even where the coal-fired generating plant had been earlier challenged so openly and intensely, there was little organized opposition to an extension of the proposed power line (a different technology) through the same area. Several leaders in one of the affected communities interpreted this lack of opposition as evidence of local support; nevertheless, survey interviews indicated that, among local adults having any opinion at all on the power line, a majority opposed it. The tendency to interpret quiescence as support appears to be so entrenched in homogeneous structures that it may hold even where there is recent evidence to contradict it. In a more pluralistic structure there is a greater degree of organization of interest groups that bring their views on issues to the attention of leaders as part of the routinized conflict processes. The urban leader, because of the structurally diverse sources of communication, is made aware of the variety of views held within the community and is less likely than the small-town leader to be caught unprepared by a grass roots movement.

There is additional evidence supporting the conclusion that leaders in small communities are more likely than these in urban communities to have perspectives that diverge from the rest of the community. In a Georgia study Nix and Seerley (1973) found that, in comparison with rural adults, urban adults expressed more of a "coordinative" orientation that stressed negotiation and intergroup communication. Leader groups expressed a high degree of "coordinative" orientation but did not differ between communities. As a result the leader–public difference in coordinative orientation was more than twice as great in the rural community as in the urban community.

Similar results come from a study of two Minnesota communities, one a small town in a mining-forestry-resort area and the other an urban center. Leaders and samples of the general population were asked to evaluate the distribution of scientific information for use in decision making. Leaders in both communities evaluated such distribution more highly than did the general public. The difference in orientation toward scientific information was greater in the small community than in the larger urban community in a way that paralleled the difference in coordinative orientation found by Nix and Seerley. The conclusion was that on the question of using such information to deal with community needs, community leaders and their publics may be marching to a different drummer (Tichenor et al. 1976).

Since degree of conflict intensity is a stimulant of communication, one might expect conflict to be a factor in leader-public discrepancies. The wide-spread reporting of debates among interest groups, which accompanies an intense controversy, might well lead to increased convergence between leaders and the public in their perceptions of what those issues are.

Summary. Definition of social needs in any community is determined by the power relationships among interest groups. Generally, need definitions reflect either the express needs of the dominant groups or short-term accommodations of groups with less power, which may threaten the stability of the system if their need definitions are ignored. Mass dissemination of information and views relevant to those need definitions must be understood as dependent upon those same power relationships. The media of mass communication in any specific situation will therefore vary according to the characteristics of the community structure, such as the degree of diversity in economic, political, religious, educational, and ethnic groupings.

Available research on these processes supports a number of conclusions about the nature of mass media reporting and its consequences for reinforcement of some need definitions rather than others. Conflict as part of need definition is more likely to be reported in mass media in more pluralistic communities than in more homogeneous communities, and groups with a greater degree of established power in the system are more likely than less established groups to regard this media reporting as favorable to their own organizational interests.

Degree of pluralism in the social structure conditions the way in which community leaders perceive influences on needs as well as the role they regard media as playing in determination of those needs. External agencies are likely to be perceived as more influential in determining local needs in more pluralistic regional structures, although there is a tendency for leaders in small communities to perceive local agencies rather than nonlocal agencies as dominant in any structure. The community weekly newspaper is not seen as a primary agency for need determination but is ascribed a supportive role by leaders, primarily through informing and editorializing about needs that have been determined first by the power groups. This secondary supportive role may also be observed in conflict situations in that media tend to be part of a process of acceleration of conflict rather than initiators of it. Evidence to this effect raises considerable questions about the role of media as an independent Fourth Estate in the system.

Conflict over needs is not necessarily a negative force in their assessment but may be a positive factor in the sense of stimulating articulation of needs, communication about need perspectives of different groups, and acquisition of information about needs throughout the community. Finally, conflict and community structure may be joint determinants of the degree to which leaders and members of the general public have similar definitions of issues. Both conflict and degree of pluralism may increase the degree of similarity, while the consensus nature and general absence of controversy in small rural communities may contribute to situations in which leaders have perceptions that may be especially divergent from the rest of the community.

U.S. experiences in needs assessment

CHAPTER 6

Group approaches

LORNA CLANCY MILLER ● RONALD J. HUSTEDDE

ALEXIS DE TOCQUEVILLE'S DESCRIPTION of nineteenth-century America captures the workings of democracy at its best:

> These Americans are the most peculiar people in the world. You'll not believe it when I tell you how they behave. In a local community in their country a citizen may conceive of some need which is not being met. What does he do? He goes across the street and discusses it with his neighbor. Then what happens? A committee comes into existence and then the committee begins functioning on behalf of that need. And you won't believe this but it is true. All of this is done without reference to any bureaucrat. All of this is done by the private citizens on their own initiative.

Some critics have claimed, however, that professional leaders and bureaucrats with technical expertise have come to dominate and control needs assessment discussions. As a result, private citizens tend to be less involved and more inclined to "let the professionals decide what's best."

If spectator citizenry threatens modern democracy, it is important to find ways to encourage citizen involvement in public affairs such as needs assessment. Most of the action taken by or on behalf of individual citizens occurs through organizations or groups. It is obvious that all groups have particular interests. Labor unions are expected to strive for higher wages and better working conditions. Ecology-oriented groups will push for cleaner environments. Corporations will strive for higher earnings for their stockholders. Their perceptions of needs are colored by their own biases and the common interests of their members.

This chapter will review several innovative group approaches to needs assessment. Included are discussions of town meetings, public hearings, the charrette, citizen-directed futures assessment, the Delphi and nominal group approaches, the jury workshop, and consciousness raising. Each of these approaches has its appropriate applications. Crucial to evaluating which group process to use in a given situation is a critical evaluation of each proposed needs assessment project in relationship to the sponsoring entity, the intended users of the findings, the diversity of participants and beneficiaries, and anticipated results and action. Available time and resources are also important delineators of the endeavor.

In the Foreword, Kellerman raises some difficult questions for needs assessment practitioners. She points out that the mere fact that a needs assessment effort is under way is admitting that special methods are required to reach some populations. Kellerman asserts that to understand any given needs assessment project, the practitioner must know who initiated the activity, why it was deemed necessary or desirable, and why the resources were made available to poll the concerns of that particular population. She underscores the importance of "uncovering genuine concerns of the population" rather than asking for a response to the issues as articulated by others. Kellerman also points to the "moral and political responsibility to see to it, at least insofar as possible, that these needs are addressed."

Key variables. With Kellerman's pointed questions in mind, four key variables are recommended here to provide a theoretical framework for some of the decisions in the selection of the group approach. They are based on a multidisciplinary survey of social science literature plus the experience of the authors in the practice of community and organization development. These key action variables include organizational context, group characteristics, idea generation, and leadership. Attention to these variables can enhance the possibility of a successful needs assessment effort.

ORGANIZATIONAL CONTEXT. In Chapter 3, Rothman and Gant present three general approaches to community organization, which put the group approach to needs assessment into an organizational context. They describe locality development as a community change approach that involves a wide spectrum of local people in goal determination and action. Strategies emphasized in this organizational context include democratic procedures, voluntary cooperation, self-help, development of indigenous leaders, and education. Social planning involves institutional change, emphasizing the amelioration of problems through a technical institutional response. Strategies in this approach include rational analytical deliberation by professionals and/or experts who apply preferred means to known ends. Social action is presented as a change process, with the goal of restructuring the power and material relationships, and is aimed at basic systemic alteration. Strategies of this process include mobilizing the general populace, clearly articulating problem concerns, confronting established power, and developing indigenous leadership.

Twain has outlined three models of social change that influence how needs assessment is conducted (Twain 1983). His three models focus on service delivery, institutional change, and political action.

Service delivery. The service delivery model is one of the best understood means of focusing on social problems. Those designing service delivery needs assessment programs generally view the problems of the target population as being due to circumstances in the environment. For example, criminal activity may be due to limited financial resources because of inadequate employment. Unemployment may be due to a lack of skills among people in the target population. An agency or group that has the responsibility of providing service to the affected clientele may tend to address the problem as though it can be cured. Crime can be solved by stimulating economic activity. Unemployment might be treated through job training.

The service delivery model asks for a diagnosis or assessment of the problem. Generally, the assessment is conducted by professionals because it is assumed that only they can make a proper diagnosis. The target group is treated as a patient. Although this approach bypasses direct client involvement, this model remains as the most frequently used means for assessing social problems.

Institutional change. Twain's second model focuses on institutional change. It is concerned with the responsiveness of community institutions and systems in dealing with social or economic problems. This particular model is directed at program failures such as prisons that are "crime schools" or at primary schools whose graduates are functional illiterates. The causes of the "crime school" problem might be overcrowded prisons or inappropriate rehabilitation programs. Schools may offer little incentive for teaching excellence. The blame for program failure is often directed at management for failing to achieve an adequate level of performance. At other times the policymakers are held accountable.

Institutional change efforts focus on ways to aid the entity so it can meet current demands. Management may be retrained to upgrade competencies, or outside consultants may be hired. At other times the focus will be on the program itself. A common theme in social programs is a shift toward prevention. The program may be overhauled to minimize production problems. Health programs, for example, may deal with preventive care rather than treating illnesses.

The responsibility for change in the institutional model often lies in the hands of management and policymakers. In contrast to the social delivery model, the institutional change model draws upon trainers, program developers, and other consultants who work with management or policymakers. It also differs from the social delivery model in that change takes place in a broader system rather than a clinical setting. It appears that Twain's service delivery and institutional change are subsets of Rothman and Gant's social planning.

Political action. The political action model identified by Twain parallels Rothman and Gant's social action practice. It focuses on mobilizing citizens to achieve change and is generally concerned with inequities and resource allocation. Advocates of this model often regard redistributing power in the community as critical in dealing with the problem. The Saul Alinsky model of grass roots activity and responsibility is often mentioned as most representative of this focus. In the Alinsky (1972) model, neighborhood groups confront city hall, financial institutions, or corporations to force change. Alinsky often viewed his version of political action as a battle between "the haves" and the "have nots." His groups attempted to gain more power through well-orchestrated strategies.

It should be asserted, however, that political action does not always involve confrontation. Other attempts to bring diverse groups together to identify needs, establish goals, and implement change assume that distinct classes and groups have many common interests and long-range change occurs more effectively through cooperation and consensus than through confrontation. The New England town meeting frequently illustrates this democratic model. Here, local people from all walks of life share common concerns and reach conclusions about needs identification and priorities through consensus or majority rule. Rothman and Gant use the locality development model to distinguish this less confrontational change process from social action.

A common cause for mobilization of special-interest groups is that agencies or officeholders are perceived to be inappropriately using resources. For example, federal monies may be used to stimulate downtown development, yet neighborhood action groups may believe such monies are better allocated to housing programs. Those advocating the political action model would argue that only the general populace can fully grasp the situation and put a priority on concerns. In many instances, the target for change is the established power structure. In other cases, citizens work with the power structure to achieve consensus about a community problem. In each case, community groups move from a passive to an active role in assessing community needs.

A key factor separating political action/locality development from other models is that client participation is viewed as one of the most important aspects of change. It is argued that feeling empowered and helping yourself and others may create more change in the long run than the service delivery or institution models. Proponents of citizen mobilization claim it leads to a significant focus on self-help and to a shift in authority that also helps others to build competence.

The political action model does not limit the helping role to professionals. It calls for more nonprofessional participation. One of the problems in this method, however, is that professionals tend to take charge or give advice. Another problem is that groups struggling to gain equity may become so entrenched that they become a handicap. Nevertheless, there has been a shift to a concept that pays attention to alienation and powerlessness. In many programs directed to targeted populations, individuals are not as likely to be passive patients. Rather, they are viewed as having special interests that need to be incorporated into addressing complex problems.

Each model has advantages and disadvantages. The service delivery approach to change can be patronizing and expensive. Political action can be troublesome and time consuming. It is important that an agency or group analyze the problem before looking at how it should be addressed. Too often, professionals pursue the method with which they are most familiar rather than developing what the client group needs the most.

GROUP CHARACTERISTICS. The second key variable relates to group characteristics. Olson's (1968) work discusses how group size may determine the quality of decisions that occur in group approaches to needs assessment. There are several trade-offs involved. When the group is large, typical participants will feel that their actions will not matter much and that the outcome will be the same regardless of their efforts. Hence, the individual often will not study the issues carefully. Larger groups also tend to have more diverse views and consequently have more difficulty in making decisions.

The larger the group, the more likely the leadership will be authoritarian and the communications networks more centralized. Hare (1982) presents several effects of an increase in group size: member's feelings of identity and commitment are diminished, group solidarity becomes more difficult to maintain, a large group requires more leadership control, and the contribution of the average member may be less. These disadvantages are in part offset by the advantage that a large group has a greater pool of skills and resources. The smaller the group, the less likely divergent and often enriching perspectives will be available. Smaller groups, however, usually can arrive at decisions more rapidly. Hare concludes, based on the research findings of Bray et al. (1978), that "it was not the actual size of the group that was important but the functional size." Consequently when the function of the group is to look for general points of view, reactions, and affirmation of the group norm, the group can be large. If needs assessment specificity and action is required, the group may divide and subdivide to achieve its objectives. When creativity and originality is desired, individuals may be more productive working alone. Those involved in needs assessment need to look at group size not only in relation to the problem but also in the context of who participates.

When one speaks of participation in needs assessment, several questions are raised. For whom is the needs assessment being done? Who will take part? Perhaps the answer to each question is a handful of professionals (as outlined in the service delivery model) or laypeople (as explained in the political action model). Many situations may call for a middle ground where a broad diversity of professional and laypeople share their perspectives, air their differences and values, and arrive at a conclusion through accommodation.

There are no easy responses to these various perspectives. As noted in Chapter 3, agencies and groups that attempt maximum feasible participation find there are many obstacles to full participation, especially among laypeople. Some organizations may feel that their goals will be undermined if their clients get too involved. Others who have encouraged participation in needs assessment by those with the greatest needs in society—the poor and other oppressed peoples—have been met with minimum or marginal involvement. These people often live on the periphery of society and are more prone to a sense of impotence and negative self-image or apathy.

Parenti (1970) offers some insights based on his study of low-income residents in Newark: "If I were to offer any one explanation for nonparticipation it would be the profound and widespread belief of so many ghetto residents that there exists no means for taking effective action against long-standing grievances and that investments of scarce time, energy, money and perhaps most of all, hope, serve for naught except to aggravate one's sense of disaffection and impotence."

Those espousing the service delivery, institutional, and political action models have made some noteworthy attempts to stimulate participation by people with the greatest needs. Some serious questions still need to be asked, however. Who is doing the assessing and for whom? What is the assessor's position in terms of status? How does the assessor benefit from the needs assessment process? If the assessor benefits more than those with the most obvious needs, one might also question the quality of the needs assessment instrument.

There are other important concerns to consider when doing needs assessment through groups. Which groups are most likely to articulate their needs? No matter how carefully the group needs assessment tool is designed, the most likely participants are those who tend to have a certain stability of residence and higher social status (Alford and Scoble 1968). Some groups have better developed skills at participation than others. The consciousness-raising approach in this chapter was especially designed to assist special-interest groups that consider themselves to be outside established policymaking networks.

IDEA GENERATION. The third key variable in group needs assessment involves creativity or idea generation. Research indicates that the higher degree to which members of the group have shared beliefs and attitudes (group norms), the more likely the group will support the status quo rather than seek out new solutions (McGrath 1985). In such homogeneous groups, McGrath lists a number of steps that can be applied to needs assessment to expand the perspective and lift barriers to inventive group exchange:

1. Require a wide information search (reward such behavior).
2. Encourage, reward, and indeed require dissent in the group.
3. Make a broad search for alternatives (preferably by people other than those who will evaluate and choose).
4. Charge some group members with the task of representing positions other than their own.

Creativity, however, is essentially an individual act, a premise recognized in the two-group needs assessment approaches in this chapter (futuring and nominal group). In each case, these approaches start with the individual working alone, generating as many ideas as possible and spending no time in evaluating them. Only later on in the process are the ideas presented to the group for review and evaluation.

Another spur to creativity is the recognition and rewards accorded to individual autonomy. McBride (1969) maintains that creativity is nourished best in voluntary associations that foster individual autonomy and dignity. He asserts that the association should attempt to incorporate goals that liberate the creative potential latent in its members. He recommends that associations avoid imposing fixed tasks and roles or attempting to psychologically condition members. If rigid boundaries are set for those involved in needs assessment, it will be difficult for them to develop a new set of needs that accurately reflects changing problems. When responsibility is taken away, it is argued, citizenship no longer exists. The citizen ceases to be a problem definer or solver. As a result, the technician or technocrat takes over.

McBride points out the paradox of voluntary associations. The political nature of voluntary groups emphasizes joint action. Hence the association is prone to use some form of coercion, at least the gentle art of persuasion. In addition, voluntary associations also need a certain amount of unanimity to clarify needs and goals, which often leads to member coercion or manipulation. The paradox is not easy to solve and raises some important questions. To what extent does the information gathered accurately reveal the real needs of the community? Have the data been twisted to meet the needs of an advocacy group? How accurately do the data reflect the concerns that are central to most people's lives?

There has been some obvious manipulation of groups. Some agencies and organizations have asked clients to approve or rubber-stamp decisions previously made by an administrative or professional core. Others are hesitant to give their clients too much voice, lest their agencies lose control. Some types of group participation are manipulative. Clients are "educated" or "cured." Other types are forms of tokenism. Clients are informed and consulted about needs but are not provided with any kind of assurance that their ideas will be taken seriously.

Co-optation is viewed as another deviant of true participation. It is a means of capturing or neutralizing the opposition of dissidents by including them as participants without surrendering control of the decision-making process. Such an approach appears democratic and hence often wins the support of the general population.

The ideal of individual responsibility and creativity is still an unrealized goal within many voluntary associations. However, the value of such responsibility can be maximized within the group when that value is held in high esteem. Although the paradox remains, an association can receive many benefits from its members' insights about needs assessment if it can seek ways to help them reinterpret and redefine their own roles and concepts.

LEADERSHIP. The potential for identifying and training native (indigenous) leaders is the fourth key component of most group approaches for needs assessment. Since it is designed to encourage problem solving and autonomy at every level, participants have opportunities to contribute in self-selected roles both as leaders and as followers.

The choice of leadership styles used in managing a needs assessment project, however, is likely to have direct bearing on the quality and quantity of leadership resulting from the experience. The most generally recognized style of leadership features hierarchical relationships and analytical, rational, quantitative thinking. The traditional, authoritarian, top-down style of leadership has proven to be very effective in homogeneous, closed-system circumstances. When solving problems that are largely short range and technical in nature and lend themselves to the application of preferred means to known ends, the direct power style is task oriented and efficient (Rosener and Schwartz 1980). This style is particularly appropriate when pursuing institutional change and social planning activities.

Another style of leadership practiced on all levels of human relationship is referred to as "transactional." The emphasis in this form of interaction between leaders and their constituents is an exchange of favors, support, and negotiated power. This style frequently is characterized as the "I'll scratch your back if you scratch mine" approach. It is important not to think of this process only in a pejorative sense, however. Such transactions make up the bulk of the relationships of everyday living, especially in groups, and political entities. Kellerman (1984) refers to this social exchange as leadership with emphasis on mutual payoffs. Neither of these leadership models, however, are likely to tap the potential leadership capacities of indigenous leaders in the group needs assessment project.

In more pluralistic community settings—with complex technological, social, political, and economic systems—leaders cannot assume that most people want the same things. Consequently, authoritarian means used to obtain the desired ends of officialdom may not be justified. If people affected by policy have not had ample opportunity to articulate their concerns, those in leadership positions will continue to risk withdrawal of public support or will be pressured in the courts. Kanter (1981) suggests that, "as public expectations rise, but problems become more intractable, and as popular sentiment views the claims of leaders with skepticism, there will be pressures to change leaders. Continuity and stability of leadership are an increasing problem in both the private and public sector."

Community groups with disparate interests often seem willing to meet if government will let the people have their say and will respond reasonably to group expressions. Citizens contributing their time and resources have every right to ask "who controls" when citizens, officials, and professionals are brought together. People must be able to trust the process and be convinced that it is a creative experience that will be taken seriously by those in power positions. If the decisions of public officials are not made in accordance with the information gathered, questions of public accountability should be expected.

There is a growing recognition of another leadership style well adapted to cases where values are diverse and a multiplicity of systems overlap.

Referred to by Burns (1978) as "transformational leadership," this approach recognizes the value of intuitive qualitative thinking and serves to synthesize, enable, and integrate. The style embraces and integrates pluralistic differences rather than focusing on a homogeneous set of goals. Leaders create an environment in which followers can discover their own talents, resources, and intentions. The leadership role is essentially one of enabling rather than controlling. To develop and maintain the trust of followers, the leaders must possess a high level of integrity, taking a stance of commitment to the community and vision for collective advancement. Transformational leaders articulate their intentions and goals and act in an open and responsive way to the needs and intentions of the followers, providing strong direction while simultaneously sharing power. Top leaders in the participatory mode focus on mission and strategy, empowering others to take responsibility (Kanter 1981). Burns (1978), in describing the "transformational leadership" style, noted that "whatever the separate interests persons might hold, they are presently or potentially united in the pursuit of higher goals, the realization of which is tested by the achievement of significant change that represents the collective or pooled interests of leaders and followers." Both the charrette and the futures group needs assessment approaches provide great potential for the practice of transformational leadership and the development of indigenous leaders.

There are limitations to a participatory leadership style. For example, involving many people in decisions is more time consuming and therefore likely to be a more costly venture. Careful attention must be given to deciding which problems warrant the greatest investment of time and resources. There may be major information or knowledge gaps that, in spite of efforts to foster participation, may still give unequal power to experts and officials. Citizens may come away from the experience feeling they have endorsed decisions they do not truly accept. Those in power may not want to give up their authority for making unilateral decisions. While redistribution of power may not be the purpose of citizen participation efforts, it may be perceived as such. A mix of leadership styles is probably the more appropriate means for organizing in most circumstances where complex technology and a plurality of values are to be considered.

Once the practitioner has determined the organizational context of the proposed needs assessment and has decided that it is appropriate to work in a group environment, a review of the other key variables can help to identify the specific approach or combination of group approaches that would be most effective. Each technique has special attributes that are well suited to differing group characteristics, levels of creativity, and leadership styles. Other considerations include time and financial limitations and the social and cultural context. Some approaches highlighted in this chapter may be too time consuming for an association dealing with a crisis that requires immediate attention. Society's norms and mores can also impose constraints on how group needs assessment is approached and which leadership style would be most effective. In any case, attention to the four key variables and restraints can maximize the intended effectiveness of the group needs assessment process.

Citizen participation. Each of the eight approaches to citizen participation that follow is illustrated with a case study and a discussion of its strengths and limitations. It is important to note that some of these approaches include steps beyond needs identification, including goal determination and consideration of alternatives and action.

TOWN MEETINGS AND PUBLIC HEARINGS. Perhaps the most widely recognized and traditional mechanisms for regular and constructive citizen participation in the government process are town meetings and public hearings. These structures are the antecedents of most other group approaches to needs assessments, affording citizens opportunities to assist officials in determining community priorities; developing consensus on issues; and tempering social, economic, and political differences. Citizens meet current leaders and see potential leaders in action making real decisions. Both character and skills can be assessed.

Town meetings. The New England town, concentrated in a six-state area, is still the first level of government in nearly 1400 municipalities. Most are hamlets with population of less than 2500 (Ross and Millsap 1966). The long tradition of democratic validity inherent in the town meeting was illustrated eloquently when historian James Hosmer wrote about the annual meeting in his New England home community. His account could have been a report of the meetings of the region in more recent times. Describing the event as a time of celebration and festivity, he wrote (Jaberg 1968):

> Following the carefully arranged programme or warrant, from which there could be no departure, because ample warning must be given of every measure proposed, item after item was considered, — a change here in the course of the highway to the shire town, how much should be raised by taxes, the apportionment of money among the school districts, what bounty the town would pay for its quota of troops for the war, a new wing for the poorhouse, whether there would be a bridge at the west ford. . . . Watching it all, one could see how perfect a democracy it was. Things were often done far enough from the best way. Unwise or doubtful men were put in office, important projects stinted by niggardly appropriations, unworthy prejudices al-

lowed to interfere with wise enterprises. Yet in the main the result was good. This was especially to be noted, – how thoroughly the public spirit of those who took part was stimulated, and how well they were trained to self-reliance, intelligence of various kinds, and love for freedom. . . . Is there anything more valuable among Anglo-Saxon institutions than this same ancient Folk-mote, this old-fashioned New England Town-meeting?

Town meetings work on the premise that society benefits most when citizens understand the programs and goals of their government and when this understanding is achieved by open and spirited debate with broadly based public participation. Officials conduct the meetings under rules of parliamentary procedure, and every citizen is afforded the opportunity to speak. Decisions are made by majority rule. Area residents are informed of the issues to be discussed well in advance of the event, affording all concerned ample time to prepare for their participation.

Modern public forums, labeled town meetings, have been used throughout the United States by public officials to foster discussion of issues and gain public support. It is important, however, to differentiate these special purpose events from the New England town meetings, which are legislative bodies. Matters discussed at the New England town meeting carry the force of official consideration and votes taken are decisive, while the ad hoc town meetings promote community dialogue and understandings and are, for the most part, advisory to officialdom.

There have been some concerted efforts to institutionalize the town meeting idea outside the New England region. One comprehensive endeavor to use this concept was initiated in the Minnesota Twin Cities area. Small group briefing sessions designed to introduce the objectives of the town meeting attracted 12,000 persons to help determine the urban issues that they felt were most important. The specially organized town meetings were coupled with the discussion of relevant issues at regular and special events of churches, schools, and civic and community organizations and through the media; the effort was concentrated in a period of one month and engaged countless citizens in focused dialogue on community-identified concerns.

Public hearings. Public hearings have been widely criticized by social scientists as an unrepresentative method of assessing public opinion. Nevertheless, this approach is one of the most traditional and widely used methods for enhancing citizen involvement in assessing needs. Hearings are required by statute at all levels of government, and many agencies rely on them as their single method of measuring public acceptance of policy.

The public hearing format varies little from one setting to another.

Prehearing notices are placed in newspapers, inviting interested parties to respond to a focused issue or proposal. The proposal, plan, or issue is presented at the hearing site by the sponsoring agency, and testimony is received from those who have indicated their intention to speak by registering at the door. Written copies of testimony may also be submitted. The testimony is recorded and a proceedings report becomes public record. After deliberating on the proceedings, the sponsoring agency takes the action it deems appropriate.

The public hearing has limitations as an effective citizen participation approach. It is often dominated by vested interests whose representatives are more likely to be aware of scheduled hearings and have the resources and knowledge to present powerful testimony. Studies show that regulated industries are responsible for 90 percent of the presentations at federal regulatory agency hearings (Checkoway 1978). In contrast, the average citizen is not likely to read the legal sections of the newspaper where most hearing notices appear and is therefore unaware of the event. The hearing location is often inaccessible or the time inconvenient for citizen involvement, particularly for low-income and minority citizens. Citizens may also be intimidated by the technical or complex language. Finally, there is no assurance that the testimony will in any way temper agency decisions.

Most of the above limitations could be remedied if agencies improved advance publicity, reduced cost barriers (i.e., work release time), and made physical arrangements more accessible. Community organizations could also use the public hearing more effectively as a means to voice collective concerns. Most hearings are covered by media representatives who are looking for newsworthy events. Well-organized testimony and special campaigns to get high supporter attendance from community groups can influence officials. Groups with an independent and powerful agenda can achieve citizen ends, not as a result of the hearing structure, but from citizen mobilization with reference to that event (see Chapter 4).

THE CHARRETTE. Mayor Paul Soglin of Madison, Wisconsin (1973–1978), stated that "the value of citizen involvement in the planning process was dramatized in the recent State Street charrette proceedings. The charrette brought hundreds and hundreds of citizens together to share their feelings and hopes for State Street. The charrette was an illustration of the benefits of grassroots democracy in governmental planning." The State Street charrette (1973) was conducted in a pattern of two phases, lasted six weeks, and involved over 700 people. The participants were from nearly every walk of life and represented every district of the city.

State Street, connecting the Capitol and the University of Wisconsin, is probably the most used mile of street in Madison. The problem to be addressed was how to develop that mile to serve not only the needs of those who come to the area for commerce and cultural purposes but of all city residents. The problem was not the technical task of finding a workable concept but rather the social task of producing enough trust and cooperation to have any plan accepted. After the Madison Common Council considered a number of approaches for obtaining information from those most affected by the State Street project, they turned to the charrette approach and appropriated $30,000 to accomplish their goals.

This community needs assessment process is patterned after the classical model of the architectural charrette. The term charrette can be traced to nineteenth-century Paris, when it was used to describe the crash effort of students preparing for comprehensive exams. The architectural students who lived in garrets around Paris had their sketches picked up in a hand-drawn cart (i.e., charrette) and delivered to the École des Beaux Arts for jury grading. Typically, the students scrambled to finish their projects, so this term has come to mean a final, comprehensive, deadline-oriented effort (Schuttler 1971).

The modern charrette approach was created in 1967 when its innovators were searching for ways to produce architectural decisions for school building designs. Walter Mylecraine and Tom Clary (Office of Construction Services in Health, Education and Welfare, U.S. Office of Education) were looking for techniques that would render plans for federally funded building projects more relevant to the real needs of communities. The idea has changed the procedures of decision making in countless other social, political, and physical environments across the country.

The purpose of the charrette is to offer the community an open public process that involves public and private agencies, citizens, and outside experts in a planning partnership. This collaborative team works in a capsuled time frame to identify and put a priority on community concerns; outline several models of development, including cost estimates; and negotiate the most acceptable plans.

The charrette organization resembles a political campaign, with open-ended membership and participants exercising considerable autonomy as they select and develop their leadership/follower role(s). Established decision makers, citizens, subject matter experts, and the media provide the major elements of the group dynamics. The resultant goals defined by the charrette should reflect the shared values of the community. Resources and commitment of the community are brought together at a carefully chosen time, taking advantage of funding cycles, elections, competing activities, and political pressure to produce decisions that receive public attention and momentum for action. The process involves forming a steering committee;

organizing task groups; and holding a charrette conference, public forums, and a final presentation.

Steering committee formation. A steering committee, composed of a balanced representation of community groups and officialdom, makes policy decisions regarding purpose, budget, and participant recruitment. Open membership in all committees legitimizes the claim that public participation will be decisive throughout the length of the project and no one group will dominate the process. If the membership of the steering committee becomes too large, an executive committee acts as mandated by the committee as a whole.

Task groups. Once the steering committee reaches consensus over the priority of issues, the committee members self-select task groups based on the issue most important to them. Support from the community is then recruited, and the data collection and analysis phases are initiated. The task groups must define the issue; determine responsibility for various aspects of the concern; and identify alternative solutions, their consequences, and the resources required for resolution.

The charrette conference. The charrette conference is a plenary session, usually running from 5 to 10 days. It is designed to integrate all the previous work of the task groups and to develop a workable set of goals. The conference as described by Barry Schuttler (consultant for the Madison project and involved in the process from its earliest conception) is "a creativity marathon that winnows out the feasible from the conceptual, leaders from spokesmen, supporters from self-seekers and goals out of problems."

This final stage opens with an explanation of the week's agenda followed by a division of the participants into brainstorming groups referred to as "creativity generators." The facilitator core—composed of a community resident leader, experts, and recorders—stays with the same set of issues while the rest of the group rotates to another. The core builds a base of information for a selected area of inquiry, while the rest of the participants become familiar with the overall picture to understand the scope of the problem, including causes, relationships, and goals.

Public forums. Results of each day's activities are presented at a public forum held each evening by leaders who have been identified by the charrette. The written reports of recorders and the graphics developed by architect students enhance the presentations, helping to build community and political support step by step. These events offer political leaders and the media opportunities to view the ideas being generated at the proceedings and to transmit them to the general public. Public officials are asked to be guests of honor at an evening forum held midway through the process, often solidifying their commitment to the emerging product.

The final presentation. As Schuttler characterized the event, "The final presentation is a little like opening night at the opera or the first gavel at a national political convention. There is an air of expectancy as notables are picked out looking at the dozens of graphics, charts and models that rim the room. Hasty meetings and whispered caucuses are taking place everywhere and what the special guests are discovering is that what looked like an amateur effort doomed to a fizzled defeat now begins to look like a professional planning conference with a scope of solutions and new concepts they never expected and have seldom if ever seen in a community setting."

Results. A stroll down State Street will underscore the resulting connections between government, culture, learning, and commerce that were achieved through this example of citizen participation needs assessment. The redesign of the street, with emphasis on people's use and activities in all seasons, causes a connective resource to take on renewed vitality and utility for the residents, students, merchants, artists, and politicians. The conversion of the Paramount Theater and Montgomery Ward store into the Madison Civic Center, a multiuse creative arts center, complete the "connective tissue" (Burns 1979).

CITIZEN-DIRECTED FUTURES ASSESSMENTS. Whether we are considering the futures invention approach (Ziegler 1978) or the preferred future process (Lindaman and Lippitt 1979), the format for a futuring method of needs assessment is like other community forum approaches. They are based on public meetings at which residents are invited to express their opinions about community problems and needs. In the futuring process, however, the participants are encouraged through the use of special exercises to consider a desired or intentional future, looking forward 5, 10, or more years. In each instance, participants are assisted in their individual efforts to articulate their personal values and commitments more effectively. The forum setting provides the opportunity to identify community residents who share common goals, thereby enhancing the collective capacity of the community to pursue intended futures. The futuring method presumes that community members have intentions, know what they are, and can develop strategies to meet them. It also presumes that participants can identify alternative problem definitions, consider alternative solutions, and identify other people who share the common concerns (Ziegler 1978).

Futures assessment techniques originated in program planning and design in space industry and applied behavioral science research. Futuring needs assessment strategies assist the participants in disengaging from old thinking patterns about their surroundings. The exercises are designed to help citizens participate effectively in forming social change rather than adapting to the status quo or "expert" predictions of trends.

In their goal setting guide, Lindaman and Lippitt (1979) suggest some warm-up exercises that pit the participant group's futuristic thinking against the main themes and opinions of several renowned futurists such as Margaret Mead, Bertrand de Jouvenal, and Glenn T. Seaborg. The groups are led to reflect on historical events and to sort them according to dominant and emergent themes (i.e., Lewis Mumford). This process enables participants to discover the patterns of change. By analyzing historical periods, a better understanding of the incremental steps required to achieve an intended future is possible.

Idea generation. In the futuring process the participants at first work individually to state their concept of the future of the particular subject area being considered. Each citizen formulates a problem area with evidence of assumptions, consequences, strategies, and tactics. The following questions might be asked in this process: What is the concern? Who is affected by it? Who owns it? Who should/can/might do something about it?

At this stage, participants are not encouraged to interact. Individuals in the group can thus begin to clarify issues and generate alternative ways of perceiving the problem. This can eventually lead to a reframing of the questions, perhaps taking a much different view from that of public officials. Asking the reframed question may in turn lead to entirely different solutions and consequences (Helmer 1983). A second benefit to allowing individuals to formulate the questions is that they often assume "ownership" of the problem. As a consequence, they are less likely to engage in denial (i.e., "proliferation of nuclear waste is not a problem") or withdrawal ("don't tell me about the inhuman conditions at Janesville Penitentiary, it's not my problem")(Healy 1979).

Lindaman and Lippitt suggest an exercise designed to sensitize participants to conditions that release or block action, thereby exploring their internal feelings affecting motivation.

Idea clarification. In the second step of the process, participants work in three-person facilitating groups to help each other clarify their goals. In this stage the focus is on questions that help understanding. It is important to note that preference or feasibility judgments are not given by participants in facilitation groups. Instead, they focus on defining the concern, who shares the concern, the competencies (skills, intentions) involved in doing anything about it, and why the matter is important.

Through identifying and clarifying individual goals within small groups, people gain the trust and cooperation needed to develop group leadership and collective action. If no one in the group shares an individual's concerns, she or he can recruit others or join a group that is addressing other shared concerns.

Review and critique. During the third step, participants work together in policy teams, usually 3 to 10 people, to discover possible collective agreements about needs, strategies, and actions. In policy teams, people decide how to measure success, how much time they can invest, what resources they can focus on the concern, and what skills or competencies they would need. The group uses the research work of Kurt Lewin in force-field analysis to examine the restraints and supports for action. Finally, participants meet in plenary session to review and critique their work and organize for appropriate action (Healy 1979).

These exercises have been successfully applied in organization and agency boards, annual meetings, city councils, student and professional organizations, church committees, and community meetings. For instance, Jackson County, Michigan, has engaged in a countywide project to reach 25 percent of the county's 150,000 residents. In March 1984, Ronald Lippitt (professor emeritus at the University of Michigan) and two Jackson associates were hired to initiate the project.

More than 100 county residents were trained to conduct small futuring sessions to help set the agendas. The sessions were designed to promote a positive feeling about the future of the community. Each group made a list of what it is proudest of, sorriest about, and what it wants Jackson to look like in the next decade. By the time they reached the community assembly in November 1984, over 2870 adults had attended futuring sessions and over 2300 students in grades 6 to 12 had participated. The community assembly for all interested community participants was aimed at continuing the dialogue begun in the small group sessions. From the original 31 task force committees that spun out of the community assembly, only two disbanded and two have consolidated into other groups. Most are meeting at least twice a month and pursuing active objectives in relation to the needs identified by the futuring process (Lippitt et al. 1984).

Another Michigan community served as a model for Jackson residents. In 1980 the Ypsilanti conference worked on 22 priority needs ranging from bike paths and improvement of the downtown and riverfront area to greater minority participation in community life and low-cost housing improvements. Some of the Ypsilanti conference task forces are still active. Lippitt and his associates have worked in 80 communities to date.

Another futuring project was conducted in 1974 when Governor Dan Evans of the state of Washington selected a 165-member, statewide task force to examine alternative directions for the state's future growth and development. The Brookings Institution of Washington, D.C., adapted the "future-intention" approach for use in the state, based on the work of Ziegler (1978). Chaired by Edward B. Lindaman, the alternatives-for-Washington process was regarded as one of the most imaginative long-range planning efforts in a series of other "Year 2000" efforts launched across the country (Everitt and Dyckman 1976). The futuring activities of the Washington statewide task force are mentioned in more detail in Chapter 11.

The Civic Literacy Project, initiated by a group of adult educators and citizens in Syracuse, New York, is another of the several hundred future-intentions projects conducted nationwide since the early 1970s under the direction of futurist Warren Ziegler. At the time of project initiation the city was experiencing pressures from many complex and controversial issues, including the closing of neighborhood schools, New York State school integration standards, waste disposal, and steam plant controversies. A special prosecutor had also been appointed by the governor to investigate allegations of political corruption in the county, and people anticipated the closing of a local penitentiary. An overriding concern of the community (largely shared around the country) was the general alienation of citizens from the government processes. Low voter turnouts at elections, frustrations with the Vietnam War, and Watergate were all manifestations of the condition. A congressional study verified that more than one-half the public felt profoundly impotent to influence public decisions (U.S. Senate 1977). Additionally, there was at least the appearance of a complete transfer of the right of ownership of problems and solutions from citizens to government.

Against this backdrop, the future-intentions project was developed. Its major goal was to offer Syracuse residents an opportunity to acquire knowledge, understandings, and skills for the clarification and empowerment of their intentions as citizens, thereby acquiring what project leadership termed "civic literacy."

At the end of three years, the future-intentions project participants were well on their way to their Year 2000 goals. In addition to the network of people committed to and skilled in addressing specific concerns, a wide range of activities were stimulated by their experience. In one case, an educational needs assessment resulted in an information referral service for adult, parent, and youth education alternatives. In another, work by legislators, lawyers, judges, service providers, and citizens achieved court reform and alternatives to incarceration. One project participant described her experience and reflected on her role as an assistant future-intentions facilitator for the Criminal Justice Workshop (Healy 1979): "There was an expectation by some Criminal Justice Workshop participants that a specific point of view on the problem was going to be presented. However, this is never the case with Future-Intention workshops. They seek to enable individuals to discover for themselves the nature of their commitments. The slant of a participant's goal is determined only by the experiences and values he or she brings to the workshop."

DELPHI TECHNIQUE. The Delphi technique was developed to get a reliable consensus of opinion among people with exceptional knowledge about a particular subject area. It was originally conceived in 1953 to solicit the perspectives of military officers regarding the amount of bombs needed in the event of war. Since then, Delphi has been employed to deal with a variety of complex questions. The method uses repeated individual questioning and feedback to arrive at a consensus. There are usually three or four mailed questionnaires involved.

Delphi can be useful when individual personality styles might be distracting in a personal setting. It avoids the direct confrontation of people with opposing views by being more receptive to individual thought. There is not the pressure to conform. It has also been used to avoid the costs of participant travel to a central meeting place.

The technique should be used only if it meets several conditions. First, there must be adequate time allotted. Normally, it takes a minimum of 45 days from the development of the first questionnaire to the final report. Second, since the Delphi takes place within a written context, it is crucial that participants have well-developed writing skills. Third, there should be some assurance of high participant motivation, since no one will be visibly present to stimulate a response.

Generally, a small group of staff members will begin the Delphi process by asking what kinds of needs they wish to assess, who will participate, and what they will do with the information. Respondents should be selected and contacted in a manner that makes them involved in all aspects of the process. A sample size should be selected; 10 to 15 people may be adequate if they are unlikely to vary a great deal. In other cases there may be several hundred participants.

There are usually three to four questionnaires involved. The first asks the participants to write a response to a problem issue. Some typical questions might be, What are the weaknesses of our professional organization?

or What are the major problems of the states' land use planning programs? Participants may also be asked to categorize their statements under headings such as education, management, and organizational structure.

After the questionnaire is returned, the responses are summarized and developed into a second questionnaire. The respondents are asked to rank their concerns, support or disagree with the various group respondents, and clarify their stance. The purpose of the second questionnaire is to identify areas of agreement and disagreement on priorities. The analysis of the second questionnaire usually includes a vote tally and a summary of the comments made. The third questionnaire is developed from the summary of the second.

Respondents are asked to review their prior response and make additional comments. They are also asked to vote on the order of importance of items listed. The third questionnaire is often the final one. It attempts to bring additional insights as well as closure to participant involvement. If there are sharply divided areas of disagreement or other closure problems, additional Delphi questionnaires may be used.

Once the questionnaires have been completed, a final report is sent to the participants. They have invested a great deal of work in the Delphi study and deserve feedback. The final report is a summary of the third or final questionnaire. It also summarizes the goals and process and the conclusion or action reached because of the study.

There are many variants of Delphi. Some Delphis conclude with the second questionnaire. Others have five questionnaires. Some Delphis have allowed respondents to use cassette tapes to record their responses. Other Delphis have sent additional questionnaires only to those who disagree with the majority. This approach, however, may intimidate the participants and pressure them to conform with the others.

The School of Nursing at the University of Wisconsin–Madison used Delphi to identify nursing roles for the future. Several hundred people were involved. The first questionnaire asked people to project the major nursing responsibilities 10 years into the future and to provide a brief example from their own experience that led them to believe this was an important and desirable change. The responses were summarized and included in a second questionnaire. Participants were asked to choose the top seven responsibilities they felt were most important to add or delete from the nursing role. There was adequate space for additional comments. Participants were assured that their response would not be binding and that this was a preliminary vote.

The third questionnaire asked participants to speculate about responsibilities the nurse would have or give up in 10 years. This questionnaire contained the number of people who voted for and against certain responsibilities. There was also a summary of the comments about each role. Participants were asked to influence the final vote and suggest implications for the future. For those responsibilities on which they wished to comment, they were limited to three short and precise statements.

The fourth questionnaire separated the responsibilities listed in the first and second into 18 major categories. The comments from the second and third questionnaires were summarized. Potential issues for each major category were also identified. Participants were asked to select the seven most important issues concerned with nursing roles, which would be discussed at an upcoming conference. There was an additional column for respondents to explain their vote or comment on the issue. The last page of the Delphi was allotted for any important issues of role realignment that were missed and should have been considered for the nursing conference.

The Delphi has many limitations in the field of community needs assessment. It does not appear to be applicable when soliciting feedback from the general public in a city or village setting. It is better oriented to experts who have well-developed writing skills and to situations where personality styles and potential conflicts should be minimized. The time required to complete the Delphi and the staff required to develop the questionnaires may prohibit its use in many communities. Nevertheless, it should be considered as a helpful needs assessment tool. It is often blended with other needs assessment approaches to better understand community needs.

NOMINAL GROUP TECHNIQUE. The nominal group technique is a well-established approach to decision making that has often been applied to community needs assessment. It is a synthesis of sociopsychological group studies that was developed by Andrew Delbecq and Andrew VandeVen in 1968. It has been applied to health, social service, education, industry, and government issues. The term nominal was coined by researchers to describe the process that brings people together but minimizes verbal communication.

Nominal group can be viewed as a brainstorming technique where people work in each other's presence but write their ideas independently. It is an appropriate group process for identifying a major community problem or need, identifying elements of that need, and establishing priorities where the judgments of individuals are aggregated into a collective decision. Nominal group is a structured meeting technique that allows for more creative and judgmental decision making according to several scientific studies. It differs from routine meetings in that it attempts to maximize the input of every individual present and minimizes the domination of the most vocal people as well as the noninvolvement of the most reticent participant.

Question. The format is preceded by a question or problem that is clearly defined. Some examples are: What is wrong with our downtown? or What are the health-related problems of our community?

Idea generation. The nominal group format begins with 5 to 10 people at a table facing each other. If there are more than 10 people present, enough tables should be arranged to accommodate them in small groups. The participants are welcomed and told about the task at hand. They spend the first few minutes in silence by listing their ideas on a piece of paper. The silent atmosphere gives people the chance to work uninterrupted and avoid the dominance of aggressive members in idea generation.

Idea presentation. After a 5- or 10-minute period, each person presents one idea from his or her list in round-robin fashion. A group recorder writes the ideas on a large sheet of paper or flip pad in full view of all the participants. The recorder is instructed to list each idea in a terse phrase and does not attempt to change the wording or judge the idea. If the phrase is too cumbersome, the participant is asked to skip a turn and reword the idea. The round-robin listing continues until all the participants have exhausted their ideas. Normally, the list contains about 25 items. The round-robin process gives everyone the chance to share ideas and increases the group's ability to deal with a large number of often conflicting perspectives.

Idea clarification. The third part of the process calls for a clarification of each idea listed on the flip pad. Participants are allowed to express their reasons for agreement or disagreement about each item. Argument, however, is discouraged. The purpose of this stage is to enhance a clearer understanding of the ideas listed, while minimizing the influence of high-status or aggressive members.

Priority rating. In the fourth step group members select from two to seven priorities from the list. They are asked to rate each item independently on a small card or rating form. The cards are collected and shuffled to retain anonymity. Votes are tallied and the results are listed on the flip pad in front of the group. The independent voting in writing eliminates social pressures. Expressing the group's judgments as a mathematical function increases judgment accuracy.

Discussion and voting. After the priorities are established, the group discusses the vote, makes additional clarifications, and voices agreement or disagreement. If needed, there can be a final vote in which group members are asked to use more refined voting techniques such as rating. As earlier, the voting should be done anonymously and silently. This particular step may lead to a more accurate recording of group judgments and bring a sense of closure to the meeting.

There are many variants of nominal group technique. In Delavan, Wisconsin, a city of approximately 5000, people adopted the nominal group technique to determine community needs. A progressive woman mayor and other key civic leaders wanted more than needs assessment. They hoped to stimulate citizen involvement in determining needs as well as a community action program to implement the findings. It was also hoped that additional leaders would emerge out of the process. They worked with a University of Wisconsin Cooperative Extension Service community development agent, who encouraged them to choose the nominal group technique and orient it to suit their overall goals. Business and civic groups supported the approach by offering volunteer or monetary assistance for advertising and other purposes.

In an attempt to avoid other meeting conflicts, city residents were offered the chance to attend one of three public meetings to voice their views. The purpose of each meeting was to find out, "What's wrong with Delavan" and to encourage community involvement in addressing those needs. The meetings were well publicized. The local grocery stores stuffed meeting notices into shopping bags. Most retail outlets had posters in their windows. Children took school announcements about the meetings to their parents. The meetings were also mentioned in church bulletins. The local banks paid for a large ad in the Delavan newspaper, which also featured several articles about the upcoming meetings. Leaders of the city's minority groups (such as the Spanish-speaking, the deaf, and the elderly) were individually contacted to encourage their people to participate, and arrangements were made for translators for the deaf and Spanish-speaking as well as access for the physically handicapped. In addition, a local women's club called every home in the community to further encourage participation.

About 300 people in the community attended one of the three public meetings. Many people were involved in publicizing the meeting. Those who came felt that their opinions really mattered and that they could bring about change to address community needs. New leadership began to emerge through committee work. Within a year and a half, many of the committees in Delavan had addressed the priority items listed in the nominal group meetings (Hustedde 1985).

The nominal group technique has been incorporated into a wide range of needs assessment efforts. In 1977 the Arts Council of San Antonio, Texas, initiated a program called City Spirit. From its inception, one of the major objectives of the program was to establish a continuing process of community input into arts planning through district and neighborhood meetings. It was not viewed as just an isolated project. The Arts Council believed arts development could not take place in a vacuum but should be linked to broader community concerns of social, economic, and political development.

The primary emphasis of City Spirit's first year was to identify arts programs and resources in San Antonio, a city of one million people. Bilingual communication networks were also sought because of the city's large bilingual population. In that first year, inventories were completed on churches, schools, community centers, and settlement houses engaged in arts programs. Lists were compiled of every known key volunteer, professional artist, performer, and administrator in the city. A survey was completed of all art funding in San Antonio. After all the information was gathered, City Spirit had a clear picture of San Antonio's art constituency. Unlike most American cities, however, the majority of the people in the community did not relate to traditional arts institutions but found their outlets for expression through the neighborhood, church, or social club.

It was decided that there would be two citywide meetings and eight neighborhood/district meetings in various parts of the city to attract the arts constituency. The meetings were cosponsored by neighborhood cultural and ethnic groups. The City Spirit program chose the nominal group technique for each meeting because it afforded all those attending the opportunity to participate and contribute their ideas. Also, an ordered list of priorities emerged through its use.

The participants were asked to list their ideas in response to the question, What cultural arts programs and facilities would you like to see develop in San Antonio over the next 25 years? Some of the priorities identified included (1) the formation of a coalition to develop a Westside Cultural Center, (2) an Eastside Cultural Center, (3) an arts clearinghouse to schedule arts events, (4) arts education starting at an earlier age, (5) use of the "Hemisfair Facilities" as a year-round art center, and (6) encouragement of an "artistic atmosphere so that everyone will want to participate" (Broomall and Canon 1977).

The nominal group technique was a tool with which the arts program could address the complex cultural programs confronting the city. According to City Spirit organizers, it offered a mechanism through which arts needs could be perceived. The preliminary identification of the arts constituency was also critical in that all the individuals and agencies involved in the arts had a common ground at the meetings in which to explore and communicate some of the major problems facing the city. Priorities for the future were achieved with maximum citizen participation and creativity.

In spite of the Delavan and San Antonio success stories, one should realize that nominal group technique has its limitations. For routine meetings that focus on information exchange, other formats might be more apt. It requires a well-trained overall facilitator and small-group facilitators that may be unavailable in some settings. The technique, like many others, does not assure that the ideas obtained from the meeting will be accepted by the rest of the organization or other groups. It also requires great planning effort to get out representative citizens in large numbers. However, within the group itself the process tends to yield a high member acceptance of outcomes.

JURY WORKSHOP. The jury workshop approach toward community needs assessment was developed by Heberlein (1976b) of the University of Wisconsin-Madison. The workshop attempts to mix professional expertise and advice with the values and intentions of citizens. It allows for complex questions to be made understandable to the general public without domination by professionals. It also avoids the domination by a vocal minority group, often found at public meetings. In many respects the jury workshop is similar to the conduct of an American jury at a public trial.

Names are drawn at random from a voter registration list, and those people are invited to attend a meeting and offered a small compensation for their work. Out of 50 names randomly drawn, perhaps 12 or 15 people register for the meeting. Like the American trial, the meeting often starts with testimony from expert witnesses, who are invited to present contrasting perspectives of a community problem or need. These witnesses are often interdisciplinary in their approach to the problem and respected in their fields. After witnesses have testified, the jury asks additional questions in order to become better informed. At some point, jury members convene and begin their own deliberation. They may draw on other small-group needs approaches such as the nominal group technique to eventually reach a conclusion about identifying or dealing with the issue. The jury workshop may last several days or just a few hours, depending on what needs to be accomplished.

The German government has used a similar approach by selecting citizens to develop various government plans. They work for a three-month period and are compensated by the government for the time they spend away from their regular jobs (Foster 1980).

Heberlein conceived the jury workshop for Madison when the city was interested in getting public input about the application of salt to public streets during the winter. It appeared to be a relatively noncontroversial issue in the city. Surveys or public meetings could have been conducted. A survey was viewed as expensive and time consuming. It was believed a public meeting would be dominated either by environmentalists who wanted to curb salt use or by salt industry advocates. It did not appear that the general public, a truly representative group of citizens, would attend a hearing. Furthermore, it was assumed that the reactions of the public would be based on inaccurate or incomplete information because it was believed they were not completely aware of the complexity of the salt problem. So the jury workshop emerged as a response to the limitations of public meetings and surveys.

The strength of the jury workshop is that it leads to responsible and representative decision making based on up-to-date information. Pros and cons are presented to a relatively impartial group that can make a thoughtful decision. It is assumed the jury is truly representative of citizens at large rather than an especially vocal minority group that tends to control public meetings. If citizens are poorly informed about a particular subject, a survey would be of little use. Hence the jury workshop is especially useful when professional groups or technicians are asked to provide information.

The workshop, however, has limitations. If the public is well informed about a particular issue, surveys may be more appropriate. If it appears that more people should be involved in decision making, a public meeting might be preferred. Citizens who are particularly upset about a certain issue may resent a jury deciding their fate and may disrupt the decision making by sponsoring their own public meetings. In any case, the jury workshop is useful and should be viewed in light of its obvious limitations.

CONSCIOUSNESS RAISING. Consciousness-raising (CR) groups have been instrumental in defining issues in which stereotyped sex, racial, and social roles have blocked individual freedoms and full community membership. The CR techniques serve to expand the capacity of those who feel disfranchised to participate more fully in the identification of their needs. Such groups have addressed landlord-tenant tensions, racist practices, environmental and health problems, hidden practices of government, and many other issues that have had impact on the participants' personal lives. In essence, the participants question current organization practices in light of their own experiences.

It is important to note that CR can be a helpful needs assessment tool when used creatively and adapted for the context at hand. A successful CR approach in one setting is not easily transferable to others. With this cautionary note in mind, it might be useful to briefly examine two of the most commonly known CR models, that of Paulo Freire and the women's movement in the United States.

The Freire model. Paulo Freire, a Brazilian educator, applied a CR philosophy within the context of adult literacy programs in developing countries, especially Latin America. Freire wanted to do more than teach people to read and write. He believed education should liberate people to define and identify their own environment and to act on it in a creative way. He perceived traditional education as an enslaving mechanism that defined "reality" and called for people to conform to it. Freire claimed that the conventional educational approach had been used to maintain the status quo by an elitist structure rather than to encourage societal questioning and change. He also perceived a need for a democratic participation experience for people because the government did not provide them with such opportunities.

The Freire approach to reading begins with key words that are an important part of local culture. He asks the people to reflect on words such as "slum," "land," "food," "work," and "salary" as they learn to read and to write them. So, as people learn to write the word "favela" (slum), they also are asked to discuss their problems of housing, food, clothing, health, and education in the slums and how they perceive the slums as a problem situation. When learning the word "land," they are asked to relate their personal situation to the land in terms of irrigation, natural resources, landlord-tenant relations, and economic domination questions. The Freire model also uses drawings of local situations to foster more discussion about people's surrounding environment, to assess needs, and to encourage community action. The questions are developed by a facilitator to encourage dialogue in an atmosphere of "love, hope and mutual trust" (Freire 1970).

Freire helped to widen people's perceptions of their social and organizational structure and to stimulate an open articulation of community needs. This awareness often leads to questioning of government and business officialdom, the formation of cooperatives and alternative organizations, and greater involvement of participants in attempting to reshape their surroundings. There has been some debate whether Freire's model is applicable to developed countries. However, some groups have redesigned the Freire approach for industrialized settings and claim it has been moderately successful. In any case, the Freire model for needs assessment and community action is an important CR tool that is still evolving.

National Organization of Women model. CR in the women's movement emerged in the late 1960s when American women who were involved in the civil rights struggle questioned their limited roles in the movement and in American society generally. Other women were seeking ways to express their discontent with lower salaries, limited employment opportunities, and inadequate sources of identity and self-esteem. They believed that their needs collided with the happy housewife image of the 1950s. Women instinctively shared their experiences with one another, which evolved into a political instrument known as CR.

Carroll (1984) writes, "Movement women, having had their fill of domineering and unresponsive leaders, attempted to structure their own groups and organizations as nonhierarchical and leaderless in order to eliminate the exercise of 'power'." CR became a needs assessment approach and a strategy for constructing theory as well as a new movement with as little structure as possible.

Women began meeting in small groups to critique an oppression they perceived as both external and internal. These small groups provided such an ambience of mutual trust and intimacy for women to share their most intimate struggles and needs that thousands of groups sprang up around the country.

The National Organization of Women (NOW) has been instrumental in encouraging the growth of CR on a national, state, regional, and local level through extensive workshops. NOW views CR, whether for men or women, as raising consciousness and increasing the awareness of female oppression in a sexist society (Evans 1979).

The CR process. CR has several similarities with the futures intervention approach in that it begins with a focus on individual concerns before looking at broader community needs. This approach assumes that all needs assessment is superficial unless group members share their private and often painful experiences with one another. Not to be confused with therapy or personal problem-solving groups, CR focuses on social rather than purely personal concerns. The approach works on the premise that it is difficult for individuals to theorize, abstract, or look at general needs assessment without first concentrating on their personal situations. The personal component allows group members to share aspects of their personal beliefs and circumstances rather than to conform to someone else's definition. Through personal sharing, group members can assess which parts of their social or organizational system have failed them.

The second phase of CR is to look at the social system, how it actually works, and how it can be modified to meet the needs of the group. The participants look at how the system has conflicted with their own personal expressions and interests. After assessing these needs, they then attempt to reduce the number of compromises they make and to bring about some change.

The CR group is usually small (8 to 10 members), heterogeneous for the sake of trust and openness, and relatively unstructured. Groups usually continue to meet for 8 to 10 weeks and focus on a number of major issues. At each group session, participants, in round-robin style, start with an expression of self-praise. It is intended as a recognition of each person's own qualities and strengths rather than praising everyone except themselves.

The introduction of the topic is fairly brief. A detailed explanation is not offered because most of the detail will be furnished by the participants. The lead-off question is designed to be answered by everyone in a circle sequence. Each participant takes several minutes to speak without interruptions or questions. For many people who are accustomed to interruptions, this breathing period gives them a new freedom of expression that increases their self-respect. The recommended lead-off question for a NOW session on equality might be, Have you ever been discriminated against because you were a female? In a sentence or two, help us understand your answer (NOW Guidelines 1983).

Generally there are about 8 to 10 follow-up questions. On occasion, simple role playing is used to help members express their feelings. The summary recognizes that individual experiences tie in with political reality. The sessions are not intended to be mere gripe sessions but attempt to look at the causes of problems and take a course of action.

The action step usually occurs when a question is asked such as, What can we do, individually and as a group, to combat the concerns we've discussed here? The group lists ideas and may choose one or two that can be addressed in a short time. For example, they might investigate how many girls are in industrial arts classes at the local high school or study the issue of comparable worth in employment.

CR critique. CR has increased the awareness of many people and enhanced their potential to influence unresponsive leaders and institutions. "Its power lies in its trust in each individual—in the personal" (Johnson 1985). Some critics assert, however, that "telling it like a story" puts people into the position of refighting old battles (Stanley and Wise 1983). They argue for a theory and practice that will explain reality in terms of organizational experience and needs. Other theorists believe that knowledge about needs does not necessarily come out of shared experiences. They believe in an objective reality that is derived through scientific research. They class personal experiences in the realm of novels and poetry—a contradiction of scientific rationale. Some CR practitioners argue that personal experiences are just as scientific and truth revealing as a research-tested theory. In fact, every person might be viewed as a laboratory, their life experiences the test of any system's usefulness and validity (Johnson 1985).

One constraint of the CR approach is that it requires skillful leaders. To facilitate rather than thwart the process, the leader must respect the perspectives in the group and not attempt to change any member's behavior. The leader must develop well-framed questions that allow members to reveal their needs. It is critical that the leader maintain an atmosphere of trust in the group and not presuppose answers. Another limitation of this approach is that it tends to take several months of meetings. CR, however, has been accomplished in shorter time spans and on less comprehensive topics; some groups have designed their own questions and issues for exploration. Adaptation to the context is the key to successful use of the CR approach to group needs assessment.

Summary. The eight group approaches to needs assessment highlighted in this chapter are not mutually exclusive. They can be combined in unique ways. For example, the Delphi technique has been used to determine an overall needs assessment question by professional groups scattered over a region. Yet when these groups gathered at their regional meetings, they used the nominal group process to explore the question at hand. Other situations may also call for creative responses. CR could be integrated into the futurist approach. Nominal group is frequently used as one step of a more comprehensive group process such as the charrette or citizen-directed futures assessment.

Some approaches have also been adapted for wider uses. For example, women's CR has been modified by other groups to deal with rural problems, welfare programs, or peace issues. In any case, a combined or adaptive approach should not be so cumbersome as to confuse the client participating in the assessment.

Tables 6.1 and 6.2 have been designed to assist the practioner in choos-

TABLE 6.1. Organizational context of group approaches to needs assessment

Group approaches	Locality development	Social planning	Social action
Town meeting	Officials and citizens work for change in cooperative effort	Not applicable	Democratic model for change with majority rule
Public hearing	Not applicable	Usually initiated by officials	Citizens may mobilize around hearing issue
Charrette	Citizens, professionals, and technicians examine alternatives	Not applicable	Not applicable
Futures	Citizens examine intentions	Ad hoc idea generation by officials	Citizen-initiated goal setting
Delphi	Not applicable	Professionals exchange expertise	Not applicable
Nominal group	Structured idea generation	Ad hoc idea generation	Citizen-initiated idea generation
Jury workshop	Not applicable	Selected citizens, input to officials	Not applicable
Consciousness raising	Special-interest consensus building	Not applicable	Special-interest group goal setting

ing a group needs assessment tool. In Table 6.1 most of the group approaches can be modified to fit each of the organizational models. However, some approaches are better adapted for use within certain organizational contexts. In Table 6.2 highlighted key variables can be found in all group approaches. However, some approaches are better adapted to

TABLE 6.2. Key variable context of group approaches to needs assessment

Group approaches	Group characteristics	Idea generation	Indigenous leadership
Town meeting	Large group, homogeneous; structured, official agenda, ongoing activity	Set agenda, limited numbers of issues, traditional views expressed	Political visibility for individuals with leadership potential
Public hearing	Large group, homogeneous; structured, official, special-purpose agenda	Views of vested interests dominate	Low potential for leadership development; official and expert dominance
Charrette	Large group, pluralistic; special or series project of limited term	Quality ideas, high level of shared decisions by citizens, tech and officials	High potential for leadership development; individuals self-select roles
Futures	Large or small pluralistic group; total community or entity, unstructured, limited term	High emphasis on new ideas and new ways of asking questions	High potential for leadership development; individuals self-select roles
Delphi	Large or small structured, dispersed group; homogeneous or pluralistic	Isolated thinking, high-quality technical judgment	Low potential for leadership development; independent experts pool judgments
Nominal group	Any size group; special-purpose, short-term, structured, homogeneous, or pluralistic	Many ideas generated by independent participants	Medium potential for leadership development; independent member, quality involvement
Jury workshop	Small, structured, pluralistic group; special-purpose, limited-term	Limited issues cross-community plus technical information	Medium potential for leadership development; independent members pool judgments
Consciousness raising	Small, unstructured, homogeneous group; time-consuming process	Ownership of ideas due to personalizing the issues	High potential for leadership development; quality, special-interest group involvement

enhance certain citizen participation values. To summarize, there are four key variables to consider:

1. Organizational context. The intended thrust of social change. An association should determine if it is involved in locality development, social planning, social action, or a combination of the three. Regardless of the model chosen, an association should be aware of the movement for increased citizen involvement.

2. Group characteristics. If the association wants an action-oriented group, it should select a relatively small group of people. If it wants a diversity of opinion and skills, it should find a relatively large number of needs assessors. Any size group can be subdivided into functional groups of appropriate task size. Before an association determines the extent of participation in its needs assessment program, it might ask these questions: Who is doing the assessing? For whom is the needs assessment being done? Whose needs are the greatest? Who will be most likely to articulate and not articulate their needs?

3. Idea generation. A major question in any needs assessment program is how to maximize accurate data reflecting the real needs of participants. Many responses may be constrained because of rigidly defined roles and concepts by the agency and/or group members. Participants may also be manipulated or educated to draw certain needs assessment conclusions. When seeking new solutions or the reframing of questions, the key to triggering creativity seems to lie in maximizing the rewards for nonconformity and individual selection of roles. Returning responsibility/autonomy to the citizen is likely to offer higher probability of long-term public acceptance. However, it should be mentioned that there may be legitimate limitations to citizen participation inherent in the purpose or imposed by the group or organization initiating the needs assessment. Less participant involvement in the framing of the questions is likely to be appropriate when the purpose of the needs assessment is to measure public acceptance of limited options or highly technological questions. For example, in the jury workshop case discussed earlier, citizens were considering a narrowly focused question regarding the use of salt for icy conditions, and that method was used to measure public reaction.

4. Leadership. The type of leadership involved in the needs assessment program can aid or hinder the process. An association that has a goal such as stimulating community participation and developing indigenous leaders, might choose or train a "transformational" leader. These participatory leaders create an environment that allows their colleagues or followers to discover their own talents and resources and emerge as leaders themselves.

If the organization or institution is essentially addressing short-range technical problems, the more traditional authoritarian style of leadership may be more effective.

CASE ANALYSIS. An illustration of a needs assessment case analysis is presented to demonstrate the use of the matrix and other resources of the book. This is not an example where the matrix was actually used but a very interesting needs assessment case that involved several approaches, thus it lends itself well to the illustrative purposes of the authors.

The Unified Services Board of Green County, Wisconsin, at the recommendation of the Division of Mental Hygiene of the Wisconsin Department of Health and Social Services, let a contract to conduct an analysis of the effectiveness of services in the county and the establishment of priorities for future programmatic decisions. In light of the organizational context, the discussion in this chapter, and the matrix, this needs assessment effort could most aptly be described as a social planning project with an emphasis on measurement of past performance and future needs.

Four approaches were chosen to reflect individual client and professional perspectives of the service system. The design of the project involved two group approaches listed on the matrix plus two surveys and the ethnographic approach (*sondeo*) described in Chapter 13:

1. Nominal group. As the matrix indicates, this approach is useful for social planning of any size group and fosters expression of individual creativity that is likely to reflect individual values. It was chosen to obtain preliminary impressions of Green County human service needs as well as some indication of how the board and staff evaluate them.

2. Survey/county fair. The first survey measured the community values associated with human service programs. Based on a list of types of persons that frequently need human services, respondents were asked to identify those with the most serious needs and the level of resources the county should provide.

3. Survey/family. In response to negative reactions regarding the "poor people" who require human services, which surfaced in the two previous needs assessment activities, this survey was designed to obtain self-definitions of their problems from the client families.

4. Delphi. As indicated by the matrix, this method of needs assessment taps the contribution of experts who can provide high-quality technical judgment. It was used in this project to identify new or enhanced human services needed, as viewed by professionals who operate within the system.

5. Ethnography (*sondeo*). This approach provides information about

the incidence and geographic distribution of specific problems and provides opportunities for human service staff to interact with the leadership of the county. As community leaders identify persons in need of services on the plot map, they graphically demonstrate for themselves the extent of services needed. The identities of potential and existing clients are transformed from statistical definitions to human dimensions. This approach changed local perceptions from a status quo ("we take care of our own") outlook to an atmosphere that was ready for local human service improvements.

All the methods generated large amounts of qualitative data. Taken together, they enabled the county to develop a three-year plan that would strengthen and revitalize both the informal and formal system of human services (Webster 1977).

The discussion of the eight group approaches and the four key variables offers some helpful clues for dealing with the question of how to assess community needs. These are not easy formulas for success. Nevertheless, maximum citizen involvement can be a principle of group approaches to needs assessment.

CHAPTER 7

Community level surveys

DONALD E. JOHNSON ● LARRY R. MEILLER

THE NEEDS ASSESSMENT SURVEY has emerged as an important tool in the arsenal of techniques used by community developers and other social change practitioners. In Chapter 1, Summers recognizes the importance of recently enacted legal requirements for citizen participation. This in part stimulated the increased use of surveys and other related techniques of public participation.

The needs assessment survey is not a recent social invention, however. The community score card, a precursor of the modern survey questionnaire, was used as early as 1917 (Wileden 1970). Local citizens, usually meeting in small group settings, scored their community on the basis of standards established by outside experts (e.g., a prescribed number of volumes in the local library or of medical doctors per 1000 residents). In time, some states adopted community betterment programs that utilized modifications of the score card system as a method of promoting competitive changes among participating communities or that enabled communities to become "certified" (Peck et al. 1983).

The community check sheet type of questionnaire gained widespread usage from 1940 to 1960. Citizens, assembled as members of a civic organization or in ad hoc groups, selected and/or ranked the most serious among dozens of potential community problems listed on the sheets.

Modern survey methodologies—which stressed proper sampling techniques, improvements in response rates, refinements in questionnaire and

126

interview schedule construction, and the like—began to be developed extensively in the 1930s. This came about in response to social concern over the wide disparities in levels of living within and among rural communities and counties in the United States. As sociologists and other social scientists made progress in refining the tools and methods of survey research, a kind of survey elitism began to develop among some researchers. Laypeople were excluded from participation in the survey process except for serving as respondents. Even today the conventional wisdom in some social scientific circles is that research quality is sacrificed when laypeople become involved in survey operational procedures.

The dilemma of the desire for citizen participation and involvement and the need for a scientifically accurate and reliable survey has been noted by Warren (1970:26). On the one hand, accuracy and reliability can be attained by outside experts, but the report usually "is destined for the library shelves." On the other hand, if the survey is unscientific and hastily put together by an action-oriented citizen's group, the facts and generalizations will be questioned. However, Warren argues that "there is no reason why widespread, interested participation and support should be separated from scientific accuracy. . . ." He argues also that survey validity should not be adversely affected by a citizen group's desire for action. If this is true, the survey should be examined in more detail as a public involvement technique.

Technique of public involvement. As noted above the community survey has not been rated highly as a technique for generating citizen participation and involvement. Typical of assessments of the community survey is that based on the model of public involvement proposed by Heberlein (1976a), who defines four major functions of public involvement: informational, interactive, assurance, and ritualistic.

The informational function consists of two components: to give information to the public and to get information from the public. As Heberlein notes, a technique that serves one component may be virtually worthless for the other. He rates the survey as a potentially excellent technique for getting information but poor in terms of giving information to the public.

The interactive function involves people and groups working together on problems. This implies a rapid exchange of information back and forth as citizens and change agents or agencies work together to reach decisions, in this case the identification of community needs. In its purest form the questionnaire and the survey operate more in the stimulus-response mode. That is, all citizens (respondents) are stimulated in the same manner by identical questions and are asked to respond. There is no sharing of information in a give-and-take manner; thus the survey is rated poor in terms of its interactive function.

The assurance function ensures that the public knows or is assured that its views have been heard and taken into account. Heberlein rates the survey as only fair in accomplishing this.

The question addressed with the ritualistic-legalistic function is whether the involvement technique being utilized either satisfies legal requirements for public involvement or adheres to social or community norms that support the democratic process. When properly conducted, the survey has excellent potential for satisfying this function.

In addition, Heberlein advocates rating involvement techniques according to their representativeness. Because it is virtually impossible to involve the entire population of most communities in needs assessment, it is important that those who are involved represent an accurate or representative cross section of the population. Or, as Hobbs notes in Chapter 2, the procedure must be methodologically sound. Readers also should note carefully the sampling techniques discussed by Dillman in Chapter 11. When the sample is properly drawn, the survey can yield results that are very accurate representations of the larger population.

When properly conducted, the survey is an excellent way to obtain information from the public; it usually meets ritualistic (legalistic or normative) requirements and is representative. It is a poor technique for giving information, is not interactive, and is only fair in assuring the public that all viewpoints have been heard and taken into account.

Improving the interactive function. Perhaps the most basic weakness of the community survey, when used in isolation from other techniques, is that it is not interactive. In actual practice, change agencies or agents usually supplement the survey with other procedures and practices that modify the weaknesses identified by Heberlein. To achieve other citizen involvement goals (such as developing a sense of community identity, helping citizens gain self-esteem and personal growth, promoting enthusiasm and motivation for change, and reducing alienation), the survey often is incorporated as a step in much broader processes designed to maximize public involvement and interaction.

For example, Voth (1975) describes a typical community development process as beginning with the formulation of a communitywide steering committee conducting one or more surveys of needs and priorities and of study and action committees to deal with community issues such as housing, health services, and recreation. Such processes typically last from six months to two years or longer, with much emphasis placed on citizen participation in all phases. In Chapter 10 Ryan discusses three major strategies for incorporating surveys in broader action research perspectives. These are designed to increase the participation (and hence the interaction) of citizens in general, or segments of the citizenry, in all phases of the change process, which includes needs assessment surveys.

Interaction between change agents, survey specialists, and the public can be promoted in the survey process itself. The authors of this chapter have experimented with several techniques for involving and interacting with the citizenry in general and with various community groups and agencies in some 40 Wisconsin community surveys from 1975 to the present time. Some of these experiences are summarized in Tables 7.1 and 7.2.

In addition, evidence can be provided that in some cases the survey process itself actually can be strengthened by citizen and agency involvement. Through the use of extensive citizen participation, Maugham and Winger (1982) have developed a method of survey of needs assessment in which results are available to the community within 24 hours of survey completion. The authors' experience is that from 8 to 10 weeks will be required, on the average, for the entire survey process in a typical commu-

TABLE 7.1. Presurvey activities

Survey phase	Interaction with the community
Legitimation	Meet with groups, organizations, agencies, or local governments to decide or agree that a survey is desirable or necessary in the first place.
Sponsorship	Sponsors of the survey also legitimize the presence of the change agent and those assisting with the survey. Interaction may occur with local government or one or more of its agencies; local organizations such as the Chamber of Commerce, Jaycees, Community Club, or other service groups; and ad hoc groups of citizens, either self-appointed or appointed by local government. Sponsors also may provide financing for the survey or solicit contributions from local groups, organizations, and businesses.
Policy inputs Timing Financing Establishing community boundaries or the area to be surveyed Final approval of questionnaire Deciding who (what groups) will be surveyed Seeking volunteer assistance Methods and timing of publicity	The sponsoring group(s) usually works with the change agent and the survey specialists in making major decisions about how the survey will be carried out.

TABLE 7.2. The survey process

Questionnaire construction Deciding on the type of question: open-ended vs. structured, use of standard format vs. community-specific questions tailored for the community, or both Deciding whether additional questions should be solicited from community groups	A local committee, perhaps the sponsoring group or an ad hoc committee of broad community representation, decides with the survey specialists on the specific content of the questionnaire. The survey specialist will finalize questions in acceptable form for committee discussion and eventual approval.
Sampling	The group(s) or committee assists specialists in drawing a random sample of citizens, (e.g., from the city directory utility billings, fire numbers).
Questionnaire distribution	The group(s) or committee assists in stuffing, addressing, and stamping envelopes to be mailed; or a group of volunteers may stuff packets and then hand-deliver to residences, explain purpose to respondents, secure cooperation of respondents, pick up questionnaires at a later date, and follow up by returning to residences until completed questionnaires are obtained.
Coding of data	After preparing codes, or precoding on the questionnaires, specialists train local volunteers to code data.
Data entry	Local volunteers enter data in computers located in the community itself or on a floppy disk that is then sent to a different location (e.g., to a university) for transfer to a computer.
Data processing	Data processing (unless by slow, laborious counting) usually is done on large computers (e.g., in a university setting). However, as home and business computers and related software grow more sophisticated and as local citizens become more adept in their use, data processing in the community itself may become a common practice.
Analysis of results	Analysis usually is done by survey specialists. However, interaction is stimulated and survey interpretations are improved when a preliminary analysis of the results is presented to the sponsoring group and/or the steering committee for discussion and suggestions.
Public presentation(s) of results	Local groups (e.g., the steering committee) interact with the change agent or specialists who will present survey results to the public (e.g., at an open public meeting). Local people make arrangements for the meeting and may participate in the presentation of survey findings. They also may arrange for additional publicity of results in local newspapers or for later presentations of results at meetings of relevant groups and community organizations.
Action committees or groups	One or perhaps several new study and action committees or groups may be formed to deal with important community issues and needs (e.g., recreation, elderly housing, education, health services). Or the existing sponsoring or steering committee may locate relevant groups or organizations to deal with the community needs that were identified.

nity in which citizens are extensively involved. This is not an unreasonable amount of time, especially if communication lines are developed to ensure a continuous flow of information to the community (discussed in the next section).

The examples cited above and in Tables 7.1 and 7.2 indicate some of the possibilities for the "marriage" of community involvement and the survey process. However, the use of various participatory techniques raises the question of the costs, if any, of such participation. For example, it might be expected that the training required to ensure high-quality participation of community volunteers would add to the time necessary to complete the survey. Compared to having the survey carried out by a professional firm, some time undoubtedly will be lost in a typical survey. However, this is counterbalanced by the educational value of the experiences provided to the volunteer participants, the actual monetary savings that result from the volunteer labor provided, and the value of the increased sense of survey ownership by the community in general. Warren (1970:25) notes, for example, that "it is important to develop citizen interest that will bring about action. Many excellent factual surveys gather dust because the broad base of citizen support, or the organizational and agency base for action programs, was not developed. One of the best ways to avoid this is to involve in the survey process the people and agencies that will be called upon later to support and implement the survey findings."

Improving information flows. Strictly speaking, the survey instrument itself provides precise but minimum information to respondents and does not communicate at all with the remainder of the population (i.e. with nonsurvey participants). For this reason, Heberlein (1976) rates the survey as a poor technique for giving information to the public. However, surveys do not occur in a social vacuum. Those who conduct them are required to communicate effectively with the citizens of a community if they expect a high rate of cooperation. To that end, survey specialists always provide additional information to prospective respondents.

When the ultimate purpose of the survey is to generate data that will be useful in promoting community change, survey specialists will provide a wealth of information to the community-at-large. These types of information are summarized below.

INFORMATION TO RESPONDENTS

1. Why respond? Information regarding the value of the survey. The purposes or uses for which the data will be utilized. Who (what groups or

organizations) will use the data generated by the survey. How the community will benefit. How the individual respondent may benefit.

2. Scientific sampling. Requirements of being selected as a matter of chance or probability. The respondent as a representative of others in the community. Why a high response rate is important.

3. Guarantees of anonymity and confidentiality. Why the respondent will not be identified. The release of grouped data rather than individual responses.

4. Timing. When the respondent will be contacted (if an interview). When questionnaires should be returned and how. When survey results will be announced and in what forms.

INFORMATION TO THE COMMUNITY

1. Introducing the survey. Announcements, either in the local daily or weekly newspaper and/or on local radio or television, that a survey will be conducted. Announcements stress the value and ultimate purposes of the survey. How the information generated will be utilized and by whom. Who is sponsoring (legitimizing) the survey and how it is being funded.

2. Presurvey activities. Formation and activities of the local steering committee or other group(s) involved in the survey. Composition of the committee and how it was appointed or formed. Invitation for interested groups or individuals to participate and in what ways (e.g., attending meetings, submitting questions for inclusion in the questionnaire).

3. Announcements of dates. When and where planning meetings will be held. When interviewing will begin or when questionnaires will be distributed. When and how questionnaires are to be returned.

4. Promotion of survey response. Guarantees of anonymity and confidentiality. Restatements of the survey purpose(s) and potential value to the community. Urge responding to the survey.

5. Progress statements. Announcements in the local media with respect to progress to date. Urge return of questionnaires. Announce survey completion and that coding and computer analysis are under way. When results are expected and in what forms.

6. Invitations to the public. Invitation to public meeting(s) where results are to be presented. Who is sponsoring the meeting(s) and who will be presenting. Time, date, and location of meeting(s). Whether printed copies of survey results are available and from whom.

7. Media presentations. Preparation of a newspaper article (preferably a series of newspaper articles) that presents and explains the survey results. Radio or television programs that highlight the results.

8. Other community presentations. Presentation of survey results, us-

ing visual aids such as overhead transparencies and slides to groups and organizations in the community.

9. Follow-up presentations. Presentations in the media or group meetings such as Where do we go from here?

If the survey is to be an effective technique for community needs assessment and results are to be utilized in processes of community change, it is evident that a wealth of information must be provided for respondents and the community in general. The survey itself does not provide such information, but those who plan and conduct surveys must do so to assure maximum community participation and impact in the community as a result.

Improving indirect effects. Surveys often produce indirect effects in the community, which may not be consciously intended and recognized. For example, when information is disseminated in the community that introduces the survey to announce presurvey activities and dates, promote survey response, etc., a general air of expectancy may be created. A survey is being initiated, and from it an expectation is created that certain actions may be undertaken in the future by local government or community groups. In this sense, the survey begins to assume two of its important functions: enhancing support for locally initiated community improvement efforts and improving the residents' sense of community (Blake et al. 1977). The survey helps residents realize that others in the community may be desiring change and improvements. A sense of community pride and spirit may begin to be generated.

Other indirect and desirable effects of surveys can be created through careful selection of diverse respondent groups and by the use of third-party communication facilitators (e.g., the mass media) in the community. For example, virtually all general community development or change surveys include a cross section or representative sample of the residents of the area. If the community is small, a 100 percent canvass of residents may be attempted (Surveying Community Attitudes 1977). Some practitioners, however, regularly include other respondent groups in the survey. Blake and his colleagues (1977), for example, list the identification of the positions of important local organizations as a major function of the needs assessment survey. They survey community organizations having formal or informal policy concerns related to community improvement, in addition to surveying local government and its agencies.

Nix (1982:4) and associates in Georgia also include other groups in addition to community resident samples. Special importance is attached to the viewpoints of two types of leaders, the first being those occupying important formal positions in the largest and most active organizations. This includes top leaders in government, politics, industry, business, finance, etc. A second type of leader interviewed by Nix (1982:3) includes the top influentials identified by reputation for power in the community. Nix includes these and other leader samples on the assumption that relatively few (1 percent or less) of the population are involved in most community decisions and that successful community action depends in part on involvement of lay community leaders.

In the mid-1970s, Meiller and Broom (1979) developed an elaborate sampling strategy for community needs assessment surveys. Based upon a model first suggested by Salmon and Tapper (1973), the Meiller-Broom approach involves sampling the opinions of at least three groups—the public (citizens), local elected officials, and community leaders. A fourth group (public servants) identified by Salmon and Tapper as important in the community development process conceivably also could be surveyed, at least in larger communities where they would contribute a large and professionally trained group.

Salmon and Tapper's (and Meiller and Broom's) contention is that these represent the major decision-making groups that exert power or influence in community change. Furthermore, the assumption is that for the most part communication linkages are weak between most pairs of groups, thus making understanding and agreement on community problems and solutions somewhat problematic. Salmon and Tapper assume that strong two-way communication linkages exist only between citizens and leaders. However, as the reader will have noted, Chapter 5 argues that leader marginality (operating in both the local community and the larger society) can lead to mistaken perceptions of what other community residents think about local problems and needs. Chapter 5 also notes that the smaller the community, the more likely it is that leaders' perspectives will diverge from those of the community-at-large. Leaders in small communities often are surprised and offended when citizens express needs that the dominant leader group has not recognized in the past. It is completely safe to accept the contention of Chapter 5 that there is never full participation or full knowledge about what everybody else thinks about local problems and needs.

This problematic nature of participation and knowledge led Meiller and Broom (1979) to experiment with a model of community consensus, as first proposed by Scheff (1967). Depending upon the amount of communication that takes place within and between groups in a community, various states of consensus about problems and solutions can exist; e.g., between any two groups it is possible to find any one of the following four states:

1. Monolithic consensus. The majority of each group *agrees* with the other on community needs, and the majority of each group *understands* there is agreement.

2. Dissensus. The majority of each group *disagrees* with the other on community needs, and the majority of each group *understands* there is disagreement.

3. Pluralistic ignorance. The majority of each group *agrees* with the other on community needs, but they *misunderstand* (i.e., believe there is disagreement).

4. False consensus. The majority of each group *disagrees* with the other on community needs, but they *misunderstand* (i.e., believe there is agreement).

Meiller and Broom (1979) argue that the best states in which a community can exist are monolithic consensus and dissensus. If most people or groups are in agreement about community needs and know they agree, they are in an excellent position to move toward the planning of solutions to those problems. Or, if they disagree and know it, they can talk out the problems, suggest compromises, and come to some resolution of community needs. On the other hand, little or no resolution of community problems will occur when groups are in the other two states of consensus.

Thus we begin to see that the community survey has potential far beyond its original objective of simply identifying local problems and placing them in some order of priority for action. The survey can be used to identify positions of important community groups as well as to determine how members of each group perceive each other and members of other groups. The varying status of agreement and disagreement and the various perceptions, accurate or mistaken, can be reported to the community following the survey.

It is in the reporting of the states of consensus that the survey may have its greatest indirect impact on the community. Using a quasi-experimental design in which feedback of consensus findings was attempted in two "treatment" communities, but not in a control community, Meiller and Broom (1979:77) found a number of significant changes in the treatment communities: (1) citizens generally became even more aware of community problems and issues and began to view them as more important; (2) the various groups surveyed became more accurate in predicting the priorities of the other groups; (3) newspaper articles that reported specific problems mentioned by the three groups stimulated more people into discussions about community problems; (4) the response to the survey by citizens, elected officials, and community leaders was enthusiastic and supportive; and (5) many credited the survey with stimulating action to resolve the problems.

Since the Meiller-Broom experiments, the consensus approach described above has been applied in some 30 additional communities by the chapter authors. Although additional rigorous evaluations have not been conducted, they have noted similar positive results in many of the communities. In addition, it has been observed informally that elected officials frequently move closer to the positions and priorities of the citizens following publication of survey results in the local press. Thus the authors suggest that utilization of third-party communication facilitators (i.e., the mass media, especially the local newspaper) is vitally important to the success of any community change effort that involves surveys.

A note of caution is in order, however. The reader will recall some of the major points made in Chapter 5. For example, although the press informs community citizens what to think about, know about, and have feelings about, the publication content usually is influenced by the medium's responsiveness to and support of the government and business power centers of the community. When this type of information control occurs, it can lead to a fairly rigid social control in the community. Although conflicts about community needs are reported regularly by the media of the most pluralistic centers (i.e., the large cities), the social control mechanisms of the more homogeneous small towns may inhibit such reporting. Therefore, the authors suggest that social and economic pressures on local editors may be significantly reduced, or even eliminated, if the change agent and/or survey specialist will prepare the articles that compare the viewpoints and perceptions of the various community groups and submit them to the local editor for publication. The experience of the authors has been that the editors are most cooperative and appreciative.

Measurement of needs. The measurement of community needs, and of individual perceptions of how other people will express those needs, has been carefully researched by Meiller and Broom (1979) and by the authors. The basic strategy employed by Meiller and Broom involves collecting certain types of information from survey respondents, which might result in the introduction of tension in the community system when reported.

Warren (1972) notes, for example, that the community as a social system is in a state of continuous change as it responds to forces that impinge upon it from the outside environment. When those forces result in stress or tension, either the structure of the system or the belief system that supports the structure must change or accommodate to maintain the existing equilibrium, or it must move to a new equilibrium (Stinchcombe 1968, Chapter 5). Even when groups are in perfect agreement (monolithic consensus), the introduction of that knowledge to the community will set many to wonder, Why, if most people agree, and we know that we agree, isn't something being done to resolve this problem? Even this mild form of tension can motivate the community to further action.

What types of information are most useful in introducing tension to the community, and how are they collected or measured? Again, a theoretical model has proved to be useful in directing Meiller and Broom and the authors in resolving this question. Measurement techniques have been devised, based upon a "co-orientation model" developed by McLeod and Chaffee (1973), that indicate three types of information useful in evaluating the state of consensus that exists in any community.

First, what *understandings* do individuals have of community problems and needs? That is, how do they define problems and how serious do they rate them? Here the survey should attempt to determine whether individuals (groups) share common knowledge about community problems or needs. For example, assume that citizens and elected officials, on the average, rate juvenile delinquency as a serious community problem. However, most citizens define the problem as one of lack of communication and the existence of feelings of mistrust between youth and the local police force. Elected officials feel the problem is based upon the need for more police officers and the failure of the public to support higher taxes to employ them. In this case, there is common or shared *agreement* that the problem of juvenile delinquency is serious. However, no common *understanding* exists between the two groups regarding the basic nature or causes of the problem. How can one measure understanding and agreement?

The authors advocate the use of unstructured or open-ended questions as a strategy for determining whether understanding exists between individuals or groups. This may be done in two ways. First, one may simply ask respondents to list and describe the three (or four or five) most serious problems existing in the community. It is then possible to determine whether the members of any two groups are basically defining the situation in the same manner (i.e., whether there is a common *understanding)*. If the same problem area (e.g., juvenile delinquency) is mentioned often by both groups, there is *agreement* on the seriousness of the problem or community need.

After repeated measurements in dozens of Wisconsin communities, the authors have modified the open-ended question approach. The modification is to present a list of general problem areas that exist in most communities and then to request the respondent to define or give the content of each potential problem area, regardless of its degree of seriousness. Over the years, 18 different areas have emerged from the various community surveys. If the community is interested in a general or extensive survey of needs, the following may be included:

Streets	Recreation and leisure-time activities
Traffic	Housing
Parking	Environment and pollution
Shopping for goods and services	Human relations
Condition and appearance of the	Crime and law enforcement
downtown	Local government and government
Economic development	services
Public transportation	Community growth and planning
Health care	Public utilities
Education	Other

These general categories have proved useful in capturing most of the specific concerns that exist in the typical community in Wisconsin. On occasion, the list has been modified or expanded to fit the peculiar nature of a community, based upon the recommendations of a citizen steering committee (e.g., adding "pedestrian and bicycle safety" in a survey of needs in an urban neighborhood and "waterfront conditions" in a village located on the banks of a major river).

After respondents list their specific concerns in each general area, they are then requested to rate the seriousness of each area. In this case a seven-point scale is utilized, where 1 represents no problem at all, 4 represents a moderate problem, and 7 indicates a very serious problem. By comparing both content and average ratings for citizens, elected officials, and community leaders, it is possible to determine the actual amount of agreement existing between any two of the various groups.

Determination of the states of consensus in the community depends upon a final measure. Each respondent is requested to predict how most members of his or her own group and how most members of the other two groups will respond. Specifically, respondents are requested to list the three or so problem areas they believe the others will rate as most serious. The accuracy of each group's assessment of the others is determined by comparing the group's perceptions of the others with what the other groups actually stated as the major problems existing in the community. If there is common understanding and similar ratings for any particular problem area and the groups accurately predict that there are similar ratings of seriousness, a state of monolithic consensus exists for the problem area. Conversely, any one of the other three states of consensus may emerge as a community characteristic. By feeding information to the community on content (understanding), agreement (ratings of seriousness), and accuracy (predictions of other ratings), the authors have been able to introduce tension into numerous community systems. This has resulted in changed levels and types of consensus as well as the motivation of community groups to further study their needs and to take remedial actions.

Other methods of needs assessment. Nix (1982) employs methods similar to those described above in assessing county or community needs. That is, he includes open-ended questions that ask respondents to describe the most important needs or the things that need to be done to make the area a better place in which to live. He then asks the respondent to rank the needs in terms of their importance. This is followed by a listing of over 40 services and conditions that can be rated on a five-point scale, ranging from excellent to very poor. These services and conditions are very similar to those used by the chapter authors and include things such as job opportunities for youth and adults, recreation for various age groups, availability of housing, various local government services, health care issues, parking, traffic, and issues relating to public and vocational schools.

In the approaches used by Nix and by the authors, it is important to note that the open-ended or unstructured questions always precede those that are more structured. The primary advantage in listing the unstructured questions first is that those who are conducting the survey are not making suggestions to, or putting words into the mouths of, those who are responding to the survey. By simply asking people to name or describe the most important needs or problems of the community or by asking for specific needs that may exist in a general category, such as "public transportation" or "shopping for goods and services," the respondent is influenced to think about those that currently are important or most salient.

The primary disadvantage of unstructured approaches is that they require individuals to be fairly precise in communicating their concerns. Some have difficulty in expressing themselves (verbally in interviews or in writing on questionnaires), and on occasion it is difficult for survey researchers to understand the real nature of the specific concerns being expressed. A second minor disadvantage of unstructured questions is that they are more difficult to code (i.e., to assign numbers to the responses for the purpose of entering into computers and doing statistical analysis). The authors, however, have developed extensive codes for the 18 open-ended questions utilized in the consensus surveys, and they find that ordinary citizens are capable of learning and using the codes in a relatively short time.

Most survey approaches to needs assessment rely upon structured questions as the principal mechanism for determining needs and their importance or seriousness in the community. The survey approach designed at the University of Missouri-Columbia is typical (Surveying Community Attitudes 1977). The questionnaire is divided into several general areas, such as retail facilities, recreational facilities and services, health services, education, community services, and industry (similar to the consensus approach of the authors). Numerous specific questions are then asked under each general area. For example, with respect to community services, the respondent is asked whether "the following municipal services are satisfactory." A dozen such services (e.g., police protection, water, sidewalks) are then listed, and the respondent simply checks "yes," "no," or "no opinion." This approach has the advantage of ease and speed in responding and makes coding of data an extremely easy task. Disadvantages to structured questions include the possibility that the list of specific concerns may be incomplete and the feeling by some (e.g., elected officials) that it is too easy for respondents to check needs that in reality do not exist (the "kid in the candy store" complaint). However, structured questions can be most valuable in determining community needs, especially when they are well designed and the community itself is permitted to add and/or modify questions to fit its peculiar circumstances. Simply put, there are no absolutely "right" or "wrong" approaches to needs assessment. It is a matter of selecting from a variety of approaches that have proven effective and have their own special advantages and disadvantages.

Summary. Community citizens can play a variety of roles in the survey process in addition to serving as passive respondents. The authors believe this involvement can be attained without necessarily losing any significant level of survey integrity and accuracy. By increasing the types of interaction between change agents, survey specialists, and the leaders and citizens of the community, the likelihood is increased that survey findings will lead to further action aimed at the resolution of community problems and issues.

The involvement of citizens is being made easier in many communities because of the increased sophistication of the public. People in general are more informed today about surveys, sampling, and the like, and the technology of the computer age has entered many of the smallest villages and community centers in the United States. Because of advances in technology, it is no longer always necessary to send data from the local community to the university or large urban center to be processed.

Suggestions have been reviewed for increasing the amount of communication occurring in the community as surveys are carried out and following their completion. The local press has long been considered a conservative force in the typical community, uncomfortable with conflict and serving primarily to promote the image of community harmony and well-being. The authors suggest that this medium can be a potent force in informing the public about all phases of the survey; in encouraging participation of various kinds; and in reporting results that change the perceptions of citizens, leaders, and elected officials. While not promoting conflict or dissensus directly, the press can accurately report information that may lead to those states. The kinds of questions asked in the survey and the comparisons of feelings and perceptions of diverse community groups can influence the equilibrium of the community system, resulting in tensions that can motivate purposive action.

This is not to suggest that the techniques emphasized here are the only, or even necessarily the best, ones for improving the effectiveness of community surveys. A number of different approaches exist (e.g., see Chapter 10), and the change agent is well-advised to shop around for techniques that best fit his or her circumstances and those of the community. A number of cookbook or how-to-do-it manuals and publications exist and may be obtained for the asking (Surveying Community Attitudes 1977; Reinhard et al. 1985). Such manuals typically assist change agents and communities in deciding policy questions (how to organize, scope of the survey, geographic area to be covered, how to construct questionnaires, sampling, distribution of questionnaires, etc.). They usually provide examples of questions that may be borrowed or adapted to the circumstances of the particular community in which the change agent is working. And finally, they may provide examples of news releases designed to promote higher rates of questionnaire return and to improve the flow of information to the community.

The authors emphasize the limited impact a survey may have when it stands alone, i.e., when it is viewed as the sole mechanism by which community residents can participate in assessing common needs. However, when the survey is properly designed, and combined with other techniques that improve communication and promote participation and more accurate understanding, it emerges as a powerful tool in the hands of the change agent. It should always be followed by group techniques that will permit a maximum of interaction and communication among those who are considering change in the community.

CHAPTER 8

Large-scale surveys

DAN E. MOORE ● JAMES A. CHRISTENSON ● ANNE S. ISHLER

THE MAIN REASON for conducting a large-scale survey for needs assessment is that many public decisions, policies, and programs affect large populations and geographical areas. The rationales developed in earlier chapters for engaging in a needs assessment process apply to the multicounty, state, regional, and even national level as well as to the community level. That is, it is just as important for citizens to be involved in these public decisions as it is in decisions affecting smaller groups within a more delimited area.

Citizen feedback is the cornerstone of a democratic and responsive policy. The President's Commission on National Goals (1960) stated that participation by all citizens in the analysis and resolution of public issues is essential. The need for an assessment of social well-being and for citizen input to and involvement in the decision-making process have long been acknowledged at the national, state, and local levels. The New England town meeting has been the exemplar of citizen involvement in solving local problems. However, once one moves to larger communities such as Chicago, regions like Appalachia, or the state level the mechanics of the town meeting are unworkable.

How do you assess needs of larger communities, counties, regions, states, or nations? In the 1950s and 1960s, many large communities began goal studies. Chicago, Los Angeles, and Dallas, to name a few cities across the United States, involved segments of the public in problem identification and goal formulation conferences, hearings, and workshops (Wheaton and Wheaton 1972). During this time most federal, state, and local agencies were feeling increased pressure to provide programs responsive to the citizenry. Beginning in the late 1950s, many legislative and regulatory statutes in transportation, health, and land use required that the needs of clientele be determined (Burdge 1982). The most popular participation mechanism was the public forum. However, forums began receiving criticism for involving a small and often nonrepresentative segment of the public in discussing critical issues. Public forums had come to be seen as ritualistic exercises rather than sincere efforts for public participation. Heberlein (1974:204) notes that "one strategy to eliminate the unrepresentativeness of participation at the public hearing is the public opinion poll; whatever its other limitations, a carefully conducted survey can insure a representative sample of a given population within statistical estimates of probable error."

Public opinion polls and large-scale surveys are not by definition needs assessment techniques. We see the results of polls almost daily on TV and in the press; private polling organizations are legion. Most major universities have survey units to conduct social science research. Surveys and polls involve gathering information (attitudinal, behavioral, or some combination thereof) from the general public or select segments. However, such information is meaningless until placed within a political/policy context. To be relevant, the data must be interpreted, must be used. If the information is to be used within the decision-making structure of society, decision makers must be involved in forming questions and interpreting results. And if information is to accurately reflect citizens' positions and behaviors, citizens also must be involved in formulating questions and, more importantly, in interpreting findings. Survey information is powerful only when translated within a policy context that involves both decision makers and citizens. Citizen participation and leadership involvement can create a situation through which large-scale surveys can serve as a major feedback process in a responsive society.

In the following pages, we will look at why large-scale surveys are popular, why needs assessments are conducted, and in particular, how large-scale needs assessments can be effective modes of public participation. Our concern is not with the mechanics of how to do large-scale surveys. A discussion of the techniques involved in drawing samples and conducting surveys—whether face to face, by telephone, or by mail—are available in several excellent books (Sudman 1976; Dillman 1978; Groves and Kahn 1979). Dillman presents the key aspects of design in Chapter 11. We will focus primarily on our own experiences in relating mail and telephone surveys in Pennsylvania, Kentucky, and North Carolina to citizen participation and public decision making.

Popularity of large-scale surveys. There are several reasons why large-scale surveys have become widely used. Technology has become available to assess the needs of select clientele inexpensively, accurately and quickly. Sampling, probability estimates, and related statistical principles developed during the World War II years became accepted by decision makers and the general public as legitimate ways to represent American society. As a consequence, the number of public and private organizations and institutes involved with large-scale surveys greatly increased.

LOW COST. Large-scale surveys have become affordable to most federal, state, and local agencies; universities and colleges; and private organizations. Telephone and mail surveys are available at a reasonable price. Dillman and his associates (1974) reported costs of less than $3 per completed questionnaire; in 1984 the cost could run between $10 and $20 per completed questionnaire if all expenses were considered. Face-to-face interviews can exceed $100 per completed interview and thus are an option for only the most affluent organizations and agencies.

ACCURACY. Expensive surveys are not necessarily accurate. Part of the reason for widespread adoption of mail and telephone surveys is their low cost with high levels of accuracy. Most surveys will obtain response rates between 70 and 85 percent (Dillman 1978), which is comparable to the response rates of face-to-face interviews. Small samples such as the familiar 1500 respondents reported on the nightly news, with an accuracy of 3 percent, can adequately describe the sentiments of 250 million people in the United States, or the population of a state, or some subregion.

Convincing the average layperson of one's ability to generalize to large populations from such relatively small samples is sometimes difficult. Involving people who will use the results in the early stages of designing the sample and in making trade-offs between sample size and costs helps somewhat. Discussing the relative merits of a random sampling process in contrast to basing conclusions on contacts with friends and next-door neighbors also helps clarify the validity of a carefully drawn sample.

TIMELINESS. Telephone survey results can be generated within a 2-week turnaround. Some specialty surveys can have a 24-hour turnaround; that is, the information can be gathered, processed, and released to the public within 1 day. For example, the Survey Research Center at the University of Kentucky interviewed (by telephone) 400 households throughout Kentucky regarding the TV stations they were watching on election eve 1980. The information was gathered in a 5-hour period, processed in another 3 hours, and was ready for release the next morning. Mail surveys often take several months from the time the first questionnaire is sent out until the last is returned. However, with adequate planning the results can be released in a form ready for use shortly after the last mail questionnaire is returned.

Uses. Conducting a large-scale survey requires considerable resources and effort. There is a temptation after the data are collected and compiled to assume that the work has been done. To the contrary, the data do not represent conclusions nor are they directly translatable into public policy. Needs assessment fits within the larger context of a decision-making process. As such it can help define problems, gather information, and assist in choosing among alternative courses of action by measuring citizens' reactions to alternative policies. But needs assessments including large-scale surveys do not make public policy.

The following examples from recent large-scale surveys illustrate their various uses; information collected can be used to assess public sentiment, rally a public, justify a stand, and explore program/policy alternatives.

ASSESSMENT OF PUBLIC SENTIMENT. A 1970 statewide mail survey in Washington helped to make large-scale mail surveys popular. The Washington survey showed that for less than $2 per sample unit, a response rate of approximately 75 percent could be obtained in approximately three months (Dillman et al. 1974). In 1973, studies in North Carolina, Arizona, Indiana, and again in Washington State were conducted using the same techniques. Over 50 statewide mail surveys assessing citizen sentiment on public problems and policy choices can be traced to these early studies (e.g., see Burdge and Warner 1975; Christenson 1976; Burdge et al. 1978; Beaulieu and Korsching 1979; Moore and Ishler 1980).

A brief description of a few of the early studies will illustrate the ways in which succeeding needs assessments built on the successes and limitations of earlier ones. The 1973 North Carolina study by Christenson (1973) is an example of citizen needs being assessed at a statewide level. The Cooperative Extension Service in North Carolina supported the survey, since its mission was to service these needs. A major objective was to systematically study and set priorities on citizens' concerns. The advantage of the statewide survey was that it provided information representative of the entire state on a wide range of issues.

The information from the 1973 survey was disseminated in seven popular documents to interested members of the general public; however, the major users were university officials and government agencies. For example, the state budget office used public preferences on tax expenditures along with other data in establishing state goals. State and regional planners used the problem identification section to assess the relative seriousness of community problems in various regions of the state.

The major shortcoming of the 1973 study was that the public input gathered did not contain information useful to decision makers at the local level. The study used a proportional sampling technique that provided appropriate state data but subsamples large enough for analysis in only a few heavily populated counties. The Cooperative Extension Service, which has local county offices, found the information interesting but irrelevant, since county samples of sufficient size were available for only 4 of the 100 counties in the state.

In a 1975 statewide study in North Carolina, an attempt was made to develop public input that would provide information for state and local decision making and program planning. Data were generated through a proportional and oversample procedure so that information was available for each county (Christenson 1975). Nine popular publications were developed, which contained information for specific counties within seven geographical areas of the state. Local agricultural extension leaders were trained to use the information as a basis for discussion with local advisory groups and interested citizenry in formulating six-year county goals. From a state and regional perspective, the availability of county data enhanced the usefulness of the public input at the multicounty and state levels. State and regional planners could compare county-to-county, county-to-state, and county subjective data (available from the study) with known objective data.

The most important insight gained from these two studies was that information only has an impact if it gets back to the grass roots level in a usable form. Such efforts require either large samples or less expansive geographical coverage. In fact, the impact on decision making at the state level was more evident when the public input also was meaningful to and used in decision making at the county level.

Subsequent studies such as those in Kentucky (Burdge and Warner 1975) and Illinois (Burdge et al. 1978) have emphasized the importance of involving information users in the early stages of large-scale surveys. For example, in Illinois numerous state and local officials were visited during the formulation of questions for the questionnaire.

A common complaint about surveys is that respondents do not have enough background to make intelligent choices among policy alternatives (Dillman 1977). However, the issue really is one of framing questions for which the relevant publics have answers, which can provide useful information for the decision-making process.

One example from a presurvey visit to a public official will illustrate the point. A state energy planner scoffed at the idea of a public survey assisting in solving the energy crisis, one he viewed as highly complex and international in scope. But he did see the relevance to his work of knowing how many people were using wood stoves and how many had increased the insulation in their homes. Needs assessment researchers must be sensitive both to what the potential information user wants to know and what the public is able to provide.

RALLYING A PUBLIC. Garkovich (1982) describes the use of a countywide survey by the Chief Executive Office (CEO) of the Jessamine County, Kentucky, Planning Commission in revising existing land use plans. The CEO wanted to rally the public behind a master land use plan and its enabling zoning regulations in order to protect the public welfare. To maximize citizen input in the development of the comprehensive land use plan, the Jessamine County Planning Commission devised a multistage program.

First, a series of public forums, eventually attended by 280 citizens, sought to inform the public of demographic and economic changes in the county since 1970 and to obtain citizen comments on issues facing the community. Two citizens' advisory committees composed of representatives from community organizations, different geographic areas of the county, and special-interest groups (developers, large farm operators, real estate agencies) developed goals and objectives for the comprehensive plan.

Second, a countywide mail survey of Jessamine County households was conducted for the planning commission to use in assessing the public attitudes toward growth planning and zoning. The sample, stratified by geographic location in the county (the two incorporated places, and the unincorporated areas), provided a countywide basis for the development of goals and objectives for the land use plan by the advisory committees.

The county mail survey thus became a tool for shaping the direction and outcome of discussions by citizens' advisory committees. Members of these committees received a copy of the survey results, which highlighted the public support for growth management and land use planning. When discussion developed as to the importance of preserving agricultural land or restricting residential developments to specified areas, the survey was used to demonstrate public support for these efforts (see Garkovich 1982).

In Pennsylvania the issue of farmland preservation was a top priority for citizens (Moore and Ishler 1980). In this instance, regional and county planning committees have used the survey results to show how citizens in their respective jurisdictions view farmland preservation in contrast to neighboring counties or regions.

JUSTIFYING A STAND. Data from a soundly executed study can identify problems and be used to justify a particular position or public policy. For example, in Pennsylvania the state Department of Transportation was interested in public sentiment regarding once-a-year versus twice-a-year auto inspections (Moore and Ishler 1980). The survey results may have been instrumental in formulating a new policy recommendation to shift from a twice-a-year to a once-a-year plan. It is difficult to determine with any certainty the relative importance of any one factor in determining policy decisions. In this case the administration used the survey results in presenting its recommendation to the legislature. Data from the same survey were also used to justify positions of various groups on state job creation policy and funding for roads.

In the above examples the survey was conducted by a university, and the public results were used by another group to justify its stand. Sometimes surveys or survey questions are commissioned with the specific intent of substantiating a particular position. For example, in 1982 a consumer group asked the Survey Research Center at the University of Kentucky to include a series of questions on the "bottle bill" in a statewide survey. The groups wanted to provide information to the state legislature showing that citizens wanted a five-cent fee attached to all plastic and glass containers and were willing to pay slightly higher prices for products to facilitate the implementation of the charge. Armed with survey information that supported their position (three-fourths of the public favored passage of the bill), the consumer group lobbied with the legislators and reported the information through the news media. Of course, the bottle industry also lobbied with legislators to defeat the bill, complaining that the bill was impossible to implement and too costly. The "bottle bill" was not passed. This is one among numerous examples of how survey results do not automatically decide policy directions.

Another group sought data from the University of Kentucky Survey Research Center on public support for a "lemon car bill." This legislation would have required automobile sales companies to insure their products and/or state conditions of the car before sale. The survey questions concerned general support for the idea (public support was high); however, increased car cost to implement the program was not supported by the public. The information was used to defeat the bill in the Kentucky state legislature. The data were made public because of the policy of the University of Kentucky Survey Research Center to disclose all information gathered. However, the information was never pushed by the consumer group, since it did not justify their stand.

Political candidates often utilize surveys to document their chances of winning an election, document public support for their positions on certain issues, or demonstrate their popularity. However, most political candidates hire private polling operations, which are not required to make their information public. Thus results are often selectively released to justify the position of the candidate. While such surveys are methodologically sound and tap the sentiments of the public, the information generated is not used to assess needs but to support a preestablished position.

The use of survey results to justify various political positions raises an interesting dilemma for the needs assessor. Who controls the information generated by a large-scale survey should be established early in the project. Who nominally sponsors the project, who funds the research, and the policies on data release and use by participating organizations are all issues of import. For example, one of the recurring themes in this book is that a commitment should be developed early (and continuously) with the users, in many cases the decision makers. Almost by definition, persons within the political arena have unique interests to represent or protect. This is true for even "unbiased" actors such as universities. A major university that has been party to conducting a large-scale survey may not be interested in having results showing a low public priority for higher education released during legislative debates on university funding.

Another potential conflict might arise when multiple constituencies are involved in the various stages of survey design, implementation and use. Large-scale surveys in particular may have a variety of constituents since multiple objectives are often being addressed. Which constituent gets the most questions in the survey? Whose questions get asked first? Even those unschooled in research methods can sense that the phrasing of questions may influence how questions are answered. Who decides on question format?

As suggested in Chapter 11, there is a substantial body of research suggesting the most valid and reliable techniques for survey work. In general, it is best for the technical details to be left to those trained in survey research methods. If the methodology including the sampling strategy is called into question, the resulting data may be of little use to anyone. At minimum, the issues raised here should be thoroughly discussed and resolved early. The size of the undertaking in large-scale surveys means that once key decisions (such as printing the mail survey questionnaires) are made, it is extremely expensive and time consuming to change.

EXPLORING POLICY ALTERNATIVES. Many of the large-scale efforts may be criticized for being conceptualized and implemented as one-shot surveys covering a wide variety of issues. Consequently, the coverage of any particular issue in a study is rather superficial, and the relationship between needs assessors and policymakers is not sustained. One project, however, illustrates a more elaborate model for doing policy surveys. Called "Alternatives for Washington," the study was initiated by the governor to guide state government program planning and provide criteria for making budgetary decisions (Wardwell and Dillman 1975).

The goal-setting process centered around a statewide task force of about 165 people. This group was given the assignment of producing alternative goals for Washington. They met four times for three-day workshops that consisted of classroom sessions, in-depth exchanges of information and perceptions, and futures operating exercises. These 16-hour-day sessions resulted in a large number of possible state goals being articulated and analyzed for the impact each would likely have on achieving the other goals (Dillman 1977). These activities were augmented by areawide meetings in 10 geographic areas of the state involving another 1500 people in similar though briefer futures creating sessions. Following the area meetings, the state task force reconvened and finalized 11 alternate futures for the state and a large number of specific goals.

The next activity of the task force was to present these choices to state residents. An intensive media campaign, which included weekly television programs, was mounted for the purpose. This effort to educate the people of the state on the various choices was followed by a survey that assessed people's preferences. The plan was to provide the results to the state task force, which in turn could use them in deciding the choices to recommend to the governor and legislature.

The questions to be included in the survey were developed through intensive interaction between the participants and the researchers. The researchers observed all sessions of the task force and attempted to convert the delegates' conclusions into questions suitable for surveys. The delegates in turn evaluated the extent to which they felt the intents of their alternative futures were captured by the questionnaires. Several repetitions of this process were required to produce a satisfactory set of survey questions.

Implementation was further constrained by the requirement that the surveys could not be started until the media campaign was concluded, but results had to be available within one month. This very short time horizon was necessitated by the mandate of the governor that final task force recommendations be available to the legislature when it convened. A full consideration of the constraints and questions the task force wanted to have answered led to doing multiple surveys: a statewide survey of the general public by telephone (to get the quickest possible feedback), area surveys of the general public by mail to explore geographic variations (as a possible basis for substate variations in policy recommendations), and mail surveys of all participants in the statewide task force and areawide meetings (to get an informed perspective on the issue). The point of doing four surveys was that each might complement the others and contribute something unique. The mail and telephone methods were used because both could perform within the prescribed time constraints inexpensively enough to get adequate numbers of responses for generalizing results to various population subcategories.

Results were presented to the statewide task force and its subcommittees as they became available. Appropriate cross-tabulations were included so that the views of particular subgroups in the population (e.g., high- and low-income people) could be examined. The influence of the survey results on the final recommendations of the task force was considerable, as evidenced by an examination of the final report (for a more complete presentation, see Dillman 1977).

The design, execution, and use of these surveys conforms very closely to the synchronized survey model discussed in Chapter 10. The decision makers in this case were the statewide task force. A series of policy discussions by this group preceded the surveys and produced its design and content. The surveys were carefully timed so that the results would be available when the final policy decisions were to be made. In the making of those final decisions, the surveys constituted one of several pieces of information used by the group.

The recommendations of the statewide task force were used by the governor in much the same way as results from most surveys. Specific findings were used to justify proposed legislative actions. Dillman (1977) notes that "policy recommendations were incorporated into the governor's 1975 state of the state speech and integrated into 20 of the 30 pieces of legislation that he recommended to the legislature in that year. However, whether the task force recommendations were indeed the actual causes of his decisions or only justifications is something that perhaps only he knows."

Evolving model for large-scale needs assessments. Each of the numerous large-scale surveys cited here, beginning with the work of Dillman and others in the early 1970s (Dillman et al. 1974), has built upon each preceding work. Modifications in the process have included designing sampling procedures to permit generalizations to subunits of the larger population; working closely with citizen's groups and local, regional, and state decision makers in study design and question content; and developing innovative ways to deliver survey results to users in an understandable and usable form and in a useful time frame. As a way to summarize some of the key elements in this evolving model, we will briefly highlight the Pennsylvania study of Moore and Ishler (1980).

The study was developed at Pennsylvania State University at the initiative of the Cooperative Extension Service. In contrast with studies that are tightly focused on a single problem, this had multiple objectives, some of which were quite broad in scope. However, the following were more or less clearly defined and agreed upon by all actors:

1. Develop priorities for education programs and program areas for the Cooperative Extension Service.

2. Develop a range of information on citizens' preferences for state and local community policies in the 1980s.

3. Use the opportunity of the survey to gather information on citizen characteristics and behaviors to inform basic research in the areas of migration, energy behavior, and community service demands. Obviously, these objectives overlap to some extent, but the critical criteria for including items in the survey was whether or not the information was seen as useful by at least one of the following groups: educators at Pennsylvania State University, public decision makers in various offices throughout the state, and researchers.

After defining the broad purposes of the study, specific methods were chosen. Because the information was to be used by state, regional, and local decision makers, it was decided that the sample size should be large enough to permit generalizations about adults residing in relatively limited local areas. Specifically, the intent was to generalize the findings to each of the 67 counties in Pennsylvania. To address such a large and geographically diverse sample of people, a mail survey was selected as the vehicle.

The basic objectives and survey parameters were established in consultation with an advisory committee drawn from across the university. The decision was made early by the advisory committee to seek funding for the study solely from within the university so that the critical decisions would remain within the control of the survey group and outside various political arenas. A variety of departments, institutes, colleges, and university administrators were approached about participating. While there was no quid pro quo, the general understanding was that financial investment in the study would permit the sponsor to ask a limited number of questions within the broad objectives outlined above. Sufficient funding was collected in this manner, and each of the sponsors was invited to participate on the advisory committee along with a number of research and extension specialists (Moore and Ishler 1980).

A word about funding and survey costs is in order here. Earlier, we suggested that costs in 1984 might run $10 to $20 per completed questionnaire. Exact costs are difficult to specify. Inflation is one major factor. Another is just what costs are considered. Is staff time contributed? Is overhead paid or contributed? Are only paper, printing, and stamp costs to be covered? Do costs include printing reports, conducting public meetings, evaluating the benefits of the entire project? Dillman suggests that the best studies are those that are most carefully planned and pay the most attention to detail. This advice implies a methodology for calculating costs. If each step in the process is carefully specified, the requisite support for each step can be calculated. In-house organizational support, sometimes seen as free, often has social costs. One way to keep these costs to a minimum is to involve the implicated people in planning and get mutual commitments so that there are no surprises. Furthermore, ways can often be found to maximize organizational benefits so that, on balance, costs are reduced. Each undertaking will require a unique combination of dollar and organizational costs. Care should be taken to calculate each of these in the beginning of a project. The Pennsylvania project attempted to follow this procedure. The advisory committee was very useful in analyzing the costs and benefits.

Next, to ensure that the information would be useful to decision makers in the state, more than 100 interviews were conducted with legislators, cabinet officials, local government officials, leaders of civic groups, and staff and citizen advisory committee members of the Cooperative Extension Service. The purpose of the overall study was explained during these interviews. Each interviewee was then given the opportunity to respond to the question, If you could ask 20,000 Pennsylvanians five questions that would help you make decisions in the 1980s, what would you most like to know? Each of the individuals contacted was enthusiastic about participating (especially after we explained that the survey would not cost them anything and was being conducted by Penn State as part of its public service mission). Interviewees responded during the interview and were also given a simple two-page questionnaire with which to communicate additional thoughts.

These decision makers and potential users of the results were not only important in developing ideas for the survey; but, more importantly, the interviews began a process, a relationship, between the university and a number of organizations. In short, an audience for the results was being created before the study was conducted. Throughout the entire project we were demonstrating that the university could cooperate and would deliver. The 100 individuals and groups were contacted for information before the questionnaire was constructed and were also involved in reviewing each draft of the questionnaire. They were kept informed at each stage of the data collection process and were the first to receive results. These individuals and organizations were key actors in the dissemination and use of the survey information.

Dillman's total design method was followed in every detail (Dillman 1978). One aspect of conducting the survey deserves emphasis, since it highlights the close interaction with relevant audiences. If there is a single key element to the success of any survey, it is to carefully pretest the survey instrument. Dillman has prescribed pretesting with three distinct groups.

First, fellow researchers and other experts in research methods and the substantive policy areas to be studied were asked to react. These people assisted in helping to make question wording compatible with previous research and helped avoid errors of fact and technique. A second group included in the pretest were potential users of the research information, such as government officials. They were helpful in assuring that the questionnaire responded to their data needs. (In this case the persons interviewed earlier were used.) A third group was made up of "real people," a sample of the general population within close proximity to the university. These people were chosen to simulate actual respondents. Some were mailed the questionnaire; others were asked to fill it out in the presence of researchers for immediate feedback. The total pretest process was interactive in that once feedback was received, a new draft of the questionnaire was developed and then subjected to further pretesting. The final questionnaire went through eight complete drafts before final printing; it was not short, consisting of 10 pages and over 200 questions and requiring approximately 30 minutes to fill out. The pretesting procedure coupled with the other components of the total design method led to a response rate of over 73 percent.

The amount of information generated when over 14,000 individuals complete a 10-page questionnaire is almost overwhelming. Only because a systematic plan had been developed in line with the study objectives was it possible to use this information in a timely manner. The first publication was a 16-page tabloid that summarized the statewide results for most of the questions in the survey (Moore and Ishler 1980). The intent with this popularized format was to communicate quickly with respondents (who were promised results if they desired), sponsors, and those users who were interviewed to develop the questions. The three-color tabloid also served as an advertising piece for potential users of the data base. This publication was in print less than one month after the last questionnaire was returned. It focused on statewide results. Later publications dealt with subpopulations and geographic areas. The release of the tabloid along with press releases and press conferences generated wide interest in the printed and electronic media throughout Pennsylvania.

As noted earlier, the first project objective was to help develop program priorities for educational programs in the Cooperative Extension Service in Pennsylvania. To this end the researchers worked closely with state, regional, and county staff to frame questions and produce usable reports. In addition, a set of regional publications was targeted for extension lay advisory planning committees. In addition, we produced a 10-minute slide/audio show that was used to introduce the study to new audiences. Twelve copies of this slide/audio presentation were made available to extension staff members in each region of the state. By conservative estimate more than 20,000 people saw this presentation during the first year. The data and reports in various forms have been used by program planning committees at all levels.

The second objective was to provide current information on public policy issues to decision makers at state and local levels. In addition to the tabloid and a variety of workshops, special reports were prepared to users' specifications. For example, the state Department of Aging was interested in priorities for senior citizens' services as indicated by the elderly themselves compared to the rest of the population; further, the department was interested in differences between the rural and urban elderly. We were able to use our extensive data base to produce a report that answered their specific policy questions. The initial users and requesters of special reports were the organizations interviewed to elicit questions, but a number of other organizations throughout the state also requested them. In all, more than 220 such publications, tailored to user needs, were produced in the year following the survey.

Summary. Large-scale surveys, to be vehicles for public participation, must be sensitive to local issues, useful to appropriate decision makers, and relevant to policy issues. To achieve this, those involved in developing and conducting large-scale surveys need to work with ultimate users of the information, use the state of the art in survey methodology, and develop an interrelated set of questions through interaction with users that will elicit meaningful information on policy questions.

It is important to realize that seldom if ever will the results of the needs assessment or a citizen survey definitively answer policy questions. But such work can provide important and timely information to decision makers. The context and clientele of decisions can be more fully elaborated. And finally, the needs assessment activity can set in motion a process of continuing discussion among various actors in the policymaking arena, whether these are governments, public agencies, or voluntary associations.

CHAPTER 9

Role of secondary data

PAUL R. VOSS ● STEPHEN J. TORDELLA ● DAVID L. BROWN

THE PRIMARY FOCUS of this book is on traditional survey and less traditional nonsurvey techniques for determining community needs. However, another approach that should always be part of any needs assessment process is the fullest possible exploitation of secondary data. There is a wealth of existing data in survey archives, research centers, and libraries awaiting further analysis. The benefits as well as the problems of using secondary data will be discussed here.

What are secondary data? Secondary data consist of statistical information gathered for a purpose other than the immediate or first application. For example, they may consist of survey responses conducted elsewhere. Such surveys may have set out to answer questions similar to your own but for a different area or different type of population. On the other hand, the survey might have been carried out for reasons entirely unrelated but may have included a question or two that could help bring clarity to another study. For example, census data gathered and published as part of the Census Bureau's decennial enumeration of the nation's people, families, and households may be useful in assessing a local community's needs.

Where are the data found?

PREVIOUS SURVEYS. It may be surprising for some to learn that data from thousands of surveys conducted over the years have been systematically preserved, catalogued, and archived precisely for others to use. Major data archives in this country include the University of Michigan's Inter-University Consortium for Political and Social Research, the Roper Center at the University of Connecticut, and the Louis Harris Data Center at the University of North Carolina. In addition, dozens of colleges, universities, and research centers around the country have smaller, sometimes specialized, data archives. In fact, it would be difficult to think of a question that someone, sometime, somewhere has not asked in a survey. These surveys can show researchers how other investigators have worded relevant questions and how similar groups of people living elsewhere have responded.

CENSUS DATA. Certainly the largest body of secondary data anywhere is that made available by federal government agencies such as the Bureau of the Census, Bureau of Economic Analysis, Bureau of Labor Statistics, and National Center for Health Statistics. The Census Bureau is the best known of these agencies. It annually conducts many national surveys and carries out several censuses every five years that provide detailed information on business, agriculture, and governments. The most well-known product of the Census Bureau, however, is the decennial Census of Population and Housing.

The most recent census, conducted in 1980, was an enormous undertaking, costing more than a billion dollars. It provides information on the number and characteristics of the population of states, counties, local units of general government, school districts, congressional districts, and election wards and precincts. For many of the more urbanized parts of the country, the census also provides data for neighborhoods and other community areas down to the level of the city block. The use of this kind of demographic data in assessing community needs will be emphasized here.

For virtually all communities there simply is no data series that goes back so far in time and offers comparably reliable counts or estimates of basic social, demographic, and economic information as the Census of Population and Housing. We contend that community needs assessments should always include an early consideration of the community's demographic makeup. This approach should serve as a supplement rather than a substitute for the survey and nonsurvey methods discussed elsewhere in this volume. Sometimes the census may include all the information one seeks. More often, however, it is likely to provide only the first level of understanding of the nature of a community.

ADMINISTRATIVE RECORDS. Another extremely important kind of second-ary data that may play a role in a well-executed needs assessment is administrative record data. These data are generally gathered by government or other statistical agencies for program administration. Examples include revenue data such as the number of tax filers or the aggregate number of exemptions claimed by persons in your community filing state income tax returns, new household utility connections or disconnections, vehicle registration information, and voting registration records. These kinds of information are gathered by state departments of revenue, public electrical utilities and co-ops, state departments of transportation, and local town clerks respectively. The difficulties encountered in obtaining and using such data will be discussed later in this chapter. The important point is that such data exist and can often be effectively employed in assessing community needs.

LOCAL HISTORICAL RECORDS. One final type of secondary data does not fit neatly into any of the above categories. This miscellaneous grouping of information includes such items as county or other local histories, county atlases, old maps, parish records, newspaper archives, and other local records. These types of records can yield important information about the history of local problems and public attention to such issues. Properly researched, they can help the community analyst develop a more complete picture of the historical context within which current issues arise.

Using secondary data in needs assessment.
For exhaustive treatments of secondary data use, it is best to consult books written specifically for this purpose (e.g., Hyman 1972; Stewart 1984; Kiecolt and Nathan 1985) or the several recent volumes published by the U.S. Department of the Treasury (1982, 1983, 1984a, 1984b) on the use of administrative records data. Some of the general ways in which secondary data may be helpful are discussed below.

DESCRIBING COMMUNITY STRUCTURE AND CHANGE. Secondary data analysis is a convenient first step in community needs assessment because a statistical portrait of a community can be developed with a minimum of technical expertise and at a modest cost. Secondary data, particularly the census type, are widely available in published volumes for all counties in the United States and in a comparable format for various decades. Such data are also available for places of 2500 or greater population. A more limited set of indicators is also available for smaller places. These printed data are available from a wide range of public agencies and an increasing number of private firms. Many of these agencies will provide data to the community on microfiche and in computer-readable form. The latter traditionally has included data on magnetic tapes. Increasingly, however, with the explosive growth of microcomputer use in local communities, agencies are making data available in the form of "down loadable" files and on floppy disks.

With limited fiscal and professional resources, most communities, regardless of their size or location, can use secondary data to develop a statistical baseline for understanding structure and change. Moreover, because the data are collected in an identical fashion for all communities, it is possible to compare conditions in one's local area with other communities. Such comparative analysis contributes to the identification of problems and opportunities in one's locale.

In some instances secondary data analysis may be all that is needed for assessing community needs. A statistical portrait of the community, particularly one that compares it to other areas, may be sufficient to call attention to problems and opportunities. A statistical profile may provide a sufficient basis for rallying community support for economic and social programs and for needed capital improvements. Again, the ability to compare local conditions to national or regional norms can be very persuasive in justifying such actions. Because secondary data can be organized to portray trends over time and to illuminate the implications of different directions of future change, they aid in anticipating and planning for future growth and development, or conversely for decline or stagnation. Statistical data are also useful for judging eligibility for various types of government aid to communities. This is important in and of itself and can be a pivotal factor in mobilizing public support for local programs.

Some community leaders prefer secondary data analysis to other needs assessment techniques because of familiarity, convenience, and/or cost. But other leaders choose this type of information for judging community needs because they believe it gives a more representative picture of the sentiment of the entire community. Typically, secondary indicators summarize individual responses in some type of statistical aggregation. These statistical data help officials separate communitywide issues from the narrower issues of special interests.

In other cases, a statistical analysis of census data may be only the initial step in assessing community needs. In these instances, secondary data analysis helps to identify appropriate issues for public concern. General domains of concern are identified through secondary analysis; then a deeper probing of public sentiment is derived from one or more of the survey (or nonsurvey) techniques discussed throughout this book.

CONSTRUCTING SAMPLING FRAMES FOR COMMUNITY SURVEYS. After examination of descriptive and comparative data for a locale has been carried out, an opinion or attitude survey may be selected as the most desirable approach to ascertaining specific community needs. Here too, secondary data can play a crucial role. Administrative records often provide the basis for drawing a representative community sample for gathering local opinion. In different circumstances these sampling frames might include such familiar sources as the local telephone directory's white or yellow pages, a city directory, local voter registration lists, or property tax rolls. They could also involve such lists as local utility customers, drivers license holders, or vehicle owners. These lists may be available from commercial organizations or state agencies as long as confidentiality and other similar restrictions are not abridged.

CHECKING FOR BIAS IN DATA FROM OTHER TECHNIQUES. Secondary data constitute an invaluable resource for determining whether survey results are truly representative of community opinion. This is important for establishing credibility of the survey effort. Demographic data gathered on each survey respondent can be aggregated and compared with similar census data for an area. Some allowance may have to be made for the passage of time since the most recent census, and the census data may have to be updated on the basis of known trends. But the census, updated or not, constitutes the most reliable basis for determining whether a survey constitutes a representative slice of community opinion.

CHECKING THE VALIDITY OF SURVEY AND NONSURVEY DATA. As needs assessment results are being studied, some further questions may emerge. Do the perceptions revealed in these data accord with reality? Why are the perceptions of some groups in the community different from those of others? Is it possible to identify which of several conflicting perceptions is most valid? The analysis of secondary data may hold the key to answering such questions.

Not long ago the state of Wisconsin hired a well-known market research firm to conduct a survey of business leaders throughout the state. Executives from some of the state's major corporations had long been critical of Wisconsin's corporate and personal tax structures. Repeated attention to this criticism in the media eventually led to major concern, indeed, widespread belief, that attitudes about the business climate in Wisconsin were responsible for some businesses leaving and that this reputation was preventing new businesses from locating in the state. The survey revealed, perhaps not surprisingly, that Wisconsin's business leaders viewed the state's tax structure very negatively. These leaders felt that the tax burden on businesses located in Wisconsin was out of line with that in other states and Wisconsin was driving businesses away as a consequence.

Simultaneously, the state contracted with a major accounting firm to actually compare Wisconsin's corporate tax burden with several other states within and outside the Midwest. Simulations using secondary data sources were carried out to measure the tax burdens in various states on several hypothetical businesses that represented well the kinds of industries located in Wisconsin. The results of both studies were released to the media. Considered together, the two studies showed that the perceptions of business leaders did not match reality. While the tax burden of doing business in Wisconsin was evaluated very negatively in the survey, the accounting study revealed that corporate taxes were lower in Wisconsin than in each of the other states in the study. Overall taxes in Wisconsin also ranked very near the average. (See Wisconsin Department of Development 1984.)

Secondary data can often be used in ways that are analogous to the Wisconsin business climate study, e.g., to validate (or invalidate) the perceptions and attitudes revealed in community surveys. And while it may be argued that perceptions, correct or not, form the basis of behavior and other attitudes, it nevertheless is important to know whether perceptions accord with the facts. Having commissioned the accounting study along with the survey, the Wisconsin Department of Development knows better how to allocate its resources to improve the state's business climate. It may seek to reform the tax structure, but at the same time it will devote attention and resources in countering the false image of the state's taxes.

DEVELOPING PROPOSALS. Secondary data are helpful in securing grants. The data may raise the question of whether the grant is even necessary. But once the decision is made to seek external support, solid demographic data usually are essential for making the application.

How to find the needed data. There is an abundance of secondary data resources. Local community librarians have a wealth of such data at their fingertips. Moreover, reference and documents specialists as well as many general librarians today have received formal training in the use of statistical publications and generally know where to turn when uncertainties arise concerning either the availability or the correct interpretation of such data.

The Cooperative Extension Service in several states has become quite active in providing statistical material to communities through the Community Resources Development (CRD) program. County agents are frequently knowledgeable about statistical resources and generally have connections with a wide array of resources, university specialists, and organizations. There may also be a city, county, or regional planning agency involved in managing your local area's development. This agency's staff should be contacted.

In every state there is a relatively new organization called the state data center. This network of data organizations, established in the late 1970s at the urging of the Census Bureau, provides decentralized access to federal- and state-generated data. Through a structure of state-level lead agencies and scattered substate affiliates, the state data center program generally obviates the need to go directly to the Census Bureau or one of its regional offices to obtain census information or guidance.

Private data firms also exist to provide specialized data access and analysis. These firms generally serve private-sector business needs such as market and site selection analysis. There are also firms providing services especially geared to community analysis, and these should not be overlooked as a source of data in the needs assessment process. Generally, however, you will find the commercial data firms to be a more costly purveyor of data than the state data centers.

In some respects, this discussion of assistance in acquiring census data has been organized in terms of increasing cost of access. Data from the public library is generally free, and information from private data firms can be relatively costly.

Sources. Exactly which sources of secondary data should you turn to for your needs? This section will address the sources of data and the types of information they can yield for your community needs assessment.

DESCRIPTIVE AND PLANNING STUDIES. Descriptive and planning studies carried out elsewhere can define problems and questions and set the stage for further needs analysis locally. They can place local questions into national, state, or regional context or compare local issues with those of similar communities located elsewhere. Descriptive studies can trace the problems over time, something that is time consuming and often difficult at the local level. Finally, they isolate the factors that are important in the analysis of a problem or set of questions facing the community. These are often the factors on which you will want to collect information for a particular community, either through secondary sources mentioned elsewhere in this chapter or through your own survey or nonsurvey analysis. A major shortcoming of such studies is that they are usually for a very specific community other than your own or they apply to the country, region, or state as a whole.

PUBLISHED AGGREGATE DATA FOR LOCAL POPULATIONS. Most data that are useful to local decision makers trying to understand their communities' needs, problems,and opportunities are easy to work with and obtain. These are called aggregate data because individual survey or census responses have already been aggregated or grouped for publication in statistical volumes, on microfiche, and on computer tape. The great advantage of aggregate data is that they are available for so many areas, in the case of selected census data right down to the level of the city block. When derived from the census and other federal sources, these aggregate measures are uniform nationwide so that data for a city block in Fargo, North Dakota, is directly comparable with those for a block in Fort Lauderdale, Florida.

An inherent disadvantage of aggregate data is simply, "What you see is what you get." If you want less geographic or subject matter detail than is shown in a census or other reference source, subject categories can be collapsed and geographic areas added up. However, more detail is usually impossible to obtain. For example, if the topic of concern for a community is the status of the elderly and a source has one table that shows income distribution and another that shows age distribution, it is impossible to derive income distribution by age from the two separate tabulations. In contrast, counties can be added together to make up development districts, substate planning areas, or other multicounty units. Similarly, five-year age categories can be added to represent groups of interest such as the elderly or youth.

In this vein the encouraging news is that the volume of aggregate data available is so vast that many desired tables are already incorporated in the original reports. Among the topics in the 1980 census volumes, for example, are the poverty status of specific groups such as the elderly and the labor force status of women by whether they are married or whether they have children and, if so, their ages (usually used to gauge the demand for day care). The extensive use of microfiche as a publication medium for the 1980 Census of Population and Housing has made much data available merely for the cost of copying; whereas, previously, an expensive computer retrieval process would have been necessary.

The volume and detail of secondary data are so great that we shall not try to cover them completely in this discussion. However, Table 9.1 provides a guide to the most commonly available sources. In this table, several subject matter topics of data available for counties and smaller places are displayed across the top and the data source is noted on the left. Entries represent available data and the smallest geographic area for which they are available. If data are available for the smallest unit, a city block, it can be assumed that such data also exist for all the larger places containing that block. These larger areas are as follows: the first larger area is a "block group," simply groups of blocks designated by the Census Bureau, that have an average population of 800. Where no data are available for city blocks (generally in rural areas and in places of under 5000 population), the smallest designated area is the "enumeration district," which also averages 800 residents, but this number can vary widely. In areas that are part of officially designated metropolitan statistical areas (MSAs) the next largest unit is the "census tract," which generally conforms to natural and neighborhood boundaries, with an average population of 4000. The larger geographic units are the more commonly known ones — the village, city, township or town, and county. The significance of these areas for community people is that so much data are readily available.

The data in Table 9.1 show that the Census of Population and Housing is an important source of information at the local level. In published census volumes an extensive set of information is shown for every place of 2500 population and over and more limited information for smaller places. Within MSAs there are also printed volumes that show information for census tracts. Tract data are also published for some larger cities outside MSAs. For places too small to appear in the printed volumes, there is the microfiche publication program. Fiche includes an extensive set of information covering virtually every topic covered in the census. At the city block level (in cities of 5000 or more) there is a limited set of information (the equivalent of one line in a printed document) showing summary measures of basic demographic and housing information. Even more aggregate information is available on computer tape.

The full range of census topics is much greater than that shown in Table 9.1. Basic demographic characteristics of people in an area (age, sex, race) are included, but so are such important issues as marital status and household structure. Income and poverty measures treat many different sources of income and also the balance of family financial resources and family size to determine poverty status. Labor force measures include employment and unemployment, occupation, industry, hours worked, commuting, and other factors. Other social characteristics cover such things as educational attainment, school enrollment, and migration. Housing characteristics are also extensive, covering many measures of housing quality, value, and structural characteristics.

No other single statistical source covers as many topics, in as much detail, for such detailed geographic units, and with such reliability and validity as the U.S. Census of Population and Housing. Its main shortcoming is that it occurs only every 10 years. Every effort to make it more frequent has failed.

Given the infrequent nature of the census, the next question is how to make community information relevant to the present current period. The

TABLE 9.1. Sources of aggregate data based on area residents

Sources	Total population	Age, sex, race	Income and poverty	Labor force	Other social characteristics	Housing
Census of Population and Housing[a]						
Reports	Tract	Tract	Tract	Tract	Tract	Tract
Microfiche	Block	Block	Block group	Block group	Block group	Block
Computer tape	Block	Block	Block group	Block group	Block group	Block
Current Population Reports	U.S.	U.S.	U.S.	U.S.	U.S.	...
Annual estimates[b]	Cities, villages, townships, and counties	...	Cities, villages, townships, and counties	County[d]	...	...
Projections[c]	Counties (occasionally smaller places)	Counties	...	...	...	...
American Housing Survey[c]	MSAs	MSAs	MSAs	MSAs	MSAs	Larger cities
Vital statistics[b]	County and some sub-county	County and some sub-county	...	...	...	...

[a]Every 10 years.
[b]Annual.
[c]Variable frequency.
[d]Not all states.

other sources of information in Table 9.1 will help in that task. The Current Population Survey (CPS) is a source of many statistical publications annually and of detailed computer tape files; CPS tabulations are available in several series of publications called the Current Population Reports. These reports cover all the topics in Table 9.1 except housing; however, they generally provide information only for the United States as a whole and for major geographic regions. The survey of income and program participation (SIPP), another program of the Census Bureau, provides information on a wide range of income- and program-related topics. These sources provide published data for the United States for recent years, and the computer files from these surveys often offer the potential of special tabulations for subnational regions and states. The U.S. and state data are useful for revealing recent socioeconomic and demographic trends, which may be reflected in the local experience and, in the absence of alternative indicators, often are used to update local demographic indicators. Current Population Reports are available at document depository libraries and at state data centers and their affiliates. Data from the SIPP survey are similarly available.

State government units often create/make estimates of the current population of local areas. In some states these estimates are used in state revenue sharing programs. They generally are available at local libraries, and through state data centers. The Census Bureau, in its Current Population Reports series, also publishes local population estimates. These estimates are available annually at the county level and every other year for municipalities and minor civil divisions.

The next question frequently asked after ascertaining where a community is now is, Where is it likely to go in the future? Population projections are useful for this. In most states either a university research unit or a state agency is responsible for producing county-level population projections based on past trends. These projections specify only the simplest demographic characteristics: age, sex, and sometimes race. However, these characteristics usually are basic to the service needs of the population. County population projections can be used in concert with trends at the subcounty and city level to estimate how a community is likely to grow. A few states and local planning units have even produced projections for cities, villages, and townships in their boundaries. Some caution is in order in this regard, for local projections are likely to be volatile, and they usually project only the total population. Many private data firms carry census data and proprietary updates of those data for small areas of the whole country. The data generally are available for political geographic areas or for places defined by geometric expressions such as a three-mile radius around a street intersection. The base data apply to about 67,000 geographic units — census tracts in tracted areas (mainly large cities) and minor civil divisions (usually cities, villages, towns, and townships) elsewhere. The forte of private data firms is their ability to instantly profile and project any area a person would like to define by adding up data from the component parts. Delivery of the profile is also quick. But the same provisos about small-area projections mentioned above also apply to their data.

Labor force estimates are often created by state departments of labor and industry for local areas. Administrative record data from unemployment compensation insurance programs can yield a wide range of employment data, including estimates of employment and unemployment and estimates of covered employment and wages by industry. Not all states have extensive statistical reporting programs, but many do and most are rapidly increasing their capabilities.

The American Housing Survey (formerly the Annual Housing Survey), is conducted by the Bureau of the Census for the U.S. Department of Housing and Urban Development. Results of this series of surveys of larger cities show much detail about the housing stock of an area, demographic and socioeconomic characteristics of area populations, and many neighborhood characteristics and problems such as airplane noise, crime, or community satisfaction.

Vital statistics (data on births, deaths and illness, marriage, divorce) are also available on the local level from state agencies. For counties and some smaller units, these vital events occurring among residents can be ascertained from state government publications. These data, together with a recent population estimate, make it possible to tell whether growth in an area is due to more births than deaths or to more people moving in than out, often an indicator of the growth of an area's economy.

DATA ON LOCAL ECONOMIES. Table 9.2 describes data on community economic structure rather than the labor force. This distinction is useful to

TABLE 9.2. Sources of aggregate data based on area business and institutions

Source	Retail trade	Other industries	Income	Government
Economic censuses	City	State and some substate	Variable	...
County business patterns[a] Bureau of Economic Analysis[a]	County	County	County	...
Books	County	County	County	...
Computer tape	County	County	County	...
State departments of industry and labor[b]	Variable	Variable	Variable	...
Census of governments[c]	...	...	...	County

[a]Annual.
[b]Variable frequency.
[c]Every 5 years.

those interested in community economic development because it is necessary to know about the current and potential labor force living in an area as
well as the kinds of industry operating there. The listing is not exhaustive
but covers the most commonly used resources available for local areas.

Economic censuses occur every five years, based on the completed
year's business for those ending in 2 and 7. Of the economic censuses, the
census of retail trade has the most detail available for local areas. For
counties and communities of 2500 population and over, data are available
on the number of establishments, payroll, and type of establishment. For
cities or counties with 500 or more establishments, more detailed tabulations are available by type of establishment. Examples of data available for
every county and place include the number of stores and annual sales for
drugstores, furniture stores, gas stations, eating and drinking places, and
other establishments. For areas with over 500 establishments, the retail
trade data also include an estimate of local income generated through their
payrolls. Retail trade is often one of the most important sectors of a community's economy, so these data can be quite useful in gauging its economic
prospects.

Other economic censuses include those of agriculture, wholesale trade,
service, construction, manufacturing, and mineral industries. Where there
is a sufficiently large number of establishments in a substate area, data are
available for that industry. However, it is much more common for data on
these industries to be available for only very large metropolitan areas,
states, or the nation.

Shortcomings of secondary data. Perhaps the most bothersome feature of secondary data is the lack of control over how they were collected
and tabulated. For example, a few years ago two of the authors were
involved in a project requiring a demographic analysis of the welfare population in Wisconsin. The state maintains a central computerized data base
of all applicants for assistance in three federal "means-tested" public assistance programs: Aid to Families with Dependent Children (AFDC), food
stamps, and medical assistance (Medicaid). The state is a respected leader
in the computerization of its welfare programs and is regarded as a model
for other states. Despite this level of sophistication, secondary analysis of
these data was difficult because quality control procedures were focused
only on information that directly affected eligibility criteria and grant
levels. Other household characteristics were often not screened for correctness by the intake worker, and internal program cross-checks for inconsistent, incorrect, or missing data were not conducted. This massive data file
and the various programs related to it performed well administratively, but

it was far less useful for secondary analysis of the state's welfare population.

Another bothersome feature of secondary data is the variation in quality over time. This often is apparent in the process by which the data are classified back to geographic areas of origin. Errors may occur, for example, when mortality data are adjusted from place of occurrence to place of residence so that accurate local vital rates can be computed. Minor changes of emphasis in the collection and adjustment processes can have significant effects on the geographic classification at different dates and can seriously alter the measurement of change.

Nevertheless, since the secondary data set is usually almost a "free good" to the community analyst, it provides inexpensive, if not always convenient, access to information about community change and the community's citizens. The challenge lies in the creativity required of the analyst to extract the needed information.

Summary. Secondary data analysis is an integral part of the community needs assessment process. The trick is to know how to articulate secondary analysis with the survey and nonsurvey techniques discussed in other chapters of this book. We have suggested that secondary data should be used throughout the needs assessment. They can give a first approximation of community change and structure and point to problems and opportunities. Moreover, secondary data analysis can help local decision makers understand how their community compares with others. This can help local officials appreciate the shared nature of their situation or its uniqueness.

But secondary data are useful at other stages in the needs assessment process. They can assist in developing sampling frames for community surveys. They are useful for checking for bias in survey data and in data derived from nonsurvey techniques. And they are useful for evaluating the validity of information from other needs assessment methods. Moreover, once community needs are identified, secondary data are invaluable for preparing grants for public program assistance. So secondary data are an essential element in the needs assessment process. Properly used, they can supplement the more detailed, community-specific information generated from community surveys and by other nonsurvey techniques. This often leads to less parochialism, data representative of the entire community, and greater utility from the needs assessment experience.

Whether community needs are assessed through secondary analysis, the various self-report methods, or more commonly, a combination of both, the goal is the same—increased citizen involvement in public decisions. In all instances this means a systematic attempt to use scientifically sound research tools to get a picture of the people who will be affected by public decisions and actions or to solicit ideas from the public on the need for new programs. While the self-report methods are possibly more direct, secondary data are in essence public reports once removed. They are aggregated reports of individual answers to demographic and economic surveys. Therefore, the difference between secondary data and information from survey and nonsurvey needs assessment techniques is one of degree, not kind. Both types of information are useful in choosing among alternatives for future public action.

CHAPTER 10

Use of action research

VERNON D. RYAN

CITIZEN SURVEYS REPRESENT one of the most frequently used methods for conducting a needs assessment analysis. In addition to enabling diverse citizen input to play an important role in the political process, these surveys help to correct distorted interpretations that may result from participation by only a fraction of the public (Milbrath 1981). Even critics of needs surveys acknowledge that they are useful for measuring the degree to which any segment of a population recognizes a problem (Rosenfeld 1974).

The survey methods proposed in this chapter are similar in design to what is commonly referred to as action research (Lewin 1946). Once action research has been defined and placed within the context of development, illustrations will be made of various needs assessment techniques that are consistent with an action research perspective. Strengths and weaknesses of each technique will be discussed, followed by a case study of an ongoing program that incorporates numerous features of action research.

Needs surveys as action research. According to Voth (1979:72), "action research is research used as a tool or technique, an integral part of the community or organization in all aspects of the research process, and has as its objectives the acquisition of valid information, action, and the enhancement of the problem solving capabilities of the community or organization." Included in this definition is the understanding that any research conducted as action research becomes an integral part of the setting under study. By placing a premium on usable knowledge, action research takes into consideration the entire developmental cycle where analysis, fact finding, conceptualization, planning, implementation, and evaluation are involved to solve problems and generate new knowledge (Lewin 1946).

In addition to the importance assigned to the entire decision-making process, action research is unique in the attention it gives to the relationship and understanding between the researcher and user of survey results. Emphasis is placed on the common values and standards that are needed to link the two parties (Rapaport 1970). The overriding theme in action research is that people will be more likely to change if they participate in exploring the reasons for and means of change (Gardner 1974). Without collaboration, recommendations for change tend to stimulate insecurity and rationalization among the audience of survey results. When they are involved throughout the survey, a sense of ownership arises, which creates a certain responsibility for seeing to it that some decision and/or action follows (Chein et al. 1949).

Alternative approaches. Various methods have been developed to take advantage of the action research perspective when conducting needs surveys. Three of the more popular are synchronized surveys, self-administered surveys, and participatory research. When discussing the merits of each method, we will limit our attention to use in needs surveys conducted at the community level.

SYNCHRONIZED SURVEYS. Recognizing that many inputs are involved in policy deliberations, Dillman (1977) coined the term "synchronized surveys" to refer to needs surveys that are completed to provide information from the point of view of policymakers. The survey itself, in addition to other available information, is a product of policy discussions so that issues and alternatives are clearly defined by relevant decision makers prior to conducting the synchronized survey. Therefore, unlike "one-shot" surveys or surveys conducted independent of policy considerations, synchronized surveys rely upon a continuous interaction with policymakers.

Synchronized surveys are particularly useful in situations where a decision-making body is responsible for a well-defined task. The researcher interacts with decision makers at an early stage to make certain that the research design and survey instrument are consistent with the type of information required to make policy decisions. In some cases, a two-stage survey procedure as proposed by Cohen et al. (1977) may be useful. In the initial phase, an open-ended survey format is adopted to collect information on a broad range of issues and concerns. During the second phase, a closed-ended format is used to provide information on specific policy decisions. The content of the latter survey is determined by the issues and concerns coming out of the initial survey but is structured in a manner consistent with policy concerns.

As Dillman (1977) points out, when a survey is carried out as an element of a sustained policy process, an important relationship exists between the policy process and the needs assessment survey. The survey becomes a product of that process. In fact, the survey is not done until policy issues and alternatives are clearly defined by relevant decision makers. Also, the format and content of the survey is based on the operating constraints and assumptions that limit the policy alternatives available.

From the perspective of decision makers, the realization that a needs assessment survey will be included in the policy processes has an effect on their actions and ideas. They now must face the reality that critical decisions are to be expected as a result of the survey findings, so any personal assumptions and preferences are more likely to be forced out into the open at a relatively early stage. Therefore, not only does the survey rely on input during earlier stages of the policy process but the policy process itself is affected by the fact that a survey is forthcoming.

Reports on the uses of a synchronized survey for policy purposes have been minimal to date. Dillman (1977) discusses the use of a synchronized survey in the state of Washington to guide program planning by state government and provide criteria for making budget decisions. Included in the process was a statewide task force that produced alternative goals for the state, another 1500 people who attended areawide meetings to assist in clarifying alternative goals, and a series of four separate surveys to assess Washington residents' goal priorities. Results were then presented to the statewide task force and used for making recommendations for legislative action. The researcher was an active participant in all phases of the project.

Garkovich (1979) discusses another example of a synchronized survey that was used in a single county as one facet of a multistage effort to develop a comprehensive land use plan. Beginning with a series of in-depth interviews with local officials and key citizens, a set of specific issues and policy areas were identified and placed within specific constraints as specified by local officials. A questionnaire was developed to obtain information on these policy areas and distributed to three randomly selected samples of local households. The sample was stratified by three geographic locations on the assumption that three groups with distinct life-styles existed within the county. Wide dissemination of the survey results to the appropriate groups and officials followed shortly after completion of the study.

A critical dimension in the study discussed by Garkovich (1979) was the prior decision to use the survey as one phase of a multistage program to maximize citizen involvement in the development of a land use plan. Various sources of secondary data were also included in the overall program, such as a survey of community facilities and population projections. Public forums were held to obtain citizen input.

The final stage of citizen involvement was the formation of advisory boards to represent the needs and interests of citizens in the area. Results of the survey and other sources of information were presented to these boards. Subsequent meetings included the articulation of specific land use goals and formulation of policy alternatives to achieve them.

In both cases the action researcher obtained important information from the public policy standpoint throughout the process. Other sources of information were also brought into the study to facilitate policy decisions. In neither case did the project terminate until the survey results were fed back into the decision-making process and used as guidelines for assessing policy alternatives.

In spite of the several advantages associated with synchronized surveys, certain limitations should be recognized. Dillman (1977), for instance, points out that researchers adopting a synchronized survey sacrifice their independence in planning, conducting, and reporting survey results. Another problem associated with synchronized surveys is the time frame demanded of the researcher. Unlike surveys conducted independent of decision-making groups, timing is dictated by how and when critical decisions are to be made. The researcher performs a subordinate role to the scheduling of events as determined by the policy process. The importance of careful planning and the timeliness of survey results cannot be underestimated when conducting synchronized surveys.

A final potential problem involves the dilemma associated with collaborative research in situations where the other party represents political decision makers. When doing such research, the threat is always there that the interests and priorities of the involved parties may not be in the best interests of the general public. Knowing when such a situation exists and how to deal with it once it is believed to be present are traits of the skilled researcher using a synchronized survey procedure.

SELF-ADMINISTERED SURVEYS. In many communities there are insufficient funds to hire a trained professional to assist community residents in conducting a needs survey. Even when funds are available, mere logistics make it virtually impossible for an outside consultant to be present in the community during every phase of the research process. A format called the "self-administered survey" has been developed and is available to communities that are planning to complete a needs assessment survey with little or no direct assistance from trained researchers.

A community self-administered survey, as the name implies, takes place when a group of community residents decides to do its own survey. There is nothing unique in the procedures other than the fact that a group of nonresearchers takes on the role of action researchers to complete a needs survey. To help in this new role, manuals are available to outline the steps to be taken in such an effort. The Cooperative Extension Service, in particular, has been responsible for developing these procedures to be used as guides in community self-administered surveys (cf. Reeder and Gilpin 1957; Baumel et al. 1964; Denney et al. 1977).

Most of the steps suggested for a self-administered survey fall into one of three action phases. They include presurvey, survey, and postsurvey activities. During the presurvey phase, special attention is given to organizing for the forthcoming survey. Who is to take overall responsibility for seeing to it that the survey is conducted? Generally, it is suggested that an ad hoc committee composed of representatives from numerous sectors of the community be formed to oversee the entire project. This committee can also determine how and when to seek public input on matters such as suggested content of the survey. Other topics such as publicity and development of a time-table are major concerns during the presurvey action phase. All these activities are accompanied with the message to get organized and seek citizen input prior to conducting the survey.

The second action phase represents the research component of a needs survey. At this stage an expert in survey designs normally consults with individuals involved in the study. In the typical self-administered survey, however, there is little more than the available manuals to offer suggestions on how to conduct a community attitude survey. Basically, these manuals offer a crash course on survey research skills. Critical areas such as how to design a questionnaire, defining the boundaries of the population to be included in the study, and how to select a probability sample when selecting the individuals to receive questionnaires are included. These manuals also discuss methods of distributing questionnaires as well as techniques for tabulating results once data are collected.

As Dillman points out in Chapter 11, this phase is the most difficult part of the survey process to communicate to a nonresearch audience. However, at the expense of detail, attempts have been reasonably successful when discussing the merits of sound research. Matters such as how to draw a probability sample of residents to complete the attitude survey and how to interpret sample results as population estimates can be dealt with effectively as long as the material is discussed at the appropriate level of detail.

Illustrations are particularly useful when addressing these complex issues.

The final action phase involves postsurvey activities, those that take place once the survey has been conducted. When individuals are involved in a self-administered survey, it is not unusual to find them getting so involved with the research activities that they lose sight of planning and implementation, which are both important steps in the action process. Therefore, to ensure proper use of survey results, careful consideration needs to be given to interpreting results, disseminating findings to the appropriate parties, and proposing further actions based on the findings. All these postsurvey activities are crucial for the completion of a successful self-administered survey.

In overview, the self-administered approach for conducting a community needs assessment epitomizes the importance assigned to active participation. Procedures adopted in such surveys reflect this importance. Denney et al. (1977) take this position when they suggest the use of volunteers to distribute and pick up questionnaires rather than using a mail or telephone method. The idea behind their suggestion is to broaden the action research process to include as many participants as possible.

The self-administered method of conducting a community needs assessment has several advantages. First, it has the potential of maximizing the educational benefits of the parties involved. The greater reliance on laypeople to serve as action researchers not only provides them with the opportunity to have input into the process but also makes them aware of the methods associated with action research.

Another advantage of the self-administered survey method is the vested interest or ego involvement that is associated with participating as an action researcher. With such a vested interest, the probability that something will occur as a result of doing the survey is increased. Other advantages associated with this method include the minimal financial resources needed to make such a survey and the greater assurance that needs will be defined within the context of the local decision-making process.

Just as the recognition awarded to the local political process can be viewed as an advantage, one can also see this as a limitation. When relying on the initiative and capabilities of local residents to serve as action researchers, individuals who are in positions of power may take control over the entire process. Issues are defined and findings are interpreted according to their personal views. What may potentially result is an action research process that protects the interests of the more powerful residents at the expense of others in the community. When this occurs, there is a tendency for the survey and its results to strengthen the status quo, since those who have something to lose as a result of subsequent action would be in control of the research process. The solution is to ensure that community-minded people play critical roles as action researchers.

A second limitation of self-administered surveys is the lack of flexibility involved in doing the needs assessment. As untrained action researchers, local residents have a tendency to strictly follow the outline suggested in the manuals. But as pointed out earlier, one of the benefits of action research is that the process itself can and should vary depending upon the circumstances surrounding the survey. Through continuous feedback, modifications may be advisable even after the process begins. Unfortunately, however, untrained action researchers are seldom aware of when and how to implement modifications as needed.

PARTICIPATORY RESEARCH. Technically speaking, participatory research is different from the action research perspective. Yet, since it is similar in its reliance on the involvement of parties who will be affected by the research, we concluded that participatory research should be discussed here.

Looking first at similarities, action and participatory research are both committed to mobilizing people for their collective decisions and actions that will enable them to become more aware of themselves and their own realities. Both stress the importance of learning through involvement, and both see the research process itself as an integral part of the community under investigation. They are also similar in that both stress the common values and standards that link researchers and clients (Brown and Tandon 1983).

Differences between the action and participatory research perspectives are for the most part tied to their unique ideological positions. In action research, which is a product of westernized countries, consensual ideologies are dominant in how problems are defined and development strategies selected. All parties are assumed to have a common interest in the research, and collaborative strategies are encouraged with the understanding that greater efficiency and effectiveness will be of benefit to everyone. Thus action research relies on legitimate authority and an acceptance of the existing distribution of resources (Brown and Tandon 1983).

In contrast, participatory research has grown out of the traditions of Third World countries. Here it is assumed that groups have conflicting interests, cooperation between groups is not expected, and those opposing the parties involved in participatory research will actively resist suggested change. In participatory research, a commitment is made to assist the oppressed to better their lives through greater equity in resource distribution and enhancement of self-reliance. Often this means adopting strategies that question the legitimacy of authority and relying on other conflict methodologies (Brown and Tandon 1983).

In participatory research, an early recognition exists that subsequent proposals may be resisted by parties not involved in the research process. In addition to mobilizing people for their collective creation of new knowledge through integrated activities (Hall 1981), opponents are clearly defined at the outset and appropriate methods are employed throughout the research process in anticipation of their resistance to proposed change.

Participatory research is widely used in developed countries. For example, Gaventa and Horton (1981) detail a project where participatory research was used to study landownership patterns in the Appalachian region. Local citizens and staff members of the Highlander Research and Education Center joined to propose a study of landownership in the area in hopes that the information collected would be useful for influencing regional policies to limit the activities of absentee landlords. Through a task force of citizen groups, funding was finally received after considerable delay from parties who, in the researchers' views, felt threatened by the proposed research.

Once under way, the research involved the training of local people in research skills, developing a network of groups committed to using the forthcoming data, and mobilizing a larger constituency to influence policy decisions. The task force held workshops in which researchers and citizen group representatives designed the forthcoming research, including data collection procedures and preparation of survey instruments, and considered alternative land reform strategies. Eventually surveys were conducted with people living in the region, case studies developed, and reports prepared to document in detail citizen concerns and expectations about landownership. At each step, decisions were made in anticipation of facing resistance from parties opposed to land reform policies. Results were disseminated to the news media and other local citizen groups.

According to Gaventa and Horton (1981), this project succeeded in accomplishing the goals of participatory research. Research skills were taught to task force members and, in turn, passed on to other residents. Networks were also created for further mobilization and were helpful in educating participants about current landownership patterns and taxation inequities. All the while, the strategies employed throughout the process were based on the realization that conflicting interests existed and opposition of land reform would eventually surface to challenge the proposals recommended by the parties involved in the research. Participatory research is particularly useful in situations where opposition is anticipated. Strategies can then be designed at the outset to respond to the anticipated attacks from those who are threatened by the results of the research. It is also a useful technique for researchers who are committed to doing surveys to reflect the needs of oppressed populations.

Participatory research also has its drawbacks. Similar to any action research, the demands for timely results and the possibility of losing control of the research are continuous concerns. One should also realize the difficulties associated with training oppressed groups. Typically, limited levels of formal education among participants require different training techniques. It also demands considerable patience on the part of the researcher and a realization that research as used in formal needs assessments is seldom a part of the participants' everyday lives.

The researcher conducting participatory research needs to be aware of the limited amount of financial support available when working with groups that may benefit the most from such research. Unlike action research with a community's leadership, participatory research often requires shoestring budgets where prudence becomes the overriding principle in research planning.

Finally, researchers considering participatory research should realize the possibility of being charged with taking a position in their endeavors. Cries of biased findings and a potential loss of credibility as a truth-seeking researcher are more likely to be directed at investigators who explicitly take a stand on an issue prior to conducting a study. Whether the charge is legitimate is a matter of debate, but the fact remains that participatory research frequently prompts such a response. Faced with the right conditions, this research can be a valuable tool when conducting needs assessment surveys. The most important condition to consider is the degree of conflict associated (or anticipated) with the issues studied and/or their probable solutions. It not only will benefit the final outcome but will also serve as "a process by which the 'raw' and somewhat uninformed — or, at least, unexpressed — knowledge of ordinary people is brought into the open and incorporated into a connectable whole through discussion (and) analysis" (Hall 1981:12).

Case study: CD-DIAL. To illustrate the use of action research in needs surveys, a summary of the objectives and procedures of a specific program will be presented. Based on personal experience while serving as director of CD-DIAL (Community Development: Data, Information, and Analysis Laboratory), I will discuss some of the advantages and limitations of using action research in community surveys. As will be apparent in the discussion that follows, CD-DIAL blends the procedures used in synchronized and self-administered surveys.

CD-DIAL began in 1978 with support coming from Title V of the Rural Development Act. Operating out of the Department of Sociology and Anthropology at Iowa State University, it continues to receive joint support from the Cooperative Extension Service and the Agricultural Experiment Station within the College of Agriculture.

The program was established to provide assistance to Iowa's communities where residents express interest in conducting an attitude survey. The incentive for doing such a survey varies by community but usually evolves around a special problem such as declining school enrollments or loss of retail trade. As a result, groups such as local school boards or chambers of commerce request assistance to do a further study of the issue. Typically, smaller communities with little or no professional staff are most in need of assistance.

When a request for assistance is made to the county extension office, and passed on to the area (multicounty) community resource development (CRD) specialist and staff, an action research process is initiated. Although variations in the process are common, five major steps are normally included in the action research.

ISSUE AND ROLE CLARIFICATION. Shortly after the request is made for assistance, a meeting or series of meetings are held to identify the purpose of conducting a survey. The parties making the request are asked to clarify the benefits expected as a result of the survey. Ideally, they are also challenged to look into the future by discussing alternative courses of action that may be taken, depending on the survey findings. This projection serves two purposes. First, it enables committees to think beyond the survey itself and helps them to consider the viability of subsequent actions and programs. A second advantage is that it makes committees realize the importance of including other parties in the research process. By planning beyond the survey, they may see that eventual actions and programs will depend on others who are not represented on the committee. In anticipation of what might follow the survey, these parties may be included at this stage.

The role of both the extension field staff and the CD-DIAL staff is to help members of the survey committee to clarify their objectives for conducting a survey. We also attempt to sensitize the members of the committee to the importance of including a broad representation of people living in the community. One way of doing this is by suggesting that the original special-interest topic or topics be expanded to include other sectors of the community. Why, the committee is asked, should the survey be limited to questions on retail trade when other sectors such as local government, schools, medical services, and social services are equally important to the community's future? Eventually, other parties are usually included to represent the interests and needs of these sectors. The result is a broad-based representation on the survey committee to work on what has now evolved into a total community effort.

During this initial step, an understanding is reached about what is expected of all parties involved. Everyone must agree on the assigned role responsibilities. Since the survey is to continue as a community project and not as one conducted by an outside research team, the committee remains in control. This means carrying out major roles in the forthcoming survey. The CD-DIAL staff serves as advisers on matters related to research design and analysis. The county and CRD extension personnel are responsible for assisting committee members in day-to-day planning activities and serving as a liaison between the local survey committee and our staff. Their abilities in providing process-related assistance are invaluable to whatever benefits result from the surveys.

PRESURVEY ACTIVITIES. Once the committee is organized and role responsibilities have been assigned, attention turns to preparing for the survey. The first activity involves formulating questions. This begins with input from the community. In some cases, the survey committee takes on this responsibility by itself. On other occasions, the committee will contact key individuals and organizations in the community and ask them to submit suggestions. Still others will solicit suggestions by circulating a public notice in the local news media or leaving suggestion boxes in retail outlets. The latter approach is the most time consuming and invites input that lacks focus and direction, but it has the advantage of providing everyone with the opportunity to make suggestions.

To facilitate the process, the CD-DIAL staff provides members of the committee with examples of previous questionnaires. Discussions follow on the strengths and weaknesses of alternative formats. Throughout these discussions, committee members are cautioned to remember their initial intent so that the format selected will provide them with the type of information needed.

When the committee has obtained the input requested and organized the questions by subject matter, it becomes the responsibility of the CD-DIAL staff (with the assistance of the CRD specialist) to develop a draft of the research instrument. This can become a very time consuming task, often involving a series of negotiations between staff and the survey committee. The goal is to develop an instrument that relies on locally understandable and acceptable terminology but to maintain defensible operational definitions. It is not uncommon to find situations where compromises regarding the instrument are necessary.

A pretest of the instrument follows. Committee members distribute questionnaires to local residents who have had little or no input into its development. From 25 to 30 residents are asked to complete the questionnaire and an attached evaluation form. This form asks respondents to evaluate the instrument in terms of the relevancy of the subject matter, clarity of wording and instructions, and time required to complete the questionnaire. They are also asked to make suggestions on additional content or rephrasing of questions.

Once all the pilot instruments have been collected, they are turned over to the CD-DIAL staff for review and analysis. Suggestions and comments are taken into consideration when developing the final draft. When this draft has been reviewed and approved by the survey committee, the questionnaire is ready for printing.

While the pilot test is going on, our staff is preparing a sample of residents who will be receiving a questionnaire. By now the population has been defined. Depending on the content of the questionnaire, the population is either a school district, a defined trade area, an incorporated place such as a community, or a county.

A 95 percent confidence level is usually selected for the survey results. A simple random sample is most often used, although stratified samples may be suggested when the population is heterogeneous. Based on these decisions, the size of the sample is determined.

As in every phase of the survey process, considerations leading up to a decision on the sample size are shared with the survey committee. They share in the discussions on the interpretation of anticipated results when using a 95 percent confidence level. They are also told of the importance of obtaining a high response rate to minimize response bias as a result of incomplete coverage. As participants in these decisions, members of the survey committee buy into the methodological procedures adopted, which during the later interpretive phase eventually serve to minimize unwarranted attacks on the research design.

FIELD WORK. Once the questionnaire is prepared and the sample drawn, field work begins. In most cases, publicity precedes the distribution of questionnaires. Information is provided on why the study is being conducted, who is involved, and when the field work is to take place.

A personal delivery and pickup procedure is used. Local volunteers are recruited by members of the committee to distribute questionnaires. Before distribution, a training session is held by a member of the CD-DIAL staff and the CRD specialist to inform the volunteers of their responsibilities. Packets are assigned to volunteers, and forms to keep log sheets are discussed. The importance of a high response rate is emphasized to everyone. At the conclusion of the session, a location is designated where volunteers are to return completed questions and log sheets.

POSTSURVEY ACTIVITIES. When all questionnaires have been returned, they are sent to the CD-DIAL staff for editing and coding. The first feedback to the survey committee is in the form of frequencies to summarize results on each question. The CRD specialist and a CD-DIAL staff member then meet with the committee to identify requests for secondary analysis. Usually this involves cross-tabulations that will show how certain groups in the community responded to specific questions. For instance, opinions about the school curriculum may vary, depending on whether school-aged children are present in the household. This kind of cross-tabulation can provide useful information for administrators involved in curriculum development. With proper guidance, such analysis is critical to the action process, since it requires the participants to move beyond mere description and toward a more useful explanatory framework. How effectively this transition is made will eventually have much to say about the manner in which the results are utilized.

Depending on the scope of the issues addressed in the questionnaire, the number of iterations between feedback and discussion will vary. Results in many cases are carried to other groups by members of the committee to make certain that important requests for data analysis are not overlooked. As judged by the CD-DIAL staff, multivariate analysis is sometimes employed to seek answers to questions raised by members of the committee. When this happens, the members are carefully led through the analysis to make certain that the results are properly interpreted.

A shared responsibility develops in interpretation of the survey results. Members of the committee are in the best position to place the results within the context of the local situation. As an example, high levels of dissatisfaction with the local law enforcement agency may be accounted for by dissatisfaction over a single police officer's handling of one particular situation. With such knowledge, generalities might be tempered so that the conclusion does not lead to a definitive statement about the entire agency.

The CD-DIAL staff also plays a major role in the interpretation phase of the process. Members of the committee often benefit by comparing the findings of their survey with the results of other community studies. Such comparisons are readily available through a computer file consisting of results from more than 30 community surveys. Another role of the staff is to help in interpretation of sample data as population estimates. This includes the use of statistical tests of significance. With proper instructions, members of the committee come to realize the importance of distinguishing between statistically significant and nonsignificant results. The distinction is made throughout their interpretation of the findings.

At some stage of the data analysis, dissemination of results beyond members of the committee (and the groups they are representing) is discussed. For general dissemination, a written report is prepared by the CD-DIAL staff, which includes frequencies on all questions and some of the more pertinent cross-tabulations. Various forms of bar and pie charts are used in this report to add clarity to the presentation. Once this report has been reviewed and edited by members of the committee, 100 copies are printed and made available for public consumption.

Other forms of dissemination are used, depending on the preferences of the committee. Local newspapers may run a series of articles to summarize the results of the survey. Another approach is to hold a town meeting where the results are presented and discussed. In other instances, graphs and charts are prepared and presented to various groups such as the city council, school board, or local service clubs and organizations. Whenever possible, members of the committee are called upon to prepare and feed the results back to the community.

FOLLOW-UP. The interpretation and dissemination of survey results lead into the final step of the action research process. During this step, the results of the survey become a topic in local decision making. In some situations, specific actions result from this process, as in cases where a new program is started or a city council chooses a particular course of action based on survey findings.

An effort is usually made before the survey is conducted to place the survey committee into a decision-making framework. Members are asked to lay out alternative courses of action based on a range of survey outcomes. With the assistance of the CRD specialist, the committee returns to this discussion. Based on the survey results, the merits of alternative actions are reviewed and evaluated. These discussions usually branch out to other groups and organizations in the community.

During these follow-up activities, the CD-DIAL staff assists the CRD specialist in making certain that the survey findings receive the proper interpretation. The statistical interpretation when using sample data as population estimates often requires staff involvement. Another example is in policy formulation where survey committees want to project the results of public referendums based on the degree of support expressed by respondents. In such cases, we caution the committee concerning the differences in surveys and public referendums to make certain that they are sensitive to issues such as variations by time (i.e., individuals may change their attitudes), format (i.e., the "undecided" vote in a survey must take a position on a referendum), and representativeness (i.e., who votes on a referendum is usually less representative of a population than respondents to a well-designed survey). For each of these reasons, the committee is instructed that the survey results should not be used to reify results of a pending referendum.

Based on past experiences, we have found that this final step of the action research process is critical to the effectiveness of the total program. From the community's perspective, the ultimate assessment of its survey will depend on what impact the results will have on local decisions and actions. From the perspective of CD-DIAL, we recognize the importance of showing direct benefits as a result of the survey. But in terms of a locally initiated project relying on community input, we are more concerned with the discussions and decision-making process used to reach a decision. Whether a community chooses to take action is of less importance than whether the study was conducted and results were interpreted rationally and in an equitable fashion.

Other than facilitating the committee's decision-making process, the CD-DIAL staff and the CRD specialist are available to help in locating other resources as needed. For instance, secondary data often complements the results provided through the survey. Making contacts with agencies that offer technical assistance on a specific subject matter or seeking block grants or other funding possibilities to help finance a community project are other ways that the staff serves the committee.

In reflecting on our associations with representatives from over 50 Iowa communities since 1978, some of the advantages and shortcomings of conducting needs assessments from a combined synchronized self-administered perspective can be identified. Whereas the synchronized approach typically limits involvement to the outside researcher and policymakers, we see benefits when residents are also included as active participants. In many cases, they bring another view into the process as consumers of local services, as taxpayers, and representatives of other interests that may or may not be considered by local decision makers.

The active involvement of an outside researcher also has advantages over the self-administered survey model. As outside researchers, we are able to bring out issues or problems that for a variety of reasons remain suppressed by local residents. As an example, small-town ideology often stresses equality among residents, and it is usually left up to the outsider to question its existence. Our experience has been that most residents are willing to listen to our questioning of local values, at least more so than when a local resident raises the same question.

As a third party, the CD-DIAL staff adds legitimacy to the final research product. Had the community done the survey alone, questions would probably be raised about the research design and potential bias in the survey instrument.

Finally, the capabilities of the CRD specialist in developing process skills is critical to the success of the program. In many instances, survey committees get bogged down by their overall planning responsibilities. Fortunately, the CRD specialist is available to make suggestions on direction and procedures and to provide encouragement to those who become overwhelmed by their responsibilities.

In addition to the benefits, we have also seen examples of the limitations or shortcomings associated with this form of needs surveys. One of our greatest fears has been the threat of strengthening the status quo as a result of doing the surveys. Normally, involvement in planning surveys comes through membership in local organizations, leaving nonmembers out of the process. This is but one example of the ways that the interests of some residents can be emphasized in the research process at the expense of others. And since residents in more favorable social and economic positions are usually more involved, we must continue to monitor the degree of input received by others.

Another danger of conducting this type of action research occurs when the survey committee's curiosity and interest in conducting the needs assessment take precedence over the primary objectives. On occasion, we find it necessary to temper their enthusiasm with their new role to make certain that conducting the survey does not replace the ultimate goal of the study. It is also necessary to monitor our own behavior to make certain that we are not preoccupied with the method or procedure to the extent that our primary purpose of strengthening their problem-solving capacity is overlooked. One final drawback in our CD-DIAL program is seen when survey committees fail to understand that the study itself is but a small step in the direction of community improvement. Unless the needs assessment survey is presented at the outset as merely a method to obtain worthwhile information and not as a panacea for community problems, the participants may become discouraged by their unfilled expectations. This is particularly true in cases where they have invested much of their own time and effort in the many tasks associated with the survey.

Summary. The educational benefits gained from local participation in the action research approach for conducting needs surveys cannot be overstated. People who are actively involved learn to appreciate the value of sound research. Collectively, they also benefit from the assurance that salient issues will be included in the study.

Another advantage of action research is the emergence of what Warren (1972:312) refers to as a special action system. Essentially, the survey committee operates as a special action system represented by a number of diverse community groups. When planning and conducting the needs survey, this committee engages in both task performance and system maintenance behavior. It also facilitates subsequent discussions and actions because of the commitment it makes to carrying out the project.

Other benefits include the opportunity for local residents to participate in various development roles (beginning with the planning of the survey on through implementation) and the emergence of new interaction patterns on issues relevant to the entire community. The development of these new patterns of communication is particularly important, since they bring together individuals who typically limit their interactions to other individuals operating within their specific interest sector. Finally, action research is particularly useful in times of shrinking budgets. Communities unable to finance a needs survey conducted by an outside consultant should consider this option, since local participation is the major resource required.

CHAPTER 11

Elements
of success

DON A. DILLMAN

FREQUENTLY, scientifically valid surveys are pitted against citizen-sponsored needs assessments, with the requirements for each being viewed as incompatible with those for the other. For example, involvement of citizens in writing questions, which is done as a means of building ownership that will lead to citizen use and acceptance of the survey results, is often seen as a barrier to the construction of adequate questionnaire items. The thesis of this chapter is that requirements for scientifically valid surveys and citizen involvement can be met when doing needs assessment surveys.

Case study. It is not always clear what elements are necessary for a successful survey. Consider, for example, the following case study:

The self-appointed leader for the community survey worked long and hard to assure its success. Taking his mandate from the mayor's opening comments at a council meeting that until a thorough assessment of community needs had been done she would oppose any new city expenditures, he started making plans. In a subsequent conversation, the mayor applauded his intentions and assured him that the council would certainly be indebted to him for taking the leadership for a needs assessment survey.

His next step was to seek help from a university extension specialist who was well known for helping communities do self-surveys. The specialist shared many copies of surveys done in other communities throughout the state. Based upon these and his experience of 20 years of living in the community the survey leader drafted a questionnaire. The extension specialist obligingly critiqued it in a three-page letter that closed with, "Your community leaders will most certainly learn a great deal about the true needs of the citizens from this well-written questionnaire."

When the local newspaper offered to encourage citizens to respond to the survey, the leader expressed his appreciation. But when the editor asked to see the questionnaire, the survey leader skillfully declined the request with a furrowed-brow and anguished assertion that he certainly would like to oblige the editor; however, if word got out on what the questions were, perhaps some people would campaign to see that the questions were answered in a way supportive of their point of view. The leader also said it would be best if the city council members did not see the questionnaire so that no one could accuse any of them of stacking the results with their favorite issues. The editor decided not to publish anything at all.

A sample of 450 citizens was laboriously drawn from city voting records, using a table of random numbers. The graphically pretty and well-designed questionnaire was prepared for mailing. The offer of some friends from his Lions Club to fold questionnaires and stuff envelopes was gratefully accepted and they were dutifully thanked when finished. But to assure that names of all randomly selected respondents were kept confidential, the leader spent a long week personally addressing each of the envelopes. He did the same thing for the follow-up contacts, which assured an acceptably high response rate of nearly 80 percent.

Faced with the nearly overwhelming task of counting answers and preparing results for the city council, the university extension specialist came to the leader's rescue with coding sheets, students who helped do the coding, and promises of a quick computer analysis.

For two months, neither the council nor the survey leader heard anything about the survey. Then the university specialist called to say he would have the results ready for the following week's council meeting. With considerable anticipation, the mayor cleared the agenda to receive the results. The newspaper editor was especially invited to the council meeting.

It took several trips from the car for the university extension specialist to bring in everyone's four-inch stack of printouts complete with row, column, and cell frequencies. The extension specialist made a marvelous presentation that utilized color transparencies, and the presentation was nicely applauded by the council and the half-dozen members of the audience. The mayor commended the extension specialist for putting on a nice show. The council members complimented her on the nice transparencies and wished out loud that more people would make that kind of presentation to the council. In response to the urgings of the survey leader and university extension specialist, they also commented on the results.

One of the council members wanted to know if 358 people were enough to speak for the community because that meant that many people who wanted to be surveyed were not. Another said it was such a nice survey that it was really too bad there were not any questions on changing parking meters in the downtown business district, which she thought was the main need for the council's money. Another council member made a similar comment about the need for animal protection facilities. Still another council member, who rarely spoke at meetings, said that some of the results were so different from the opinions of some of her friends that she wondered how much it would cost to do the survey again and find out if people were really giving their true opinions especially on those "strange ladders with the seven steps."

The council unanimously passed a resolution thanking the survey leader and extension specialist. The newspaper editor took their picture beside a stack of printouts, which council members returned just for the occasion. The next day the picture appeared on page one of the paper beside an article, "Pair Thanked for Community Service."

And that was pretty much the last anyone heard of the community needs assessment. Most citizens in the community did not know it had been done, the printouts were stacked away to collect dust, and despite the mayor's admonitions to the council, business went on pretty much as usual. The city budget remained unchanged.

Students of needs assessment techniques often have widely divergent reactions when they are asked to comment on the above experience. Some feel the survey was a success, that is, a scientifically valid survey was accomplished. Others feel it was a total failure and are quick to point out that nothing happened as a result of the survey; for example, no new interactions were started, there was no written report used to meet legal requirements, and no decisions were influenced. The reasons suggested by some for the lack of use of the survey was that it was not done by the community, it was done by a particular person for the community, and members of the community had no ownership over it. And it is argued that if community volunteers had worked together to develop the survey and had implemented and summarized the results, the chances of the mayor and city council making use of the information would have been far greater.

Involvement principles. Frequently, scientific surveys are pitted against citizen surveys with the latter being touted as true needs assessment that are likely to make a difference. Some of the involvement principles that can be inferred from such surveys are:

1. It does not make so much difference what questions are asked as long as questions citizens want to ask are included.

2. It is more important that everyone has an opportunity to fill out a questionnaire than whether the results are representative, as from a scientifically drawn representative sample from which a high response rate is obtained.

3. Maximum publicity, delivery, and pickup of the questionnaire door to door by friends and neighbors encourage higher response and more honest answers.

4. Coding and summarizing the results by citizens enable people to learn what everyone has said and, thereby, increase the likelihood of results being used.

A person who is well trained in survey research methods is likely to react with alarm if not disdain to the above principles. From a formal research perspective, if citizens want to ask inadequately structured questions, the results will be inadequate. Trading representativeness and high response for letting everyone fill out a questionnaire means results cannot be interpreted. Publicity produces prior discussion and the possibility of bias. People are less likely to give honest answers to friends than to strangers. Volunteer summarization invites errors and encourages individual interpretation based on the few questionnaires seen by each individual.

What often strikes a well-trained survey researcher as contamination and bias may strike a community developer as involvement and commitment. What a researcher might see as clean data strikes a citizen as sanitized beyond recognition and likely use. Herein lies the dilemma of success; how to combine the implementation of a scientifically based survey, done according to the principles and rules necessary for its scientific success, with procedures necessary for the results to be used.

Considerable tension often exists between producing accurate results and fitting the needs assessments into a decision-making process, both of which have been identified as fundamental questions that must be faced when deciding upon a needs assessment technique. The tension is made all the more intense by other criteria such as the intended purpose of the assessment and cost considerations.

Fundamentals. In this chapter the requirements for successful needs assessment surveys will be examined in some detail. In addition to the scientific requirements for doing valid surveys, we also consider requirements to assure their use and impact.

WHAT IS A SURVEY? A survey is a very limited but potentially very powerful tool. A well-done survey can tell the proportion of people in a population who have a certain attribute and the proportion who do not. It is the only needs assessment method that has this capability (although certain other methods, for example, analysis of reports and consultation of census data, involve secondary uses of surveys). It is this quality that makes the survey a unique scientific tool. At the same time, we must recognize that if we do not know what questions to ask, a survey cannot be done. In addition, if the questions we wish to ask are ones people cannot possibly answer, the desired information cannot be obtained and a survey is an inappropriate tool. However, the fact remains that when we wish to talk about the proportion of people having or not having a particular attitude, opinion, belief, possession, housing situation, or whatever, the survey method is not only appropriate but necessary.

USE OF SURVEYS. A planned needs assessment survey is designed to increase the likelihood that results will be utilized. The use of surveys in communities is based upon a sociological view, revealed by a long tradition of community research (Warren 1972).

Communities are not idyllic groups in which all people are involved equally in community affairs. In addition to elected officials, most communities have informal power structures that influence community decisions. Many formal associations and organizations seek to influence decisions from time to time. Citizen involvement in community decisions is often individualistic, but sometimes it is articulated through campaigns, coalitions, hearings, and other meetings. The normal processes of community life include conflict, competition, and cooperation. The needs assessment survey is a mechanism often used to articulate and help resolve community issues. Such a survey, to be successful, must do much more than accurately reveal what percentage of residents favor a particular course of community action; a successful needs assessment must be used in decision-making processes.

Basis of success.
A list of elements for success must be somewhat arbitrary. Yet there are certain things that must happen if a survey is to produce valid data and serve its intended purpose. Our discussion is focused around nine tasks, all of which are necessary for the implementation of a survey. They describe the places where surveys typically break down. The most important point is that all nine must be satisfactorily accomplished for a needs assessment survey to succeed. There are no options. Upon hearing this statement, a friend once pointed out that to win the baseball world

series, it was only necessary to win 57.1 percent of the games (in a seven-game series). Such a winning percentage is not good enough for needs assessment surveys. The implementer must win at each of the steps; failure at any one can provide the fatal blow to the intended use of the survey results.

RELATIONSHIP TO USERS. We start with an important step that surprisingly is often excluded from survey method texts. One of the most frequent reasons survey results are not used, and certainly a reason in the example with which we started this chapter, is that the intended audience has not been consulted ahead of time and little thought has been given to the intended use for the survey results. People who struggle to specify what information is desired from the survey, evaluate alternatives for administering the survey, and commit time to the effort are more likely to make use of the results. They also seem somewhat more likely to understand the limitations of the survey data and the appropriate and inappropriate uses for them.

This issue is not as simple as declaring that the more involvement the better. Sometimes involvement produces pressures or decisions such as "let anyone who wants to fill out a questionnaire do so," so that the generalizability of results becomes open to question. Sometimes a group of volunteers becomes so heavily involved that the involvement of others who wish to influence the questions is resisted. Ownership of a survey effort by the few risks rejection by the many.

Few issues are more important, or as often ignored, as exactly how results are to be used in the end. Once started, a survey tends to take on a life of its own. Questions may be revised to the point where they simply do not provide the data that people desired when they started the survey. Thus a part of beginning a survey is to clearly establish the objectives and specify what one intends to do with the results. One outcome of such discussions is to provide guidance for the next step, that is, writing questions.

WRITING QUESTIONS. Writing questions is not a magical ritual in search of the perfect ones that unfailingly produce valid answers. Novices who take pen in hand too often search for the questionnaire items that will measure attitudes and beliefs with the precision with which a thermometer measures temperature. They are inevitably disappointed. People do not hold attitudes and beliefs with the same precision they hold, for example, age or years of education. In addition, the most extensive study of wording effects to date (several hundred experiments and 34 separate surveys) shows that response to attitude questions varies depending upon the context in which the question is asked, order of the questions, allowance for "don't knows," and construction methods (Schuman and Presser 1981). The raw materials for writing questions are simply words, with which most people have some facility and as a result tend to overestimate their ability to write survey questions. However, vague questions produce vague answers, and questions that are too precise may produce no answers at all. Open-ended questions are intolerable in some situations and essential in others. These issues are only the tip of the questionnaire writing iceberg.

Many explicit principles for wording questions must be followed when writing them (Dillman 1978; Sudman and Bradburn 1982). The reader is advised to use references liberally when working on what is the most difficult yet most essential part of doing a survey.

Religiously adhering to all the question writing principles in these references will not solve all the problems associated with needs assessment surveys. A question, or set of questions, that accurately measures a particular attitude may be rejected because it lacks credibility to the likely user. We recall an effort to measure community satisfaction by asking whether people were very, somewhat, slightly, or not at all satisfied with their community. The typical result was that most people chose the "very" category, thus making the response not very useful when trying to identify the types of people that tended to be most satisfied. As a substitute a well-tested satisfaction scale was proposed, known as the delighted-terrible scale. The answer choices included delighted, mostly satisfied, satisfied, neutral, dissatisfied, mostly dissatisfied, terrible (Andrews and Withey 1976).

A politically sensitive member of the citizen group declared that she knew of no county commissioner who would take the answers to such a question seriously. After additional discussion, the question was eliminated despite its measurement advantages. Similarly, citizen groups will often discard a series of abstract agree-disagree questions that are to be combined by means of Likert, Thurston, or other scaling procedures. Explaining to a county commissioner that older people are 3.6 on a scale whereas young people are 3.2 may also be difficult to do.

At the other extreme, we have faced situations in which items of critical interest to sponsors of needs assessment surveys, for example, "the belief that the county engineer was technically competent," posed another kind of difficulty. Most citizens are simply not qualified to judge an engineer's technical competency. The consultant to the group faced a dilemma; to reject this and similar questions could exact a cost in volunteer commitment. Sometimes, and for good reason, items are included in needs assessment surveys even though they ignore certain principles of wording. The writer of needs assessment questions must be not only competent in principles of question wording but sensitive to the self-perceived needs of would-be users and the influence of group dynamics on citizen involvement that will affect the use of survey results.

CHOICE OF METHOD. Prior to the 1970s, the only survey method with scientific credibility was the face-to-face interview. The mail questionnaire was thought to be incapable of generating acceptable response rates. The telephone had simply not been seriously explored for its survey capabilities, a result of the infamous 1936 *Literary Digest* survey in which the use of telephone directories (but not the telephone itself) resulted in a prediction that Landon would beat Roosevelt in that year's presidential election. The bad prediction was partly the result of most households and particularly lower income households not having telephones, a situation that no longer exists in most areas of the United States. The drop-off pick-up questionnaire, though credible, was not much used for needs assessment because of having little or no cost advantage over the face-to-face interview.

During the 1970s, the situation changed dramatically. It became apparent that barriers to high response rates for mail questionnaires, especially for community needs assessment surveys, were not as great as once thought (Dillman 1977, 1978; Heberlein and Baumgartner 1978; Butler and Howell 1979). The telephone was proven capable of producing lengthy interviews, with data fairly comparable to that obtained by face-to-face interviews (Dillman 1978; Groves and Kahn 1979). Through random digit dialing, most households became accessible for interviews. Most importantly, however, the face-to-face interview skyrocketed in cost. It was the victim of higher energy costs, higher labor costs, and the greater difficulty of locating respondents, a situation that is associated with smaller household size and the increasing proportion of families in which all adults are employed. Taken together, these changes mean that face-to-face interview methods are now seldom used except for the most important and well-funded surveys, being commonly replaced by the telephone and, in some situations, the mail. Even the decennial U.S. Census relies heavily on mail questionnaires and telephone follow-ups.

Certain questions about the equivalency of the alternative methods remain (particularly in the area of sampling) but do not appear serious enough to prevent the widespread use of telephone and mail procedures. Many times, the questions once thought to require face-to-face interviews can be modified in ways that make it possible to ask them in the mail and telephone situation (Dillman 1978; Sudman and Bradburn 1982).

It is difficult to specify differences in expected response rates among methods, an action that a colleague has described as comparable in difficulty to shooting at a moving target in a wind storm. Response rates for general public surveys vary dramatically by population and by how much one is willing to spend for locating hard-to-reach respondents. However, in general, response rates for face-to-face interviews and telephone interviews are about the same, and response to well-done mail surveys runs 10 to 15 percent lower. As a result, the response rate is much less a factor in choosing methods than in the past.

Cost is difficult to specify, especially for needs assessments in which volunteer efforts are frequently substituted for some of the normal expenditures. In general, face-to-face interviews are by far the most expensive and mail the least expensive. The decreasing costs of long-distance telephone calls and the possibility of using interviewers with relatively little training in a centralized interviewing situation have brought telephone and mail costs closer. The increasing availability of word processing equipment for handling the mail questionnaires raises the question as to whether the gap will continue to narrow. There have been many instances in which community needs assessment surveys could have been executed less expensively by telephone (because of no toll charges and the use of volunteer interviewers) than if done by mail.

The important point of this discussion is that the choice of method is no longer an issue with the monumental implications it was thought to have only a decade ago. Successful needs assessment surveys can often be accomplished by any of the three methods discussed and the cost may not be significantly different between the two alternatives and face-to-face interviews.

While each of the methods is capable of producing scientifically acceptable information, the nature of the needs assessment activity may discourage the use of a particular approach. In general, people experience more discomfort with telephone interviews than other methods and exhibit more impatience than with face-to-face interviews. The majority of the people interviewed by telephone in a national survey would have preferred another method to the telephone, whereas only 1 percent of those involved in the face-to-face interviews would have preferred the telephone (Groves and Kahn 1979). Sponsors of community needs assessment surveys might reasonably conclude that a survey will be better accepted by community residents and ultimately generate more support if done by an alternative other than the telephone. The newness of telephone survey procedures may be a factor in choice of method.

Another factor that cautions against telephone surveys is the situation in which the person conducting the survey has little survey experience and there is no money to hire a person to supervise interviews. The complexity of doing telephone interviews is greater than for mail surveys, and lack of expertise is the reason for some people avoiding the telephone survey. Exact procedures for conducting a mail survey can be communicated fairly easily to a person with little survey experience, whereas there is more difficulty in doing so in a telephone situation. Also, training and supervising volunteer interviewers is a difficult and demanding task.

At the same time, telephone surveys can be done far more quickly than mail surveys, thus increasing the likelihood that results can be obtained before citizens lose interest. Also, one does not have to risk the possibility of issues changing dramatically between the time interviews begin and the time they finish.

Mail questionnaires, particularly the drop-off pick-up version, are especially attractive in certain needs assessment situations. When a survey objective is to have a very large number (or even all) households in the community participate, the advantages of the mail questionnaire become substantial. The other methods do not lend themselves as well to being handled in such large quantities.

Increasingly, the choice of method has come to depend more on needs assessment objectives and resources available to those conducting them than the data-producing capabilities inherent in a particular method. Both the telephone and mail will be used extensively in the future. Greater use will also be made of the telephone as citizens become more sophisticated about the ability of small samples to represent large populations and gain comfort with the telephone, both of which seem probable as we gravitate toward becoming an information society (Dillman 1983b). One of the pressures stemming from the advent of the information society is the demand for fresh data, retrievable at the push of a button. The telephone is a far more integral part of the emerging technology than the energy-intensive delivery and retrieval of mail questionnaires.

QUESTIONNAIRE CONSTRUCTION. There is far more to a questionnaire than a randomly ordered listing of questions. Not only does the order in which the questions are asked make a difference in how people respond (Schuman and Presser 1981), it also makes a difference in whether they respond at all (Dillman 1978). Questionnaires need to be constructed in a way that order, bias, and resistance to responding are overcome. In practice this means, among other things, starting questionnaires with interest getting, and easy-to-answer questions and holding personal questions, especially income, until the end. Extensive discussion of specific questionnaire construction principles are provided in Dillman (1978) and Sudman and Bradburn (1982).

Choice of survey method has a dramatic effect on questionnaire construction. Mail questionnaires must look nice, need very clear directions, and require a visual display that encourages easy comprehension. Face-to-

face and telephone instruments do not have to meet these stringent requirements, although telephone questionnaires usually need a format that can be
easily handled while the interviewer holds a receiver in one hand. Face-to-
face questionnaires must be drafted in a way that coordinates with visual
cards that are handled by the respondent.

Choice of method also influences the way the questions are asked. The
use of telephone interviews is totally dependent on what a person hears, one
word at a time. The nature of the mail questionnaire is such that screen
questions tend to be avoided and response choices are seldom included in
the stem of the question. Listing response choices after the question usually
suffices. In contrast, screen questions are easily administered over the telephone and response choices are typically included in the stem of the questions. Open-ended questions, on the other hand, are frequently avoided in
mail questionnaires because of poor performance. For similar reasons the
offering of many and/or lengthy response choices is avoided in telephone
questionnaires. Whereas one can be asked to rank several items in a mail
questionnaire, this is more difficult to do over the telephone. Face-to-face
interviews offer far more flexibility in how questions can be asked and thus
how the questionnaire is constructed.

When confronted with the limitations of question formats, survey
sponsors are frequently inclined to focus on these limitations as a reason
for using another survey method. Except in situations where a survey must
rely heavily on open-ended questions (and therefore the mail questionnaire
will not perform well), we have seldom found questionnaire construction
requirements posed by a particular method to be a persuasive reason for
switching from one choice to another. The method-selection reasons discussed in the previous section and citizen involvement goals are generally
far more compelling. We are impressed with the extent to which modified
question structures necessitated by choice of method can provide information necessary for the needs assessment situation.

On the surface, successful questionnaire construction seems like an
activity that should be done solely on a scientific basis, by an individual
who understands the varying construction requirements posed by mail, telephone, and face-to-face situations. In general, there are other phases of
doing a needs assessment where public involvement can be more productive.

However, whether intentionally or inadvertently, needs assessment
questionnaires often become public relations documents. Survey sponsors
often want to review a questionnaire before giving their stamp of approval.
People who are asked to understand and use the results often want to see
exactly how the questions were asked and in what order. There have been
instances where sloppy telephone questionnaires containing an excessive
number of arrows to identify "if then" paths throughout the questionnaires,

extensively detailed interviewing instructions, and unnecessary boxes placed around answer choices made it impossible for a reasonably well-educated official to read the questionnaire without help. Much of a study's credibility can be needlessly lost and not recovered by after-the-fact explanations of how telephone interviewers are accustomed to such hieroglyphics.

Support for mail needs assessment questionnaires that use the total design method has developed in many states because questionnaires have been attractive and easily understood by people without survey training. Booklet cover designs contain appropriate titles, and graphic designs create interest in results and credibility for the needs assessment (Dillman 1983a). In some instances, citizens have designed the cover to reflect particular characteristics of a community or state that help interest people in completing the questionnaire.

Telephone and face-to-face questionnaires can be constructed with public relation concerns in mind. The results contrast sharply with the internal working document mode used in many if not most scientific surveys.

SAMPLE SIZE. It is ironic that the most important development in survey methodology in this century is probably the most misunderstood aspect of needs assessment surveys. It concerns the power of small random samples for estimating the distribution of characteristics in large populations. Typical of the prevalent misunderstanding is the frequency with which survey consultants are asked the following question, What percentage of the people in the population need to be surveyed for my results to be accurate? The question as worded is inappropriate for reasons described below.

Perhaps the most important principle of sampling is that the ability to find out the distribution of a characteristic in a population depends mostly on sample size and hardly at all on the number of people in the population, except when that population becomes very small. This principle is illustrated by Table 11.1, which shows the number of completed questionnaires from a random sample of the designated size needed for various degrees of

TABLE 11.1. Size of sample needed from populations of varying size for specified levels of accuracy

Population size	To be accurate within:		
	± 2%	± 4%	± 10%
3,000	1234	517	97
20,000	2222	606	100
100,000	2439	621	100
1,000,000	2500	625	100
100,000,000	2500	625	100

Assumptions: Dichotomous variable with nearly 50 percent of answers in each response category; 95 percent confidence level.

accuracy. For example, 100 questionnaires are needed for any size population over 20,000 to be accurate within 10 percentage points. A careful statistical description of what we mean is as follows: 19 out of 20 times that we draw random samples of 100 people from our population, the result would be within 10 percentage points of the value we would have obtained by surveying all members of that population. As a rule of thumb, increasing our sample by a factor of 4 decreases our likely sampling error by one-half.

Perhaps an analogy will be helpful for the person who finds the argument of the power of sample size somewhat dubious. Sampling is based on probability theory, as is the rolling of dice or flipping of a coin. The assumption of randomness, that is, every member of a population having an equal (or known) chance of being selected, is similar to saying we have an "honest" coin. If we flip a coin 10 times, we have 1 chance in 1024 of getting 10 heads. In essence, when the same proportion of people in a sample hold negative opinions as hold positive opinions, the chances of randomly drawing people who hold mostly negative or mostly positive opinions is quite small.

Those who conduct needs assessment surveys are seldom satisfied with 100 respondents, and for good reason. Although that number is adequate if one is satisfied with $\pm$ 10 percent accuracy on a dichotomous (e.g., yes/no) question, it is not adequate if one wishes that level of accuracy for questions in which there is wide variation (e.g., income and education). Neither is it sufficient if one wants $\pm$ 10 percent accuracy for a particular segment of the population (e.g., women only or people over 60 only). Because of the desire to be accurate in describing many characteristics (the answers to some of which exhibit wide variation) and in order to talk about differences among subgroups, those who conduct needs assessment surveys are well advised to increase the size of their samples well above 100 people.

Sometimes sponsors of needs assessments will listen to a presentation on sample size and respond with the suggestion that if every household in a community of 10,000 people is given a questionnaire and only 15 percent respond (a reasonable response rate for a mass mail questionnaire without follow-ups), their sample size would be adequate. This argument confuses sampling error with another source of error, that is, nonresponse. Our discussion of sample size requirements assumes that every person is randomly selected for the survey and cooperates. A low response rate raises the possibility that those who responded are in some way different from those who did not. Thus the assumption of randomness in who responds, the cornerstone that underlies any discussion of the power of small samples to accurately represent large populations, cannot be made. In the context of low response rate, any discussion of sample size loses a great deal of meaning.

Some needs assessments are done for the main purpose of comparing different groups. Use of simple random sampling would require huge increases in overall sample size to have enough questionnaires from groups that represent a small proportion of a population (e.g., mobile home owners or people over 65). This is one of several problems leading to the use of stratification and other types of sampling methods that allow use of small overall samples but do so in more efficient ways than permitted by random sampling. Descriptions of the use of stratified, disproportionate stratified, cluster, multistage cluster, and other sample designs are available elsewhere (Miller 1983; Babbie 1982). More than any other aspect of the survey process, the development of sample designs is one where a sponsor of needs assessment surveys is well advised to seek assistance (Scheaffer et al. 1979).

SAMPLE SOURCES AND BIAS. It is one thing to announce an intention to survey the citizens of the community or state and quite another to obtain a representative sample of them. The superiority generally attributed to face-to-face interviews in the past was based less on its facility as a means of eliciting information from people than on its ability to reach random samples of the general public. The rise and acceptance of telephone interviews have been propelled by the fact that most households now have telephones, and despite increasing proportions of unlisted numbers, random digit dialing sampling methods can reach virtually all households with telephones.

The single greatest, although by no means insurmountable, barrier to greater use of household mail surveys is in finding accurate lists of households from which to draw samples. The slightly lower response rate is a much less significant problem. The method so far developed for eliciting high response depends upon knowledge of the householder's name and thus necessitates some sort of list as opposed to maps with dwelling units or random lists of telephone numbers necessary for the other methods. There are no generally available up-to-date lists of household telephone directories, the only source other than drivers license lists that may be available for an entire region or state. Also, telephone directories do not include unlisted numbers. Although rural counties usually have fewer unlisted numbers, metropolitan areas often have large proportions (20 to 40 percent of the households). Also, the United States has traditionally been a geographically mobile society, thus the published directories are quickly out of date. More importantly, some portions of society are more prone to be missed by use of telephone directories as a combined result of not having a telephone, having an unlisted number, or the listing being out of date.

For example, in a 1979 face-to-face household survey in Washington State, respondents were asked whether they had a telephone and if their number was correctly published in the currently available directory (Dillman and Mason 1979). Overall, 79 percent reported that the number was correctly published. However, only 69 percent of the 18- to 29-year-olds, 63 percent of the unregistered voters, and 61 percent of the people with incomes less than $5,000 were available in the current directory. At the other extreme, over 90 percent of the households with greater than $25,000 incomes, 88 percent of the suburban households, and 85 percent of college graduates had numbers listed in the current directory.

Frequently used alternatives to the telephone directory include city directories, utility listings, voter registration lists, and drivers license lists, the advantages and disadvantages of which have been discussed elsewhere (Dillman 1978). Use of each has a potential for certain biases and may not be available in certain states or cities.

Needs assessment surveys, that community or state leaders define as being done "for the public good" may result in having access to information that makes it possible to improve the quality of lists or even obtain lists that would otherwise be unavailable. There have been instances in which telephone companies have provided up-to-date operator listings and utility companies have provided access to their listings. A state having a law prohibiting sale of lists of drivers licenses may make that list available for needs assessment surveys that have state agency sponsorship. Thus the shortcomings of the lists may be overcome.

One of the most troublesome issues in some needs assessments is who from a given household should respond when there is more than one adult. The reason this frequently becomes an issue is that achieving representativeness requires randomly or systematically selecting who responds. Sponsors of needs assessment often find it frustrating to tell a citizen who wants to respond that they are only interested in their spouse's or living partner's opinion. Selection of respondents from within a household is sometimes made all the more difficult by the frequently used procedure of identifying the number of adult females and the number of adult males and then asking for "the oldest female" to respond, for example. This depersonalized process does not make intuitive sense to many people and often results in efforts by volunteers to circumvent the process. Sometimes it also results in people being offended and is interpreted as a sexist procedure resulting in the opinion of one sex being preferred over that of the other. This is especially true of mail surveys when letters say, "In your household we would like an adult male to respond."

Recent research offers an encouraging new possibility for respondent selection that is probably more understandable and has the appearance of being less sexist. O'Rourke and Blair (1983) asked for the adult who had the most recent birthday to respond and found characteristics of respondents compared well with those who were selected by conventional enumeration methods. Another advantage of this procedure for needs assessments is that it is easier for interviewers to understand and use. Although it has not been tested for mail surveys, there appears to be no barrier to its use here.

Except for face-to-face interviews and extremely well-financed household surveys that allow repeated callbacks to overcome not-at-homes, perfect sample frames are exceedingly rare. Some bias is virtually inevitable, and the task of the survey sponsor becomes learning as much as possible about the potential nature of that bias in seeking to minimize it in situations where prevention is an impossible dream.

SURVEY IMPLEMENTATION. Inadequate survey implementation is one of the most serious threats for successful needs assessments, especially where there is considerable reliance on voluntary assistance. Specific procedures for implementation are readily available for face-to-face interview (Survey Research Center 1976), telephone (Dillman 1978; Frey 1983), and mail (Dillman 1978, 1983a) surveys. Each of these discussions emphasizes the need for follow-up contacts to reach all the sampled households.

One of the things to learn from these discussions is that many activities must occur simultaneously and implementation requires prior planning and coordination. The work is not over once the interviewers start contacting households or the envelopes go into the mail.

Regardless of method, no aspect of the implementation process is more important to achieving satisfactory response or more likely to be poorly done than thorough follow-up. Entry of most adults, regardless of sex, into the labor force and the increased likelihood of adults to be involved in activities away from home mean that well over half the first face-to-face and telephone interviewer calls do not result in completed interviews. In the case of mail surveys, repeated follow-ups are the single most powerful stimulator of high response; a successful needs assessment cannot be done without them. Follow-ups, regardless of method, are more difficult than initial contacts. Face-to-face interviewers have to travel out of their way to recontact missed households for which they know the likelihood of response is less than for households with no previous contact. Telephone interviewers have to spend extra time explaining the nature of the needs assessment to someone who has received a partial explanation from another member of the family previously contacted by phone. In households where the previous contact has been made, the interviewer may often have to overcome reluctance. Also, telephone interviewers often must check for correct numbers and interpret comments made by other interviewers who previously tried to complete the interview. All forms of interviewing require development and maintenance of information about previous contacts, and the cost of follow-ups is usually higher than for first contacts.

Volunteers often find the first round of surveying interesting and the latter tedious, with the result that it becomes difficult to obtain help for the essential follow-ups. The problem of volunteers is compounded in the situation where it has been decided to survey every household in the community. Typically, service clubs are asked to drop off and pick up self-administered questionnaires. The allegiance of the volunteers tends to be to their club and not to the survey in particular. Training for the project may have been sandwiched into the noon hour, after lunch, and before the mandatory 1:15 PM adjournment.

There have been instances of the higher income parts of town (where most service club members reside) being well surveyed, while residences in poor neighborhoods did not even receive the original questionnaires, let alone follow-up contacts. The success of such efforts can be greatly improved by selecting service clubs that come as close as possible to representing all segments of the community and providing training that emphasizes the importance of follow-up. Providing specific address lists to be checked off for delivery as well as pickup also helps. The formation of special cleanup contact crews to work after the enthusiasm and perseverance of service club members has been exhausted is also useful.

Volunteers for conducting telephone interviews have been used successfully. It is perhaps one of the most attractive features of telephone interviewing. The success of this approach is greater if there is a centralized facility where interviewers can be closely supervised, making sure that interviewers do not call people with whom they are acquainted (so that interview procedures revert to conversational exchanges). Success is also more likely if there are extra jobs to be done so that interviewers who have difficulty on the telephone can be assigned to other important roles in the survey process. Supervising volunteers requires considerably more tact and patience than the normal employee-employer relationship. However, the use of volunteers often has a very substantial payoff. If the volunteer interviewers will be responsible for presenting and interpreting results to others, the interviewing helps them understand the strengths and limitations of survey data in a way that other techniques typically do not. Their commitment to successful completion of projects may also be secured by the long hours experienced in use of the telephone. Experience on the telephone often makes the difference between whether citizens believe the results are valid or not.

DATA CODING AND ANALYSIS. Data coding refers to assigning numbers to each response so that it can be entered into a computer for numerical analysis. Analysis refers to determining, finally, the distribution of the characteristics as coded in the population that was surveyed. The popularity of needs assessment has increased in almost direct proportion to the increased ease of coding and analysis of the data once it is received. Developments in computer technology have made it possible to do needs assessment more quickly with far less effort.

The most important principle of success is to talk, preferably in great detail, to the person who has taken on the responsibility for the data analysis and to do this prior to finalization of the questionnaire. Few fields are changing more rapidly than computer science. Different computer systems require different coding and analysis processes, and the rapidity of change means that a wide variety exists in the computer procedures being utilized by various individuals and organizations. Proliferation of microcomputers has added an additional range of coding and analytic possibilities to an already crowded field. The focus of early discussions with computer analysts is likely to be on what questions you wish to answer with the data and whether precoding of the data (assigning appropriate numbers to response choices) should be added to the questionnaire to facilitate coding and analysis.

The most worrisome aspect of coding is the likelihood of error. Coding, which often involves transferring numbers from questionnaires to correct columns of coding sheets, virtually always produces some error, as does entry of the rather sterile appearing numbers into the computer. For this reason the standard procedure of most analysis is to enter all data into the computer twice and when the second entry does not correspond to the first, to recheck the questionnaire. Procedures are also followed so that impossible numbers (e.g., a 3 when the only answer choices for a particular question are 1 or 2) cannot be erroneously entered.

Reconverting raw numbers to interpretable tables with appropriate labels also results in errors, and we have known of people reporting results they thought were from one question when actually the results were from another. Only one or two experiences of this nature can result in the credibility of all questions in a survey being seriously undermined. Trained computer analysts learn to look for such errors and can sometimes include appropriate checks in their work to ensure that such errors do not happen.

The capabilities of computers are increasingly impressive, the larger the number of respondents and the greater the number of questions. Rapid advances in computer technology have resulted in less time being required between data collection and analysis. Computer-assisted telephone interviewing (CATI) allows interviewers to code operations during the interview with results being summarized the minute interviewing for the day has concluded. These developments are important because one of the great difficulties in needs assessment surveys has been the lag between data collection and analysis. Often, involvement of citizens in data collection generates substantial enthusiasm and a readiness to take action. But this enthusiasm can completely disappear if people must wait several months for the results.

When a considerable lag between data collection and analysis seems inevitable, hand tabulation may be used to obtain quicker analysis of certain questions and maintain volunteer enthusiasm during the lag period. We have developed the technique of using small file cards (3" × 5" or 4" × 6"), which have been printed with coded choices near the outside edges for the questions of critical interest. These cards are then hand coded. By dealing the coded cards into piles (much as one would deal a deck of playing cards and count the number in each of the resulting piles), citizens can provide their own frequency distributions. By redealing each pile according to the answers to a second question, cross-tabulation tables can be achieved. In rare instances when a needs assessment survey involves relatively few respondents and questions, the entire survey can be summarized with less time and effort than would be required for a computer analysis. The advantage of a quick reporting of results to the sponsoring needs assessment survey group is substantial.

DATA PRESENTATION. In principle, data presentation is one of the simplest parts of a needs assessment survey. The task involves identifying which information is relevant to answering the questions that led to doing the survey, organizing the data in a comprehensible form, and presenting it. Unfortunately, more needs assessments probably fail because of inadequate data presentation than for any of the other reasons so far discussed. Failure at this stage is particularly distressing. Anticipation is highest as sponsors of needs assessment finally have the opportunity to see the results of their considerable work. What should be an exciting climax can become anticlimactic, confusing, and just plain boring.

There are many ways to improve data presentations. Among them are the use of effective visual support, sorting and organizing data to address the original issues that led to doing the survey, supporting verbal with written presentation and vice versa, using statistical techniques that are appropriate to the audience, and providing a qualifying context for data.

Fundamentally, comprehending survey results involves understanding, remembering, and comparing numbers. The ability of most people to remember numbers recited to them verbally and then to mentally compare them with later numbers is very limited. Most surveyors realize this and support their presentations with overhead transparencies or slides. All too often such visuals consist of typed tables from written reports that, when projected, are too small to be read and/or too confusing to be understood.

It is important to realize that presenting all the information frequently has an overload effect, with the result that confusion and failure to pinpoint important relationships of central interest occur. The use of written summaries to supplement such presentations is helpful in avoiding the data simplification that deters presenters from reducing results to more easily comprehensible forms. The preparation of written summaries often lags behind verbal summaries, making simultaneous presentation difficult. This problem has frequently led us to reprint the original questionnaires, substituting percentages for code numbers of answer choices.

A well-trained data analyst is familiar with the battery of statistical techniques for efficiently summarizing data. When random sampling is done, use of such techniques, ranging from t-test to log linear odds analysis are deemed useful. The difficulty of reporting such information is apparent when audiences do not understand it or, as often happens, it is substituted for presentation of the normal percentages. We recall the embarrassment felt by nearly everyone in the room when a well-intentioned analyst started a presentation to county commissioners with his overall conclusion that the "use of six demographic variables accounted for 30 percent of the variance in the dependent variable, that is, the use of county recreational facilities." His statement was supported by a chart that showed the associated F-test and little more. The silence in the room was deafening as the commissioners contemplated what questions to ask and the analyst attempted to give further explanation, which became less and less comprehensible. Such analyses are useful but can also be tremendous barriers in the use of needs assessment data; people are reluctant to make decisions based on information they do not understand.

Another difficulty sometimes encountered in data presentation is the failure to understand the context surrounding survey data, particularly from that associated with samples of populations. Data analysts are used to thinking in probabilistic terms about data accuracy; people in the political arena sometimes think of data in absolute terms. We recall one survey presentation with the finding that 51.7 percent of a statewide sample of 1800 people favored the proposal. Recipients of the information tended to view the result as an election outcome; that is, a victory is a victory no matter how close. Discussion of how sample size affects confidence in the results, how exact wording of questions affects answers, and how attitudes are prone to change are all important issues in helping to understand survey results.

Dramatic changes are occurring in our ability to prepare effective visual presentations. Microcomputers as well as mainframe computers can easily turn raw data into a variety of graphic forms. Press-on letters and a variety of materials have changed the preparation of visuals so that good visual support is no longer only the province of the professional artist.

Differences exist in the type of visual presentation that is most effective in particular situations. Whereas the projection of 35-mm slides is probably effective for large formal presentations, the use of transparencies on overhead projectors is more effective in smaller groups where discussion of individual findings is to occur. Not having to darken a room completely and being able to face the audience and add notations to individual transparencies combine to give a considerable advantage to overhead transparencies when one is working with a group and attempting to make the bridge from survey data to action.

Summary. This chapter is very different from one that might have been written a decade ago on doing successful needs assessment surveys. Although the nine necessary elements for success have not changed, the procedures for achieving success are in most cases quite different. In particular, the coming of age of mail and telephone surveys has provided new opportunities for doing needs assessments and has demanded the development of new procedures for their effective use. The proliferation of far more powerful and more accessible computers has drastically improved the speed with which surveys can be done and revolutionized our methods for coding, analyzing, and presenting results.

The most dramatic change of all is the bringing of technology and skills for doing such surveys closer to where the need for them exists. Doing valid surveys was once the primary if not exclusive province of highly trained professionals. The development of procedures for doing mail and telephone surveys has made it possible for people with less training and commitment to the enterprise to conduct competent surveys. The proliferation of telephone survey laboratories and the abilities of individuals to do one-shot surveys over entire states or regions provides evidence of that trend. We know of one instance in which a volunteer organization secured funds from the state legislature to do a statewide survey on water quality for state policy purposes. The organization sought volunteers from the membership to conduct the interviews. Their success was possible in part because help on technological aspects beyond their competency (e.g., final questionnaire construction and drawing of sample) could easily be obtained from others.

Needs assessment technologies will continue to change. We are entering an information age in which provision of information will substitute for other elements of the production process (Dillman 1983b; Hawken

1983). From a societal perspective, surveys are a feedback mechanism by which one can obtain knowledge of many conditions. The essence of substituting information for other inputs in the productive process is to know what input is needed when and where so that we become more efficient in the conversion of inputs to outputs, whether this is the use of iron ore or health and welfare services.

The basic elements are in place for communities, organizations, and states to look more frequently at the allocation of resources and citizen priorities and to do so in closer articulation with the decision-making process. The massive community or needs assessment that took months to plan, months to execute, and many more months to summarize and is expected to serve as a representation of priorities for several years to follow will likely go the way of the passenger train — nice to have but not the most efficient or desirable way of getting from one place to another.

Communication and computer technology, including easily acceptable banks of question formats and household sample frames have paved the way for rapid investigation, conducting, and reporting of surveys. Since the time of Watergate, U.S. society has relied on overnight surveys for important issues affecting our country. We expect that needs assessment surveys that rely on slower traditional modes of origin and implementation will have considerably less impact on decisions than those that rely on the technology in predominant use by the larger society. Exciting times lie ahead for those doing needs assessment surveys.

Needs assessment in international development

CHAPTER 12

The context

LORNA MICHAEL BUTLER ● ROBERT O. BUTLER

NEEDS ASSESSMENT is on the verge of establishing itself as a promising international development tool. Achievement of this status depends to a great extent on the abilities of academics and practitioners to understand and interpret the opportunities and realities faced by developing nations and donors. In our development work experience, needs assessment is rarely given the recognition it deserves, and its potential contributions are seldom considered early or frequently enough. Often project design teams are organized with no one on them having a background in needs assessment. Consequently, the project design may overlook systematic involvement of local users.

There are many opportunities in advance of and during project implementation to which needs assessment can contribute. The rewards are substantial. In more than one instance we have spent valuable days talking with remote villagers and ministry field staff about their needs and problems. Their comments are consistently, "We have never been asked before. We are pleased you will listen, but will it make any difference?" The purpose of this chapter is to provide a base of understanding about the potentials that exist for needs assessment in international development work within various settings.

There are so many different levels of people involved in development, each with diverse interests and goals, that it makes the task of needs assessment extremely complex and vitally important. For example, we have been involved with the Egypt Major Cereals Improvement Project. The charge was to integrate farming systems research into this program. An assessment of needs had to respond directly to at least five different organizational systems (USAID Washington; USAID Mission Cairo; New Mexico State University; Government of Egypt, including the Ministry of Agriculture; Consortium for International Development). Within each there is a complex hierarchy of individuals with very different backgrounds, expectations, and reasons for involvement. This does not even begin to recognize local leaders and farm families and the sociopolitical structure with which they are affiliated. It is no small task to devise a means of communicating with the most significant actors among this group, at the same time conforming to decision makers' time deadlines. Here was a situation where a needs assessment could significantly affect project directions when there were essentially two years remaining in the contract.

Consultants' contributions will be far more valuable if they have a good grasp of the developing-country situation and that of the donor project; the following pages examine the opportunities that exist for needs assessment in these two contexts. With this background, Chapters 13 and 14 illustrate the application of needs assessment in several developing-country contexts and propose a set of guidelines or rules of thumb for planners and administrators as they consider needs assessment in international development. Many examples are drawn from the authors' personal experiences in Africa and the Middle East.

The developing-country situation. In developing nations, the needs assessment environment is vastly different from the United States. Contrary to Summers' comments in Chapter 1, few developing nations view citizen involvement in policymaking and program development as a desirable state of affairs; much less do they facilitate its occurrence. In contrast to Americans, citizens of developing nations tend to be less well educated, possess fewer resources, and have more limited opportunities to voice concerns to policymakers. This is even more probable among selected cultural groups, especially if they are poor or female. Given this situation, the range of needs assessment methods should be expanded beyond survey alternatives addressed by Dillman in Chapter 11. Neither mail nor telephone survey methods would be effective in developing countries, since mail and telephone services have not been sufficiently expanded in rural areas. Therefore, the use of these methods would exclude vast numbers of people.

Today most agricultural development programs are directed to the rural poor. Understanding the circumstances surrounding this clientele is an extremely important aspect of accurately assessing their needs. The decision-making atmosphere also has a marked influence on needs assessment design. Historical circumstances surrounding Third World leaders and decision makers have precipitated a unique set of values and attitudes that challenge even the most resourceful research methodologist. Another critical dimension is the availability of resources. While this may appear obvious to those of us who have worked in developing countries, our own experiences in being associated with ample resources and democratic processes frequently lead us to overlook the obvious. The sections that follow address these three important contextual elements in the developing country situation: the clientele, the decision-making atmosphere, and resource limitations and potentials.

THE CLIENTELE. Who are the clientele? The majority of people in developing nations are the rural poor. Compared to the rest of the population, the poor are more susceptible to poor health, malnutrition, and a low life expectancy. These and other factors make communication problems more severe. This may be related to cultural or language differences or social distance. When working in Malawian villages during the dry season, we found people simply did not have enough physical energy to participate in long interviews. At that time of year, food supplies are limited and illness is common.

The World Bank (1980) identifies 38 low-income nations, all estimated to have a per capita income of $360 or less. Although agriculture is their principal occupation, a growing number of people, especially in Asia, have little or no land. This sector is also frequently dependent on seasonal employment or migration from one location to another. The mobility of the population frequently leads to their exclusion from needs assessment studies. This factor is well illustrated in Lesotho where a high percentage of working-age men migrate to South Africa for employment in the mines. Any research effort meant to include this sector must determine when this population group is likely to be home. Even when miners are not working, they frequently spend their leave time visiting relatives in other areas of the country.

We also need to expand our visions of the clientele. Development must concern itself with those people who manage and control national institutions and policies. Public officials, political leaders, and civil servants, through the organizations they influence, have a major impact on incentives and opportunities for a better life. For example, if policies prevent farmers from adequately fertilizing family food crops in preference to cash crops (as in Egypt), farmers are unlikely to be motivated to increase family food production. Only by observing farmers' responses to this frustration did we learn how fertilizer is inconspicuously reallocated to the preferred food crops. When farmers were questioned, they noted no problems.

Little attention has been given to building an understanding among organizational leaders of the value of public participation. While in Lesotho, we had the opportunity to collaborate for several months with a team of livestock and range administrators and specialists in designing a livestock development program. In the early stages, there was considerable apprehension among administrators regarding public participation in the planning process. By the time the assignment was completed and there had been sufficient time to build mutual trust and understanding of the entire team's perspectives, there was considerable support for integrating citizen participation methods into the final recommendations. It takes time to educate management about the potential contributions of needs assessment. Similarly, it also requires commitment on the part of the practitioner to learn how methods can contribute to administrators' needs. In this situation, the multidisciplinary nature of the team and the time spent together working on the problems strengthened the application of the methodology.

Leaders and members of local organizations also represent a critical audience. Collective abilities must evolve at the local level for strengthening national systems of action. Neglect of this dimension will have long-term negative effects on the transfer of acceptable technologies and policies to the people who need them most.

Knowing the clientele is only part of the problem. Needs assessment must ensure that the clientele's voices are heard and heeded. Approaches should ensure the widest possible public participation in setting goals and formulating policies and plans. Increased public participation gives planners and administrators a more realistic picture of people's preferences as well as increased public support for programs. For the masses, involvement in planning and decision making holds potential for increased local control. While these factors may seem obvious, they are not at all well understood in all developing nations. We have observed administrators in prominent positions who are quite certain they know what people's needs are. Only with adequate time are they able to experience the personal rewards associated with encouraging broader participation. Unfortunately, there is rapid turnover in administrative positions. Rarely is there time for young administrators to recognize this leadership principle.

Even in the 1980s small farmers and slum dwellers, who make up the majority of developing-country populations, are frequently nonparticipants. Their individual resources are minimal; their productivity is small. They are dominated by the rich, educated, and powerful; therefore, neither their voices nor their votes are heard (Mendoza 1983:ix–xii).

THE DECISION-MAKING ATMOSPHERE. The context of development in the 1980s has changed considerably. For a good many years, a centralized power has exercised great authority and control over local affairs. This has triggered a deepening distrust of technicians and officials associated with central ministries and national organizations. Smaller or less powerful nations were frequently dependent on or manipulated by colonial governments, donor nations, or multinational organizations. More powerful entities often experienced little opposition from less powerful ones. This was attributable to such factors as differing access to resources, perceived abilities to function independently, long-standing colonial histories, high levels of poverty, and so on.

Today the tables have turned. Resources, even in the weathiest of nations, are limited. Population growth, redistribution, and carrying capacity are critical factors receiving attention from leaders throughout the international community. The priorities of developing nations have shifted. Individual levels of self-confidence have risen. International travel, educational attainment, and communications technology have expanded everyone's horizons. No longer are leaders of less industrialized nations content to have outside experts guide or control decisions that will affect national institutions and clientele.

The communications revolution is also radically changing the political atmosphere in the Third World. For the first time, low-income people are a political force to be recognized. Peasants are a common sight on worldwide television networks. They are able to direct instant attention to needs and concerns. The world is more aware than ever of the political influence of peasants in all societies.

Literacy is also advancing rapidly. Traditions are disappearing as the poor are learning that there are alternatives to poverty and oppression. There is a tide of rising expectations as the poor are becoming aware of the unequal distribution of the world's resources (Waterlow 1982:28).

RESOURCE LIMITATIONS AND POTENTIALS. Developing nations are continually faced with resource limitations. The problems of advancing population numbers and the pressure on biological resources is a subject that has received considerable attention (e.g., see Brown 1981). Rural areas compared to urban areas possess a smaller share of infrastructural services (e.g., water, transportation, electricity, public sanitation, health care, schools). This rural-urban dichotomy in some respects is comparable to rural U.S. communities. However, the degree to which it exists in Third World countries is far greater. More people are affected. The problems have more drastic consequences.

Everywhere the poor tend to reap a smaller share of the benefits of research and development programs and policies. In developing nations this has sometimes been the outcome of years of self-interest on the part of external investors. Capital cities were situated in areas where expatriates preferred to live. Industries were located for the convenience of export arrangements rather than in rural areas where labor was available. Traditional elites as well as central government officials frequently resisted grass roots participation. Decentralization rarely occurred. As a result, rural people have had few opportunities to develop the necessary organizational skills to assure a more equitable distribution of resources.

Available resources can be used to greater advantage. No persons are better informed about their own situation and needs than the individuals directly concerned. Needs assessment methods can be adapted to take advantage of the indigenous expertise of farmers, pastoralists, family members, shopkeepers, civil servants, traditional leaders, politicians, and ministry officials.

Farm families have a long history of informal research experience. Over the years, farmers continuously learn from their surroundings, solving problems as they occur and making necessary adjustments. This science of the farming family or nonformal research has been a survival mechanism over the centuries, which academic researchers have been inclined to ignore in their search for technological solutions (Axinn 1981:1–2). This concept is inherent in the farming systems research approach to development now receiving international attention (see Chapter 13).

At the same time, needs assessment can be a learning tool through which participants become partners in the total needs assessment process: design, implementation, verification, and interpretation. In this approach the social scientist or practitioner can play a central role as capacity builder. Methods can strengthen the social learning and problem-solving abilities of local and national institutions. Ordinary people can be encouraged to become action researchers. "Uneducated" villagers are valuable sources of data. Through active participation in needs assessment, local people can channel their knowledge into their own institutions and eventually into action. The challenge that practitioners face is how to achieve a high degree of fit between program design, clientele needs, and the capacities of collaborating institutions and organizations (Korten 1980:17).

It is our intent here to draw attention to the uniqueness of the developing-country situation, thereby appealing to social scientists involved in needs assessment work to sensitize their efforts to this environment. This chapter will also address the donor project situation. Although developing nations are frequently inundated with external aid, surprisingly little attention is given to applying needs assessment to the donor situation. The difficulties associated with project implementation are as much a part of one side as the other. The critical concerns of developing nations and the very real problems they face demand that needs assessment practitioners consider the relationships between the developing-country situation and the donor situation. Needs assessment can address several purposes concurrently:

1. Building the capacity of local, national, and donor organizations to respond to the real problems and concerns of local people.
2. Taking advantage of indigenous resources, human and physical.

3. Serving as a learning laboratory to strengthen people's knowledge and skills for participating in public decision-making processes.

4. Collecting accurate, reliable, and useful information.

5. Developing mechanisms for responding to short-term objectives that are compatible with long-term goals.

Opportunities in developing-country settings. The time is right. A combination of factors exists today that is conducive to the application of multipurpose needs assessments in developing-country settings. The use of development projects in international assistance has grown steadily since the 1950s. Perspectives on their success have been mixed. It does seem, however, that we are more willing to acknowledge past mistakes and inadequacies with respect to meeting the needs of the poor. There is also much to be learned about strengthening organizational capacity to sustain the benefits generated by investments. Lessons learned from successful community and rural development efforts are still appropriate and often transferable to other cultural settings.

Five different factors are discussed below: (1) the value of indigenous knowledge, (2) clientele gap, (3) capacity strengthening, (4) cultural diversity, and (5) the information revolution. The very existence of these factors in developing nations implies that there are significant opportunities for application of needs assessment to international development work. There is also an increasing recognition that the problems of development are not entirely technical. As social scientists we are frequently asked to collaborate with physical scientists and administrators in resolving development issues. When we are involved with project planning and implementation, our contributions will be greatly enhanced if we are sensitive to these factors.

THE VALUE OF INDIGENOUS KNOWLEDGE. One of the primary reasons for doing needs assessment is to communicate with a particular clientele. This implies we believe that the clientele's knowledge is important. Indigenous knowledge in this case refers to the knowledge of all developing-country clientele regardless of educational background, residence, position, or economic status.

There has been a prevalent assumption that people possessing formal education and training somehow have access to superior or more valuable knowledge. This has sometimes been contrasted to the "inferior" knowledge of uneducated and untrained people. This perception of the superiority of science-based knowledge has predominated everywhere—among industrial nations and Third World professionals, civil servants, and even village or community workers. We continue to see evidence of this belief system, for example, in differential wages, top-down management approaches, extension training, university curricula, research methods, development project design. Frequently, without thinking, we imply that local people's knowledge is unimportant, imprecise, or even wrong (this problem is extensively addressed in the January 1979 *IDS Bulletin,* beginning with the editorial by Chambers 1979).

Ever since anthropologists' early field work, academics have been concerned with indigenous people's knowledge of their environment. Only recently has this concern permeated international development activities. Customary development philosophy transmits knowledge from scientists or experts to village people or to less educated counterparts, rarely the reverse. Perhaps the acknowledgment of the need for more of a systems or multidisciplinary approach to problem solving has had some impact. There has also been a rude awakening to the fact that the availability of scientific knowledge did not assure the spread of Green Revolution technology to the people who needed it most.

Recognition of the worth of indigenous knowledge may call for basic value and behavioral changes among development planners and practitioners. Sometimes we are insensitive to our authoritarian styles and one-way communication tendencies. This may be exhibited by excessive use of academic language, not hearing local people, not recognizing people's capabilities, or not allowing adequate time for our own exposure to other people's worlds.

A more major philosophical shift may be essential. Commitment to reversing directional flow of technical knowledge from outside (professionals, officials, practitioners) to inside (farmers, village families) to inside-outside implies a major change in current development practices. Perhaps a development team might receive its first in-country orientation from village leaders and farmers who would show how their livestock is fed or herded, their family food is obtained, or neighborhood trade is conducted. In our experience, projects frequently begin with team members telling local leaders and villagers what the project plans to do rather than first listening to villagers' needs and observing local behavior patterns. As a result, project personnel frequently waste time by testing technologies that farmers have already found to be unacceptable.

Howes and Chambers (1979:7) suggest that the problem may lie with the fact that professionals and experts depend on scientific or formal knowledge to legitimize superior status. By creating a dependency among clientele, we reinforce our need for personal assurance of maintaining control over the situation.

As we work with counterparts in developing nations, the concept of indigenous knowledge takes on more meaning. We have observed that

Third World nationals are increasingly intolerant of our unwillingness and inability to hear and see life as they see it. This can be illustrated by two contrasting perspectives concerning possible solutions to Lesotho's lowland food production problem. The area frequently suffers from drought, poor soil conditions, and a shortage of adequate male labor as a result of migration to the South African mines. A high proportion of subsistence farms are managed by women and children. One of the major crops on which women depend is sorghum. It supplements women's limited income in that it is a primary resource for the brewing and sale of beer. Many women contribute labor to some aspect of the brewing economy, thereby assuring at least one source of cash or in-kind income. The use of sorghum as a food for women and children is also reinforced by cultural beliefs. Therefore, its importance in the lives of women and children cannot be underestimated. Yet we have often heard agricultural scientists and development officials discussing the need to change the local variety of sorghum to one that is suitable for livestock feed. In their views the shortage of cattle forage could be advantageously supplemented through production by lowland farmers who could sell it to livestock owners. Obviously, there are at least two different views on the problem. More communication was needed between the differing perspectives so that villagers' perceptions about their situation were not overlooked. Too often, technical solutions have had negative impacts on local people simply because no one took the time to listen to and observe them.

We not only need practical suggestions about how to assure the use of indigenous knowledge but also have a responsibility to sensitize nationals who have effectively learned our bad habits. Unfortunately, the same attitudes toward the clientele often exist in developing nations as in the curricula that many of us have taught. A student from an African nation expressed concern that his research methods class placed little value on designing a survey instrument in the field where questions must be mutually understood. He observed that research designs and tools were largely products of researchers' offices, sometimes far from the site where the data were to be obtained and applied. His conclusion was, "Now I understand why my friends' research does not please my people."

Our ability to apply more creative methods for obtaining local perspectives can produce rewards for development, for example, by (1) more accurately predicting clientele's willingness to accept recommendations; (2) improving communications between inside and outside sectors, that is, between project participants and donor or host country representatives; (3) building clientele's confidence in their own knowledge and capabilities; (4) producing more cost-efficient information in terms of accuracy, relevance, usefulness, and timeliness; (5) recognizing unique differences among villages, ecological regions, and cultural groups; and (6) generating greater public support for decisions.

CLIENTELE GAP. One of the most perplexing institutional problems developing nations face is the growing gap between decision makers, professionals, and civil servants and the people they serve. The widening social distance between this administrative class and the public is one of the primary symptoms of administrative incapacity (Bryant and White 1982:29). Although not the total solution, needs assessment can be a valuable mechanism for decreasing this gap. The process can begin in the early phases of legitimization and continue through all phases, including the application and dissemination of findings.

Reasons for this gap are many and varied. In some respects, the situation is not unlike the United States. Civil servants and administrators frequently lose touch with their rural backgrounds. They may be several generations removed from rural life. Compared to rural people, civil servants often have greater access to resources. Educational experiences may have taken them to other countries and exposed them to new values and specialized skills. Earning a government wage probably assures more comfortable housing, access to transportation, and a standard of living in excess of that experienced by the average rural resident.

It is difficult to eradicate the second- or third-generation colonialistic mindset of the elites that administer developing-country bureaucracies. According to Roy (1982:72–73), current Third World extension systems will never adequately reach the majority of the disadvantaged because of the "almost 'imperial' research which is being extended." The author goes on to say that "even agricultural research has left its 'grassroots' moorings and taken off into more esoteric varieties. . . . "

Access to resources can also have adverse effects. Jones (1971:150) notes the tendency for countries to place excessive emphasis on pure science and affiliation with an international intellectual elite, rather than on solving local practical problems.

While there is a historic underpinning to this class-related social distance problem, it has major structural implications. Although needs assessment alone is unlikely to stimulate the needed changes, it can sometimes serve as a tool to bring about awareness of the problems and even to help in the search for solutions. Extension field staff are the critical link to the rural people whose needs we are attempting to meet. Yet it is this level of staff who receive the poorest training and the least pay and have the fewest incentives to do a good job. Without exception, in every developing country in which we have worked, the situation is the same. These field agents are rarely asked what kind of research would be helpful to the farmers with whom they work, and they are probably never involved in carrying out research, let alone under local farm conditions. Chances are the experiment station researchers do not trust them to interpret the findings of ongoing studies. In Lesotho we actually heard researchers say they had no interest in traveling to the field to talk to farmers. One went so far as to say, "I don't understand why I should write up my findings for extension staff. What I do is my business, not theirs!"

Studies of field staff in developing nations reveal the tendency for staff to align themselves with community elites. Bryant and White (1982:183–84) argue that this is a way of coping with tensions brought on by differing access to resources, stressful environmental conditions, and internal organizational pressures. Regardless of the reason behind it, this behavior contributes to the growing gap between clientele and government representatives.

In Malawi and Lesotho we have been in positions to observe the process used by extension and community development field staff to set up visits between outside officials and village leaders. In Lesotho these outside officials often included Lesotho nationals as well as expatriates. The goal was to facilitate discussions with local people to give officials a better understanding of villagers' needs and concerns. In almost every case, field staff called on the same village leaders every time, and usually they were the more articulate, better educated, and wealthier village representatives. In one instance, a village farmer who spoke excellent English was contacted to meet with dignitaries but asked to speak only the local language. An interpreter was called on to translate his comments to the visitors. The inevitable outcome is an increasing gap between field staff and other people that are rarely called on to provide information. This leads to a growing discrepancy between what officials perceive to be the situation and the real situation, which is rarely represented.

We have observed the growing body of evidence indicating that government personnel do not comprehend the needs of the poor. The problem is exacerbated because the people who need to be most aware of the situation are neither poor nor rural. The very nature of civil servants' positions tends to render them outsiders, comparable to expatriates. In most African nations, studying agriculture at a university is considered one of the least desirable goals among young people. Few incentives are provided to encourage rural young people to consider the agricultural profession so that someday they might return to the rural area as a trained agriculturist. As a result, many young people who do enter the agriculture professions do so only as third or fourth choice, and they are probably from an urban background. Because rural young people have poorer schools and less money to pay school fees, they are less likely to go on to a university than their urban counterparts. Once again this illustrates an underlying structural conflict that contributes to the condition.

Chambers (1981b:2–5) identifies the major obstacles that lead to misperception or lack of perception about the needs of the rural poor:

1. The context of cognitive problems. The world of professionals and civil servants, compared to the rural poor, is an extremely different socioeconomic environment. There are vast extremes in everything from wealth and status to power and prestige. Professionals and young officials are quickly caught up in the advantages of an urban-based life-style, promotional opportunities, and the pressures of advancement. Without realizing it, they become involved with development problems at a policy level only, with only brief selective visits to rural areas. Attention gradually moves toward those with whom they have most in common, not the rural poor. Identification of needs therefore reflects this conflicting cognitive context.

2. The integrated nature of rural poverty. Five interrelated dimensions make poor people difficult to reach: poverty, physical weakness, vulnerability, powerlessness, and isolation.

3. Rural development tourism. The phenomenon of the "brief rural visit" underlies much of the difficulty administrators and decision makers have in understanding the problems of the poor. Outsiders are like tourists in that they have three things in common: an urban origin, a need for information, and a shortage of time to do the job. These factors, along with the likelihood that the poorest people tend to be invisible, result in inadequate, inaccurate, or superficial information.

Training is needed that can help sensitize government personnel at all levels to the needs of the poor. The FAO's *Agriculture: Toward 2000* draws attention to the past neglect of human relations skill training to improve two-way communication between local people and participatory organizations and civil servants (UN 1981:104–5). However, it is doubtful that training alone will alleviate the problems. Many of the difficulties are tied to structural and institutional conditions that are rarely seriously addressed by development projects or government officials. Administrators place little priority on expanding resources in the field where they are most needed. For example, resources are not allocated to employee incentives such as transportation and quality housing.

The situation is illustrated in Jordan. Most agricultural production occurs in the Jordan valley, approximately one hour's drive from the major population center. Yet the Ministry of Agriculture provides no housing for agricultural field staff in the valley and no incentives for civil servants who must commute this distance to work. Even though more time is required to go to work, employees are expected to arrive at the same time as other government staff who are located at headquarters. In recent years, Jordan, like many developing nations, has also suffered from limited financial resources available for in-country travel.

In Lesotho many field staff are located 10 or more hours drive from ministry headquarters. Communications with superior officers is extremely limited due to poor roads and limited phone services. Decisions about field agents' jobs are made at headquarters, far from the location of areas benefited. The pattern is to await orders from top-level administrators. As a result, recommendations may be made that are totally inappropriate for people who live in remote areas.

These examples are symptomatic of many Third World situations. Often they represent long-term structural phenomena that mirror customary cultural patterns. We often make the mistake of suggesting that developing-country societies are communal by tradition, when actually a close look at ethnographic data may show a very hierarchical pattern of decision making. Lesotho is an example of a situation where this type of analogy has been inaccurately applied because needs assessment methods neglected systematic behavioral observations and one-to-one discussions with local people.

CAPACITY STRENGTHENING. By capacity strengthening, we mean building or extending current resources. This might refer to human resources like skills and confidence of staff or leaders, or it might refer to physical resources such as buildings or equipment. Developing nations are continuously faced with the need to make the best possible use of available resources. Without exception, their greatest assets are people—a resource that is often unrecognized and underestimated, particularly in isolated rural areas.

Individual needs and concerns are most effectively identified and expressed through local collective associations. However, local autonomy, on its own, provides little leverage for change. Assuming that development emphasizes improvement in the productivity and welfare of the majority of people, it is essential that both local and national organizational capacity be strengthened.

Previous to the 1970s, international approaches to community involvement were largely associated with early community development efforts by colonial governments. They grew out of a recognition that multipurpose village-level workers could supplement government agency personnel by organizing local communities to identify felt needs and resources. In the French colonies *animation rurale* was a local development strategy to promote rural modernization. In fact, most community development approaches had little to do with village people's concerns, needs, or capabilities.

Early community development efforts declined, largely because few people recognized the complexity of the development process. Not enough was known about the rural sector to avoid attempts to transfer inapplicable group mobilization strategies from Anglo-American settings to vastly different situations. The downfall of these efforts stemmed from failure to create a local organizational base (Uphoff et al. 1979:19).

Local organizational capacity. Today there is increasing recognition of the need to strengthen the capacities of developing-country organizations and bureaucracies to assure that people and communities are the prime movers of development processes. People everywhere want to assume control over their own lives, and they are more willing than ever to speak out to this effect. Considerable agreement also exists in development agencies to support the need for widespread participation in decision making in development processes. While the atmosphere for local involvement in decision making and planning may have all the right appearances, it may also be full of conflicts.

Government leaders may fear loss of control over money, people, and programs. In many developing nations there has been an extensive history of centralized administration. As a result, official attitudes and behaviors often conflict with new requirements. Sometimes there is deep distrust between technicians and ministry officials or between government officials and rural people.

New development management strategies are badly needed. For example, Korten and Alfonso (1983:2), both associated with the Asian Institute for Management, Manila, predict a fundamental change in structures, procedures, and internal organizational cultures. They advocate organizational reform based on social learning processes that respond to needs of rural people. This includes (1) planning methods based on better knowledge of the poor and their environments, (2) methods of changing government agencies that simultaneously strengthen personnel's knowledge and skills, and (3) changes in linkages between institutions and the people served to eliminate barriers to collaborative problem solving.

The FAO (UN 1981:102–3) notes that "farmers, and especially small farmers, cannot face natural and economic challenges alone and unorganized." Progress in agricultural development to date has been a joint effort attributable not only to technological innovation but also to strengthened institutional structures for farmer support and motivation. Structures need to be firmly based in local communities to enable smallholders and the landless to have access to needed resources. Organizational systems must be shaped and operated through active local member participation. Grass roots organizations can ensure that farmers and their family members will be heard at national policy levels (see similar statements of policy by World Bank 1980 and USAID 1982).

While commitments like the above are reassuring to social scientists and development practitioners, little is actually known about local organizations. Much disagreement exists over their capacity to actually stimulate development and participation. Uphoff and his associates (1979:35) conclude, after extensive analysis of 16 Asian case studies, that one cannot assume that local organizations must promote participation in decision making, evaluation, or even implementation and development benefits.

However, it is hard to overlook the promise of strengthened local capacity. Accomplishment of rural development objectives has been a major outcome in Asia. In both Africa and Asia it has contributed to more effective small-farmer involvement and improved two-way communication between project participants, project management, and extension (Uphoff et al. 1979). In Botswana it has been a major factor in achieving agricultural development goals (Willett 1981:215–17).

Esman and Uphoff's (1982:31) analysis of 150 case studies leads them to conclude that building local organizations does not presume this to be the only, or the best, means of assuring rural development. However, there are some specific tasks that local organizations can carry out effectively. They can, for example, articulate local peoples' interests and perspectives to help ensure that government is more responsive to individual and group needs. Local organizations have been very successful in gathering planning and goal setting information.

The Lesotho Farming Systems Research Project has been effective in working through village committees to involve farmers in adaptive research to identify production problems and to obtain input on how the project can more effectively address farmers' needs. The mechanism has also been useful as a means of transferring improved technologies.

Local people need training to contribute effectively to organizational problem solving. Most evidence indicates literacy is not essential to effective participation unless the attitudes of the bureaucracy are contradictory. The major problems arise with training approaches that have a top-down orientation. Training needs to provide skills in organizational operation as well as in technical skills for solving identified problems. Leadership training also seems to be essential. If the clientele are omitted from the training process, it is doubtful that needs assessment methods can bridge the communications gap between local needs and development resources of the projects. Training at both levels builds a problem-solving team. The clientele must be part of that team.

National organizational capacity. The effectiveness of local organizations is dependent on linkages to regional and national institutions. This implies a need for the right kind of skills at all levels in public and private organizations. Division heads, researchers, district officers, and field agents all need supportive skills and attitudes to facilitate participation.

Top-down attitudes, management approaches, and teaching styles tend not to be conducive for building local capacity. If research findings do not get to or are not accepted by the farmer, this indicates a weakness in the institutional capacity. An example of this breakdown is the tendency for ministries of agriculture to make blanket recommendations for fertilizer use throughout the nation or across a major region. Such recommendations are often given without considering local differences in soil type, moisture conditions, availability of fertilizer, or farmers' incomes. Somewhere communications between farmers and those making and carrying out decisions are breaking down.

Chances are, neither civil servants nor clientele have been trained in the knowledge and skills needed for participation. Paternalistic attitudes, common in the bureaucracies of many societies, are contrary to the necessary attitudes of cooperation, collaboration, and acceptance. Without these, government agents may never comprehend the potentials and capabilities of local people. If people have been subject to a history of colonial edicts and authoritative direction, they may lack the needed confidence to make productive contributions. A fundamental reorientation of norms may have to take place before government officials actually become accountable to rural people. This perspective was echoed by Ivan Illich at the twenty-fifth anniversary conference of the Society of International Development: "Government and the economy must become subordinate to the people" (Bednar et al. 1982:36). This in itself may not be politically feasible or practical, particularly if it means radical changes.

Training is an essential ingredient to strengthening national institutional capacity. Only in rare circumstances do professionals, administrators, or junior officials possess adequate social science skills and the right attitudes to make the participatory concept work. The goal is to get the professional or government official collaborating side by side with the clientele in problem solving. The team will be most effective when each member is learning from the other. This is an essential component of successful needs assessment.

CULTURAL DIVERSITY. Historically, development efforts have ignored cultural diversity. All the people in a country, or at least within an ethnic group, have been assumed to be homogeneous. Technical information is presented as if everyone has access to similar resources and values and aspirations are the same. There has been little attempt, until the relatively recent introduction of farming systems research, to identify small homogeneous groupings within larger ecological or cultural regions (see Chapter 13 for more discussion of farming systems research).

Many factors have a bearing on how individuals and groups make daily decisions. Past experiences have much to do with how we perceive today's needs. So do the opinions of other family members, friends, and people whose respect we value. Perceived rewards and risks that accompany one choice relative to another are also influential factors.

Environmental conditions make a significant difference in values, attitudes, and behaviors. For example, people living in a fuel-deficient area may be hesitant to eradicate a particular rangeland weed when it has historically served as a source of emergency cooking fuel during excessively dry periods. In villages located near tree-lined streams and rivers, destruction of the same weed may be viewed quite positively.

Field research in East Africa on cultural adaptation to different ecological environments substantiates this. The Culture and Ecology in East Africa Project examined the adaptive process of change in culture, society, and individual behavior among four different groups in Tanzania, Kenya, and Uganda. The study found significant differences in values, attitudes, and personality attributes among communities of farmers and pastoralists. These differences were based on distinctive environmental adaptations (Edgerton 1971).

An earlier study of one of these same ethnic groups, the Hehe in Tanzania, found at least five basic land use and settlement systems, each of which influenced interpersonal relationships and political systems (Winans 1965:441–42). Microadaptation is a reality, even in what appears to be a homogeneous cultural group. There is therefore a need to tailor research programs and technological recommendations to the specific conditions of each community. Each area needs to be examined for its unique natural, social, and economic characteristics.

Social change over time also turns once similar communities into those with many differences. This is illustrated by nations like Botswana, where population has increased, people have become more mobile, villages have expanded, and new settlements have been established. This precipitates a breakdown in traditional authority and increasingly diverse groups of people sharing resources. Willett (1981:281) notes that people in these newer settlements are not used to working together, nor do they recognize the authority of each other's leadership. This heterogeneous cultural base frequently causes complications in defining needs, planning, and managing resources.

Needs assessment methods need to recognize cultural diversity and the value of this quality. This can be accommodated by selective or stratified sampling in quantitative studies or by identifying culturally representative groups or informants for qualitative studies. There may be a need to test the validity of findings among different cultural groups or to systematically involve the groups in evaluating proposed recommendations. It is wise to encourage local people, even in the most isolated rural area, to apply their own unique perspectives and capabilities to managing their own futures. In support of this, Rashmi Mayur (1984:22), Director of the Urban Development Institute, Bombay, India, expresses fear of Third World homogenization. In his words, "We need varieties of cultures to survive."

THE INFORMATION REVOLUTION. A colleague of ours was approached by a visiting Indonesian university administrator, who asked, "What are American universities doing to take advantage of satellite technology?" With over 13,000 islands in Indonesia, it is little wonder that this question is viewed as of some importance by national planners and decision makers. Think of the possibilities for linking people, information, and ideas across such a dispersed nation. Data could be quickly shared from one island to another. Policymakers in ministry headquarters could have immediate access to needed decision-making information, which now takes months or even years to obtain.

In the west we are bombarded with rapidly advancing communications technology. Yet the telecommunications revolution is probably just beginning for developing nations. To some extent information, as we know it, is already available in remote areas through tape cassettes, loudspeakers, microphones, and television. Now, with the merger of the microchip and high-capacity networks made possible by optical fibers, microwaves, satellites, and digital circuits, the potential for applying these to development work is almost endless.

There are three primary areas where this new technology might be used: communications, information storage and retrieval, and computing. All three could have major implications for needs assessment work overseas. The questions are: Will policymakers, politicians, and planners in developing nations recognize the potential? Will it be feasible to adapt available technology to the needs of development? Will it be possible to develop the needed specialized skills and knowledge at management levels and in the field to support the utilization of this technology?

Satellite technology opens the potential of interactive communication with remote rural areas. Small isolated villages can have satellite hookups with a minimum of infrastructure, at low cost, and without highly skilled personnel. Videoconferencing could replace days of travel under difficult conditions and offer the advantage of talking with groups of people simultaneously (Wellborn 1984:59–62).

International projects have studied the potential use of satellite telecommunications for classroom teaching, teacher training, university courses, health diagnosis and education, and agriculture extension. The medium will provide a much less costly means of communicating with remote areas. However, it will probably require considerable personnel training, software development, and maintenance. Major institutional commitments will be needed from user agencies (ministries, educators) to take full advantage of the possibilities and from service providers (telephone companies, radio broadcasters) to meet the special requirements of rural users. Close collaboration will have to take place between groups that have no history of collaboration (Casey-Stahmer and Goldschmidt 1984:7).

The entire area of telecommunications in itself represents a critical area of needs assessment. Research and development will be essential to adapt technologies to the requirements of rural areas. This will place entirely new demands on the type of training needed by civil servants. Those in decision-making roles will be subjected to a totally new field in which they will probably need considerable understanding of communication technologies and how to adapt them for national needs.

Needs assessment methods could feasibly move into a brand-new domain. Remote sensing by satellite can supply data for entire countries on such things as vegetation, moisture, irrigation, and crop damage. Year-round monitoring can predict harvest size and the effect of drought, disease, and improper irrigation.

Satellite communications expand the potential of group interaction processes. Social scientists will be able to collaborate across national borders, so working in a developing nation need not be an isolated experience. It will be possible for countries with similar ecological or cultural situations to work together to assess needs. Ultimately, we may be able to conduct needs assessments without stepping foot inside the country or region of concern. Language differences may be minimized through instant translation processes. Laser-read videodisks will hold 50 to 100,000 pages of easily accessible information at very low cost. Where no library services are available, it will be possible to get computer-based access to major information sources. By the turn of the century this and much more is within the realm of possibility.

Opportunities in external donor projects. Most developing nations are supported to some extent by external donor projects. Support usually consists of an outright grant or some type of resource sharing arrangement from an outside country, organization, or private corporation. Resources in the form of money, staff, equipment, infrastructure, or a combination of these may be contributed to assist the developing nation in meeting mutually agreed-upon goals. Very often the project agreement includes a commitment from the external donor and the host country.

An example of an external donor project for the country of Jordan is the Jordan Valley Agriculture Services Project. Under this agreement between the U.S. government and the Hashemite Kingdom of Jordan, the contractor (Washington State University) agrees to furnish technical assistance and commodities to increase food production. Jordan, the host government, agrees to supply selected staff and physical resources. A contractual agreement is actually implemented by representative units of the two participating governments.

Development-assistance agency evaluations note wide discrepancies between intended and actual results of projects. A variety of problems plague development projects. For example, "ineffective identification, imprecise delineation of goals and purposes, inadequate analysis of beneficiary needs, inaccurate assessments of local conditions and absorptive capacity, insufficient preparation and feasibility analysis, and overemphasis of appraisals on financial and technical aspects to the neglect of important social, cultural, and political factors" (Rondinelli 1983:317).

John Fisher (1984), Executive Director, Consortium for International Development, discussed the following reasons for failures: (1) proprietarian attitudes on the part of contractors and donors, (2) inadequacy of incentives for all parties to do a good job, (3) projects being based on erroneous assumptions about the capabilities of developing-country institutions, (4) tendency to create institutions that are beyond the capability of the host country to sustain, (5) projects not being an integral part of the total country plan, (6) projects not being economically sound, (7) resources needed for projects not delivered and sufficient local resources not available to ensure project sustainability, (8) project staffing not done to meet the real needs of developing-countries, and (9) inadequacies of developing-country managerial systems.

Some of these problems could be minimized through more adequate needs assessment. An early understanding of the capabilities of national institutions assures that project designs do not create institutions that cannot be maintained by the existing resource base, skill levels, and management capabilities. Early assessment of these capacities could influence a project design team to include appropriate management training or needed structural changes.

Certain subgroups among the poor such as pastoralists, fishermen, landless farmers, women, and isolated indigenous people are difficult to reach with project benefits, especially in short time periods. Projects directed to such subgroups require a more thorough understanding of the people involved in order to find the best method of instituting change. This includes more attention to adapting standard technologies and implementation strategies (Perrett and Lethem 1980:3).

What appears appropriate from a government or funding agency's viewpoint may not necessarily appear so to the recipient or user. During the past decade, grass roots movements have become increasingly popular. New-directions legislation passed in the 1970s recognizes that needs of users should be identified. Needs assessment can help to make these connections. The 1973 U.S. Foreign Assistance Act mandates that American bilateral assistance be extended in ways that involve intended beneficiaries in project planning, implementation, and benefits (USAID 1975).

The United Nations Economic and Social Council also recommends that governments "adopt popular participation as a basic policy measure in national development strategy" and "encourage the widest possible active participation of all individuals and national nongovernmental organizations, such as trade unions, youth and women's organizations, in the development process in setting goals, formulating policies, and implementing plans" (UN 1975:paragraph 4).

Use of needs assessment as an international development tool is relatively new. Nationals from developing nations are unlikely to be familiar with it. Therefore, the contractor will probably need to initiate needs assessment and identify its potential contributions. Ideally, if the opportunity permits, it should be considered in the original project design.

The following section addresses the donor project situation. We tend to concentrate efforts only on developing nations. Greater attention to the donor sector as well may help to assure a better investment return. This sector of development work poses major challenges to social scientists in that the donor project situation must be addressed simultaneously with the needs of the developing nation.

In the external donor project situation there are a number of operational phases throughout the project duration. Ideally, the same donor representatives are involved in project design as in project implementation; however, this is not always the case. Needs assessment can make major contributions during each phase beginning with project design.

Figure 12.1 illustrates these phases and the extent to which each overlaps with another. For example, the design of a project includes many opportunities for strengthening the capacities of organizations in the host and donor country, since the entire project is essentially a learning-adapting process. Needs assessment techniques can serve as mechanisms for project participants to learn about the environment in which they function, test strategies for accomplishing goals, and revise methods of operating. If we look at the donor project this way, needs assessment becomes an integral part of the entire development process.

The potential role for needs assessment in the various phases of external donor projects is discussed below. It may be helpful to view needs assessment as one of several tools that can increase chances of success for donor projects in the very complex process of development. Three primary phases are discussed given the close interrelationship that exists among each: (1) project design and evaluation, (2) early needs and accomplishments, and (3) capacity strengthening.

PROJECT DESIGN AND EVALUATION. The design phase is one of the most important parts of the project, yet frequently it does not receive the atten-

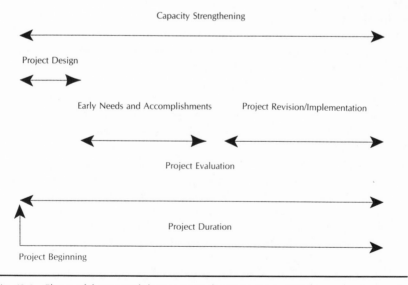

Fig. 12.1.   Phases of the external donor project showing opportunities for needs assessment.

tion it deserves. Long-term success is extremely dependent on this early phase. In some project contracts a poor design can be the most major constraint affecting implementation because of the inability to make needed changes as the project progresses. This phase probably offers the greatest opportunities for needs assessment practitioners, since so much of the project's future rests on an accurate, early assessment of clientele needs. Project design usually includes identification of the following elements and each represents an important aspect of needs assessment: (1) the problem, (2) clientele needs, (3) resources available, (4) resources needed, (5) project goals, (6) implementation strategies, (7) time schedule, (8) organizational structure, (9) feasibility of success, and (10) evaluation strategies.

Design teams are generally requested on short notice with minimal time for preparation. Team members sometimes have little or no experience in designing development projects and frequently no background in the country of concern. Rarely is design-team training given to the team members. Project design often reflects team members' biases and ignores the perceptions of recipients. Many design teams do not include social scientists, least of all anyone familiar with needs assessment. Projects may also be directed to macro needs identified by government officials, thus ignoring the micro situation of the clientele.

Proposals written to identify development needs are often based on secondary, tertiary, or outdated data. This information may not reflect the needs of local people. We have observed design teams that never go outside the capital city or government headquarters. As a result, the design reflects only the needs of ministry officials, politicians, and staff from other development projects. At the very least, we urge design teams to spend time in the field talking to village people who may benefit from the project. It is not too difficult to find a few key informants among village leaders, farmers, women heads of households, extension or community development field officers, shopkeepers, and produce marketing clerks. One must venture off the main highway to more out-of-the-way villages and visit these areas when the weather is bad and/or when migrant workers are home.

The Caribbean Agricultural Research and Development Institute recently initiated a design that incorporated a training workshop for host country nationals to involve them in the project design process. This not only helps to ensure that project design is responsive to local needs but also builds long-term ownership in project implementation.

Try not to be overly dependent on existing data, or at least attempt to check out its accuracy and validity. Many surveys and census studies conducted in developing countries are subject to inadequate supervision and weak methodologies. We have observed extension agents filling in census forms under a tree or in the local cafe. Often people who collect these data have other jobs and therefore are not motivated or trained to work effectively.

If early project design does not accurately reflect clientele needs, goals and objectives may be inappropriate or imprecise. There may also be limited knowledge of the clientele situation. When this happens there is a tendency for project personnel to spend more time than is practical in discussing and reidentifying goals and further clarifying the situation. The outcome is lost time that might have been better directed to early accomplishments.

What kinds of delivery systems and policies are needed to bring about positive impacts on the clientele? How can projects avoid detrimental effects on clientele and other unidentified audiences? "Technology has no inherent value in itself and no value to society until it is applied for the purposes for which it was created (Leagens 1979)."

If the infrastructure for delivery of the programs does not adequately function, program impacts may be negative or something quite different from that intended. When we encourage farmers to adopt cultural practices requiring the purchase of inputs, they must be available, acceptable, reasonably priced, and timely. Accurate information on these factors is needed by the organization and could come from needs assessment.

Far too little attention has been given to existing organizations and institutions. These social systems and the decisions and actions they represent are the subject of social science. Yet social scientists are more inclined to give attention to the farmer or rural household. Institutions are set up to serve the public as research stations, schools, ministries, and extension services.

While working in Egypt, we became aware of the number of outside consultants in farming systems research. According to our Egyptian colleagues, each had observed the situation and given advice. One impression they left behind was an inability to recognize the well-established system of agricultural research stations throughout the country. Egyptian scientists had reason to be skeptical of some of the consultants' proposals to forget the current experiment station approach and redirect agricultural research to an on-farm approach. Apparently, little effort had been made to involve Egyptian nationals in identifying ways that the existing institutional system could be strengthened through the addition of farming-system research.

Development project staffs need to concern themselves with strengthening collective abilities that will generate appropriate technologies and policies. Agriculture research is of no value if it does not reach farmers or is unacceptable to them. Development projects must help provide a better decision-making environment for the farmer-producer. Institutions are the mechanisms through which projects can be most effective in changing behavior to help ensure that actions result in agricultural improvement. Social scientists can assume responsibility for interpreting institutional values, beliefs, authority patterns, norms, and rewards. All have a major bearing on the quality of rural people's lives. Projects need to be effective vehicles of social learning, social change, and strengthened administrative development. Development assistance can help provide the clientele with institutions that serve individual and collective needs (McDermott 1982:2–5). Lack of knowledge or scientific information on the part of the clientele does not constitute the major or only impediment to improving their conditions. The quality of the institutions that are supposedly there to serve them is a contributing factor.

In only one project design have we observed a systematic effort to build in a needs assessment of how the ministry-donor project administrative system could be reorganized to better support proposed project goals. This occurred in the design of the Lesotho Mountain Livestock Development Project. The design team had a strong representation of nationals, but more importantly, it was led by a confident national administrator. It also contained a sociologist, an anthropologist, and an agricultural economist in addition to broad-thinking and experienced livestock and range specialists.

Esman and Uphoff (1982:95) discuss four components that rural development project design and implementation teams should consider: public investments and expenditures, government policies, appropriate technologies, and more effective institutions. Most government planners and development assistance organizations emphasize the first three and generally ignore the institutional dimension. Without effective institutions, infrastructure will not be built or sustained. Public services such as extension may be provided but will not be well utilized. Investments will yield low returns for nations that can least afford them.

Another often overlooked dimension of institutional development is that of the home institution. Changes within the institutions that implement projects may be necessary (e.g., the government agency, donor agency, or contractor organization). Universities have attempted in varying ways to get the Cinderella slipper of USAID contracts to fit their present domestic institutions. Many times this has resulted in differences between the donor and the contractor.

USAID has increased its long-term commitment to helping countries develop institutional capacity. This includes food and agriculture planning and policy analysis; basic and adaptive research, education, and training; and dissemination of improved technology (USAID 1982). Institution building requires 10 to 20 years before the capacity is fully developed to operate without external assistance. As a result, donor and contracting institutions may have to adjust their sights for longer term planning. As an example, contractors such as universities may have to project ahead in looking at faculty members' entire careers and whether some individual work can feasibly be redirected and rewarded for international roles. Assessing individual, departmental, and organizational needs could be very important to mesh the unique demands of each.

Very little has been said about project evaluation. Evaluation is not a mutually exclusive activity in relation to the needs assessment that takes place throughout the project. Data gathering for evaluation is done with several primary questions in mind. Has the project met the needs of people and organizations? How much and in what ways have needs been met? What has been the level of quality of the methods or processes used? What are the project outcomes over and above what was anticipated? How good or how bad are the results?

Current evaluation philosophy puts considerable emphasis on project impact and its potential for transferability. Therefore, care should be taken to define needs assessment questions and methods that will provide these answers. Ideally, evaluation data are collected throughout the project, beginning with the onset of project design. Many of the principles underlying successful needs assessment apply equally to project evaluation. More discussion on these can be found in Chapter 14.

EARLY NEEDS AND ACCOMPLISHMENTS. Practitioners are justifiably concerned about how to respond to clientele needs in early program phases. In collaborative project efforts, the needs of the clientele, the donor agency, and the host country are often perceived differently. Long-run success demands early positive indicators to assure continuation and support. Early visibility and signs of progress build necessary support from clientele groups and donors. Too often, project designs outline long-term accomplishments but ignore the importance of up-front, short-term accomplishments.

Social scientists are in a particularly good position to respond to this demand. Data need to be made available quickly. They must be presented in such a way that they can be integrated into plans for the next project phase or in recommending solutions to immediate problems. For example, if an agronomic cultural practice has been studied for two or more years, is it better to communicate the preliminary findings to project management and farmers or to continue the testing in isolation for a longer period until the findings indicate a higher statistical significance? Project researchers who are used to working under controlled conditions of experiment stations and laboratories seem to find it difficult to release findings before they are certain of the results. In Lesotho on the Farming Systems Research Project, it was not until the third year that on-farm testing of research results was initiated. In Egypt, during five years of cereals crop demonstration work, almost no effort was made to test these findings under ordinary farm conditions. This is too long a time lapse for farmers and village leaders to maintain interest or faith in project benefits.

Closely associated with early accomplishments is the process of project legitimization and how it is marketed to the clientele. Many times in developing countries high government officials are charged with legitimizing project activities. These officials, such as a minister of agriculture or department head, are political appointees. They may make promises that are difficult for the project to fulfill. In Lesotho, ministry officials made promises of tractors, implements, and seed, while the project document made no mention of supplying these to farmers. The credibility gap created by unrealistic promises creates a constraint that can outlive the entire project and jeopardize future development potentials.

Frequently, projects are delayed in their early stages. This is often due to the slow process of resource transfer between donors and recipients. Delay is also attributable to the problem of developing an infrastructure that adequately meets the needs of the project. In some settings the infrastructure may never be adequate in relation to project demands. This reflects a design problem. If commodities are an important part of the project, delay in purchase postpones initial program efforts and accomplishments. Problems such as these can persist, therefore receiving more attention than project goals and objectives. One must minimize constraints in setting up infrastructure and logistic support and focus on the broader overall goals.

A short turnaround on baseline or needs assessment data is essential to project creditability. If data are to be collected, arrangements need to be made to guarantee that analysis and compilation of the findings will take place in the shortest time possible. The Lesotho Farming Systems Research Project implemented an extensive baseline study. Data analysis plans called for utilization of the government-owned computer. After a number of attempts to do so, the data were finally sent to the United States for analysis. This delayed the process to the point that decisions were made without the findings. The entire process of design, training, implementation, and analysis consumed 21 months.

Lessons learned from such an effort might suggest the use of personal computers or other analysis techniques that could better ensure a more rapid turnaround of data. Use of qualitative data from a smaller sample might be more practical than a large representative sample. Situational data is important to the decision-making process of the project, but if findings are not available, the project cannot benefit from the effort. As a rule of thumb, the simpler the needs assessment method, the better it will be received and used.

Too many times, project outcomes and purposes are not broken down into short-term, achievable goals. Also, technical assistance advisors have problems in identifying immediate accomplishments that should be reported. Sometimes there is a tendency to feel that short-term accomplishments are not worth sharing. Many times this interpretation is wrong. For this reason, it is important that nationals are involved in identifying project accomplishments and suggesting simple, understandable methods of dissemination. Well-designed needs assessments can facilitate this.

CAPACITY STRENGTHENING. Capacity strengthening was described earlier as the building or extending of existing human and physical resources. As shown in Figure 12.1, capacity strengthening is an ongoing process beginning with project design. Usually, donor projects think of capacity strengthening too narrowly, that is, primarily in terms of developing-country capacity. This view does little to encourage other representatives of the donor institution (such as university faculty, staff, or administration) that involvement in development can benefit the entire institution. University capacity can and should be strengthened through the development project process.

For the donor, a strengthened institutional capacity may mean a long-term plan to reward people for their involvement in project-related activities. It may mean decentralizing responsibilities so that more than elite administrative groups are trained and involved in design, research, and project evaluation. Many things can be done to encourage individuals to learn as they participate in a development project. By planning for this to happen, the donor institution can reap major benefits.

If projects are to be successful, administrators need to use methods of planning and management that put less emphasis on control and more on incentives, exchange, and facilitation. More effective management methods include information sharing in the local language or taking advantage of village radio systems or special television programs.

In Lesotho, the traditional village meeting or *pitso* was often used by project or government officials to communicate with village people. However, it was never the effective communication system it could have been because it was not used in the traditional manner. This would have required many smaller informal village discussions preceding the *pitso*, as had been customary in the past. Then the *pitso* could merely be used to legitimize plans and decisions already made. As it is now used, none of this preliminary discussion occurs, and there is no follow-up discussion. As a result, the approach often leaves villagers with many frustrations, misinterpretations, and unanswered questions.

Continued and increased attention must be given to processes of reciprocal exchange and to methods of management based on consensus building. This can be done using frequent staff meetings where people of all levels are encouraged to express ideas and suggestions. We have experienced situations where educational level was used as a criterion to exclude local staff participation. As a result, people with the most practical field experience were prohibited from participating where they were most needed.

Group-oriented needs assessment methods would be valuable in facilitating this process. In African nations, less formally educated staff are often hesitant to express good ideas for fear of criticism from superiors. Using a process-oriented rather than a control-oriented approach is important to success (Sweet and Weisel 1979:127–45).

Methodologies that involve participation in the decision-making process result in better management. In too many cases there is a tendency to utilize a tightly controlled, top-down approach. It is difficult to facilitate skill development in an atmosphere of fear and uncertainty. Involving project staff in planning and decision making will help to increase their level of understanding and support of the project. Management must assume that staff appointed to the project generally have little if any understanding of project goals and objectives. Continued project discussion and in-service education opportunities need to be pursued if all staff are to progress together.

Assuming that institutional strengthening is a goal, working relationships among project staff are a critical contributing factor for reaching project goals and objectives. Early in the implementation phase, consensus on goals and objectives is necessary. Closely associated with the goals is the need for consensus on methodologies and means of reaching goals. Many times, the goals and objectives of a project are agreed upon, but means of attainment is an area of disagreement.

Continuous efforts to inform and involve host country government officials is also important. This is especially true for individuals who are initially involved. There is a danger in not keeping people informed of project changes and modifications. In collaborative efforts this becomes more complicated and difficult to ensure. Project designers and those involved with needs assessment need to plan for the flexibility necessary to keep in tune with changing social, political, and economic situations.

The donor and contractor must consider how people at all levels of government will be involved in programs. Information targeted to reach particular cadres of officials must be planned if desired institutional changes and capacity strengthening is to be achieved.

Institutions become a reality through organizations such as a research station, a university, or a soil conservation service. Projects need to address institutions in international development assistance programs. The clientele needs a better decision-action environment. Institutions are the mechanisms through which behavior can be changed so that actions yield increased agricultural production. If the desired change of behavior of the recipient is going to take place, plans must be identified to strengthen and change the organizations that reach farmers (McDermott 1982).

Capacity strengthening is dependent upon a team approach and the ability of the staff to work together. Team building can be accomplished around a needs assessment model. Taking findings to staff for their interpretation and clarification can result in more accurate assessments and recommendations. It also builds team ownership in the outcomes.

In the Lesotho Farming Systems Research Project, not enough resources were spent in attempting to reach all levels of ministry staff. Decisions directly affecting the project were made by ministry officials with little or no understanding of project purposes and goals. In retrospect, increased attempts should be made to plan for the involvement of ministry officials in project planning and needs assessment implementation activities. Needs assessment has the possibility of being a tool to facilitate project management when used to involve and inform all levels of management. These desired outcomes will not take place without advance planning.

Capacity strengthening is important for not only the recipient country but also the donor agency. The donor agency may need to strengthen its decision-making capacity prior to implementing successful projects. Parts of the donor institutions may lack experience in handling international responsibilities. At the donor-contractor level, service units may be ineffective in setting up specialized training, commodity purchase, and international communication procedures. There may be particular needs in building abilities of campus departments to backstop field work and to improve faculty member understanding of what needs of overseas colleagues are.

Universities are frequently project contractors. There are many institutional modifications that a university might consider to more adequately support project needs. Individual and unit responsibilities could be assessed in order to assign project responsibilities to people who have the interest and background to do an effective job. There is a tendency to add on tasks to people's current domestic responsibilities. It would be useful to systematically assess department support capabilities in order to more effectively use their expertise where it is most needed. This could add to the quality of specialized project team training or to project evaluation procedures. Frequently, people called on to assume these responsibilities do not have the needed expertise. They are merely top-level administrators who are given "plums." Universities also need to adapt methods of reporting and budgeting so that their formats are acceptable and useful to the donor agency and in-country project needs. Revised purchasing systems are needed to facilitate monitoring of international shipments from point of purchase to delivery.

Currently, many universities are administering development contracts under the same institutional structures and processes as research grants. Modification of existing systems are necessary to respond more adequately to unique project implementation needs. This aspect of the donor project represents a relatively untouched area for needs assessment.

Summary. The international development situation to which needs assessment must respond is a complex environment in which there are conflicting needs and expectations. The fact that both developing nations and external donors must be viewed as active participants in the process creates a multidimensional situation. Each of these sectors consists of a myriad of levels, groups, and institutions, each having much to gain or lose from any needs assessment activity. This multidimensionality makes the design of participatory needs assessment imperative and at the same time difficult to achieve.

CHAPTER 13

Applications

LORNA MICHAEL BUTLER • ROBERT O. BUTLER

No single development program package has universal applicability. Similarly, no single research method has yet been developed that can be readily transferred from one setting to another. The problem of transfer is exacerbated, since most research methods evolve in Western settings.

Little attention and commitment has been given to adapting methods to non-Western conditions, particularly where agricultural development is concerned. In our experience, consultants are frequently given too little time to do the job. This often results in little or no involvement of host country nationals. This may be compounded by the extreme sociocultural distance between those carrying out the study and the people whose needs are being assessed. Users rarely conduct their own needs assessments.

With more than five decades of development experience behind us, it may be productive to examine our past mistakes and contributions. Vast amounts of data have been collected in developing nations, primarily

The authors wish to acknowledge, with appreciation, the valuable contributions of the following colleagues who critiqued, edited, and up-dated case study presentations: Nepal, *Gaun Sallah* — Dr. Donald A. Messerschmidt, Associate Professor, Department of Anthropology, Washington State University; Guatemala, The *Sondeo* — Dr. Peter E. Hildebrand, Professor, Food and Resource Economics Department, Institute of Food and Agricultural Sciences, University of Florida; Sudan, Farming Systems Research in North Kordofan — Tim Frankenberger, Department of Anthropology, University of Kentucky; Botswana, Local Institutions in Mopipi Communal First Development Area — Freddie Zufferey, Ministry of Local Government and Lands, Government of Botswana.

Our conclusions have been influenced by Robert Chambers (1983), and by personal communication with colleagues like Freddie Zufferey (Botswana), Malcolm O'Dell (Synergy International), Coleen Brown (Egypt), and Rick Bernstein (Michigan State University). We are also indebted to the many international development practitioners, both social and physical scientists, who took part in a 1985 Washington State University Department of Rural Sociology and Cooperative Extension Service study on "the roles of sociologists and anthropologists in farming systems research."

through censuses and surveys; little of this data has actually been applied to development planning. Only recently has the concept of needs assessment begun to penetrate development seminars and conferences, project papers, contracts, and plans of action. At last we are beginning to recognize the challenge of putting our skills to work on behalf of the people who need them most — the poor, the landless, migrant laborers, and other sectors of the Third World population whose voice is seldom heard.

There is often a socioeconomic gap between the civil servants or practitioners who staff a development program and the rural people who constitute the users. Even when we view ministry officials as clientele, a cultural gap probably still exists between this sector and the professionals who are responsible for identifying needs.

Under these circumstances, needs are hard to identify. Up until very recently, the sample survey has been the primary method used to obtain these data. In spite of the optimism expressed by Dillman in Chapter 11, the usefulness of survey methods in developing societies is far more controversial than in Western societies.

In other cultural settings we find that problems and needs are not easy to sort into predetermined categories. We are now more aware of the need to view problems holistically as users do, and this is not so easy when using structured formats. Rarely have we been able to utilize needs assessment data directly. They usually have to be interpreted for use by decision makers. This has some limitations, especially in relation to technical information. We cannot expect people to know about things they have not experienced.

Techniques that are effective in this country may not work where people are accustomed to different analytical styles. Rank ordering, for example, may not produce the desired outcomes. In Malawi, a village extension worker was asked to give us a ranked list of job-related problems that should be considered in making her job easier. Her response was, "If you have nothing, and someone offers you a choice of either a car, a house, some cattle, or a trip to the city, what can you say? It is like being offered an ox-cart when you have no oxen."

The one thing we have learned, regardless of setting, is that people's priorities of need change over time. This makes it extremely important to select methods that can monitor changing perspectives and can anticipate future acceptance and long-term sustainability.

Most development planners and administrators now agree that assessment of needs can contribute to program design and implementation. However, there is little consensus on how much investment there should be in needs assessment and to what degree these data can really contribute to ongoing program decisions. While there is little agreement on the best methods to assess needs, there are some definite trends toward which leaders in the profession are moving. These directions, as summarized in Chapter 14, have evolved from lessons learned in overseas agricultural and community development beginning around the 1950s.

Generally, there seems to be increased acknowledgment of the need to emphasize human resource development in the process. This means designing methods that enhance human capabilities. Political analysis is also being used more often. There is increasing recognition that people everywhere want to participate in controlling their own futures. Methods are leaning more in a holistic direction, integrating subjects that people naturally associate together. Not so long ago, social organization research was conducted in isolation from crops research or marketing research. Now they are coming together.

Methods are becoming less rigid and exhaustive and more time efficient than in the past. There is more commitment to reducing bias against the poor and others normally excluded from development processes (Chambers 1981a, b).

While this may seem remote to those of us affiliated with more authoritarian and traditional organizations, there are certain "reversals in learning" and in management that are being given increasing recognition. These are clearly articulated by Chambers (1983:201–15).

Reversal in learning refers to the need to learn directly from the people we are trying to help. Simultaneously, we must devise methods that enable professionals to experience the world as the clientele see it. Chambers (1983:202–9) suggests six ways of learning from our clientele, which is essentially what needs assessment is all about, although sometimes we forget who the teachers really are: (1) sitting, asking, and listening; (2) learning from the poorest; (3) learning indigenous technical knowledge; (4) joint research and development involving farmers, family members, and scientists collaboratively; (5) learning by physically working alongside farmers or other clientele; and (6) using simulation games to train rural development professionals.

Reversals in learning depend on complementary organizational support, or "reversals in management." Chambers (1983:212–15) suggests we start by changing our styles of communication to facilitate more joint planning and involvement of subordinates or clientele. Organizational policies may also need review to provide needed field worker support. Stability and service are most needed in rural areas. The third management reversal seems to be the key to the entire issue. It involves decentralization, or shifting power to the clientele to assure empowerment of the local people.

We are also more conscious than ever of the need to balance identified needs with the realities of long-term sustainability, meaning that data on needs must be integrated with technical expertise and a sound understanding of the country. For example, the very best needs assessment may be a total waste if not in tune with available management capacity and financial support.

Past development programs were frequently based on inadequate predictions of technical feasibility and their suitability to small farm conditions. They suffered from limited knowledge of the sociocultural and institutional environment in which they were to be implemented. Future development must not only reach a mass of low-income people but also contribute to the viability of their development through improving local people's planning and implementing capacities (Lele 1975:175–92).

This chapter describes recent needs assessment trends that are bringing a note of optimism to the field. They are described within three broad categories: group, individual, and integrated approaches. Each category includes a description of the method, a synopsis of strengths and weaknesses, and several case studies that illustrate application of the method. In reviewing these examples, we critique the way in which the methods meet some of the unique problems of international development.

Essentially, we are advocating needs assessment decentralization — in planning, deciding, doing, evaluating. As local people are given the opportunity to practice the skills necessary to assume these and other responsibilities, our programs will take on new meaning. They may even begin to meet people's needs.

Group approaches

DESCRIPTION OF METHOD. Group organizational approaches, particularly at the local level, are critical rural development mechanisms. Individual citizens, especially those who are poor or landless, are powerless without organizations to provide services, to express needs, or to communicate problems to higher levels. Groups can activate the potentials of people, giving them an entrée into the system, thus enabling them to take control over their own lives (Uphoff and Esman 1974; Uphoff et al. 1979).

Needs assessment is an ideal type of responsibility for local organizations to assume in that it can meet several development-related objectives. In particular, it provides a mechanism for capacity strengthening. It also is an effective way to obtain valid data about local people's needs and concerns by involving them directly in the process. Needs assessment groups can also be formed through natural or informal groups, for example, extended family or other existing social groupings such as neighborhood groups, work or labor exchange groups, and age-mate or religious groups. New groups can be formed. It is better, however, to begin by identifying existing groups or organizations. If the purposes of the needs assessment can be accomplished by working through existing groups that are understood by local people, this is probably the best approach (for an excellent analysis of international research findings on this subject, see Esman and Uphoff 1984).

There are a number of ways a group can assume major responsibility for needs assessment. Most methods involve a semistructured approach in which individual ideas or opinions are gathered or combined to do some or all of the following: describe the current situation, clarify problems, generate solutions to problems, analyze consequences of alternative solutions, recommend actions, plan action strategies, evaluate actions. The more responsibility a group assumes, the more the process is likely to enhance member capabilities. Techniques that can be used are discussed below.

Focus groups or panels. The group, or part of the group, serves as a source of information about selected local behaviors or practices, problems, impacts of recommendations, or policies. Participants are selected because of their knowledge of the subject and their ability and willingness to discuss the topic. The purpose of the group is to focus on and provide information about one topic on which they are well informed. The group may also arrange for involvement of other groups in needs assessment. In some cases, the group assumes primary responsibility for design, implementation, analysis, and follow-up of a community or group survey.

Team ethnography. Ethnographic interviewing in the anthropological sense usually involves key informants in long-term interaction with an investigator. Team ethnography replaces the single investigator with an interdisciplinary or "mixed interest" team, as in the Guatemalan *sondeo* (Hildebrand 1981:425–32), which is used to understand limited-resource farming systems or the "interdisciplinary post-harvest team" piloted at the International Potato Center in Peru (Rhoades and Booth 1981). The approach is distinguished by ongoing intensive dialoguing among team members. The entire team becomes totally immersed in the problem-solving process.

Participatory action research. Different sectors of the population collectively conduct their own research and initiate actions. The process opens channels of communication among administrators, researchers, and local residents. It facilitates collective participation. It is a learning process in which a role reversal occurs between those with and without formal education (Hall 1975; Swantz 1975; Fals-Borda 1981). Participatory action research has evolved largely in response to Third World nations' growing dissatisfaction with survey research. Followers of the approach see survey research as an oppressive and alienating methodology inconsistent with principles of human learning and development (Fals-Borda 1981:58). The real issue in participatory action research is political power, which is manifested at the village level. Those who are committed to it identify with the following set of rural development values: equality of access to economic resources; equal rights for all (political, social, cultural); participation of clientele in all social decision making (work, welfare, politics); and the end of the separation between mental and manual labor and the use of technology appropriate for this purpose (Wignaraja 1984). To be compatible with this long-term process of structural and cultural change, needs assessment may only be a small effort initiated by committed individuals and groups. Central to the process is the concept of multiplication through training of catalysts or vanguard groups.

Citizen advisory groups or task forces. Advisory groups or task forces are not unique to international needs assessment. This method of involving citizens in planning and doing has been practiced with varying degrees of success worldwide. An advisory group or task force can be formed for many purposes—to serve as a voice for the community or organization, generate information, define policy or establish criteria, offer advice, or carry out specific tasks. The purpose of the advisory group or task force should be clear and limited in scope and duration. Too many responsibilities may confuse group members, thereby lowering the quality of the outcome. Group members are most productive when they know the beginning and ending of their responsibilities. The greatest danger with advisory groups and task forces is in their loss of purpose and, as a result, the participants' ultimate loss of interest. Productivity can be enhanced by a reward system.

STRENGTHS AND LIMITATIONS. Each technique has obvious strengths and limitations depending on application. In general, group involvement brings researchers closer to subjects, and there is considerable potential for two-way communication. Researchers concerned about rigor and objectivity may experience some frustration with this approach, since the data may reflect the most vocal group members and there is less opportunity for control. Major strengths and limitations of the group approach are outlined in Table 13.1.

CASE STUDY APPLICATIONS

Nepal—gaun sallah *or "village dialogue".* The *gaun sallah* or "village dialogue" approach to local needs assessment and planning builds upon Nepal's local level Panchayat government system and current efforts toward decentralization (Messerschmidt 1983, 1984). Although originally implemented for

TABLE 13.1.   Strengths and limitations of the group approach

Strengths	Limitations
Facilitates local participation	Does not provide quantitative data
Facilitates input from people who may not normally participate in the development process	Not generalizable to larger population
	Requires a skilled leader, "catalyst," or "broker"
Strengthens communication among/between investigators and subjects	May take considerable time to develop group leadership and participatory skills before actual data collection can begin
Can bridge cultural barriers	
Motivates involvement and enthusiasm	May not provide realistic linkages to macro-setting
Stimulates creative group energy	
Provides a more accurate picture of local situations, group processes, and social relationships	Harder to implement among larger groups (over 15 to 20), especially if heterogeneous in composition
Can be low cost	Assertive personalities can dominate
Generates data quickly	May raise participant expectations unrealistically
Builds leadership skills and organizational capacity	Can be sidetracked with extraneous information
Links data to action	
Provides qualitative data	

national resource development, the approach has been adapted for use in population, health, and appropriate energy and watershed planning. Internationally, the strategy has been adopted by the Centre for Integrated Rural Development for Asia and the Pacific, headquartered in Bangladesh. This is an 11-nation rural and agricultural development program throughout South and Southeast Asia.

Gaun sallah represents a continuum of flexible steps to needs assessment and planning subject to available resources and project demands. It is essentially a strategy for assuring villager and user group participation in local, project, and regional planning and development. It combines resource assessment with planning, thereby speeding up the entire process and making it more meaningful at all levels. It is a comprehensive strategy, following the style of rapid rural appraisal (discussed later), which works best in partnership with local extension education and training. Underlying this is the assumption that the more you can train local people to assume their own responsibilities, the less will be the need for outside support and involvement.

Egypt—Basaisa village project. Basaisa is a rural community in the Nile delta. A participatory action research project began to emerge in 1970. Objectives for the project are (1) learning how to use available resources to improve quality of life in ways that residents themselves determine; (2) promoting local innovations to meet energy demands, reduce drudge labor, and stimulate income-generating activities, especially among women; (3) monitoring impacts; and (4) providing a transferable model (Nelson and Arafa 1982).

The project began when student volunteers, researchers, and village young people initiated an informal training program. They began by teaching Arabic literacy, carpentry, and children's play activities. Local problems and needs were identified concurrently. Initially, small action projects were identified.

Expressed needs of villagers are addressed through training and service activities. These are structured to develop an awareness of the potentials of collective action. Data collection methodologies such as ethnographic surveys, genealogies, and key informant interviews are integrated with action and research activities through idea-generating discussions with villagers. This group discussion element seems to be the key to the project's success.

Project emphasis has now shifted to strengthening the community's organizational infrastructure and transferring the model to neighboring villages. Linkages have expanded to organizations beyond the village. Economic and social development has been stimulated through community participation in idea generation, planning, identification of potential impacts, assessment of responsibilities, and documentation of outcomes (Arafa and Nelson 1982:2–3).

Guatemala—the **sondeo.** The *sondeo* is a spanish term meaning to sound out. It is a rapid reconnaissance survey approach originally developed by the International Science and Technology Institute in Guatemala in response to budget and time limitations. It is an interdisciplinary team approach designed to acquaint agricultural technicians with the area in which they are going to work. The team uses the *sondeo* to define the existing farm production system; it consists of agronomic and socioeconomic representatives. The team's goal is to generate, through on-farm and research station experiments, acceptable improvements to existing production systems. The *sondeo,* therefore, provides direction to the first year of work (Hildebrand 1981).

The *sondeo* is a rapid method of obtaining qualitative information. Its strength is in its timeliness, low cost, and holistic orientation. Team members jointly interview local people, explore the area, make observations, discuss findings, and reach agreements about the farming system of the region and possible methods of improvement. Questionnaires are not used and writing is kept to a minimum.

The *sondeo* approach makes several assumptions. One is that the team has previously familiarized itself with the area through "windshield surveys," walking visits, review of maps and reports, and talking to informants. It also assumes that the team knows how to conduct ethnographic or informal interviews and has made some decisions among its members about critical things to observe. The more dialogue that occurs among team members and between the team and farm family members, the higher the quality of data produced. Ideally, farmers or other farm family members should be perceived as team members.

In our experience the *sondeo* approach can be adapted in a variety of ways for either overseas or domestic needs assessment. In Washington we have used it to identify county extension program priorities, to identify alternative strategies for strengthening a well-developed county 4-H youth program, and to define areas of potential technological improvement in a Southeast Asian refugee farm project. In Jordan it has helped establish extension and research staff training needs. It is an effective tool for citizen involvement, team building, collaborative problem solving, and enhancing field staff program development skills.

The success of the *sondeo* seems to rest with the ability of the team to understand and integrate three basic social science field methods: the ethnographic interview, key informant approach, and team or group consensus. While it requires some time commitment from those involved (a minimum of one week to a maximum of three weeks), it generally enhances the two-way communication between the clientele and professionals and generates problem solutions that are acceptable to local people. Most importantly, the broad participation it fosters usually helps to legitimize activities in the community and build local ownership.

CONCLUDING OBSERVATIONS. For many needs assessment practitioners, group action represents the central process in linking the learning process to sustainable development. Nonformal education becomes an empowering process that allows individuals through joint planning and action to exercise more control over decisions, resources, and institutions that affect their lives. As a needs assessment tool, it goes beyond generating data. It links data to action.

While individual and group approaches share common elements, the differences make their applications uniquely appropriate to varying situations. Both require a high level of rapport between the party or parties acting as interviewer and the party or parties acting as interviewee. The way questions are presented and sequenced is also a consideration in both. Depending on how participants in the process are selected, both approaches are vulnerable to problems of validity and bias, although the group approach offers more potential for immediate adaptation to unique cultural conditions.

However, assessment of needs through group approaches seems to involve a broader range of personal risks than the use of individual approaches. Practitioners need flexibility to work with a broad range of people and a degree of openness to the possibility that academic traditions may not be acceptable. The interpersonal dialogue that accompanies collaborative group work comes only with commitment and intensive involvement together. For some it may require considerable training if the group does not achieve a fairly sophisticated level of interaction. Without this, the group approach can end up being a glorified set of individually distinct interviews.

Group participation is deeply rooted in many cultural traditions. If social scientists can first gain an understanding of customary patterns of social organization, this can lead to a highly acceptable methodology with which people may already be comfortable.

Individual approaches

DESCRIPTION OF METHOD. Needs assessment information has been collected from individuals for a long time. In non-Western societies this has been done primarily by personal interview surveys. Mail and telephone surveys have been used very little. Many developing nations have enormous collections of survey data, some of which have never been analyzed or used. In almost every developing nation in which we have worked, there are stacks of unanalyzed forms on some ministry storeroom floor or table. This includes agroeconomic surveys in Malawi, censuses in Lesotho, agricultural statistics in the Middle East, and many more. Sometimes a foreign investigator initiates a study, departs at the end of the contract, and leaves the forms for nationals to analyze. The likelihood of continuing analysis is slim, particularly if nationals have not been fully involved in the study. Frequently, they have many other conflicting demands on their time and little access to clerical or computer help or have inadequate understanding of how the data could be productively used. There are also many examples of investigators who have collected vast amounts of information using local resources and then taken it home leaving nothing behind.

Individual-oriented methods generally involve a single interviewer asking a single respondent a set of questions. Surveys tend to use a predetermined set, whereas ethnographic interviews use a longer term, more intensive probing approach that combines more informal "dialoguing" with questions. Both extremes can be modified depending on the type of data to be gathered. Surveys can be designed with open-ended questions, and ethnographic interviews can be focused or combined with systematic quantitative observations. Needs assessment has been conducted using a variety of individual-oriented methods, three of which follow.

Population censuses. Censuses are individual enumerations, within a defined territory, of every household or unit. Tabulations are made of population characteristics and processes or other statistical information such as agriculture, labor, industry, housing, or health. Sometimes censuses exclude groups of people who are difficult to reach, such as nomads, migrants, or women. Censuses may be conducted with regularity, or years may go by before an enumeration is repeated. Censuses have some of the same implementation problems as surveys. Recruitment, training, and supervision of enumerators is demanding because of the numbers involved and the need for coordination and consistency at every level. Because questionnaires are developed in advance, assuming homogeneity of respondents and context, some of the same validity problems arise as for surveys.

Sample surveys. Sample surveys are widely used because of their adaptability. They can be designed to meet cost and time demands and describe with reasonable accuracy the degree to which certain characteristics are likely to be found among the population as a whole. As Dillman notes in Chapter 11, survey technology has improved enormously. Although this is most evident in Western societies, the trends will gradually be felt in developing nations as well. The nine elements of success discussed by Dillman are important guidelines for survey work anywhere.

In the past decade, development projects or government survey units have conducted many sample surveys to describe the current situation, for example, in the form of regional agroeconomic surveys. Since this time many farm management studies have been confined to more manageable samples. This has resulted in more timely information. In the late 1970s many development projects initiated baseline surveys to establish monitoring and evaluation benchmark data for measuring project performance. Most of these generated a vast amount of data, much of which was not used. They consumed far more time and resources than is now considered practical.

Key informant interviews. This informal interview approach has long been the principle tool of anthropologists, particularly in cross-cultural situations. Combined with other field methods, it has enabled investigators to gain a deep understanding of people different from themselves. It is essentially a way of learning from people about the occurrence and meaning of activities, events, and behaviors in their daily lives.

The approach is dependent on a small number of local informants who are willing and able to talk about their way of life or community. Often, informants are trained to conceptualize the kind of data desired, and many become extremely skilled at analyzing their own situations. The strength of the method is based on the long-term relationship developed between the informants and the investigator, the informality that builds mutual trust and confidence, and the fact that it can be effectively combined with participant observation.

Although there are countless ways of applying the key informant method, there are few examples in which it has been applied to assessing needs in association with development projects. Informally, a good many project planners and evaluators rely on key informants for information, but these relationships are rarely maintained and nurtured on a continuing basis as part of a systematic needs assessment.

STRENGTHS AND LIMITATIONS. Much has been written contrasting the qualities of surveys with ethnographic methodology (Bennett and Thaiss 1970; Gold 1977:102–7; Pelto and Pelto 1978:67–102). There are many ways by which each can be strengthened to obtain better quality data.

The misuse of survey methods in international development work has been a major concern, particularly because the technique is used so extensively. The greatest problem lies with the strong Western or academic bias of standardized questionnaire formats. Frequently, surveys are implemented with little or no sensitivity to the cultural context of respondents.

Stone and Campbell (1984:32–34) present a convincing argument regarding the contextual bias of survey research. Respondents often avoid culturally sensitive topics. The researchers cross-checked data obtained from a family planning survey in Nepal only to learn that women who reported little knowledge of family planning actually were too embarrassed to discuss the subject. In Malawi we encountered a similar problem in trying to obtain accurate information about numbers of children that had died, women's involvement in secret societies, and women's roles in national political activities. We countered this problem by building long-term relationships with local informants and obtained the needed information over a longer period.

Some topics are not easily explained by predetermined response categories. In several instances, this has been evident in trying to identify extended family member relationships, methods of crop cultivation or harvest, and actual responsibilities of different family members. The survey's dependency on single-context data clearly casts doubt on the validity of the technique in non-Western settings.

The major strengths and limitations of individual approaches are summarized in Table 13.2. The sample survey and key informant interview methods are identified because these two seem to hold the greatest integrative potential for international development. This may not be easily accomplished, however, since the two are distinctly different. They make very different assumptions about the entire research process.

CASE STUDY APPLICATIONS

Lesotho—Farming Systems Research Project baseline survey. The Lesotho Farming Systems Research Project (FSRP) was initiated in 1979. The project was required to conduct technical, economic and social, and subsequent base-

TABLE 13.2. Strengths and limitations of individual approaches

Strengths	Limitations
Sample survey	
Is generalizable to large populations	Sample must be carefully selected to ensure statistical meaning
Provides wide range of information about population characteristics	Is subject to problems of contextual validity
Can be statistically analyzed	Needs ample time and skills to design instrument, train interviewers, analyze results
Provides confidentiality	Difficult to design culturally sensitive instrument
Can be conducted by nonacademics	
Provides low-cost method to describe total population	Requires resources for typing, printing, and duplicating
Is adaptable to available resources	Requires skilled analysis personnel (and sometimes equipment that is not available)
Is adaptable to different types of problems	
May be effectively combined with other methods	Size of study can easily get out of hand, thereby sacrificing short-term contributions
	Difficult to develop rapport between subject and interviewer, so depth of insight may be limited
	Recall data is open to question
	Based on one time perspective
	Time is not available to convince some respondents to participate
	Individual questioning may not be culturally compatible in a communal or group-oriented society
	Academic bias exists in constructing the instrument
Key informant interview	
Builds trust between investigator and informant	Closeness between investigator and informant can result in data bias
Provides deep understanding of problems, causes, reasons, behaviors	Time is needed to find informants and build trust
Permits continual clarification and review of information	Biases of informants and investigator may exist
Is effectively combined with other methods	Community members that are not selected as informants may feel excluded
Encourages input from people who might not normally participate in single-session interview	There is difficulty in quantifying data
	Is not generalizable to the total population
There is no high-cost printing or statistical analysis	Informants' perspectives may not represent everyone's perspectives
Is responsive to cultural context	There is potential for extraneous information

line surveys in the three ecological areas of project implementation. In July 1980 a baseline survey was initiated. Previous to this the project team had inventoried and mapped prototype areas and villages as well as conducting informal observations and farmer discussions. The purposes of the baseline survey were to (1) provide a quantifiable description of farming practices, (2) provide a description of the population, (3) identify production constraints, (4) identify better methods of providing agricultural technical information to farmers, (5) create on-the-job training in field methods, and (6) increase farmer involvement in and understanding of the project (Butler 1982).

Baseline surveys tend to generate a vast amount of information about a wide variety of topics, and they cover wide geographical areas. These factors hint at some of the potential pitfalls to which we fall prey when we initiate a baseline survey. Conlin (1979) takes a hard look at some of the very real problems of baseline surveys and, for the most part, the observations are accurate. The baseline survey process usually provides no continuous analysis of data; therefore, early planning opportunities associated with preliminary observations are lost. Much of the data, especially concerning social relations, is not obtained through direct questioning. Many of the facts that a baseline survey produces could be much more quickly and accurately generated through other methods.

There may be circumstances when a baseline survey is justified, for example, when there is little or no existing information about an area. A baseline survey may be required to help evaluate project benefits. The baseline survey can serve a useful purpose in training staff in field methods and in giving staff firsthand experience in survey design, interviewer training methods, field supervision, and data analysis.

Other purposes of the FSRP baseline survey can be questioned. Probably too much was expected of this method. Other methods, such as key informant interviews, diary keeping, or the *sondeo* might have been used to greater advantage.

In retrospect it would probably have been better to begin with a *sondeo* involving a few of the available Lesotho nationals, some local volunteers, and some of the American team members. This would have quickly generated early planning information. This did not happen in Lesotho. Team members representing different disciplines tended to do their own exploratory surveys, occasionally in cooperation with other colleagues. As a result the merging of these findings into a systems model never really took place.

The Lesotho baseline survey was implemented through five steps:

1. Village and household inventory. The Ministry of Agriculture Research Division rural sociology staff listed every village, chief, and house-

hold. Project field sites were located 2 to 10 hours' drive from headquarters over rugged terrain. Close to 3000 households were contacted for the original sample list.

2. Instrument development. The FSRP team represented eight different disciplines. At different periods each discipline had one or more national counterparts, but the availability of national staff was irregular and unpredictable. Team members collaborated to identify priority data needs. The rural sociology unit assumed the primary role for instrument development and survey implementation, although at different points other disciplines contributed. It took about two and one half months to develop an instrument for pretesting. Final revisions were not complete until a "training of trainers" course was conducted. This took place five months from the time the survey was initiated. Both the instrument and a field manual were developed in Sesotho, the local language.

3. Training of trainers. A seven-day course was held for research division trainers on how to implement the survey and train village interviewers for data collection. Trainers eventually designed and taught a comparable course for village interviewers in each prototype area. The total sample drawn during the course consisted of 461 households with a total of 441 questionnaires analyzed.

4. Data collection. Village interviewers were recruited for a training course in each area. The course was taught by research division trainers in Sesotho. Training and data collection took about three months.

5. Data analysis. Original plans were to have all data preparation and analysis done in Lesotho. The government of Lesotho has computer facilities. However, a scarcity of personnel and other difficulties prevented the use of this option. Questionnaire coding was done by research division staff. However, all data were analyzed at Washington State University.

The Lesotho baseline survey not only was difficult to analyze under local conditions, but the amount of time required for this process (almost one year) added to the improbability that the information will ever be put to effective use. The entire process of survey design, training, implementation and analysis consumed approximately 21 months and an excessive amount of staff time. Most of the potential for data use was also diminished by project staff turnover before data analysis was complete.

Major potentials and limitations of the baseline survey are outlined in Table 13.2. The greatest difficulties in utilizing this technique in non-Western settings are associated with complex research conditions. Normally, there are difficulties associated with cross-cultural communication. These are accentuated when implementing a survey of any kind. Some cultures are group oriented and therefore uncomfortable in answering individually.

A survey requires more rapport and trust building in a cross-cultural setting than is probably practical. Local resource limitations also cause major difficulties, for example, availability of local staff, typing and printing facilities, transportation.

If a baseline survey seems to be an important needs assessment tool, it will be more helpful to development projects if the following prevail:

1. Purposes and length are limited.
2. It is focused on one population, production subsystem, or problem area.
3. Responsibilities are assumed by a committed interdisciplinary steering committee rather than a single discipline.
4. Organizers have a strong background in local languages and cultures.
5. It is combined with other methods, such as a group approach.
6. It can be postponed until early project visibility and support have been attained.

Malawi—the indigenous team and life history collection. During 1974–1975 Butler (1976) conducted a needs assessment in Malawi based on a modified version of the key informant interview technique. The method was dependent on the collaborative involvement of an indigenous investigator team that worked over a 14-month period with 12 village informants. They applied participant observation and the life history method (Langness 1965) to analysis of rural women's roles in the *Chewa* agrarian system. This information was applied to the improvement of the agriculture diploma and degree curricula at Bunda College of Agriculture. A description of the study in four interrelated phases follows:

1. Team training. The investigator team (four people) was trained and guided in ethnographic field methods throughout the research period. This includes discussions with local leaders, local farmers, young people, agricultural technicians, and college staff. This built team skills, ideas about needed data, a commitment to the problem, and a consensus about field responsibilities and methods of operating. A discussion outline guided data to be collected about life history phases from one informant visit to the next. Analyses of informant visits and preparations for coming visits became regular training-learning opportunities.
2. Key informant selection. College students conducted a population census of the villages included in the study. Names of potential informants were pulled from this list. Informants were self-designated female household heads as a result of the existing matrilineal tradition and the extensive

male labor migration. Selection was also based on age and stage in the family life cycle. After discussions with this preliminary group, 12 informants were finally selected.

3. Life history collection. Team members worked in pairs, occasionally changing partners and informants. Individual life histories were the organizing theme for discussions. Sixteen different life history focuses evolved over time. As many as four different visits took place to get complete coverage of each. These were not predetermined phases, but to the team they each seemed the logical next step. The team also recorded observations of daily activities of informants and family members. They also took part in some of these activities, for example, seed sorting, weeding, harvesting, and water carrying. Attention was directed to agricultural and other subsistence activities.

4. Data analysis. Data analysis was initiated with the first informal discussions, and observations were made in the field. Analysis continued with team members and the author participating after every field visit. Notes were kept by the team and further refined in training sessions. Conclusions about what was heard and observed were based on group consensus.

Upon conclusion of the study, findings were tested on the investigator team and on others at the college. College students also conducted a comparable microstudy with different informants. This helped to test the validity of the findings. Recommendations from the study were incorporated into curricula changes.

CONCLUDING OBSERVATIONS. There are many ways to adapt individual approaches to the needs of development programs. For example, interviews can be conducted by well-trained local people who speak the same language and know the situation. Smaller samples can be used and respondents can be visited more than once. Observations can be substituted for recall questions. Questions can be constructed in culturally meaningful ways, for example, using local examples, terms, and methods of description. Local people can be involved in design of instruments, sample selection, interview discussions, data collection, and interpretation of findings.

Individual methods of assessing needs will probably always be an essential part of needs assessment in development. The value of the approach lies with our ability to get closer to respondents. Frequently, this means taking more time to build trust and confidence. We think it also means making a major commitment to learn about the cultural context before any methodology is identified, then maintaining a continual check on whether the methodology remains in tune with the cultural context.

Indications are that the survey's more structured format is less compatible with the needs of non-Western societies. However, the demands of development projects still necessitate that we learn how to modify this technique to make it more culturally sensitive and responsive to the needs of decision makers. It seems helpful to integrate it with shorter term, more focused ethnographic approaches. Both methods, in partnership, can provide extremely valuable insights to project planners and technicians if information is timely, useful, and cost efficient. Above all, local people should be active participants in the process.

Integrated approaches

DESCRIPTION OF METHOD. If social science research is to genuinely assist the goals of development, there must be more effective integration of people, methods, and disciplines. We are probably closer to accomplishing this ideal than ever before. Social scientists are facing an exciting and challenging opportunity in development work if they will rise to the responsibility.

Current international development efforts are largely directed to generation and transfer of food production technologies. There is an increasing number of opportunities for social scientists to collaborate with biological scientists in resolving production problems. Unfortunately, many biological scientists are not impressed with our lack of precision, slow turnaround of survey data, and inability to adapt methods to short-run planning problems.

We also have trouble modifying research methods to meet practical project needs. Part of the difficulty lies with the narrowness of individual social science disciplines. Each, in reality, must be able to cross over in alliance with other social science methods, for example, ethnographic methods with survey methods or group learning methods. In addition, there must be linkages with the methods of agronomists, range ecologists, and animal scientists. Too many early diagnostic studies and baseline surveys are done by social scientists alone and the results conveyed to physical scientists when the field work is over. The two should be in the field together from beginning to end. There is also a tendency to view research methods as single-purpose endeavors. Research methods can be tools for training others and involving others in understanding their own problems. If we take these concerns seriously, perhaps we can change some of the existing stereotypes that nonsocial scientists have of social scientists' contributions.

Since the 1970s there has been an increasing level of interest in a development model that draws on principles from agronomy, cultural ecology, community development, extension, farm management economics, and other academic areas. The concept is not new but has evolved in various parts of the world as a result of isolated individual field work (see Fresco 1984 for a preliminary discussion of European contributions). The concept is farming systems research, also referred to as farming systems research and extension (FRS/E), farming systems research and development, or adaptive on-farm research. It is an interdisciplinary approach to problem solving that is intended to strengthen the partnership between small-scale farmers and biological and social scientists. It has been widely tested in Central America, Africa, and Asia. Now there appears to be a growing consensus among development organizations, developing nations, and academics that the concept holds considerable promise for meeting practical development objectives and for integration of disciplines in response to needs (e.g., see Gilbert et al. 1980; Norman 1980, 1982; Shaner et al. 1982; Collinson 1984).

The section that follows describes the FSR concept and several related techniques that seem to hold potential for needs assessment work in non-Western societies and hard-to-reach communities everywhere. Rural and minority communities in all parts of the world suffer from similar problems of limited resources and an inability to make themselves heard in the development process.

Farming systems research and extension. Research in farming systems focuses on the small-scale farm family, its resources, and the interrelationships among resources and family goals. The assumption is that farm and household decisions are intimately linked. A particular farming system evolves through decisions made by the family with respect to available resources and its own goals.

The primary aim of farming systems research and extension is to increase farm productivity in ways that are useful and acceptable to small-scale farm families. This is made operational by increasing the level of farmer participation in problem identification, searching for solutions, generating simple improvements in current technologies, and assessing the usefulness of these improvements.

Proponents of FSR/E contend that experiment station research has been top-down and commodity oriented, therefore generating fewer benefits to small-scale farmers compared to larger commercial farmers. FSR/E, therefore, begins with an interdisciplinary team that learns from the farmer about the existing farming system.

If we examine the Anglophone approach to FSR/E, four interrelated research phases are identified. Each can be strengthened by social science methods. The phases are descriptive or diagnostic, design, on-station and on-farm testing and monitoring, and extension of findings. At each phase, involvement of the farmer and the family is central. The *sondeo,* discussed earlier (or an informal exploratory survey), is an approach that has been successfully used in the descriptive or diagnostic phase.

In other phases we need to consider adapting various sociological and anthropological field methods. For example, key informants can be helpful for identifying appropriate sites for on-farm research and improving extension methods for disseminating findings. Informants can also contribute to the evaluation of improved technologies. The sample survey method may be important in predicting the acceptability of specific technology changes or examining areas of economic feasibility. Group methods are already proving useful in early project legitimization, verification of findings, and problem diagnosis. They can also contribute to the quick assessment of the potential for adoption and methods of adapting experiments to meet local needs.

Rapid rural appraisal (RRA). Development practitioners have been focusing attention on a set of strategies that are complementary to FSR/E. While they may have different labels and applications, their very existence represents a move in the right direction. An indication of the trend toward integration of techniques and concepts is evidenced by Beebe's (1985) paper, one of several fugitive publications available to help the practitioner with implementation of RRA. (See also Byerlee et al. 1980; Rhoades 1982; and Shaner et al. 1982:72–83, 278–318.) A series of provocative papers was generated as a result of several conferences on RRA in 1978 and 1979 at the Institute of Development Studies, University of Sussex. Since then we have heard such terms as "rapid rural appraisal," "rapid reconnaissance," "exploratory survey," and *sondeo* (e.g., see Chambers 1980; Hildebrand 1981; Longhurst 1981).

All these approaches mark the beginning of a very promising movement that is bringing disciplines and methods closer together. Appraisal in the RRA sense includes all areas where data are collected and analyzed to assist development decision making, including monitoring and evaluation of development alternatives. While the approach is not a panacea, it suggests ways of spending less time on data collection and more on learning about and from the clientele, particularly the poor or others frequently overlooked by development processes.

Chambers (1980:35) contends that RRA may be the key to overcoming the endemic problems surrounding the shortage of time, which shut the poorer people out. More time could be used to involve them in the needs assessment process. RRA methods stem from the difficulty that all development planners face. How do you obtain accurate and relevant information about the clientele? How do you do this in cost- and time-efficient ways so that the information will be available when needed? At the same time, how do you take advantage of local knowledge, particularly from people not normally considered in appraisals?

RRA methods balance the trade-offs between the costs of achieving greater accuracy in relation to the amount of data that will probably be used. For example, can we justify spending excessive time on sampling, developing detailed questionnaires, and interviewing large samples of respondents if the data obtained may not direct an immediate application to the problems of rural people? Particular RRA techniques that have been found effectual are use of (1) unobtrusive indicators to assess the relative socioeconomic level of people; (2) key informants who know the clientele well; and (3) games, role-playing, and group methods in team and staff training and with clientele (Chambers 1980:33–40).

STRENGTHS AND LIMITATIONS. The strengths and limitations of integrated approaches (see Table 13.3) need to be assessed within the context of application. Each technique should reinforce the others with which it is used. The total approach is the ultimate concern. Do the compromises made in modifying individual methods justify the overall benefits? It may be difficult to objectively assess these trade-offs if there is strong disciplinary identity with the specific parts; however, usually if an interdisciplinary team struggles together with data collection, design, and implementation, team members seem inclined to bury their various academic alliances. This seems to be a sign that the integrated approach is really beginning to work.

TABLE 13.3. Strengths and limitations of integrated approaches

Strengths	Limitations
Facilitates a systems or holistic perspective	Can threaten team members if they perceive their discipline is not appreciated or needed
Facilitates involvement of clientele	
Provides greater assurance that the clientele's situation will be seen from that perspective rather than from a component perspective	Start-up time may be slow
	Scientists used to rigor and tight control of variables may be frustrated by a less structured approach
Develops understanding among all individuals or groups involved	
Offers flexibility to meet practical demands	Requires detailed organization at every phase and level
Provides a more accurate picture	Can be subject to overambition
Improves communication among clientele, scientists, and practitioners	Some disciplinary representatives may never understand or appreciate colleagues' conceptual backgrounds or the collaborative mode of operation
Responsiveness to cultural context offers potential for validity	
Strengths of one method can supplement weaknesses of another—can optimize the best of all worlds	Requires that time be committed for training and continuous planning
Training and continuous planning are effectively integrated	

CASE STUDY APPLICATIONS

Sudan—farming systems research in North Kordofan. The University of Kentucky International Sorghum and Millet Socioeconomic Project is analyzing the farming system of the el-Obeid region of North Kordofan. Specific objectives of the project are to identify socioeconomic constraints impeding agricultural production, distribution, and consumption of millet and sorghum and to provide baseline data on traditional agriculturalists in the area. The study was carried out by two American applied economic anthropologists, two Sudanese graduate students in anthropology and geography, and a Regional Ministry of Agriculture home economist over a 15-month period. Collaborative input was also received from two agronomists and two agricultural economists.

Research operations began in July 1981 with a village survey followed by the following studies:

1. Initial village study. Eighteen villages were analyzed over a two-month period to obtain a comprehensive picture of the village society and economy. The informal group interview method was used.

2. Ethnographic study of agriculture production and the household economy. Intensive village ethnographies were carried out to facilitate design of a survey instrument for later use. This included 5 to 15 families from a total of three villages. Village population ranged from 500 to 3000 people. Data were generated on such things as farming practices, crop growth stages, staple food supplies, and decision making. Data on cultivated landholdings were obtained from all farmers. This was accomplished through local leader legitimization and the use of films and slides to entertain farmers during data collection.

3. Ethnographic and documentary study of markets. A six- to eight-month marketing system study was carried out, using tax receipt records for sales, ethnographic interviews, and observations. This included a biweekly survey of cereal grain prices; interviews with merchants, vendors, clerks, and farmers during marketing season; and village shop stock inventorying and monitoring. A total of 58 merchants were interviewed, representing 50 percent of all merchants. Questions on marketing were also included in a farming system survey (see below).

4. Farming system survey. A preliminary farming system survey or pretest of 40 farmers was conducted. This sample was randomly selected from the earlier study of cultivated landholdings. The original household list was compiled by obtaining the government's "sugar list," which lists every household for the purpose of providing monthly sugar rations at discount prices. Following the pretest, the survey was administered to another sample of 166 farmers, representing 12 villages.

Findings of the North Kordofan study described farmers' methods of dealing with production constraints and proposed recommendations for alleviating them. Their approaches clearly illustrated the value of a diverse set of methods for generating a vast amount of insight into one area's farming system. Small samples and intensive approaches reaped high pay-offs (Reeves and Frankenberger 1981, 1982).

Since completion of the first phase of this study, the field assessment has continued. A University of Kentucky interdisciplinary team, consisting of two sociologists and an agronomist, has been investigating the farmer networks of information transfer. This phase of field work has been able to build on the earlier findings and on the personal relationships already established in some of the villages.

The strength of this FSR/E case study has been in its ability to build from one level of data to the next, using preliminary data to support later studies. Traditional survey and ethnographic methodology have been modified so that each contributes more to the whole than to a part. According to Frankenberger (1984), during the early ethnographic or reconnaissance survey, "We let the farmers take the lead on the information given. . . . By the last village we knew the system so well. The 'snowball effect' ultimately allowed verification in later villages, and multiplied the amount of information we learned."

In reflecting on methods used, the investigators would again opt for a combined methodology approach. Breadth obtained through field work in fewer villages is well worth the sacrifice of trying to cover more territory. Personal networks are firmly established, and information is constantly checked for validity. The investigators recommend that survey interviews be kept short and focused. Two and a half hours was excessively long. Ideally, data analysis should be done immediately in the field, meaning that the needs assessment design must be controlled to ensure that this is possible (Frankenberger 1984).

Primary field work problems encountered were similar to those found in many developing-country settings: vehicle maintenance, unavailability of fuel, time limitations, conflicts between cultural norms and expatriate expectations, physical illnesses of team members, difficult travel conditions, and institutional change.

In retrospect the investigators note the importance of cultivating critical power networks in advance. These will go a long way to ensure support for your work and fuel for your vehicle. We are also reassured by comments about the accuracy of intuitive guesses about findings. Policymakers need information continually, often before investigators feel it should be released. In this study, one of the investigators noted, "You shouldn't worry too much about intuitive guesses on findings. You're probably fairly accurate anyway. Decision makers need this information immediately. Give it to them" (Frankenberger 1984).

Botswana—local institutions in Mopipi communal first development area. A series of thirteen reports plus a *Handbook for Facilitators* for Botswana extension staff have been produced as a result of a project supported by the USAID Rural Sector Grant and the Cooperative Agreement between USAID and the University of Wisconsin Land Tenure Center. The needs assessment study under review here represents one of seven district institutional analyses carried out in Botswana in the early 1980s. Each was designed to support long-term development needs of the district; however, different methodologies were used in each setting. The Mopipi study took place in the Boteti subdistrict in the central district, which lies to the east of the Kalahari desert. This area is sparsely populated by slightly over 7000 people who are engaged in dryland and *molapo* (annually river flooded) farming, livestock production, fishing, subsistence hunting, and gravel extraction. Three villages were analyzed. Two were well established and one represented a relatively new settlement.

Objectives of the study were to identify traditional and modern institutions, analyze institutional potentials and constraints, recommend strategies for strengthening these institutions, and recommend means of enhancing productive employment. Research was conducted by a team of university students and a researcher employed by the University of Wisconsin Land Tenure Center but affiliated with the Applied Research Unit, Ministry of Local Government and Lands. A combination of methodologies was applied: personal interviews with community leaders, group interviews with key institutional committees, informal conversation, and a lot of participant observation. Students resided in the village throughout the duration of the study. No sample survey took place, although a set of guidelines for collection of field data was developed.

Fieldwork was preceded by inventorying and mapping activities. This contributed to the identification of development areas (Communal First Development Areas, or CFDAs). As a result, Mopipi was identified as one of these areas. The Mopipi CFDA needs assessment is based on four underlying beliefs (Zufferey 1984):

1. Rural dwellers possess a vast informal knowledge of their environmental and socioeconomic conditions which (usually) remains untapped (if not positively discarded) by most research. The common myth that "everything must be researched for these poor people" (because they obviously

know nothing) not only is very paternalistic but scientifically *dépassé*.

2. The development process at the grass roots level encompasses virtually all walks of life, in which one component cannot easily be dissociated from the other or the modification of one may equally affect all the others. Therefore, a comprehensive approach is preferable to highly specialized (fragmented) research.

3. Involving rural dwellers as equal partners in generating and analyzing their own information develops a strong sense of confidence, mutual trust, and motivation to implementation.

4. Researchers involved in participatory processes should avoid sitting on the fence and watching, then dumping a report in the recipients' laps and leaving. They should become active participants and artisans of at least the initial implementation phase they recommend.

The research identified major problems in resource management, for example, access to arable land; quality of grazing; and management of water, wildlife, and fishery resources. Traditional institutional problems were found to be associated with ethnic diversity and lack of development-area integration. Modern village institutions were subject to attitude problems, inadequate understanding of objectives, isolated working conditions, staff illiteracy, and lack of training in such things as group skills. Extension problems were also identified as well as the problems of government institutions outside the specified communities.

Recommendations generally focused on four fundamental problems that might be addressed to strengthen local institutions: ethnic diversions and leadership competition; the process by which local institutions are created; the plurality and appropriateness of existing institutions; and the need for information, training, and group skills.

In a relatively short time, this study generated strategy recommendations to ease institutional constraints. In addition, several projects were suggested for enhancing local employment and income. The suggestions have very practical implications where local people's needs are concerned and are concisely presented for consideration by planners and administrators. Diverse people have been involved in the study beyond the researchers. This includes district staff, a core development area working group, village extension workers, community leaders, and others. The interdisciplinary team concept is an important integrating element in the design of the multidimensional strategy. The various data collection approaches are well suited to building community trust with many kinds of rural people, thus contributing to the identification of acceptable action strategies (Zufferey 1983).

The principal investigator notes, however, that desirable "is not sufficient to the successful implementation of rural development projects, however well tailored they may be to specific area residents" (Zufferey 1984). Rural development outcomes represent long-term expectations. To date, outcomes of the study have been disappointing to those involved. However, this situation is not necessarily tied to needs assessment approaches. In Mopipi the problem may be associated with institutional factors such as high staff turnover, shortage of staff, lack of integration between headquarters and district, and research project termination.

The situation raises a question that is a frequent concern when participatory processes are used to involve rural people in analyzing and resolving their own problems. Where should project support stop? When a survey methodology is used, publication and dissemination of findings usually bring closure to the project or phase. With an integrated approach, the best point for concluding project support may neither be evident nor easy to agree upon.

CONCLUDING OBSERVATIONS. What is it that ensures a concerted effort on the part of the practitioner to adopt a more integrated needs assessment approach? In our observations, practitioners who are committed to this field research philosophy hold certain beliefs and values that are compatible with putting others first.

If project administrators could develop mechanisms to screen team members for compatible belief systems, chances are that needs assessment methodologies would be more interdisciplinary and less bound by methodological rules. Data would be collected faster, and others would be taught to take responsibility for research and to involve laypeople in generating and analyzing their own data.

The successful application of integrated needs assessment approaches seems to be tied to professionals' beliefs in decentralization of resources and decision making. Even though practitioners may not be experienced in interdisciplinary work or in involving local people as partners in field research, if they possess beliefs that support this, practitioners will quickly respond to training and guidance in integrated needs assessment strategies. However, operationalizing these approaches is still very dependent on administrative and institutional support. It also seems to take a high level of disciplinary and personal confidence to operate in an interdisciplinary mode and to transfer decision making and management responsibilities to clientele.

Those of you who assume responsibility for the application of integrated strategies will find yourselves spending vast amounts of time smoothing the way at institutional and policy levels. This is time well spent. Consideration may need to be given to relocating well-trained staff to more remote villages rather than keeping them at headquarters and to providing incentives for nationals in village field work roles. More time may be needed for identifying and strengthening local resources and for allowing professionals to learn from village people. Analysis of problems should begin at the bottom, with village people analyzing their own resources, problems, goals, and priorities, not with professionals designing question-naires that have "codable response categories."

CHAPTER 14

Guidelines

LORNA MICHAEL BUTLER ● ROBERT O. BUTLER

THIS CHAPTER on the role of needs assessment in international development is essentially a summary statement. Our purpose is to draw on the contents of Chapters 12 and 13, extracting what we see as a set of guidelines or rules of thumb for the application of needs assessment in international development work. Many of these guidelines are applicable to any setting, domestic or international. However, there are certain unique conditions prevailing in developing nations that cause us to stress the extreme importance of these guidelines for practitioners involved with Third World development. Some of these unique conditions are summarized below.

Conditions unique to developing nations

NUMBER OF PEOPLE AFFECTED. The rural poor, by far the most prominent clientele represented, constitute a far greater number of affected people in developing nations than their counterparts in industrialized nations. The estimated number of people living in absolute poverty in developing nations is estimated to be between 680 and 780 million compared to approximately 100 to 115 million in developed areas. For developed areas (Europe, United States, Canada, Australia, New Zealand) this figure probably is in excess of actual numbers since "absolute poverty" does not exist to the same degree as in the developing world. In less developed countries this measure reflects the amount of income needed to ensure a minimum caloric intake. Other factors also account for absolute poverty, for example, access to health care, education, public sanitation, and transportation. Because some countries are less poor than others, poverty levels are not easily comparable (estimates are approximated based on Birdsall 1980; World Bank 1980; Population Reference Bureau 1982).

This factor is significant simply because of the sheer number of people whose lives are affected if we do a more effective job of identifying and meeting their development needs.

LIMITED PROJECT-TIME DURATION. Although development projects are projected over a longer time than in the past, those supported by USAID generally are contracted for five years. While they may be extended or redirected at the end of this period, they are often concluded or shifted into a holding pattern until bureaucratic policies and procedures are translated into the next phases. Sometimes indecision about continuation can consume project activities throughout the final one to two years of a project's life.

A high proportion of development aid is subject to the conditions surrounding limited project-time duration. While a project is being implemented, there may be ample resources to carry out needs assessments. However, when a project is over, resources stop. Staff that were once available to participate in field work may no longer be employed, transportation may be reallocated to another project, or a change in leadership may establish new priorities that do not include needs assessment. Therefore, the quality of needs assessment that is conducted before and during the life of a project is of substantial importance.

TENDENCY TOWARD AUTOCRATIC LEADERSHIP. There are many examples of situations in which aid projects fail because they have been designed and implemented in isolation from the clientele they are intended to benefit. This problem is exacerbated in developing countries because there is less tendency toward citizen or organizational involvement in planning and decision making.

Unlike in the United States, there are few affirmative action or citizen participation policies. Cultural patterns of leadership are frequently top-down, reinforced by centuries of tradition in which leadership to govern is often inherited or ascribed. Today, administrative and management styles in the Third World lean toward the autocratic as opposed to the democratic. This does not imply that there are no indigenously democratic organizations in developing nations.

There is, however, a tendency for outsiders to overlook these collective elements of traditional social organization, for example communal work groups, marketing and credit cooperatives, land management schemes, or other natural kin associations. In international development there is, therefore, a real opportunity for needs assessment to strengthen indigenous systems of public participation to ensure a more accurate assessment of peoples' needs that may easily be overlooked (e.g., see Chambers 1983).

CROSS-CULTURAL WORKING SITUATION. While practitioners may find themselves working among people whose cultures are different from their own in industrial nations, the likelihood of this occurring in a Third World nation is considerably higher. Even a national leading a needs assessment team in his or her own country is likely to encounter many different ethnic traditions and languages within close proximity.

Nigeria, for example, is inhabited by a large number of ethnic groups ranging in size from a few thousand to many million. Among them, several hundred languages are spoken. Even in a small country like Malawi, people who grow up in the northern region speaking Tumbuka sometimes have a difficult time working and speaking with people residing in the central region. Here, most people are Chewa, although there are also Yao, Ngoni, and other groups as well. While Chichewa is the predominant language, the other ethnic groups are each characterized by distinctive languages, cultures, and histories.

Underlying assumptions.

There are certain underlying assumptions that we believe are basic to the conduct of needs assessment. Our reasons for adhering to this philosophy are spelled out in Chapter 12 where we describe the context in which needs assessment is carried out. Five assumptions, discussed below, constitute an operating philosophy that often helps us make decisions about field methodologies or professional ethics and responsibilities.

1. Needs assessment is multidimensional. It can and should address more than one purpose, for example, generate support for decisions; improve communications between "inside" and "outside" sectors; predict clientele's willingness to accept changes; build clientele's confidence in their own problem-solving abilities; generate cost efficient and accurate information; and recognize unique differences among people, villages, and regions.

2. Needs assessment requires an integration of research methods. Webb et al. (1966:3–5) refer to this as "triangulation of measurement process." The need for multiple methods arises because there are no social science methods perfected that are sensitive to all possible sources of variation. The use of different methods that complement each other helps to avoid the risk of false confidence that may accompany reliance on a single method.

3. The clientele constitutes all individuals and groups who may be potentially impacted or who may impact. While local farmers or villagers are usually one of these important actors, it may also be important to direct attention to others, for example, organizational and institutional represent-

atives that may affect long-term outcomes.

4. Needs assessment is essentially a communications mechanism. The more effective the methods and the ways in which they are integrated, the less the social distance between practitioners (outsiders) and clientele (insiders). Ideally, the aim is to introduce methods that will improve understanding of the clientele's situation as they see and experience it.

5. The clientele are equal partners in the needs assessment process. No one is better informed about their resource problems, aspirations and needs than the clientele themselves. They should therefore assume equal responsibility for analyzing, planning, providing information, interpreting findings, and carrying out action strategies.

Outline for action. In this section we present useful "how to" guidelines for practitioners. These are precipitated by the preceding assumptions, which have evolved from our own development experiences and observations. Realistically, it seems imperative to design and implement needs assessment as an integral part of the entire development process. As such, it can serve as a mechanism for involving and training a wide range of clientele in development efforts. Simultaneously, it may provide support for needed changes in institutional structures that are more sensitive to local people's needs and concerns.

PARTICIPATION. Use needs assessment as a participation mechanism:

1. Clientele involvement. Involve representatives from all impacted clientele in each step of the needs assessment process — legitimization, problem definition, goal setting, analysis of alternative methodologies, development of needs assessment design, training and orientation for implementation, field work, organization and analysis of findings, reporting and dissemination, application, and/or integration of findings.

2. Involvement of policymakers. Beginning in the earliest stages, involve the people who will be carrying out programs or policies that may evolve from findings; for example, find ways to incorporate particular concerns or deadlines of administrators, policymakers, and scientists. Keep them well informed on support needs, progress, and preliminary findings.

3. Local control. Facilitate local control and ownership; for example, identify an existing organization or group to sponsor the needs assessment. Organize appropriate leadership and technical training for group members to strengthen their capabilities to participate in the total process. Consider working through a local group organizer, facilitator, or broker.

4. Team approach. Identify and develop a representative team to con-

duct the entire needs assessment. Include a mix of clientele such as a village organizational representative, a farmer, a local extension agent, a district chief, an agricultural researcher, and an administrator.

5. Responsible participation. Avoid token participation. Identify legitimate responsibilities for local leaders, farmers and family members, public officials, junior and senior civil servants, and so on.

The Lesotho Farming Systems Research Project (FSRP) baseline survey discussed in Chapter 13 probably did not adequately involve all impacted clientele in the various needs assessment processes. While there was deep involvement of Ministry of Agriculture Research Division staff, the findings might have had broader use if more effort had been made to include specialists in other ministry divisions, for example, livestock or crops. This might have helped counteract the subsequent problem in the research division when most participating research staff either left the country to attend school or to resume U.S. employment. Few remaining staff had enough understanding of the data to put it to practical use.

Over time, the baseline survey encountered considerable opposition from USAID mission representatives. Early legitimization with USAID, Lesotho government policymakers, and contractor representatives could have contributed to the support of the survey as well as use of the findings. Had village leaders or a local organization been encouraged to assume a responsible role in the survey, for example, as participants on a *sondeo* team, a less formal data collection method might have resulted. Although the survey was legitimized locally, villagers participated primarily as paid enumerators. A much more effective group involvement process could have been designed to facilitate participation in problem identification and resolution. Earlier collaboration among researchers, extension agents, and farmers might have stimulated the initiation of on-farm experiments much sooner than they actually occurred.

SYSTEMS OR HOLISTIC FRAMEWORK. Design and conduct needs assessment within a systems or holistic framework:

1. Interdisciplinary approaches. Use methods that integrate people of different backgrounds, types of training, or interests, for example, by forming interdisciplinary or *sondeo* teams (Hildebrand 1981:423) of scientists from differing disciplines, civil servants, and rural clientele. Begin this integration at the time of project design.

2. Systems interaction. Analyze the problem from a systems perspective where possible. Recognize interactions among and between different parts of the total system, for example, the social, economic, technical, and

physical environments. Diagnose critical ties between the microsituation and the macrosituation (e.g., see Redfield 1960:17–32).

3. Historical context. Consider the historical context of the situation to understand why the current system has evolved. Study the existing system to learn how and why local people do things the way they do.

4. Clientele-management goals. Give priority to methods that address the goals and concerns of the clientele. At the same time, balance these with the demands of national policy or project management.

5. Multiple methods. Employ different but complementary methods to obtain varying levels of insight. Different situations require different approaches. One method may be strong where another is weak.

The value of the interdisciplinary field team has been recognized by livestock development projects for over two decades. This is evident in examining the Masai Livestock and Range Development Project initiated in Masailand in Tanzania in the mid-1960s. The project represented early attempts by the Tanzanian government to accelerate the movement of its pastoral peoples (the Masai) into a modern economy. After several rather unsuccessful years of trying to incorporate livestock owners into group ranching associations, sociological factors were acknowledged to be basic to the problems of implementation. A historical review of the project, including roles and attitudes of team members and associated organizations, provides considerable insight into the complexities of applying a systems perspective.

A few examples are presented to illustrate the need for advance organizational and management planning to accommodate systems field methodologies. All involved institutions need to look at the implications of this approach from the point of view of their own goals, and individual team members also need to do this.

Over the years, field teams consisted of specialists in animal production, range ecology, livestock marketing, water development engineering, anthropology, and extension-rural sociology. Although on the surface this may seem an ideal combination of backgrounds to respond to the problems, 10 years later project goals had not been accomplished. Many of the problems relate to difficulties associated with the systems approach.

Each person's position description was extremely restrictive, except for the social scientists. The organizations involved had a relatively narrow perception of the technicians' responsibilities. As a result, technicians were not encouraged to study the local situation or to research how the Masai actually managed their rangeland and water. This was considered to be the role of the anthropologist. If technicians had learned more about local people's knowledge and beliefs, this might have eliminated the false stereotypes that existed about the Masai's conservatism or animal production skills. These stereotypes, which also existed at institutional levels, frequently resulted in inappropriate recommendations that eventually failed.

Apparently, team members also had an inadequate understanding of the potential contributions of each of their colleagues' disciplines. The primary reasons for having a social scientist on the project were to collect information about the Masai that would isolate possible constraints and identify social structures for facilitating project inputs and to persuade the Masai to adopt project technology. Engineers were so absorbed in technical and fiscal aspects of the project that social scientists were only minimally involved in water development. Until midterm of the project, contributions to grazing management consisted solely of providing human demographic and grazing unit boundary data. Range specialists were under pressure to produce and implement management plans in too limited a time period and without adequate understanding of local livestock management dynamics. Another aspect that became apparent was that extension, out of necessity, should have been a part of every team member's job. When extension was seen only as the role of the extension agent, the total field implementation suffered (Moris and Hatfield 1982:43–61).

TRAINING THE TEAM. Needs assessment can be a training tool:

1. Training opportunity. View every step of the process as an opportunity for imparting new knowledge and strengthening existing skills.
2. National colleagues. Develop joint working relationships with national colleagues and encourage nationals to assume leadership and responsibility.
3. Leadership. Expect national colleagues to take the lead role in guiding and training their own staff and clientele.
4. Train the trainer. Consider a "train the trainer" approach in which nationals at various levels not only develop needed confidence and skills but also have experience in relaying these to others. Farmers can also be viewed as trainers in teaching technicians about local production practices, local language terms, culturally acceptable practices and varieties, and existing organizational systems.
5. Field experience. Field experience will strengthen individual practical skills and build organizational capacity at the same time.
6. "Hands on" experiments. Incorporate needs assessment with "hands on" experiments or trials. Village people or ministry staff will become more motivated to participate when they are contributing in meaningful and responsible ways.
7. Integration of levels. Develop learning experiences that integrate

technical-level or junior field staff with more senior-level staff, rural clientele, local leaders, and expatriates. Build mutual respect for unique perspectives and capabilities of all.

8. Curricula. Well-designed training for needs assessment can provide training needed in technical fields, organizational development, and leadership. Training for needs assessment is frequently transferable to other responsibilities.

9. Multiplier effect. The outcomes of needs assessment can be multiplied by combining it with practical and theoretical classes, small scale experimentation, and training others. The process arouses interest among the clientele, encourages them to try something new, and motivates them to show others what they have learned (Bunch 1982:148–51, 196–201).

One of the primary purposes of the Lesotho FSRP baseline survey was to train trainers. Many senior agriculture research staff were responsible for supervising and guiding junior staff, and all were under pressure to identify research priorities that were relevant to farmers.

Soon after our arrival in Lesotho, the permanent secretary of the Ministry of Agriculture stopped all research activities, directing staff to carry out a nationwide survey to determine research program directions. Although our role in this effort was minimal, it was sufficient to convince us that most research staff could benefit from improved survey and field work skills. Few staff had experienced training in interviewing skills, sample selection, formulating interview questions, or data analysis. Yet they were occasionally put in positions, regardless of discipline or responsibility, where they needed these abilities. Skills for training others were also limited.

While a baseline survey is a more formal approach to describing existing production systems than might have been necessary in Lesotho, it did provide the kind of rigor needed to teach survey research principles. In retrospect, it seemed important to use the baseline survey as a tool to impart these skills, as opposed to an informal survey such as a *sondeo*. Ethnographic skills characteristic of the *sondeo* are much harder to grasp with no background in survey research or interviewing techniques. Had the staff involved been trained at a degree or higher level, they might have readily moved into a *sondeo* approach. In this situation, the baseline survey was a suitable preparation for moving into *sondeo* work.

To initiate the survey, a multidisciplinary research group collaborated on the research design. This included extension, range ecology, animal science, agricultural marketing, farm management, rural sociology, agronomy, and nutrition. This group designed and pretested a questionnaire. Eventually a team of four trainers from this group assumed responsibility for the survey. They participated in an intensive "train the trainers" course, the purposes of which were to (1) train trainers who in turn would train, guide, and supervise village interviewers; (2) familiarize trainers with the survey instrument; (3) teach field implementation methods; (4) prepare those responsible for the survey to answer local people's questions; and (5) build a team (Butler 1982).

From this point on, Lesotho nationals assumed responsibility for all aspects of the survey: legitimizing the survey at the village level, selecting the sample, developing and conducting interviewer training, selecting and supervising interviewers, and collecting and checking data. Every step of the way, the trainers worked through each problem as it occurred, including inaccurate sample listings, inappropriate interviewer selection, revisions in training methods, and team member conflicts and contradictions in local language interpretations. By the conclusion of the survey, the trainer team had reached a high level of skill in survey research. They also developed a sufficient level of ownership in the findings to utilize them in their own degree work the following year. More than once we were told by individuals who served as trainers how much they had learned in the process and how many times the skills were used.

ORGANIZATIONAL INVOLVEMENT. Integrate needs assessment into existing or acceptable organizational structures:

1. Local organizations. Tie needs assessment to existing organizational or natural group structures to strengthen local organizational capacity. Such organizations might assume responsibility for conducting a needs assessment.

2. Clientele-professional integration. Develop legitimate mechanisms for integrating clientele with professionals, practitioners, and scientists so that collaborative teams of equals evolve. This is sometimes facilitated through a local "broker" paraprofessional who organizes, trains, consults, verifies, explains, and so on.

3. Start locally. Initiate the needs assessment process at the local level to build understanding, leadership, and ownership from the inside to the outside.

4. Reinforce ongoing functions and objectives. Integrate needs assessment into organization program planning, implementation, and evaluation processes. Capitalize on existing horizontal and vertical linkages, for example, within or between ministries.

5. Constituent communication. Keep information flowing to constituency groups. Begin this early using easily understandable approaches.

The Lesotho FSRP was designed and implemented to meet organizational goals of the Lesotho government. Before initiation of the project, there had been no agricultural research unit cutting across all disciplines of the ministry. Initially, research had been conducted in each respective ministry division, for example, the crops or livestock division. At the onset of the project in 1979, a Ministry of Agriculture (MOA) research division was created to carry out farming systems and basic research and to incorporate a systems approach. Staff were gradually assigned to both types of roles, working side by side in agronomy and soils, entomology, farm management, marketing, extension, range ecology, animal science, and rural sociology.

The research division, with its farming systems research thrust, was established to be equal in status to all other MOA divisions with a comparable division head. The research director also assumed the responsibility of the FSRP director. In this way, ongoing research programs and new farming systems research programs stood a better chance of achieving integration than if each was assigned to different organizational units. Any needs assessment effort therefore became a matter of discussion across the entire research division. For example, many discussions about the baseline survey took place at research division staff meetings conducted by the research director.

The project was assigned to three different field sites. In these areas it also operated within the existing MOA structure. For example, district MOA officers were regular actors in program planning in prototype areas that fell within their districts. This included the ultimate assignment of prototype area extension agents. Although these agents were assigned to work with the FSRP, they were still very much a part of the district MOA staff. They were paid regular MOA wages and were responsible to the district MOA officer. No special incentives went with project responsibilities.

Village chiefs and their councils assumed a role in advising the project of farmers' needs and priorities. This was done through an agricultural committee structure, members of which were elected by village people to advise the project on a continuing basis. Committees received training in order to carry out their needs assessment responsibilities.

Another way local people's needs were assessed on the Lesotho FSRP was through use of the traditional *pitso* system. Essentially, the *pitso* is a public meeting that is customarily called by the chief to communicate with villagers. The project continually utilized this acceptable means of communication from the beginning — to legitimize activities, identify seasonal production problems, hear local people's viewpoints, provide information, introduce staff who would be working in the area, or solicit participants in different activities. Although there were times when the *pitso* was not adequate, it proved to be an effective tool for first-level needs assessment because it was already well accepted and used by village people.

MANAGEMENT CONSIDERATIONS. Needs assessment must meet practical management consideration:

1. Problem orientation. Data collection must address real national and local concerns. Give attention to discretely identifiable problems such as erosion control, rangeland management, forage preservation and storage, and so on.

2. Decision-making information. Focus on bottom-line decisions, especially in early phases. Try to help decision makers deal with immediate problems and crises. Provide objective information on which to base planning and policy decisions.

3. Early visibility. Start with a small, narrowly focused needs assessment that can generate understanding of the purpose and value of the needs assessment; be completed quickly; provide rapid turnaround of results and possible applications; and generate recognizable successes early on, particularly those that might be viewed as economic gains.

4. Early data availability. Provide fast data turnaround. Phase the study to keep clientele and participants interested and to maintain management's support. Provide preliminary and continuing findings rather than waiting for completion of a long-term study. Show clientele early application of their contributions.

5. Adapt to limited resources. Select cost-efficient methods that make the best use of available resources. Use existing staff and local leaders to identify respondents, understand the current situation, inventory organizations, legitimize the needs assessment, and communicate. Rural people can orient professionals, scientists, and civil servants about local patterns of behavior.

6. Dissemination of findings. Plan appropriate methods of disseminating and sharing findings with clientele, participants, and management. Avoid academic jargon and complex terminology. Incorporate local language and examples. Keep reports short and concise. Use locally acceptable visual aids.

The greatest criticism of the Lesotho FSRP baseline survey concerned its inability to contribute to these guidelines. On its own, the baseline survey was too extensive and not sufficiently focused to contribute to timely project decisions. Findings did not become available for use for 21 months. By this time the project and the research division had undergone many staff changes. Findings therefore had little meaning to existing staff. Little effort was made by project administrators to assure that findings were disseminated in anything other than a printout format. As a result, there was a tendency for only expatriate team members to make use of them.

In retrospect, if informal surveys or *sondeos* had been conducted in the early stages of the project, more timely data might have been provided with which to plan on-farm experiments as well as other project activities. Informal team surveys could have involved local farmers and district MOA staff to compensate for the research division's shortage of national staff. Local support or early visibility could have been more effectively generated through this approach.

A *sondeo* would make information about current production systems available fairly quickly, making it possible to follow up with directed surveys about particular problems. Since some team members did not join the project at its onset, their involvement in problem-oriented surveys might have eased their entrance to field work.

Reliance on a long, rigorous baseline survey did not prove a cost-effective needs assessment method. Less staff time would be needed to carry out short informal surveys. The use of group interviews (e.g., of local agricultural committees or extension staff) might also have been worth consideration. More systematic observation of current practices could also have been done collaboratively by team members and village people.

Regardless of the method used, a plan for dissemination of findings helps to assure their use. In the case of the baseline survey, this could have been effectively done through a series of field workshops in which findings about the prototype area were presented to local people, including ministry staff. Some findings actually have been incorporated into agricultural committee and extension agent training. Selected findings have also been presented in a technical bulletin for extension staff. Much more of the latter could have been done, since field staff usually have very little technical information available. However staff would probably require guidance in how to apply the findings to their work.

CONSULTANTS AND PRACTITIONERS. Needs assessment consultants and practitioners have certain ethical roles and responsibilities:

1. Outsider bias. Recognize the probability of outsider bias. This bias might be checked by local informants or focus discussion groups. Cultural bias can lead to inappropriate methods of organizing and training, as when outside professionals make plans and decisions without involving national colleagues. Allow time for testing needs assessment methods at the clientele

level and listen to the feedback (see Chambers 1980:15–28 for discussion of biases).

2. Neutrality. It is easy to overidentify with clientele or certain sponsoring institutions. Try to maintain a neutral role in which all interests are represented.

3. Facilitator role. Assume a facilitator or trainer role as opposed to the role of expert or specialist. Let national colleagues assume major responsibilities and leadership roles.

4. Use of existing systems. Avoid trying to change organizational systems if they seem to be working. Use them to legitimize and carry out the needs assessment. Consider ways of strengthening the capacities of existing organizations by expanding people's skills or involving organizational representatives in analyzing and resolving their own problems by using their own resources.

Historically, it has been the tendency for development projects to direct their resources to the "better off" members of the population. Even though project goals may identify the poor as beneficiaries, the existing power structure, including current ministry clientele, frequently is made up of people who have more resources.

In Egypt we observed cereals research demonstrations being carried out on fields of village chiefs. Laborers, rather than the farmers themselves, were hired to do the field work.

In Lesotho, in spite of the good intentions of the FSRP, government and donor officials were not in agreement as to who should constitute the target groups of agricultural aid. Some ministry leadership favored giving preference to the progressive or "better off" farmers simply because of the need to show results. Even as we worked in the field, supposedly involving the smallest farm households, ministry staff were continually in touch with larger farmers to obtain inputs, influence other farmers, and borrow land for local trials and demonstrations.

In Malawi, a village chief who had major production resources was continually visiting the agricultural college to secure help for his people to obtain fertilizer and seed, get advice on improved practices, obtain nutrition classes for village women, and so on. In cases like this, practitioners are continually having to balance their own allegiances. Very often the donor agency or contractor is also inclined to feel more comfortable with the clientele who have the most resources. In Lesotho, when we took visitors to the field, the only place they could obtain food during the day was at the home of a very progressive farmer/entrepreneur. We found it a continual challenge to keep local extension staff thinking about the needs of limited-resource farm families. They simply were not in touch with them to the degree you would expect. When visitors came who had to be suitably impressed, it was natural to depend on those people who had more local influence, were more articulate, and were easier to reach.

In Lesotho we eventually learned how to utilize the more progressive farmers to make contacts with the smaller farmers. For example, often the laborers on larger farms were widows or deserted women who had their own small farms. If it had not been for the established rapport with some of the progressive farmers, this important clientele might never have received much attention. Even so, simply because they were female and not at their own homes during the day, they were not often seen by local extension agents. When they were acknowledged, the problem of having sufficient resources (e.g., land) to participate in the program always arose.

Summary. In this chapter we have identified six major guidelines that we have found important in our needs assessment work overseas:

1. Use needs assessment as a participation mechanism.

2. Design and conduct needs assessment within a systems or holistic framework.

3. Needs assessment can be a training tool.

4. Integrate needs assessment into existing or acceptable organizational structures.

5. Needs assessment must meet practical management considerations.

6. Needs assessment consultants and practioners have certain ethical roles and responsibilities.

In a sense these guidelines constitute an operating philosophy or practitioner ideology that is basic to working in Third World development. While we are continually under pressure to produce visible results and measurable products, it is very difficult to do so without giving the human element equal time and attention. This is as important for technical scientists as for social scientists. All must first make the commitment to the clientele, then the real test is found in the many personal actions that follow. The guidelines ultimately must be absorbed as a mind-set or a belief system toward the activities of each day. Many provide opportunities for some aspect of needs assessment in any setting.

References cited

Alford, Robert, and Harry Scoble. 1968. Sources of local political involvement. *Am. Polit. Sci. Rev.*(62):1192–1206.

Alinsky, Saul D. 1972. *Rules for Radicals*. New York: Vintage Books.

Almond, Gabriel A., and Sidney Verba. 1965. *The Civic Culture*. Boston: Little, Brown.

Andrews, Frank M., and Stephen B. Withey. 1976. *Social Indicators of Well-Being*. New York: Plenum.

Arafa, Salah, and Cynthia Nelson. 1982. Utilization of solar energy and development of an Egyptian village: An integrated field project. Progress report 3, August 1980–December 1981. Cairo: American University.

Axinn, George H. 1981. Issues in farming systems research: A multidisciplinary behavioral science perspective. Farming Systems Research Group, working paper 8, Michigan State University, East Lansing.

Babbie, Earl R. 1982. *Social Research for Consumers*. Belmont, Calif.: Wadsworth.

Barber, Benjamin. 1984. *Strong Democracy: Participatory Politics for a New Age*. Berkeley: University of California Press.

Baumel, C. Phillip; Daryl J. Hobbs; and Ronald C. Powers. 1964. The community survey: Its use in development and action programs. Iowa State University Cooperative Extension Service, Soc-15, Ames.

Beaulieu, Lionel J., and Peter F. Korsching, eds. 1979. Focus on Florida: The citizens' viewpoint. Center for Community and Rural Development, IFAS, special series 1. Gainesville: University of Florida.

Bednar, James, Edward Caplan et al. 1982. International conference calls for new measures. *Horizon* (USAID)1:26–40.

Beebe, James. 1985. Rapid rural appraisal: The critical first step in a farming systems approach to research. Farming Systems Support Project, IFAS, networking paper 5. Gainesville: University of Florida.

Bennett, John W., and Gustav Thaiss. 1970. Survey research in anthropological field work. In Raoul Narroll and Ronald Cohen, eds., *A Handbook of Method in Cultural Anthropology*. New York: Columbia University Press.

Bennis, Warren G.; Kenneth D. Benne; and Robert Chin. 1969. *The Planning of Change,* 2nd ed. New York: Holt, Rinehart and Winston.

Birdsall, Nancy. 1980. Population growth and poverty in the developing world. *Popul. Bull.,* vol. 35, no. 5.

Blake, Brian; Ned Kalb; and Vernon Ryan. 1977. Citizen opinion surveys and effective community development efforts. *J. Community Dev. Soc.* 7:92–104.

Bleiker, Hans. 1978. *Citizen Participation Handbook,* 3rd ed. Laramie,Wyo.: Institute for Citizen Participation.

Bradshaw, Jonathan. 1972. The concept of social need. *New Society* 30:610–43.

Brager, George, and Harry Specht. 1973. *Community Organizing*. New York: Columbia University Press.

Bray, Robert M.; Norbert L. Kerr; and Robert S. Atkin. 1978. Effects of group size, problem difficulty, and sex on group performance and member reactions. *J. Pers. Soc. Psychol.* 36:1224–40.

Breach, Ian. 1978. Environmentalists after Windscale. *New Scientists* 258–60. July 27.

Breed, W. 1958. Mass communication and social integration. *Social Forces* 37:109–16.

Broomall, Nancy R., and Robert Canon. 1977. City spirit San Antonio. Unpublished report, Arts Council of San Antonio, San Antonio, Tex.

Brown, Lester. 1981. *Building a Sustainable Society.* New York: Norton.

Brown, L. David, and Rajesh Tandon. 1983. Ideology and political economy in inquiry: Action research and participatory research. *J. Appl. Behav. Res.* 19:277–94.

Bryant, Coralie, and Louise G. White. 1982. *Managing Development in the Third World.* Boulder, Colo.: Westview Press.

Bunch, Roland. 1982. *Two Ears of Corn.* Oklahoma City: World Neighbors.

Burdge, Rabel. 1982. Needs assessment surveys for decision makers. In Don A. Dillman and Daryl J. Hobbs, eds., *Rural Society in the U.S.: Issues for the 1980s.* Boulder, Colo.: Westview Press.

Burdge, Rabel J., and Paul D. Warner. 1975. Issues facing Kentucky. University of Kentucky Cooperative Extension Service, Lexington.

Burdge, Rabel J.; Ruth M. Kelly; and Harvey J. Schweitzer. 1978. Illinois: Today and tomorrow. University of Illinois Cooperative Extension Service, special series 1, Urbana.

Burns, James MacGregor. 1978. *Leadership.* New York: Harper and Row.

Burns, Jim. 1979. *Connections: Ways to Discover and Realize Community Potentials.* New York: McGraw-Hill.

Butler, Lorna Michael. 1976. Bases of women's influence in the rural Malawian domestic group. Ph.D. diss. Department of Anthropology, Washington State University, Pullman.

_____. 1982. Farming systems research baseline survey, methodological report. Kingdom of Lesotho Ministry of Agriculture Research Division. Pullman: Washington State University.

Butler, Lorna Michael, and Robert E. Howell. 1979. *Coping with Growth: Community Needs Assessment Techniques.* Corvallis: Western Rural Development Center, Oregon State University.

Byerlee, Derek, and Michael Collinson. 1980. *Planning Technologies Appropriate to Farmers: Concepts and Procedures.* Mexico: Centro Internacional de Mejoramiento de Maiz y Trigo.

Carroll, Susan J. 1984. Feminist scholarship on political leadership. In Barbara Kellerman, ed., *Leadership: Multidisciplinary Perspectives.* Englewood Cliffs, N.J.: Prentice-Hall.

Casey-Stahmer, Anna, and Douglas Goldschmidt. 1984. Satellites spread skills. *Dev. Forum* 12:7.

Cater, D. 1969. *The Fourth Branch of Government.* New York: Random House.

Chambers, Robert. 1979. Editorial. *IDS Bull.* 10:1–3.

_____. 1980. Rural poverty unperceived: Problems and remedies. World Bank staff working paper 400. Washington, D.C.: World Bank.

_____. 1981a. Rapid rural appraisal: Rationale and repertoire. *Public Adm. Dev.* 1:95–106.

_____. 1981b. Rural poverty unperceived: Problems and remedies. *World Dev.* 9:1–19.

_____. 1983. *Rural Development: Putting the Last First.* London: Longman.

Checkoway, Barry. 1978. The politics of public hearings. Bureau of Urban and Regional Planning Research, planning paper 78-23. Urbana: University of Illinois.

Chein, Isidor; Stuart W. Cook; and John Harding. 1949. The field of action research. *Am. Psychol.* 3:43–50.

Christenson, James A. 1973. People's goals and needs in North Carolina. In *Through Our Eyes,* vol. 1. North Carolina Agricultural Extension Service, Miscellaneous Publication 106, Raleigh.

_____. 1975. North Carolina today and tomorrow. North Carolina Agricultural Extension Service, Miscellaneous Publications 1941–1949, Raleigh.

_____. 1976. Public input for program planning and policy formation. *J. Community Dev. Soc.* 7:33–39.

Cohen, B. C. 1963. *The Press and Foreign Policy.* Princeton: Princeton University Press.

Cohen, Mark W.; Grayce M. Sills; and Andrew J. Schwebel. 1977. A two-stage process for surveying community needs. *J. Community Dev. Soc.* 8:54–61.

Coleman, J. S. 1957. *Community Conflict.* New York: Macmillan.

Collinson, Michael. 1984. Farming systems research: Diagnosing the problem. Paper presented at the annual Agricultural Symposium, World Bank, Washington, D.C., January 9–13.

Commission on Freedom of the Press. 1947. *A Free and Responsible Press: A General Report on Mass Communication: Newspapers, Radio, Motion Pictures, Magazines and Books.* Chicago: University of Chicago Press.

Conlin, S. 1979. Baseline surveys: An escape from thinking about research problems and, even more, a refuge from actually doing anything. Paper presented at the Rapid Rural Appraisal Conference, Institute of Development Studies, University of Sussex, Brighton, U.K., December 4–7.

Cook, F. L.; T. R. Tyler; E. G. Goetz; M. T. Gordon; D. Protess; D. R. Leff; and H. L. Molotch. 1983. Media and agenda setting: Effects on the public, interest group leaders, policy makers, and policy. *Public Opin. Q.* 47:16–35.

Coser, L. A. 1967. *Continuities in the Study of Social Conflict.* New York: Free Press.

Cox, Fred M.; John L. Erlich; Jack Rothman; and John E. Tropman, eds. 1970. *Strategies of Community Organization: A Book of Readings,* 1st ed. Itasca, Ill.: Peacock.

Craig, Paul D., and Mark D. Levine. 1981. Decentralized energy. American Association for the Advancement of Science, selected symposium 72. Boulder, Colo.: Westview Press.

Curran, J. 1978. The press as an agency of social control: An historical perspective. In G. Boyce, J. Curran, and P. Wingate, eds., *Newspaper History: From the 17th Century to the Present Day.* London: Constable.

Dahrendorf, R. 1959. *Class and Class Conflict in Industrial Society.* Palo Alto, Calif.: Stanford University Press.

De Fleur, M. L., and E. E. Dennis. 1981. *Understanding Mass Communication.* Boston: Houghton Mifflin.

Denney, Hugh; Red List; Bryan Phifer; Vicki Hobbs; Daryl Hobbs; Leonard Johnson; Brenda Nolte; Greg Witney; Louise Metzner: and Ed Owsley. 1977. *Survey of community attitudes: A technical and procedural manual for communities.* Manual 108, 12/77/2M, University of Missouri-Columbia and Missouri Division of Community Betterment.

Dervin, B. 1980. Communication gaps and inequalities: Moving toward a reconceptualization. In B. Dervin and M. J. Voigt, eds., *Progress in Communication Sciences,* vol. 2. Norwood, N.J.: Ablex.

Dillman, Don A. 1977. Preference surveys and policy decisions: Our new tools need not be used in the same old way. *J. Community Dev. Soc.* 8:30–43.

_____. 1978. *Mail and Telephone Surveys: The Total Design Method.* New York: Wiley-Interscience.

_____. 1983a. Mail and self-administered surveys. In Peter H. Rossi, James D. Wright, and Andy B. Anderson, eds., *Handbook of Survey Research.* New York: Academic Press.

_____. 1983b. Rural North American in the information society. *Rural Sociol.* 3:345–57.

Dillman, Don A.; James A. Christenson; Edwin H. Carpenter; and Ralph M. Brooks. 1974. Increasing mail questionnaire response: A four-state comparison. *Am. Sociol. Rev.* 39:744–56.

Dillman, Don A., and Robert G. Mason. 1979. Unpublished data, Community needs assessment study, Western Rural Development Center, Oregon State University, Corvallis.

Donohue, G. A. 1974. Feasible options for social action. In L. R. Whiting, ed., *Communities Left Behind.* Ames: Iowa State University Press.

Donohue, G. A.; P. J. Tichenor; and C. N. Olien. 1973. Mass media functions, knowledge and social control. *Journalism Q.* 50:652–59.

Donohue, G. A.; C. N. Olien; and P. J. Tichenor. 1975. Mass media and the knowledge gap: A hypothesis reconsidered. *Commun. Res.* 2:3–23.

_____. 1978. Media, conflict and citizen understanding: A holistic approach. Paper presented at a seminar on the effects of communication on conflict resolution, East-West Center, Honolulu.

_____. 1985. Leader and editor views of role of the press in community development. *Journalism Q.* 62:367–72.

Dreier, P. 1983. The corporate complaint against the media. *Quill* 71:17ff.

Edelstein, A. S., and J. B. Schulz, 1964. The leadership role of the weekly newspaper as seen by the community leaders: A sociological perspective. In L. A. Dexter and D. M. White, eds., *People, Society and Mass Communications*. New York: Free Press.

Edgerton, Robert B. 1971. *The Individual in Cultural Adaptation*. Berkeley, Calif.: University of California Press.

Esman, Milton J., and Norman T. Uphoff. 1982. Local organization and rural development: The state-of-the-art. Center for International Studies, Rural Development Committee. Ithaca, N.Y.: Cornell University.

_____. 1984. *Local Organizations: Intermediaries in Rural Development*. Ithaca, N.Y.: Cornell University Press.

Ettema, J. S., and F. G. Kline. 1977. Deficits, differences and ceilings: Contingent conditions for understanding the knowledge gap. *Commun. Res.* 4:179–202.

Evans, Sara. 1979. *Personal Politics*. New York: Vintage Books.

Everitt, Skip, and Claire Dyckman. 1976. *Bellingham 2000: A Citizens' Guide to the Future*. An unpublished Title I, Higher Education Act Report. Bellingham, Wash.: Huxley College.

Fals-Borda, Orlando. 1981. The challenge of action research. *Development: Seeds of Change* 1:55–61.

Fisher, John. 1984. Why projects fail. Address, 20th annual meeting of the Association of U.S. University Directors of International Agricultural Programs, Pullman, Wash., June 26–28.

Fishman, M. 1980. *Manufacturing the News*. Austin: University of Texas Press.

Foresite. 1978. Crystal, Minn.: Minnesota Waste Management Board.

Foster, Charles R., ed. 1980. *Comparative Public Policy and Citizen Participation: Energy, Education, Health and Urban Issues in the U.S. and Germany*. New York: Pergamon Press.

Frankenberger, Tim. 1984. Personal communication.

Freire, Paulo. 1970. *Pedagogy of the Oppressed*. New York: Continuum.

Fresco, Louise. 1984. Approaches to the study of farming and cropping systems. Draft of paper prepared for workshop on Designing Effective Farming Systems for West Africa, Iowa State University, Ames, June 11–22.

Frey, James H. 1983. *Survey Research by Telephone*. Beverly Hills: Sage Publications.

Gans, H. J. 1979. *Deciding What's News*. New York: Pantheon.

Gardner, Neely. 1974. Action training and research: Something old and something new. *Public Admin. Q.* 34(March/April):106–15.

Garkovich, Lorraine. 1979. What comes after the survey? A practical application of the synchronized survey model in community development. *J. Community Dev. Soc.* 10:29–38.

_____. 1982. Land use planning as a response to rapid population growth and community change. *Rural Sociol.* 47:47–65.

Gaventa, John. 1980. *Power and Powerlessness: Quiescence and Rebellion in an Appalachian Valley*. Urbana: University of Illinois Press.

Gaventa, J., and B. D. Horton. 1981. A citizen's research project in Appalachia, USA. *Convergence* 14:30–42.

Genova, B. K. C., and B. S. Greenberg. 1979. Interest in news and the knowledge gap. *Public Opin. Q.* 43:79–91.

Gerlach, Luther P., and Virginia H. Hine. 1973. *Lifeway Leap: The Dynamics of Change in America*. Minneapolis: University of Minnesota Press.

Gibbs, Louise Marie. 1982. *Love Canal, My Story*. Albany: State University of New York Press.

Gieber, W., and W. Johnson. 1961. The city hall beat: A study of reporter and source roles. *Journalism Q.* 38:289–302.

Gilbert, E. H.; D. W. Norman; and F. E. Winch. 1980. Farming systems research: A critical appraisal. MSU rural development paper 6, Department of Agricultural Economics. East Lansing: Michigan State University.

Gitlin, T. 1980. *The Whole World Is Watching*. Berkeley: University of California Press.

Gold, Raymond L. 1977. Combining ethnographic and survey research. In Kurt Finsterbush and C. P. Wolf, eds., *Methodology of Social Impact Assessment*. Stroudsburg, Pa.: Dowden, Hutchinson and Ross.

Gross, Edward, and George A. Donohue. 1970. Organizational diversity: The rural system as an ideal model. In Larry R. Whiting, ed., *Benefits and Burdens of Rural Development: Some Public Viewpoints*, pp. 241–53. Ames: Iowa State University Press.

Groves, Robert M., and Robert L. Kahn. 1979. *Surveys by Telephone: A National Comparison with Personal Interviews*. New York: Academic Press.

Hachten, W. 1963. The press as reporter and critic of government. *Journalism Q.* 40:12–18.

Hall, Bud L. 1975. Participatory research: An approach for change. *Convergence* 8:24–32.

_____. 1981. Participatory research, popular knowledge and power: A personal reflection. *Convergence* 14:6–17.

Hare, Alexander Paul. 1982. *Creativity in Small Groups*. Beverly Hills: Sage Publications.

Hawken, Paul. 1983. *The Next Economy*. New York: Holt, Rinehart and Winston.

Healy, Grace M. 1979. Toward the year 2000: Citizens' ownership of the future. Civic literacy project, Contract G007604807. Syracuse, N.Y.: Syracuse University.

Heberlein, Thomas A. 1974. The three fixes: Technological, cognitive, and structural. In Donald Field, James C. Barren, and Burl F. Long, eds., *Water and Community Development: Social and Economic Perspectives*. Ann Arbor: Ann Arbor Science Publishers.

_____. 1976a. Principles of public involvement. Department of Rural Sociology Staff Paper Series in Rural and Community Development, University of Wisconsin-Madison, April.

_____. 1976b. Some observations on alternative mechansims for public involvement: The hearing, public opinion poll, the workshop and the quasi-experiment. *Nat. Res. J.* 16:197–212.

Heberlein, Tom, and Robert Baumgartner. 1978. Factors affecting response rates to mail questionnaires: A quantitative analysis of the published literature. *Am. Sociol. Rev.* 43:447–62.

Helmer, Olaf. 1983. *Looking Forward: A Guide to Futures Research*. Beverly Hills: Sage Publications.

Hildebrand, P. E. 1981. Combining disciplines in rapid appraisal: The *sondeo* approach. *Agric. Adm.* 8:425–32.

Hirigoyen, Patrick, and Kevin Johnson. 1983. Searching for solutions: A report on the Minnesota waste management boards. Statewide conference on the Hazardous Waste Management Plan at the University of Minnesota, St. Paul Campus, May.

Hocking, W. 1947. *Freedom of the Press*. Chicago: University of Chicago Press.

Howes, Michael, and Robert Chambers. 1979. Indigenous technical knowledge: Analysis, implications and issues. *IDS Bull.* 10:5–10.

Hoyle, Fred, and Geoffrey Hoyle. 1980. *Common Sense in Nuclear Energy*. London: Heinemann Educational Books.

Hustedde, Ronald J. 1985. The Delavan experience. Unpublished paper, University of Wisconsin Extension, Madison.

Hyman, Herbert H. 1972. *Secondary Analysis of Sample Surveys: Principles, Procedures and Potentialities*. New York: Wiley.

Jaberg, Eugene Carl. 1968. The town meeting of the Twin Cities, 1966–1967: A case history of community dialogue. Madison: University of Wisconsin.

Johnson, Lynne A. 1985. CR in practice. Unpublished paper, University of Wisconsin Extension, Madison.

Jones, Graham. 1971. *The Role of Science and Technology in Developing Countries*. London: Oxford University Press.

Jungck, Robert. 1979. *The New Tyranny: How Nuclear Power Enslaves Us*. New York: Fred Jordan Books/Grosset and Dunlap.

Kanter, Rosabeth Moss. 1981. An agenda for leadership in America. In *New Leadership in the Public Interest*. New York: NOW Legal Defense and Education Fund.

Kasperson, Roger E., and Myrna Breitbart. 1974. *Participation, Decentralization and Advocacy Planning*. Washington, D.C.: Association of American Geographers.

Katz, E. 1980. On conceptualizing media effects. In T. McCormack, ed., *Studies in Communi-*

cation: A Research Annual, vol. 1. Greenwich, Conn.: Jai Press.

Kellerman, Barbara. 1984. *The Political Presidency: Practice of Leadership.* New York: Oxford University Press.

Kerr, Donna. 1984. *Barriers to Integrity.* Boulder, Colo.: Westview Press.

Kiecolt, K. Jill, and Laura E. Nathan. 1985. *Secondary Analysis of Survey Data.* Beverly Hills: Sage Publications.

Klapper, J. T. 1960. *The Effects of Mass Communication.* New York: Macmillan.

Korten, David C. 1980. Community organization and rural development: A learning process approach. *Public Adm. Rev.* 40:480–511.

Korten, David C., and Felipe B. Alfonso. 1983. *Bureaucracy and the Poor: Closing the Gap.* West Hartford, Conn.: Kumarian Press.

LaHayle, Tim. 1980. *The Battle for the Mind.* Old Tappan, N.J.: Revell.

Lang, K., and G. E. Lang. 1966. The mass media and voting. In B. Berelson and M. Janowitz, eds., *Reader in Public Opinion and Communication.* New York: Macmillan.

Langness, L. L. 1965. *Life History in Anthropological Science.* New York: Holt, Rinehart and Winston.

Leagens, J. Paul. 1979. Adoption of modern agricultural technology by small farm operators: An interdisciplinary model for researches and strategy builders. Program in International Agriculture. Ithaca, N.Y.: Cornell University.

Lele, Uma. 1975. *The Design of Rural Development Lessons from Africa.* Baltimore: Johns Hopkins University Press.

Lemert, J. B., and J. P. Larkin. 1979. Some reasons why mobilizing information fails to be in letters to the editor. *Journalism Q.* 56:504–12.

Lewin, K. 1946. Action research and minority problems. *J. Soc. Issues* 2:34–46.

Lindaman, Edward, and Ronald Lippitt. 1979. *Choosing the Future You Prefer: A Goal Setting Guide.* Ann Arbor, Mich.: Human Resource Development Associates.

Lippitt, Ronald; Zoe Wilcox; and George States. 1984. A design for community/county future planning for Jackson City and County. Unpublished, prepared for Jackson Tomorrow, Ann Arbor.

Lippmann, Walter. 1922. *Public Opinion.* New York: Macmillan.

Lipset, Seymour Martin. 1962. Introduction to *Political Parties* by Robert Michels. New York: Free Press.

Longhurst, Richard, special issue ed. 1981. Rapid rural appraisal: Social and rural economy. *Institute of Development Studies Bull.* 12:1-54.

McBride, William Leon. 1969. An ideal model and that "democratic" failure association. In J. R. Pennock and J. W. Chapman, eds., *Voluntary Associations.* New York: Atherton Press.

McCombs, M. E., and D. L. Shaw. 1972. The agenda-setting function of mass media. *Public Opin. Q.* 36:176–87.

McDermott, J. K. 1982. Social science perspectives on agriculture development. Paper presented at faculty seminar, University of Nebraska, Lincoln.

McGrath, Joseph E. 1985. Groups and the innovation process. In Richard L. Merrill and Anna J. Merritt, eds., *Innovation in the Public Sector.* Beverly Hills: Sage Publications.

McLeod, Jack, and Stephen Chaffee. 1973. Interpersonal approaches to communication research. *Am. Behav. Sci.* 16:469–99.

McLeod, J. M.; L. B. Becker; and J. E. Byrnes. 1974. Another look at the agenda-setting function of the press. *Commun. Res.* 1:131–66.

McQuail, D. 1983. *Mass Communication Theory: An Introduction.* Beverly Hills: Sage Publications.

Maeder, Suzanne. 1976. Comparing two plant sites. In Michael Murphy, *Northern Great Plains, Coal: Conflicts and Options in Decision Making.* Minneapolis, Minn.: Upper Midwest Council.

Maughan, Wesley T., and Jeri Winger. 1982. Computerized community assessment. Attitude Survey Guide, Utah Community Progress, rev.

Mayur, Rashmi. 1984. The Third World and tomorrow, an interview with Rashmi Mayur. *Futurist* 18:21–22.

Meadows, Donella; Dennis L. Meadows; Jorgen Randers; and William W. Beherns III. 1976. *Limits to Growth.* New York: McGraw-Hill.

Meenaghan, Thomas M.; Robert O. Washington; and Robert M. Ryan. 1982. *Macro Practice in the Human Services.* New York: Free Press.

Meiller, Larry R., and Glenn M. Broom. 1979. Communication experiments in building community consensus. *J. Comm. Dev. Soc.* 10:63–79.

Mendoza, Gabino A. 1983. Foreword. In David C. Korten and Felipe B. Alfonso, eds., *Bureaucracy and the Poor.* West Hartford, Conn.: Kumarian Press.

Messerschmidt, Donald A.; Udaya Gurung; Bharat Devkota; and Bhimendra Katwal. 1983. *GUAN SALLAH*: The "village dialogue" method for local planning in Nepal: A discussion paper, 2nd rev. printing. Kathmandu, Nepal: Resource Conservation and Utilization Project.

_____. 1984. Using human resources in natural resource management: Innovations in Himalayan development. Paper prepared for the Working Group on Watershed Management. Kathmandu, Nepal: International Centre for Integrated Mountain Development.

Milbrath, Lester W. 1981. Citizen surveys as citizen participation mechanisms. *J. Appl. Behav. Sci.* 17:478–96.

Miller, Delbert C. 1983. *Handbook of Research Design and Social Measurement,* 4th ed. New York: Longman.

Molotch, H., and M. Lester. 1975. Accidental news: The great oil spill as local occurrence and national event. *Am. J. Sociol.* 81:235–60.

Moore, Dan E., and Anne S. Ishler. 1980. Pennsylvania: The citizens' viewpoint. Agricultural Experiment Station. University Park: Pennsylvania State University.

Moris, Jon R., and Colby R. Hatfield. 1982. A new reality: Western technology faces pastoralism in the Masai project. In International Rice Research Institute, Report of an exploratory workshop on the role of anthropologists and other social scientists in interdisciplinary teams developing improved food production technology. Manila, Philippines: IRRI.

Morley, D. 1981. Industrial conflict and the mass media. In S. Cohen and J. Young, eds., *The Manufacture of News: Social Problems and the Mass Media,* rev. Beverly Hills: Sage Publications.

Myshaw, E. J. 1977. Extending the growth debate. In Kenneth D. Wilson, ed., *Prospects for Growth.* New York: Praeger.

National Organization for Women (NOW). 1983. Guidelines for feminist consciousness raising. Washington, D.C.: NOW.

Nelson, Cynthia, and Salah Arafa. 1982. Problems and prospects of participatory action research: An illustration from an Egyptian rural community. Paper presented at the 10th World Congress of the International Sociological Association, Mexico City, Mexico.

Neuman, W. R. 1976. The patterns of recall among television news viewers. *Public Opin. Q.* 40:115–23.

Nix, Harold L. 1982. *The Community and Its Involvement in the Study Planning Action Process.* Athens, Ga.: Institute of Community and Area Development.

Nix, H. L., and N. R. Seerley. 1973. Comparative views and actions of community leaders and non-leaders. *Rural Sociol.* 38:427–38.

Norman, David W. 1980. The farming systems approach: Relevancy for the small farmer. MSU rural development paper 5, Department of Agricultural Economics. East Lansing: Michigan State University.

_____. 1982. The farming systems approach to research. Farming systems research paper 3. Manhattan: Kansas State University.

Olien, C. N.; G. A. Donohue; and P. J. Tichenor. 1968. The community editor's power and the reporting of conflict. *Journalism Q.* 45:243–52.

_____. 1981. Use of the press and power of the group. *Sociol. Community Life* 4:1–2, 7.

Olson, Mancur, Jr. 1968. *The Logic of Collective Action: Public Goods and the Theory of Groups.* New York: Schocken Books.

O'Rourke, Diane, and Johnny Blair. 1983. Increasing informant cooperation for random respondent selection in telephone surveys. Paper presented at the 38th annual conference for Public Opinion Research, May 19–22, Buck Hill Falls, Pa.

Paletz, D. L.; P. Reichert; and B. McIntyre. 1971. How the media support local government authority. *Public Opin. Q.* 35:80–92.

Palmgreen, P., and P. Clarke. 1977. Agenda-setting with local and national issues. *Community Res.* 4:435–52.

Parenti, Michael. 1970. Power and pluralism: A view from the bottom. *J. Polit.* 32:501–30.

Peck, John; William Kimball; and Donald Johnson. 1983. *Award and Recognition Programs for Community Development.* Ames, Iowa: North Central Regional Center for Rural Development.

Pelto, Pertti J., and Gretel H. Pelto. 1978. *Anthropological Research: The Structure of Inquiry,* 2nd ed. Cambridge, Mass.: Cambridge University Press.

Perlman, Robert. 1977. Social planning and community organization. *Encyclopedia of Social Work,* vol. 2. Washington, D.C.: National Association of Social Workers.

Perrett, Heli, and Francis J. Lethem. 1980. Human factors in project work. World Bank staff working paper 397, Washington, D.C.: World Bank.

Population Reference Bureau. 1982. World population data sheet, 20th ed. Washington, D.C.: Population Reference Bureau, Inc.

President's Commission on National Goals. 1960. *Goals for Americans.* Englewood Cliffs, N.J.: Prentice-Hall.

Rapaport, R. 1970. Three dilemmas in action research. *Hum. Relat.* 23:499–513.

Rebuffoni, Dean. 1983. State's bedrock may offer disposal site for wastes. *Minneapolis Star and Tribune,* June 13, p. 3B.

Redfield, Robert. 1960. An ecological system. In Robert Redfield, *The Little Community.* Chicago: University of Chicago Press.

Reeder, W. W., and R. G. Gilpin, Jr. 1957. Know your community with a community self-survey. Extension Bulletin 982, New York State College of Agriculture. Ithaca, N.Y.: Cornell University.

Reeves, Edward B., and Timothy Frankenberger. 1981. Farming systems research in North Kordofan, Sudan. Report 1, Aspects of agricultural production, the household economy, and marketing, INTSORMIL Contract AID/DSAN-G-0149. Lexington: University of Kentucky.

————. 1982. Farming systems research in North Kordofan, Sudan. Report 2, Aspects of agricultural production, the household economy, and marketing, INTSORMIL Contract AID/DSAN-G-0149. Lexington: University of Kentucky.

Reinhard, Kathryn; Daniel S. Murphy; Donald E. Johnson; and Larry Meiller. 1985. Community needs assessment training and development handbook. Department of Rural Sociology, Cooperative Extension Service, University of Wisconsin-Madison.

Rhoades, Robert E. 1982. The art of the informal agricultural survey. Lima, Peru: International Potato Center.

Rhoades, Robert E., and Robert H. Booth. 1981. Farmer-back-to-farmer: A model for generating acceptable agricultural technology. *Agric. Adm.* 11:127–37.

Rondinelli, Dennis A. 1983. Projects as instruments of development administration: A qualified defense and suggestions for improvement. *Public Adm. Dev.* 3:307–27.

Rosenbaum, Nelson M. 1978. Citizen participation and democratic theory. In Stuart Langton, ed., *Citizen Participation in America.* Lexington, Mass.: Heath.

Rosener, Lynn, and Peter Schwartz. 1980. Women, leadership and the 1980s: What kind of leaders do we need? In *New Leadership in the Public Interest.* New York: NOW Legal Defense and Education Fund.

Rosenfeld, Alan S. 1974. Need surveys and the social construction of reality. *Urban Soc. Change Rev.* 7:39–42.

Ross, Russell M., and Kenneth F. Millsap. 1966. *State and Local Government and Administration.* New York: Ronald Press.

Rothman, Jack. 1979. Three models of community organization practice, their mixing and phasing. In Fred M. Cox, John L. Erlich, Jack Rothman, and John E. Tropman, eds., *Strategies of Community Organization: A Book of Readings,* 3rd ed. Itasca, Ill.: Peacock.

Roy, Prodipto. 1982. Extension with the disadvantaged: A radical view. In G. E. Jones and M. J. Rolls, eds., *Progress in Rural Extension and Community Development,* vol. 1. New York: Wiley.

Rucker, Bryce. 1968. *The First Freedom.* Carbondale: Southern Illinois University Press.

Salmon, R. J., and G. H. Tapper. The power-conflict approach. In H. B. Long, R. C. Anderson, and T. A. Blubaugh, eds., *Approaches to Community Development.* Iowa City, Iowa: National University Extension Association and American College Testing Program.

Scheaffer, Richard L.; William Mendenhall; and Lyman Ott. 1979. *Elementary Survey Sampling.* Belmont, Calif.: Duxbury Press.

Scheff, T. J. 1967. Toward a sociological model of consensus. *Am. Sociol. Rev.* 32:32–46.

Schudson, Michael. 1978. *Discovering the News: A Social History of American Newspapers.* New York: Basic Books.

Schuman, Howard, and Stanley Presser. 1981. *Questions and Answers in Attitude Surveys: Experiments on Question Form, Wording and Context.* New York: Academic Press.

Schuttler, Barry L. 1971. The charrette planning process. Unpublished manuscript. Clarksville, Md.

Shaner, W. W.; P. F. Philipp; and W. R. Schmehl. 1982. *Farming Systems Research and Development: Guidelines for Developing Countries.* Boulder, Colo.: Westview Press.

Shaw, D. L., and M. E. McCombs. 1977. *The Emergence of American Political Issues: The Agenda-setting Function of the Press.* St. Paul, Minn.: West.

Shepherd, R. G. 1981. Selectivity of sources: Reporting the marijuana controversy. *J. Commun.* 31:129–37.

Shingi, P. M., and B. Mody. 1976. The communications effects gap: A field experiment on television and agricultural ignorance in India. *Commun. Res.* 3:171–90.

Sigal, L. U. 1973. *Reporters and Officials: The Organization and Politics of Newsmaking.* Lexington, Mass.: Heath.

Simmel, G. 1955. *Conflict and the Web of Affiliations,* R. Bendex, trans. New York: Free Press.

Spergel, Irving A. 1977. Social planning and community organization: Community development. *Encyclopedia of Social Work,* vol. 2. Washington, D.C.: National Association of Social Workers.

Stanley, Liz, and Sue Wise. 1983. *Breaking Out: Feminist Consciousness and Feminist Research.* London, Boston: Melbourne and Healey, Routledge and Keagan Paul.

Stewart, David W. 1984. *Secondary Research: Information Sources and Methods.* Beverly Hills: Sage Publications.

Stinchcombe, A. L. 1968. *Constructing Social Theories.* New York: Harcourt, Brace and World.

Stoiken, Larry, ed. 1976–1983. *Alternative Sources of Energy.* Milaca, Minn.: Alternative Sources of Energy, Inc.

Stone, Linda, and J. Gabriel Campbell. 1984. The use and misuse of surveys in international development: An experiment from Nepal. *Human Organ.* 43:27–37.

Sudman, Seymour, and Norman Bradburn. 1982. *Asking Questions: A Practical Guide to Questionnaire Design.* San Francisco: Jossey-Bass.

Suominen, E. 1976. Who needs information and why. *J. Commun.* 26:115–19.

Surveying Community Attitudes. 1977. Technical and Procedural Manual for Communities, University of Missouri-Columbia and Missouri Division of Community Betterment, Manual 108, 12/77/2M.

Survey Research Center, Institute for Social Research. 1976. *Interviewer's Manual,* rev. ed. Ann Arbor: University of Michigan.

Swantz, Marja Liisa. 1975. Research as an educational tool for development. *Convergence* 8:44–53.

Sweet, C., and P. Weisel. 1979. Process versus blueprint models for designing rural development projects. In G. Hondale and R. Klauss, eds., *International Development Administration.* New York: Praeger.

Thompson, Michael. 1980. An outline of cultural theory of risk. Publication WP-80-177,

International Institute of Applied Systems Analysis. December, A-2361. Laxenburg, Austria: IIASA.

Tichenor, P. J.; C. N. Olien; and G. A. Donohue. 1976. Community control and care of scientific information. *Community Res.* 4:403–24.

_____. 1980. *Community Conflict and the Press.* Beverly Hills: Sage Publications.

Todd, Thomas M. 1980. Presentation of hazardous waste facility development to Connecticut legislature. (Thomas M. Todd, Legislative Analyst, Research Department, Minnesota House of Representatives.)

Tuchman, G. 1978. *Making News.* New York: Macmillan.

Twain, David. 1983. *Creating Change in Social Settings.* New York: Praeger.

United Nations, Department of Economic and Social Affairs. 1975. Report of the 24th session. Commission for Social Development, E/CN./5/525, New York: U.N.

United Nations, Food and Agriculture Organization. 1981. Agriculture: Toward 2000. Economic and Social Development Series 23. Rome: FAO.

Uphoff, Norman T., and Milton J. Esman. 1974. Local organization for rural development: An analysis of Asian experience. Center for International Studies, Rural Development Committee and Department of Government. Ithaca, N.Y.: Cornell University.

Uphoff, Norman; John M. Cohen; and Arthur A. Goldsmith. 1979. Feasibility and application of rural development participation. A state-of-the-art paper, Center for International Studies, Rural Development Committee. Ithaca, N.Y.: Cornell University.

U.S. Agency for International Development. 1975. Implementation of "New Directions" in development assistance. Report prepared by AID for Committee on International Relations on Implementation of the Foreign Assistance Act of 1973, 94th Congr., 1st sess., July 22, 1975. Washington, D.C.: USAID.

_____. 1982. Food and agriculture development. AID policy paper, May. Washington, D.C.: USAID.

U.S. Department of the Treasury. 1982. Statistics of income and related administrative record research: 1982. Compiled and edited by Wendy Alvey and Beth Kilss, Statistics of Income Division. Washington, D.C.: Internal Revenue Service.

_____. 1983. Statistics of income and related administrative record research: 1983. Compiled and edited by Wendy Alvey, Statistics of Income Division. Washington, D.C.: Internal Revenue Service.

_____. 1984a. Statistical uses of administrative records: Recent research and present prospects, vol. 1. Compiled and edited by Beth Kilss and Wendy Alvey, Statistics of Income Division. Washington, D.C.: Internal Revenue Service.

_____. 1984b. Statistical uses of administrative records: Recent research and present prospects, vol. 2. Compiled and edited by Beth Kilss and Wendy Alvey, Statistics of Income Division. Washington, D.C.: Internal Revenue Service.

U.S. Senate, Committee on governmental affairs. 1977. Public participation in regulatory agency proceedings. 95th Congr., 1st sess., prepared pursuant to S. Res. 71, p. 52.

Vidich, A. J., and H. Bensman. 1958. *Small Town in Mass Society.* Princeton, N.J.: Princeton University Press.

Voth, Donald. 1975. Problems of evaluating community development. *J. Community Dev. Soc.* 6:147–62.

_____. 1979. Social action research in community development. In Edward James Blakely, ed., *Community Development Research: Concepts, Issues and Strategies.* New York: Human Sciences Press.

Wardwell, John A., and Don A. Dillman. 1975. Alternatives for Washington: The final report, vol. 6. Office of Program Planning and Fiscal Management. Olympia: State of Washington.

Warren, Roland L. 1970. Organizing a community survey. In Fred M. Cox, John L. Erlich, Jack Rothman, and John E. Tropman, *Tactics and Techniques of Community Practice.* Itasca, Ill.: Peacock.

_____. 1972. *The Community in America,* 2nd ed. Chicago: Rand McNally.

Waterlow, Charlotte. 1982. The awakening peasant: Rising expectations in the Third World. *The Futurist* 16(October):27–30.

Weaver, D. H.; D. A. Graber; M. E. McCombs; and C. H. Eyall. 1981. *Media Agenda-setting in a Presidential Election: Issues, Images, and Interest.* New York: Praeger.

Webb, Eugene J.; Donald T. Campbell; Richard D. Schwartz; and Lee Sechrest. 1966. *Unobtrusive Measures: Nonreactive Research in the Social Sciences.* Chicago: Rand McNally.

Webster, Stephen. 1977. Green County human services needs assessment. Madison, Wis.: Department of Health and Social Services.

Wellborn, Stanley. 1984. What next? A world of communications wonders. *U.S. News and World Report* 96(April 9):59–62.

Werner, A. 1975. A case of sex and class socialization. *J. Commun.* 25:45–50.

Westley, B. H. 1976. Setting the political agenda: What makes it change? *J. Commun.* 26:43–47.

Wheaton, William, and Margaret Wheaton. 1972. Identifying the public interest: Values and goals. In Ira Robinson, ed., *Decision Making in Urban Planning.* New York: Russell Sage Foundation.

Wignaraja, Ponna. 1984. Towards a theory and practice of rural development. *Development: Seeds of Change* 2:3–11.

Wileden, Arthur F. 1970. *Community Development: The Dynamics of Planned Change.* Totowa, N.J.: Bedminster Press.

Willett, A. B. J. 1981. *Agricultural Group Development in Botswana,* vol. 3, Chs. 17–26. Gaborone, Botswana: Ministry of Agriculture, Agricultural Management Association.

Williams, Lindsey. 1980. *The Energy Non-Crisis.* San Diego: Worth.

Wilson, James Q. 1962. *The Amateur Democrat.* Chicago: University of Chicago Press.

Winans, Edgar V. 1965. The political context of economic adaptation in the southern highlands of Tanganyika. *Am. Anthropol.* 67:435–41.

Wisconsin Department of Development. 1984. Wisconsin business climate study. Madison: Wisconsin Department of Development.

World Bank. 1980. World development report. Washington, D.C.: World Bank.

Ziegler, Warren L. 1978. Principles for and practices in the design and initiation of civic literacy projects. New York: Syracuse University.

Zufferey, F. S. 1983. A study of local institutions in Mopipi communal first development area central district. Gaborone, Republic of Botswana, Ministry of Local Government and Lands, Applied Research Unit. Madison: University of Wisconsin Land Tenure Center.

———. 1984. Personal communication.

Annotated bibliography

LORNA CLANCY MILLER ● GARY MEJCHAR

SECTION I. Political and social contexts of needs assessment

Alderfer, Clayton. 1972. *Existence, Relatedness, and Growth: Human Needs in Organizational Settings.* New York: Free Press.

Alderfer suggests that human needs can be conceptualized in terms of three independent categories: material *existence* needs, interpersonal *relatedness* needs, and personal *growth* needs. These findings suggest a more complicated behavior motivation dynamic than posed in Maslow's satisfaction-progression need hierarchy.

Bates, Frederick and Lloyd Bacon. 1972. The community as a social system. *Social Forces* 50:371-79.

The authors state that two types of conjunctive (conflicting yet interdependent) relationships lie at the core of community structure: *exchange interstitial groups,* organized around professional-client or merchant-consumer relationships, and *coordination interstitial groups,* which function to manage relationships among two or more distinct groups with potentially conflicting interests. The authors suggest that rigorous and systematic empirical studies "of the increase, or decrease, in the number, scope and potency . . . " of the exchange and coordinational interstitial groups can provide a standardized measure of degree of "community."

Bates, Frederick, and Clyde Harvey. 1975. *The Structure of Social Systems.* New York: Gardener Press.

The authors combine primarily a general systems approach with role theory approach, symbolic interaction approach, and conflict theory in an "attempt to build a single integrated conceptual model of human society and of its various subparts." The book is divided into six sections: philosophic foundations, micro structure of social systems, macro structure of social systems, the actor as a participant in social systems, dimensional analysis and change, and a general assessment.

Bradshaw, Jonathan. 1972. The concept of social need. *New Society.* 19:640-43.

This approach to the classification of social need concepts can be used by researchers and policymakers to clarify what part of the total need is appropriate to try to meet. The interrelated definitions of social need — normative need, which the expert defines as need; felt need; expressed need, which is action oriented; and comparative need, which compares the characteristics of those who receive the service—are basic elements of the illustrated taxonomy on housing needs.

Brown, Lester R. 1981. *Building a Sustainable Society.* New York: W. W. Norton. The author states that this book is part of the continuing research program of the Worldwatch Institute (begun in 1975). The book examines three factors demonstrating severe environmental stress that could possibly jeopardize the life-supporting capacity of this planet. These factors include: (1) excessive loss of top soil globally, e.g., "at the existing intensity of cultivation, every ton of (U.S.-grown) grain exported leads to the loss of several tons of top soil"; (2) demands exceeding the sustainable yield of global biological systems, e.g., widespread overfishing, overgrazing, and deforestation; and (3) potential depletion of oil reserves before alternative energy sources are developed (e.g., attempts to replace oil with nuclear power will lead to weapons proliferation, political instability, and possible self-destruction). Two-thirds of the book is prescriptive, with the author discussing many potential ways of creating a sustainable society, making clear that such a move will require "fundamental economic and social changes, a wholesale alternation of economic priorities and population policies." The author states that "every facet of human existence—diet, employment, leisure, values, politics, and habits—will be touched." The author also cautions that of the many dimensions of the transition to a sustainable society, the most critical is time.

Burns, James MacGregor. 1978. *Leadership.* New York: Harper and Row. The author deals with leadership as distinct from mere power holding and as an opposite of brute power. He offers a general conception of the true nature of leaders, drawing from sources such as Maslow, Lasswell, and Kohlberg to support his argument that mutual need, empathy, and growth characterize all genuine leadership. The book, ranging over political history in many countries, illustrates the varieties of leadership the author has identified, including reform, revolutionary, heroic, parity, legislative, executive, and others. He distinguishes two broad categories: transactional leadership, where the interaction between a leader and his or her followers is based on some exchange of benefits and motivations remain unchanged, and transforming leadership, in which the leader and followers "engage" one another in such a way that both are raised to "higher levels of motivation and morality." Burns presents a theory of leadership as a "dynamic reciprocity between ordinary people of 'followers' and political and ideological 'leaders' that thrives on conflict and demands no consensus."

Cook, Fay; Tom R. Tyler; Edward G. Goetz; Marsarett T. Gordon; David Protess; Donna R. Leff; and Harvey L. Molotch. 1983. Media and agenda setting: Effects on the public, interest group leaders, policymakers, and policy. *Public Opin. Q.* 47:16–35.
The authors explore the impact on the general public and policymakers of a single media event—a television report of an investigation of fraud in the home health care program (NBC 1981). Although the findings indicate that the media influenced views about the importance of the issue, the change in public opinion did not lead to subsequent policy change. The policy change that followed

was a result of collaboration between journalists and government policy members.

Donohue, G. A.; Tichenor, P. J.; and Olien, C. N. 1973. Mass media functions, knowledge and social control. *Journalism Q.* 50:652–59.

The authors present a macroconceptual frame of reference as an approach to the study of mass communication processes, based on the assumption that control of knowledge is basic to the development of social power. Mass media are viewed as interdependent parts of a total social system in which problems of controlling and being controlled are shared with other subsystems. It is asserted that in a systems control approach, mass media in a less complex system are likely to emphasize the distributive aspect of system maintenance. As the system becomes more differentiated, mass media tend to perform a feedback as well as a distributive function. The study also asserts that as mass media infusion into the social system increases, segments of the population with higher socioeconomic status tend to acquire this information at a faster rate, creating an increased gap of knowledge between segments of society.

Easton, David. 1976. Theoretical approaches to political support. *Can. J. Polit. Sci. (Rev. Can. Sci. Polit.)* 9:431–48.

The author states that "the context in which political support has heretofore been considered has been preservationist, directed at how objects of the political system manage to maintain a certain level of support." He contends that there needs to be a theoretical awareness not only of official leadership and legitimacy but also of the dimensions of trust, loyalty, and confidence in the political community. He poses the question of political support in a different and more comprehensive frame of reference by turning it around — How does change occur?

French, Wendell L., and Cecil H. Bell, Jr. 1973. *Organization Development: Behavioral Science Interventions for Organization Improvement.* Englewood Cliffs, N.J.: Prentice-Hall.

In this book the authors describe *organization development* as an applied behavioral science process that seeks to improve organizations through planned, systematic, long-range efforts focused on the organization's culture and its human and social processes. The scientific method offered to implement this specific organization development approach is an orderly process of inquiry, data gathering, and the testing of hypotheses with emphasis on interpersonal, group, and intergroup behaviors and dynamics. The interventions described focus on culture, processes, and events at many levels of organization, presenting material on both the theory and the practice of organizational development. The book is relevant to academicians and students as well as organization specialists and managers who may want to try to improve their organizations.

Genova, Bistra; K. L. Greenberg; and S. Bradley. 1979. Interest in news and the knowledge gap. *Public Opin. Q.* 43:79–91.

The comparative strengths of socioeconomic status and individual interests as major factors in the consumption of public affairs news are analyzed in the context of the "knowledge gap" hypothesis. Respondents from fifteen central Michigan communities were quizzed on their interest and knowledge about the National Football League strike and the Nixon impeachment developments. Interest was more strongly related to knowledge than education, particularly for more complex information. On the second survey taken 10 days later, more new information had been learned by those with higher levels of interest.

Gerlach, Luther P., and Virginia H. Hine. 1970. *People, Power, Change: Movements of Social Transformation.* Indianapolis: Bobbs-Merrill.

This study of movement dynamics identifies five key factors that the authors believe must be present and interacting before a collectivity of any size becomes a true movement. Their approach to the analysis of movements is a result of three years of anthropological research into two modern movements—the Pentecostal Movement and the Black Power Movement. They take the position that movements are both cause and effect of social change. In this book they are focusing on movements as mechanisms of change rather than on the conditions of disorganization or deprivation that give rise to them.

Gerlach, Luther P., and Virginia H. Hine. 1973. *Lifeway Leap: The Dynamics of Change in America.* Minneapolis: University of Minnesota Press.

Based on research that examined social movements, social change, and established order responses, conducted in Minnesota and East Africa, Gerlach and Hine present distinctions between revolutionary and developmental change. They explore the concept of systems, evolutionary principles, insights into the role of movements and responses to them, and the stability-through-change idea as conceptual tools that can be used to interpret the changes society is experiencing.

Hare, Alexander Paul. 1982. *Creativity in Small Groups.* Beverly Hills: Sage Publications.

The author makes the point that "the steps in group problem-solving and in the creative process are essentially the same" and that all of the insights of group dynamics can be applied to the analysis of creativity in groups. In Part I he examines four perspectives of small-group interaction: functional categories for the analysis of content, interaction dimensions to assess process, and dramaturgical and exchange analysis. In Part II three theories of group development are reviewed in terms of one or more of the perspectives presented in Part I. Hare's examination of the traditional consensus process used by Quakers for over 300 years when seeking agreement on difficult social problems, reveals an outline of steps for problem solving and group creativity. The seven steps include problem definition, data collection, solution review, solution development at the appropriate level of creativity, pilot project test, agreement and commitment, and implementation.

Helmer, Olaf. 1983. *Looking Forward: A Guide to Futures Research.* Beverly Hills: Sage Publications.

The author observes that the last 20 years have seen the emergence of what has become known as a "futures movement," with hundreds of futures societies all over the world, numerous journals devoted to the future, and congresses attended by thousands. The author states that this book is concerned with generic methods of exploring the future and the application of such methods to long-range planning. Some of the systematic futures research methods discussed here include trend extrapolation, the Delphi technique, cross-impact analysis, simulation gaming, and scenario writing. The author states that this futures movement has included a change in philosophical attitude toward the future — a growing awareness that there are a multitude of possible futures, with associated probabilities that can be estimated and to some extent manipulated, as well as a new pragmatic attitude that technology and our environment are undergoing change and the pace of change in our time is accelerating.

Kasperson, Roger, and Myrna Breitbart. 1974. Participation, decentralization, and advocacy planning. Commission on College Geography resource paper 25. Washington, D.C.: Association of American Geographers.
This work critically examines three political phenomena: citizen participation in public policy, decentralization, and advocacy planning. The authors' overall conclusions of assessments of each of these phenomena is that, at best, they have fallen short of their set objectives and, at worst, have failed miserably. Following each rather objective assessment of the said phenomena, the authors provide ideals and propose alternatives for reducing the gap between "utopian objectives" and empirical realities.

Kellerman, Barbara. 1984. *The Political Presidency: Practice of Leadership.* New York: Oxford University Press.
This book offers a broad-based discussion of leadership and followership in the context of American presidential leadership. Kellerman joins three themes to form a comprehensive theory of presidential leadership: leadership as a reflection of the national character, leadership as social exchange, and presidential leadership as a set of behaviors that includes personal politicking. Six case studies cover recent presidents including Kennedy, Johnson, Nixon, Ford, Carter, and Reagan.

Kellerman, Barbara, ed. 1984. *Leadership: Multidisciplinary Perspectives.* New Jersey: Prentice-Hall.
Kellerman describes this book as "a first requisite step toward cooperative work in leadership studies." The work consists of a series of original essays probing leadership issues from multidiscipline perspectives: historical, psychological, anthropological, political, organizational, sociological, and philosophical. It provides interested students as well as practitioners a wide selection of theory and practice with which to build understanding of the complex exchanges between leaders and those who are led.

Merritt, Richard L., and Anna J. Merritt. 1985. *Innovation in the Public Sector.* Beverly Hills: Sage Publications.
This book is the fourth volume in *Advances in Political Science: An International Series.* It presents original papers that focus in an integrated, multidisciplinary manner on practical and theoretical knowledge in the area of creativity and innovation. The innovative process is examined at many levels, ranging from individuals to international organizations. Invention, adoption, and

adaptation of change — using specific examples from agriculture, education, technology, and law — offer an analysis that suggests what works best in an open pluralistic society.

Monette, Maurice. 1979. Needs assessment: A critique of philosophic assumptions. *Adult Educ.* 29:83–95.
The author states that "needs are not mere empirically determinable facts; they are complex value judgements." Given this normative function of needs assessment, the author states that it is essential to examine the "causes" of the determined needs. The author proposes adopting a Freirian approach, which involves critical examination of the assumptions, values, and motivating philosophies underlying the basic needs assessment paradigm itself. Such an approach "places high priority on individual autonomy and the freedom to transform reality."

Nix, Harold. 1969. Concept of community and community leadership. *Sociol. Soc. Res.* 53:500–10.
The article attempts to define the notion of "community" and provide a categorization scheme for types of leaders and forms of leadership. Community is seen as the social facts existing in "the exchange and coordinative relationships between the various special-interest groups and organizations within a locality." Three dimensions of community leaders are classified: hierarchical level and function classification, scope of influence, and orientation. The author also discusses several different possible community power structures: focused/unitary, split/bifactional, multifactional, and amorphous.

Olien, C. N.; Donohue, G. A.; and Tichenor, P. J. 1978. Community structure and media use. *Journalism Q.* 55(autumn):445–55.
The extent to which media choice is affected by community type and structure is determined by analysis of data from 19 Minnesota communities with populations under 10,000. In-home interviews found support for the position that daily newspaper reading will be lower and television watching higher in communities where the local paper is a weekly rather than a daily. Preference for type of media results in greater or lesser exposure to information about local or national affairs, which may affect the participation and understanding of public issues on the local, national, and international levels.

Olson, Mancur, Jr. 1968. *The Logic of Collective Action: Public Goods and the Theory of Groups.* New York: Schocken Books.
Applying economic analysis to the subjects of the political scientist, sociologist, and economist, this book presents an unorthodox theory of group and organizational behavior. The author challenges the assumptions of most of the literature about organizations, that groups act to serve their interests and the individuals in groups act out of self-interest. Olson says that unless the number of individuals in a group is quite small or there is coercion or some other special device to make individuals act in their common interest, rational self-interested individuals will not act to achieve their common or group interests. His collective action theory is examined within the framework of trade unionism, Marx's class theory, other special-interest groups, and orthodox theories of pressure groups.

Pennock, J. Roland, and John W. Chapman. 1969. *Voluntary Associations.* New York: Atherton Press.

This is Volume III of *Homos,* the yearbook of the American Society for Political and Legal Philosophy. It generally covers the political and legal aspects of private and voluntary associations, a philosophical analysis of their nature, and their operational significance for social and political pluralism.

Ross, Russell M., and Kenneth F. Millsap. 1966. *State and Local Government and Administration.* New York: Ronald Press.

The predominant emphasis of this textbook is on the administrative aspects of state and local governments. It covers the role of county governments, municipalities, and special districts (e.g., school, libraries, sewerage) and examines the importance of intergovernment coordination and cooperation and the growing relationships between the national and local governments. Also addressed are state regulations that affect business and labor.

Simpson, Dick, and George Beam. 1976. *Strategies for Change: How to Make the American Political Dream Work.* Chicago: Swallow Press.

The citizen participation strategies advocated in this book are designed to reform both the procedures and the substance of American politics. The authors' approach to a specific community problem or issue is to break down the process into three essential steps: define the situation accurately, evaluate a range of alternatives, and develop new tactics and institutions. Drawing on personal experiences in Chicago, the authors present two of the strategies as case studies. How to win elections through independent politics and nonviolent issue campaigns are analyzed for strengths and weaknesses. The third approach, how to take over bureaucracies, has yet to be tried but is presented in a hypothetical case to reform the Chicago school system. The book reflects the authors' seven years of experience with the Independent Precinct Organization, Citizens Action Program, dozens of electoral and issue campaigns, and deliberations with community organizers at a seminar on strategies for change held at the University of Illinois at Chicago Circle in 1968.

Suominen, Elina. 1976. Who needs information and why? *J. Commun.* 26:115–19.

On the basis of a "study of informational need" carried out by the Department of Long-range Planning of the Finnish Broadcasting Company (YLE) in 1972, the relationship between informational inequality and economic and social inequality is explored. Two dimensions of the concept "information need" are distinguished: subjective/objective and relative/absolute. Results suggest that those who have the greatest objective and relative need of information often feel the least subjective need. Mass communication appears to reinforce inequality by the media's language, terminology, and approach to issues.

Tichenor, P. J.; J. M. Rodenkirchen; C. N. Olien; and G. A. Donohue. 1973. Community issues, conflict, and public affairs knowledge. In Peter Clark, ed., *Models for Mass Communication Research,* vol. 2, Ch 2. Beverly Hills: Sage Publications.

This study, using data from 15 different community areas in Minnesota, examines whether social conflict in a community is likely to open the knowledge gap between various social strata of the population even further or to close it.

With community issues as the basic unit of analysis, the researchers measured mass media coverage, knowledge concerning the issues, perceptions of conflict, interpersonal communication, information recall from media content, and community attitudes about each issue. This study defines conflict as "a varying system condition which could be treated as either a dependent or an independent variable, depending upon the nature of the analysis." It suggests that defining the issue as controversial leads to more information exchange through the media and other institutions, and the media coverage in turn is regarded as controversial. This dynamic community process leads to resolution of the problem or diminished information flow or both. Issue relevance and community structure are identified as important determining factors in the course of the issues analyzed in these single-time studies.

Twain, David. 1983. *Creating Change in Social Settings: Planned Program Development.* New York: Praeger.

This book addresses the specialty areas of program planning, organizational development, and program evaluation at the local community level. The author suggests that "one objective of this book is to provide an integration of the three specialty areas, both theoretically and practically." He focuses on improved quality and competence of community as integrative components. The book presents a critical assessment of the current state of planned program development as well as a challenge to change agents to strive to facilitate "an enhanced quality of life through more competent community behavior." Useful techniques and procedures are provided to assist change agents in meeting these goals.

Warren, Roland. 1956. Toward a reformulation of community theory. *Human Organ.* 15:8–11.

Writing in the mid-fifties, Warren recognized the need to develop an updated theoretic framework of "community." His reformulation was based on a systems approach, focusing on the changing relationship between the horizontal axis (i.e., relationships within the locality) and the vertical axis (i.e., relationships between community-based special-interest groups and regional/state/national organizations). Warren suggested that to keep the increasingly structurally differentiated communities together, there would be a need to develop a complementary/symbiotic relationship between the task-oriented activities of the problem area specialist and the tension reducing/coordinating activities of the community coordinator.

SECTION II. U.S. experiences in needs assessment

Biddle, William W., and Loureide J. Biddle. 1968. *Encouraging Community Development: A Training Guide for Local Workers.* New York: Holt, Rinehart and Winston.

The authors designed this book to serve as a training guide and textbook for the nonprofessionals or preprofessionals who are engaged in local community improvement. It does not analyze the social arrangements that resist social reform and change but instead is devoted to exploration of ways local people can gain the collective strength to influence the changes and cope with the forces of resistance. An addendum for social science students is offered at the close of each chapter, linking the ideas of that section to social scientific research and presenting that research from a multidisciplinary perspective.

Blake, Brian; Ned Kalb; and Vernon Ryan. 1977. Citizen opinion surveys and effective CD efforts. *J. Community Dev. Soc.* 8:92–104.

The authors suggest that it is common for social researchers and community development workers to pay too little attention to how alternative citizen opinion survey approaches can/should vary with the specific objectives of the survey. The authors specify four different objectives: (1) identify problems and priorities for action, (2) identify positions of crucial local organizations, (3) enhance support for locally initiated community improvement efforts, and (4) maintain/instill the residents' sense of community. Under each objective the authors point to the procedural/substantive differences in (1) primary audiences, (2) question topics, (3) degree of community input, and (4) appropriate respondents.

Boruch, Robert F., and William R. Shadish, Jr. 1983. Design issues in community intervention research. In Edward Seidman, ed., *Handbook of Social Intervention.* pp. 73–98. Beverly Hills: Sage Publications.

The authors suggest that design sophistication alone is inadequate without well-developed managerial and legal skills, including negotiation expertise for the responsible social scientist. Numerous issues that are important to consider in design decisions are discussed, including research questions and how they are framed, the nature and complexity of the audience to whom the "answers" are intended, cost-benefit analysis of research information, and anticipation of answers and use of this information. The authors are critical of the extremely limited attention given to the implementation context of programs by designers of social intervention research as well as the fact that applied social research and substantive theory are seldom joined.

Checkoway, Barry. 1978. The politics of public hearings. Bureau of Urban and Regional Planning Research, planning paper 78-23. Urbana, Ill.: University of Illinois.

This paper examines the quality of public hearing practice and explores ways that it could be improved. The author points out four failures of the practice as a citizen participation process that is an effective instrument of democratic government. He points to the failure of prehearing procedures, challenges public hearings as a communications procedure, underscores the reasons for lack of general community representation, and questions the extent of influence on agency decisions. Checkoway offers several ways that the sponsoring agency and citizen groups could organize to improve the responsiveness of this approach to participatory decision making.

Cohen, Mark; Grayce Sills; and Andrew Schwebel. 1977. A two-stage process for surveying community needs. *J. Community Dev. Soc.* 8:54–61.

To be truly effective, the authors suggest, a survey must provide a nonbiased assessment of problems/needs that actually exist. One way to achieve this end is to provide for residents' input in the writing of questions for the needs assessment instrument. One technique to provide this citizen input is the two-stage interview process. Stage one is an open-ended interview designed to determine a wide range of problems affecting people in the area. Stage two is a briefer closed-ended interview consisting of more specific/categorized items obtained from the open-ended effort. This second stage is designed to determine the frequency and severity of the problem. The drawback of this technique is, of course, more time/cost expenditures. The trade-off is the potential for yielding more useful/valid information.

Cox, Fred M.; John L. Erlich; Jack Rothman; and John E. Tropman, eds. 1979. *Strategies of Community Organization: A Book of Readings.* Itasca, Ill.: Peacock.
This collection of articles describes and conceptualizes various aspects of community organization and social change. Part I considers the functional and historical perspective, Part II examines the context of community practice, and Part III presents a wide range of strategies to help practitioners organize their own approach to strategy choice and implementation.

Creighton, James L. 1981. *The Public Involvement Manual.* Cambridge, Mass.: Abt Books.
This manual provides practical guidance in designing and conducting public involvement programs. Strategies to reach the relevant public, suggestions for structure of public meetings, workshops, and media contacts, including advice for conflict management and an overview of other public involvement techniques, are presented. The intent of the author is to present examples of public involvement alternatives and issues to be considered rather than to provide specific prescriptions for problem solving.

Dillman, Don A. 1977. Preference surveys and policy decisions: Our new tools need not be used in the same old way. *J. Community Dev. Soc.* 8:1.
The methodological constraints and prohibitive costs of preference surveys that researchers experienced when engaged in past efforts to affect policy decisions have been largely removed with the development of reliable mail and telephone data collection methods. These developments have lead to the design of the synchronized survey approach to determine preference in policy decisions.

Dillman, Don A. 1978. *Mail and Telephone Surveys: The Total Design Method.* New York: Wiley.
The book provides specific guidance in using the total design method (TDM) for mounting mail and telephone surveys. The TDM approach to surveying is built upon the premise that to maximize both the quality and quantity of responses, attention must be given to every detail that might affect response behavior. The TDM relies on a theoretically based view of why people do and do not respond to questionnaires, and careful attention is given to the administrative details in the survey process. The author states that recent improvements in procedures for conducting mail and telephone surveys have brought these methods up to the same par as face-to-face interviews and have proven them superior to face-to-face interviews in many instances. The book provides guidance as to the advantages and disadvantages of various methods of writing questions, constructing questionnaires, and implementing telephone and mail surveys.

English, Fenwick, and Roger Kaufman. 1975. *Needs Assessment: A Focus for Curriculum Development*. Washington, D.C.: Association for Supervision and Curriculum Development.

This publication serves as a rather broad-based cookbook for "how the curriculum developer does a needs assessment." In addition to the generic steps of planning, instrument development, data collection, implementation strategies, and funding, the authors discuss the related concerns of critical assumptions of needs assessment efforts, dealing with ambiguity and anxiety, validation of performance objectives, and feedback.

Fitzsimmons, Stephen, and Warren Lavey. 1975. Social economic accounts system (SEAS): Toward a comprehensive, community-level assessment procedure. *Soc. Indic. Res.* 2:389–452.

In this article, the expression social economic accounts system (SEAS) is used to refer to an information system based upon periodically gathered, coded, analyzed, and evaluated data regarding social and economic characteristics of communities. The purposes of SEAS are to permit description at specific times of the characteristics of community residents, institutions that serve them, and activities that affect their lives. The impetus of the SEAS appears to come from the authors' observation that "while communities have a holistic character, the study of them is typically fragmented." Fitzsimmons and Lavey suggest that the SEAS can facilitate an integrative theory of human behavior and the bringing together and presenting of data that provides a "meaningful picture of overall community viability."

Freire, Paulo. 1970. *Pedagogy of the Oppressed*. New York: Herder and Herder.

The preface to this book suggests there is no such thing as a neutral educational process. "Education either functions as an instrument which is used to facilitate the integration of the younger generation into the logic of the present system and brings about conformity to it, *or* it becomes 'the practice of freedom,' the means by which men and women deal critically and creatively with reality and discover how to participate in the transformation of their world." This book presents the thoughts and methodologies developed by Freire, which address the later element of education as applied to the teaching of illiterates. Freire describes the problem as the "culture of silence" (i.e., economic, social, and political domination) and points toward *conscientizacao* (i.e., learning to perceive social, political, and economic contradictions and to take action against the oppressive elements of reality) as a viable solution to the problem.

Freire, Paulo. 1973. *Education for Critical Consciousness*. New York: Seabury Press.

The introduction to this book states that the author's central message is that one can know only to the extent that one "problematizes" the natural, cultural, and historical reality in which he or she is immersed. Problematizing is viewed as the antithesis of the technocrat's problem-solving stance. In the latter approach, an expert is removed from the reality of the problem, analyzes it into component parts, devises means for resolving difficulties in the most efficient way, then formulates a strategy or policy. Such problem solving, according to the author, distorts the totality of human experience by reducing it to dimensions that are amenable to treatment as mere difficulties to be solved. But to problematize in the author's sense is to associate an entire population with the task of codifying total reality into symbols that can generate critical consciousness and empower them to alter their relations with nature and social forces. The author critically examines "society in transition," "closed society and democratic inexperience," "education and *conscientizacao*," and the extension system.

Garkovich, Lorraine. 1979. What comes after the survey? A practical application of the synchronized survey model in community development. *J. Community Dev. Soc.* 10:30–38.
    The author uses the specific example of the development of a comprehensive land use plan to demonstrate how community development workers can utilize the "synchronized" survey technique (Don Dillman's) to (1) generate citizen involvement in problem and need identification, (2) generate more effective citizen involvement in government agenda building and policymaking, and (3) increase citizen involvement in policy implementation and evaluation.

Goudy, Willis, and F. Wepprecht. 1977. Meeting research and extension objectives: local, regional programs developed from residents' evaluations. *J. Community Dev. Soc.* 8:44–53.
    The authors remind us that "recent federal legislation, 1972 Rural Development Act, mandated the development of closer ties between data gathering and dissemination efforts in rural America." This article is essentially a report card on these Title V–generated activities (specifically in the state of Iowa). The authors make the important point that "the intent of the community studies was not to reveal specific goals or action programs, but rather, to define general concerns that could be examined further and developed by problem-solving groups working at the local and/or regional levels." Based on this overview of activities, the authors conclude that "although improvements could be made," the collaboration projects stimulated by the Title V mandate have been a success.

Gundry, Kathleen, and Thomas Heberlein. 1984. Do public meetings represent the public? *APA J.* 50:175–82.
    This article is based upon the findings from three public participatory research projects designed to measure the representativeness of meeting participants compared to the general population on demographic characteristics, opinions or policies, and opinion variance. The authors state that if meetings are well publicized, they are held so that all parties have easy and equal access, and all meeting participants are consulted about their opinions, the opinions given at public meetings appear to broadly represent those of the relevant public. This appears to hold true despite differences in the public meetings in scale (city, county, state), subject, level of controversy, and length.

Hahn, Alan J. 1970. Citizens in local politics: Nonparticipation and unrepresentation. *J. Community Dev. Soc.* 1:2.
    This paper explores relationships between "nonparticipation" and "unrepresentation," making two major points. First, decisions are made by competitive elites and there are some interests that are nearly always excluded. Second, in spite of attempts to increase citizen participation, few average or lower status

citizens actually participate in community decision making. The author contends that "community development efforts need to be aimed more at community leadership than at blocks of inactive citizens themselves."

Heberlein, Thomas A. 1976. Some observations on alternative mechanisms for public involvement: The hearing, public opinion poll, the workshop and the quasi-experiment. *Nat. Resour. J.* 16:197–212.

Given the need and at times requirement for agencies to demonstrate public involvement in a decision-making process, the author discusses the strengths and weaknesses of several alternative mechanisms for public involvement in an effort to help managers choose the public involvement technique most useful for their needs. The paper focuses on citizen involvement in specific projects or policies and is built upon the assumption that "as long as individuals trust the decision-maker to act in their best interest, they have no need to participate; however, as trust erodes, the demand for participation tends to increase." The author suggests four criteria of effectiveness useful in evaluating the adequacy of specific methods: the individuals involved should be representative of all groups affected; the individuals involved should be well informed, with knowledge of implications and alternatives; the methods should be interactive (i.e., action, response, reaction); and where possible, input should be based on actual experience and behavior.

Heberlein, Thomas, and Robert Baumgartner. 1978. Factors affecting response rates to mailed questionnaires: A quantitative analysis of the published literature. *Am. Sociol. Rev.* 43:447–62.

In a study of 98 mailed questionnaires (response rate experiments, where all were treated as respondents to a survey), two variables—the number of contacts and the judged salience to the respondent—were found to explain 51 percent of the variance in final response. Variables including government organization sponsorship, type of population, length of the questionnaire, questions concerning other individuals, use of a special class of mail or telephone on the third contact, and use of metered or franked mail on the outer envelope affected final response independent of contacts and salience. A causal model of the final response rate, explaining 90 percent of the variance, and a regression equation predicting final response rates are presented.

Hyman, Herbert H. 1972. *Secondary Analysis of Sample Surveys: Principles, Procedures and Potentialities.* New York: Wiley.

This book provides a comprehensive description of the methods and applications of secondary data analysis. This systematic review of secondary data practices is relevant to the sociologist, social psychologist, and political scientist, both researcher and student, providing lists of research designs, sources of data, and detailed case studies. The author emphasizes the rich sources of knowledge gained from 35 years of data gathering, which is now accessible to social scientists through specialized archives. An exhaustive bibliography and analytic table of contents offer easy reference.

Jaberg, Eugene Carl. 1968. The Town Meeting of the Twin Cities, 1966–1967: A case history of community dialogue. Graduate School of the University of Wisconsin-Madison.

This Doctor of Philosophy (speech) thesis examines the Town Meeting of the Twin Cities project, which was based on models from colonial New England and postwar Germany. It was a communitywide attempt to structure citizen dialogue on contemporary issues. The project was planned on the premise that communication networks of town meetings fostered interpersonal relations that must be considered a part of the mass communication process. This citizen participation effort was funded in part by the Title I, Higher Education Act and sponsored by a consortium of institutions of higher education in the area. Jaberg covers the entire project, including a review of the historical antecedents and the final evaluation that included data collected from over 6000 persons and was conducted by the Social Science Research Center of Augsburg College, Minneapolis.

Jackson, Kate, and Saralei Farner. 1976. *Community Needs and Resource Assessment Guidebook*. Washington, D.C.: National Center for Voluntary Action.
Based on the comparison between a number of different approaches to community needs and resource assessment (CNRA), this document suggests that planners of CNRAs may wish to consider (1) having the residents devise their own assessment model adapted to the needs and realities of their community; (2) having as wide a citizen participation and review as practicable, "involvement of citizens has direct bearing on the interest of the citizens"; (3) that to have data that "makes sense," there should be objective (quantitative) and subjective (qualitative) information about needs and services; and (4) that popular support or "citizen clout" for a survey effort comes from reputation, representation, and optimum sponsorship. The document also contains many excellent cautions to consider in the CNRA process as well as a useful example of a topically comprehensive survey instrument and community resource inventory checklist.

Kane, Rosalie A., and Robert L. Kane. 1981. *Assessing the Elderly: A Practical Guide to Measurement*. Lexington, Mass.: Lexington Books.
The authors provide criteria for selecting measurement instruments to help the long-term care providers to choose the best approach for assessing the needs of the elderly. The book examines whether a measure is most appropriate as a clinical tool for individual care or for producing information about groups of persons for program planning or policy purposes.

Kanter, Rosabeth Moss. 1980. An agenda for leadership in America. New York: NOW Legal Defense and Education Fund.
Kanter draws on her recent social science research to examine power, power sharing, and effective leadership. She found that "increasing the power attached to a wide variety of organizational positions can enhance the productive capacity of an organization." She contends that this observation is of special importance to business and industry as well as government and private organizations who run the risk of losing important problem-solving capacity in lower echelon employees when the approach to leadership is inflexible.

King, F. 1977. *A Technical Manual on Analyzing, Interpreting and Reporting Needs Assessment Data*. Needs Assessment Development Project, Department of State, Tallahassee, Florida.

This manual is one of six booklets in the larger *Needs Assessment System,* which is the product of the Needs Assessment Development Project sponsored by the Florida Department of Education. The major part of this manual discusses a variety of statistical techniques appropriate for the analysis of one variable (e.g., mean, chi-square, Kolmogorov-Smirnov), two variables (e.g., *t*-test, Spearman, Pearson); and more than one pair of variables (e.g., multidimensional chi-square, factor analysis, multiple regression). The conclusion of the manual provides an example of how to report needs assessment findings.

Koneya, Mele. 1978. Citizen participation is not community development. *J. Community Dev. Soc.* 9:23–29.
     The author states that the key difference between citizen participation (CP) and community development (CD) is in the orientation/location of decision-making power. CP is seen as government originated; the government decides to include citizens to a greater extent as means toward some ends. CD, on the other hand, "is citizen-originated activity that organizes and uses citizen power to reach upward toward government." This comparison of CD and CP demonstrates the varying underlying assumptions of the two approaches, that is, CD's projection of citizens' capacity for handling power and authority versus CP's assumption of the need to create and sustain a dependency relationship between citizens and government.

Korten, David C. 1980. Community organization and rural development: A learning process approach. *Public Adm. Rev.* 40:480–511.
     Although the need for participation in rural development and community organization has been recognized, interest has so far remained at a theoretical level. The author suggests that the prevailing approach to rural development emphasizes top-down, preplanned, time-bound strategies that function to strengthen the positions of prosperous traditional elites rather than integrating the rural poor into the development process. Five case studies are examined, which employ an alternative bottom-up strategy focusing on participatory planning and the linkage of knowledge with action.

Langton, Stuart. 1978. *Citizen Participation in America.* Lexington, Mass.: Lexington Books.
     Intended for a general audience of citizen leaders, government officials, and scholars, this book provides a common frame of reference for addressing critical issues of theory and practice concerning citizen participation. This collection of essays integrates four general areas of study that touch on citizen participation: democratic theory, studies of political behavior, community development and citizen action, and government-initiated citizen involvement. A multidisciplinary approach was used to identify and examine common and interrelated issues to provide background materials for the September 1978 National Conference on Citizen Participation in Washington, D.C.

Lauffer, Armand. 1982. *Assessment Tools for Practitioners, Managers and Trainers.* Beverly Hills: Sage Publications.
     Drawing on experiences of social workers and others in direct practice with individuals, families, community groups, and agencies, a wide range of assessment tools are presented in a form that can be easily learned and applied in a

variety of human service situations. Lauffer introduces practitioners to such helpful techniques as ecomapping, task analysis, nominal group, Delphi, force field analysis, gaming, and photography. Using vignettes and exercises, he provides guidelines for employing these flexible tools at many levels of intervention.

Lindaman, Edward. 1978. *Thinking in the Future Tense.* Nashville, Tenn.: Broadman.

This is a wide-reaching futurist piece integrating elements of education, theology, science, philosophy, and technology with participation in individual/ community volunteer activities. The content of this book centers around what the author views as "the awesome dual responsibility of being *able to* construct our own future and having to choose *whether to* and *how to* participate in the creative process, then . . . *to decide what options* we prefer." The author stresses that "the bases for the images that pull us into the future ought to be our own, chosen freely, the fruits of our creativity and unique perspective rather than someone else's prescriptions for tomorrow."

Lindaman, Edward, and Ronald Lippitt. l979. *Choosing the Future You Prefer: A Goal Setting Guide.* Ann Arbor, Mich.: Human Resource Development Associates of Ann Arbor.

The authors describe the contents of their book as "some of the orientations and activities we have found most rewarding in our own attempts: (l) 'to think in the future tense,' (2) to develop goal images about the future, and (3) in doing careful planning to enable us to step successfully into the future." The book contains 27 exercises appropriate for groups of almost any size, designed to help participants "work creatively and strategically" in influencing and shaping their preferred futures. Examples of included exercises are adjectives by decade, seeing society as a whole, my world-now checklist, and clarifying and specifying the future image. The authors suggest that it is crucial to choose to pursue such efforts toward creating futures as opposed to coping "reactively to the future created by others."

Linstone, Harold A., and Murray Turoff. 1975. *The Delphi Method: Techniques and Applications.* Reading, Mass.: Addison-Wesley.

Delphi is a group process that utilizes written responses, aggregating the judgments of a number of individuals to improve the quality of decision making. This method does not require face-to-face contact, making it particularly useful for involving experts, users, administrators, and resource controllers who cannot meet together physically. Delphi was originally used as an instrument to estimate probable effects of a massive atomic bombing attack on the United States and, later, as a process for technological forecasting. When viewed as a communication process, however, there are few areas of human endeavor that are not possible objects for application. The philosophical and methodological foundations of Delphi are presented in this book as well as design considerations to accomplish this form of structured communication.

Lowdermilk, Max, and W. Laitos. 1981. Towards a participatory strategy for integrated rural development. *Rural Sociol.* 46:689–701.

The authors outline seven major phases to their "participatory research development strategy" (PRDS): preliminary reconnaissance, priority problem identification field studies, search for solutions, assessment of solutions, project implementation, formal project evaluation, and project completion. The authors also stress eight "key concepts," which they view as integral to the entire PRDS process: systems approach; interdisciplinary team work; client involvement (e.g., "if client involvement is not ultimately self-sustaining, then it is not true development"); learning process, valuation (e.g., "the process of analyzing value criteria and making assumptions explicit rather than implicit"); training focus; institutional linkages; and monitoring/evaluation (e.g., "perhaps one of the weakest links in the rural development process occurs at this evaluation phase").

Meiller, Larry, and Glenn Broom. 1979. Communication experiments in building community consensus. *J. Community Dev. Soc.* 10:61–79.
Employing a quasi-experiment methodology, the authors test a survey-feedback-survey approach to building community consensus, stimulating interpersonal communication, and increasing the level of community knowledge between/within three community groups (i.e., citizens, elected officials, and community leaders). The findings suggest that through feedback (i.e., informative meetings, newspaper articles, direct mailings), respondents in the three groups became more knowledgeable about community problems and more accurate in estimating how others viewed development priorities. The authors also suggest that developing a "third-party communication facilitator" role in community development programs could serve as a catalyst to the information exchange and consensus building processes and in turn help to ensure that local planning is more responsive to actual local needs and priorities.

Miller, Delbert. 1977. *Handbook of Research Design and Social Measurement,* 3rd ed. New York: David McKay.
This handbook is an extremely comprehensive, detailed reference guide to the research process. It is divided into five parts containing discussion of specific phases of the research process. Each phase provides the reader with relevant outlines, instructions, work checklists, tables, examples, selected readings by experts in the field, and selected bibliographies. The handbook is designed to be equally helpful to teachers, researchers, and students.

Nix, Harold; G. Brooks; and B. Courtenay. 1976. Comparative needs of large and small communities. *J. Community Dev. Soc.* 7:97–105.
The authors view community as a social system whose function is to manage conflict and competition. They suggest that there are two basic types of relationships found between community groups within social systems: exchange relationships (i.e., interactions based on the exchange of goods and/or services) and coordinative relationships (i.e., generally undertaken by representatives of special-interest groups or organizations who are concerned with coordinating functions or managing relationships between varying groups in a social system). The authors hypothesize, and the findings seem to provide some support for the notion that "community leaders will indicate a greater relative concern for needs of community coordination as the community becomes larger and more complex" but that leaders of smaller communities will be primarily concerned with exchange needs.

Preston, James. 1969. Identification of community leaders. *Sociol. Social Res.* 53:204–16.

This article is essentially a comparison of three methods of identifying community leaders: action measure, organization/positional measure, and reputational measure. Based upon findings generated from a "quasi-field experiment," the author states that, although the three differing methods are best suited to identify different types of leaders, there is a tendency that "as community size decreases, the three approaches will identify the same group of leaders."

Rawlinson, J. Geoffrey. 1981. *Creative Thinking and Brainstorming.* New York: Wiley.

This is a practical book on creative thinking designed for managers at every level of organization or for any people working together to find solutions to problems. Drawing from the author's experience with nearly 800 groups of managers on four continents, the book identifies barriers to creative thinking and provides ideas for removing those obstacles. Systematic procedures for organizing and conducting effective brainstorming sessions are presented as well as a brief survey of related techniques.

Rosener, Lynn, and Peter Schwartz. 1980. Women, leadership and the 1980s: What kind of leaders do we need? New York: NOW Legal Defense and Education Fund.

In one of two papers on leadership produced for the round table discussion on new leadership in the public interest, sponsored by NOW, the authors analyze two different styles of leadership. They describe the traditional model, labeled "Alpha" for the purposes of the paper, as relying on hierarchical relationships and analytical thinking and focusing on short-range solutions for problems after they have developed. The second style, referred to as "Beta," is characterized as a newly recognized leadership style that engages followers in a participatory, cooperative mode and acknowledges concerns for growth, learning and negotiation of different value choices in a long-range time frame. The paper concludes with several issues that are of prime concern (i.e., energy, economy, environmental quality, war) and demonstrates how a balance of Alpha and Beta leadership could address these and other societal problems, thereby altering the trend toward an authoritarian and homogeneous society resulting from an overreliance on the Alpha (traditional) style of leadership.

Rosenfeld, Alan S. 1974. Needs surveys and the social construction of reality. *Urban Soc. Change Rev.* 7:39–42.

A major problem with needs surveys, according to Rosenfeld, is that respondents simply cannot accurately answer the fundamental question asked, that is, At what point in your taken-for-granted world could an intervention by a social service make a positive impact on your life? Rosenfeld suggests that what will most likely be reflected in the results of needs surveys is the socially taught/defined "reality" rather than the respondent's personal life situation. Rosenfeld also suggests that two components are essential for successful social change: the clients must recognize the problem or else explain why it does not exist, and the providers must learn what the situation looks like from the viewpoint of the recipient. Rosenfeld concludes that needs surveys can provide information on the recipient's problem recognition but are not capable of providing the viewpoint of the recipient.

Schuessler, Karl. 1982. *Measuring Social Life Feelings: Improving Methods for Assessing How People Feel About Society and Their Place in Society.* San Francisco: Jossey-Bass.

Schuessler suggests that his twelve scales successfully capture all the social life feelings that sociologists have operationally distinguished. These scales are (1) self-determination, (2) distrust people, (3) feel down, (4) job satisfaction, (5) faith in politics, (6) feel up, (7) people cynicism, (8) political cynicism, (9) future outlook, (10) work ethic, (11) demoralized, and (12) career concerns. He explains how the scales were constructed, demonstrates how they are scored, compares them to other scales, and assesses their reliability and validity. Schuessler also makes the reader aware of many of the weaknesses/problems of scales, suggesting that "one must either make do with scales that are the best possible or do without scales altogether." The book is designed to be of value both to those interested in the practical application of social life feelings scales and to those interested in the methods of scale construction and evaluation.

Schuman, Howard, and Stanley Pressor. 1981. *Questions and Answers in Attitude Surveys.* New York: Academic Press.

The authors state, "Our main goal is to determine how the ways in which attitude questions are asked in surveys affect the results derived from these same surveys." In so doing Schuman and Pressor attempt to tackle numerous problems that plague survey researchers, such as question order and response order effects, use of open versus closed questions, assessment of "no opinion," measuring the middle position in scales, balanced and imbalanced questions, form of wording, and measurement of attitude strength. Discussions of each topic contain rather rigorous assessment (both qualitative and quantitative) of the potential impact/problems inherent in the different alternative question forms.

Seidman, Edward, ed. 1983. *Handbook of Social Intervention.* Beverly Hills: Sage Publications.

The editor contends that "new knowledge is maximized at the interface of different disciplines and divergent perspectives. Consequently, this volume provides in a single source an integration, overview, and critical appraisal of a diverse array of social and community interventions." Social intervention is used to refer to an alteration of intrasocietal relationships, planned and unplanned ("natural"), intended and unintended. The effect is social change. The book is divided into six parts: (1) historical, cultural, and value perspectives; (2) research design and measurement; (3) strategies; (4) educational, psychological, and social programs and policies; (5) economic and environmental programs and policies; and (6) training issues and future projections.

Shapek, Raymond, A. 1975. Problems and deficiencies in the needs assessment process. *Public Adm. Rev.* 35:754–58.

Shapek suggests that needs listings are often initiated based on goals that are likely to be achieved, e.g., assuming that the created listings alone will provide decision makers with sufficient data to plan and implement programs effectively. He adds that such needs listings are often "fraught with inconsistency and lack of meaning." For these reasons they "are largely ignored and ridiculed." Shapek calls for three improvements that would enhance needs listings as instruments of change: (1) establish local recognition of the variables affecting the use of needs lists; (2) create more viable, community-specific lists; and (3) use needs lists as integrated planning tools.

Sorter, Bruce, and Charles Simpkinson. 1979. Coordinated networks: A method for community development. *J. Community Dev. Soc.* 10:89–100.
   The authors discuss a strategy to identify and connect needs with services/resources through coordinated networks of organized citizens, students, businesses, frontline agency staff, and local government. Needs were primarily identified and data gathered by a staff of "trained information system volunteers." Needs identification/collection methods used included questionnaires, surveys, nominal group processes, town meetings, and publications. The authors suggest that the coordination of service providers is "best facilitated through the efforts of frontline workers using barter and exchange rather than through direct financial agreements between agency heads proceeding from the top down." The authors also state that "the link between community residents, private organizations, and public agencies . . . develops best through ongoing cooperative trust-building efforts within the community network itself."

Stewart, Davis W. 1984. *Secondary Research: Information Sources and Methods.* Beverly Hills: Sage Publications.
   This text presents the secondary research process, which includes methods to locate, evaluate, integrate, and use published data from available information sources and computerized data bases. The author explores computer-assisted information searches and discusses the problems associated with integrating data from multiple sources. Issues of evaluation of secondary research are also included.

Sudman, Seymour, and Norman M. Bradburn. 1982. *Asking Questions: A Practical Guide to Questionnaire Design.* San Francisco: Jossey-Bass.
   This book concerns the type of question-asking embodied in the structured questionnaires or interview schedules used in social and market research. It deals specifically with questionnaire construction. The general thesis of this book is that questions must be precisely worded if responses to a survey are to be accurate and the survey valid. Methods for handling specific types of questions are discussed, such as threatening and nonthreatening behavior questions, knowledge questions, and attitude questions. Also covered are response options, rationale for the order of items in a questionnaire, formatting, method of administration, and ethical principals to be observed in survey research. Numerous actual questionnaire examples from Gallup, Roper, SRC, National Opinion Research Center, and SRL are included. Most of the chapters begin with a checklist that serves as an initial guide as well as a subsequent reference for actual survey construction.

Surveying community attitudes: A technical and procedural manual for communi-

ties. 1977. Manual 108 12/77/2M. University of Missouri-Columbia and Missouri Division of Community Betterment.
This publication functions as a cookbook for doing a community self-survey needs assessment. "How-to" topics covered include steps in organizing a self-survey, constructing a questionnaire, survey distribution and collection, tabulation and analysis of collected data, interpreting survey results, and using survey results in community planning and action programs. Also included are useful appendices of a sample community survey, sample news releases, sample letters to community groups, and "how-to" procedures for conducting a random sample.

Tait, John; Janet Bokemeier; and Joe Bohlen. *Identifying the Community Power Actors: A Guide for Change Agents.* North Central Regional Extension Publication 59. Ames: Iowa State University.
This publication was designed to assist "change agents," whose objective is to promote and stimulate social change in communities, in identifying key community leaders. The authors assume that obtaining support from the "community power actor" is essential to the success of community action programs. The publication examines four leader-identification methods: (1) positional, (2) reputational, (3) decision-making, and (4) social participation. A description of each method is given, and the assumptions, procedures to be used, types of power actors to identify, and advantages and limitations of each are discussed.

Warheit, George; Roger Bell; and John Schwab. 1977. *Needs Assessment Approaches: Concepts and Methods.* DHEW publication (ADM) 77-472.
This DHEW manual is essentially a "how-to-do-it" resource in conducting needs assessment studies in community settings. Although its focus is on mental health needs, its content is applicable to general needs assessment approaches as well. The manual provides a definition, discussion of advantages and disadvantages, and an "activities checklist" for five different needs assessment approaches (the first three being nonsurvey): key informant, community forum, rates under treatment, social indicators, and survey. Most of the manual, however, deals with a rather detailed overview and assessment of the survey approach, including coverage of sampling, data gathering techniques, research instrument designs, and interviewer training. Also included as appendices are a number of sample interview schedules, scales, and available census material.

Warren, Roland L. 1955. Community needs: How to identify and understand them. In *Studying Your Community.* New York: Russell Sage Foundation.
This book chapter presents some considerations to be addressed prior to conducting a survey, including a discussion of types and uses. The basic steps of the community survey process are outlined: scope and size, sponsorship, cost, organizing the survey committee, survey forms, field work, survey report, and publicity and follow-up.

Webb, Kenneth, and Harry P. Hatry. 1973. *Obtaining Citizen Feedback: The Application of Citizen Surveys to Local Governments.* Washington, D.C.: Urban Institute Publications Office.

This report explores the potential usefulness of citizen surveys to city and county government. It is based on an examination of the Dayton Public Opinion Center experience, Urban Observatory ten-city survey, and other selected projects. The study was supported by the Kettering Foundation through the Urban Institute. It discusses the various uses of surveys, their dangers and how to reduce them, a comparison of survey procedures, and some organizational options for conducting surveys.

Wireman, Peggy. 1970. Community development and citizen participation—Friend or foe? *J. Community Dev. Soc.* 1(2):54–62.

This paper examines the citizen participation requirements of federal programs and considers to what extent the community development process can help realize improved physical and social community conditions with those minimum citizen involvement demands of the bureaucracy. Wireman suggests seven elements that would maximize the community development results: holistic approach, involving the entire community, citizen participation in goal setting, self-help, rational and experimental approach, use of outside experts and materials, and emphasis on the process as well as the product.

SECTION III. Needs assessment in international development

Bennett, John W., and Gustav Thaiss. 1970. Survey research in anthropological field work. In Raoul Naroll and Ronald Cohen, eds., *A Handbook of Method in Cultural Anthropology*. New York: Columbia University Press.

The authors point toward a growing number of anthropologists who are abandoning their traditional "holistic-depictive" field approaches for computer and/or social survey approaches. The authors argue that, in certain anthropological research modalities, survey methods, with their distinctive logic and epistemology, are wholly or partly inappropriate; whereas in other contexts these survey techniques may be used reasonably effectively. The essence of the authors' concern is captured in the following statement: "The human reality must be apprehended by a variety of viewpoints, not by one alone, because this very reality is always in part a construct, always in part an image, and only by encouraging difference in perspective and approach can one obtain the needed richness of imagery, and consequently, theory.

Bunnag, Jane. 1976. Needs appraisal. United Nations Development Program, Bangkok (Thailand), report RB-382.

This paper consists principally of two checklists of preoperational research needs for development projects in developing nations. Preoperational research is focused on the possibility or feasibility of introducing a given innovation, its implications, and necessary modifications. The checklists—the first on factors relevant for agricultural program planners and the second on implications for a family planning project—group preoperational research needs as quantitative and qualitative data categories. The author contends that it is useful to systematize needed information so that the social planner may be made aware of the multiplicity of factors affecting the projected input in a development activity.

Burki, Shanid Javed, and Mahbub Ul Haq. 1981. Meeting basic needs: An overview. *World Dev.* 9:167–82.
The main thrust of this article is that the only way to eliminate poverty is to increase the productivity of the poor. However, to permanently sustain the elimination of poverty, programs designed to increase productivity must also provide the immediate area with adequate educational and health services, develop outlets for goods and services on which to spend growing personal financial resources, and have adequate funding resources available to the area to cover the very long period necessary to increase the productivity of the absolute poor to a level where they can afford basic needs.

Chambers, Robert. 1981. Rapid rural appraisal: Rationale and repertoire. *Public Adm. Dev.* 1:95–106.
The author states that the right information at the right time is vital for aware/responsible decision making but that, in rural development, information generated is often too costly and inappropriate. Two principles are stressed in rapid rural appraisal: "optimal ignorance" (knowing what is not worth knowing) and "proportionate accuracy" (recognizing the degree of accuracy required). Examples of approaches/techniques covered include using existing information, indigenous technical knowledge, key indicators, direct observation, group interviews, and aerial inspection. In all cases these techniques may be less rigid and exhaustive than many traditional methods but more rigorous in terms of time, cost, and use value.

Chambers, Robert. 1981. Rural poverty unperceived: Problems and remedies. *World Dev.* 9:1–19.
The paper suggests that in developing countries poor rural people and rural poverty generally are underperceived or misperceived by those who are themselves neither poor nor rural. Three obstacles to accurate perception are discussed: the rich, powerful, urban-based professionals are centralized and the poor, weak, rural people are at the peripheries; the integrated nature of rural poverty (isolated poor); and "rural development tourism" (i.e., short visits) by urban-based outsiders. Six biases against contact with poverty/the poor are laid out. The author concludes that although the problem is immense, implementation of measures to change the thinking/behavior of political leaders, officials, persons from aid agencies, and others involved in policy implementation is a key need for reducing rural poverty.

Foster, Charles R., ed. 1980. *Comparative Public Policy and Citizen Participation: Energy, Education, Health and Urban Issues in the U.S. and Germany.* New York: Pergamon Press.
Based on papers presented at a German-American conference on relationships between participation and policymaking held at Tulzing, Bavaria, scholars in this book address four basic issues crucial to the future of Western societies. After a discussion of the development, scope, and principal causes of the citizen action movement in the United States and Germany, this volume examines the effects and limitations of the increased interest in direct participation, with emphasis on energy, education, human services, and health policies. An agenda for participation research is also suggested.

Gold, Raymond L. 1977. Combining ethnographic and survey research. In Kurt Finsterbush and C. P. Wolf, eds., *Methodology of Social Impact Assessment*. Stroudsburg, Pa.: Dowden, Hutchinson and Ross.

The author poses the premise that fieldwork and survey methods are noninterchangeable, that researchers can conceive of, study, talk about, and treat the problems of society in quite distinct ways (i.e., field-involved sociologists see society as gemeinschaft and nonfield as gesellschaft). Despite the lack of methodological, procedural, and conceptual fit, the author argues that there is considerable potential for the work of the two to complement/supplement each other. The real problem, suggests the author, is getting the two types of investigators to work together.

Hall, Budd L. 1981. Participatory research, popular knowledge and power: A personal reflection. *Convergence* 14:6–19.

This article generally presents an overview of the underlying assumptions, methods, and goals of participatory research (PR) as well as some of the outcomes from the International Forum on Participatory Research held in Yugoslavia in April 1980. The author states that participatory research is most commonly described as an integrated activity that combines social investigation, educational work, and action. He also states that PR differs significantly from more traditional kinds of research in its commitment to the empowerment of learning for all engaged in the process. Central to PR is its role of strengthening the awareness in people of their own abilities and resources and its support to mobilizing or organizing. Also included here is a listing of contact people from the Participatory Research Network from Africa, Asia, the Caribbean, Europe, Latin America, and North America.

Hildebrand, Peter E. 1981. Combining disciplines in rapid appraisal: The sondeo approach. *Agric. Adm.* 8:423–32.

The article reviews the *sondeo* (or reconnaissance survey) approach, which essentially employs a multidisciplinary team to describe and assess farmer constraints and technology needs in advance of agricultural research. Five teams, with one social scientist and one natural scientist on each team, changing pairings each day, investigate farmer conditions for four days. Each member of the team then prepares a report that is finally amalgamated into a joint report. The *sondeo* was developed by the Guatemalan Institute of Agricultural Science and Technology—as a response to budget restrictions, time requirements, and other methodology—to augment information in regions where agricultural technology generation and promotion are being initiated.

Ickis, John C. 1983. Structural responses to new rural development strategies. In David C. Korten and Felipe B. Alfonso, eds., *Bureaucracy and the Poor.* West Hartford, Conn.: Kumarian Press.

The author first presents ideal type renderings of three traditional rural development strategies (i.e., growth, welfare, responsive) as well as the holistic strategy, which contains components from each of the previous three. He then relates the results from five Central American countries, which in the 1970s embarked on holistic strategies intended simultaneously to achieve growth, well-being, equity, and participation. The author points to weaknesses in three key areas: social intervention, institutional leadership, and system management, which appear to account for something less than successes in the projects examined. The author concludes by stating that development, defined in holistic terms, is a highly charged political process in which power, commitment, and leadership are key variables that can account for success in this capacity building process.

Korten, David C. 1980. Community organization and rural development: A learning process approach. *Public Adm. Rev.* 40:5.
The article suggests that the most successful Third World development assistance programs (based upon the findings of five Asian case study projects) are those that are "holistically perceived learning processes (for all involved) as opposed to a bureaucratically mandated blueprint design." The author states that the key is to have a development organization with a capacity for embracing error, learning with the people, and building new knowledge and institutional capacity through action.

Korten, David C., and Felipe B. Alfonso, eds. 1983. *Bureaucracy and the Poor: Closing the Gap.* West Hartford, Conn.: Kumarian Press.
The impetus for this book developed out of the 1979 meetings of the Management Institute's Working Group on Social Development (composed of four leading Third World management institutes of Asia and Latin America), where "action research" efforts were investigated as alternatives to the perceived limitations of conventional management concepts/methods. More specifically, the editors suggest that this book explores how the poor inhabitants in the many poor countries of the world can be helped to increase their productivity, develop their ability to work together for their mutual good, and enhance their bargaining power in relation to the rich and powerful in their societies. An underlying assumption here appears to be that the need to participate fully in the (economic, social, political) life of the community is a very basic and fundamental need. The book is divided into seven parts including, Creating Responsive Implementing Agencies (Part 2) and Helping the Poor Help Themselves (Part 6).

Roy, Prodipto. 1982. Extension with the disadvantaged: A radical view. In G. E. Jones and M. J. Rolls, eds., *Progress in Rural Extension and Community Development,* vol. 1, pp. 71–85. New York: Wiley.
The paper is divided into three sections. Section 1 provides a historical overview and critique of the development, extension, and research structures instituted in the Third World over the last 20 years. Section 2 offers some new methodologies for working with the poorest sections of the global population through nongovernment organizations. The final section suggests that although the existing research and extension structures have some utility, new project-specific, nonformal structures need to evolve. The author states that ultimately the poor need to participate more fully in the development process.

Stone, Linda, and J. Gabriel Campbell. 1984. The use and misuse of surveys in international development: An experiment from Nepal. *Hum. Organ.* 43:27–37.
This article examines some of the problems that arise when applying Western

survey methods in Third World countries. Findings suggest that nonsampling error for knowledge and attitudinal variables, measured in a popular KAP (knowledge, attitude, practice) survey, was far greater than what is normally computed as sampling error. The authors advise that for development-oriented research in the Third World, qualitative research methods should be interfaced with a survey to improve data validity and serve as a control for nonsampling error. A decision-making model for selection of optimum research strategies is also presented.

Swantz, Marja Liisa. 1975. Research as an educational tool for development. *Convergence* 8:44–53.
   The article discusses the basic requirements and benefits of participatory research in developing areas. The research is based on the principle of the villagers themselves being active participants in the research plan and thereby motivated to evaluate their own strengths and needs for village development (e.g., to help villagers use their many traditional skills). The author suggests that the participatory research strategy can eliminate the exploitative aspects of research, can operate as a political leveling instrument, and can be both educational and motivational.

Vergroff, Richard. 1974. Popular participation and the administration of rural development: The case of Botswana. *Hum. Organ.* 33:303–9.
   An effort to isolate variables associated with successful, locally initiated, and locally undertaken community development efforts is made. Three specific criteria are analyzed: leadership, participation, and coordination. The Republic of Botswana is used to examine local participation and the contribution of self-help to national development. Data collected from 31 villages suggest that the type of leadership available for rural development is not a key issue if the concern is with immediate outputs. Both traditional and elective authorities appear equally capable of organizing and bringing to completion local development projects.

Voth, Donald E. 1979. Social action research in community development. In Edward J. Blakely, ed., *Community Development Research: Concepts, Issues and Strategies.* New York: Human Sciences Press.
   The author provides historical background, definition, process, rationale, and goals of social action research in community development as well as suggestions/directions for training in action research. The primary characteristic of action research is the integration of research, action, and participation. The author states that action research is "research used as a tool or technique, an integral part of the community or organization in all aspects of the research process, and has as its objectives the acquisition of valid information, action, and the enhancement of the problem solving capabilities of the community or organization." The author views the goal of social action research as very similar to Paulo Freire's "development of critical consciousness."

Waterlow, Charlotte. 1982. The awakening peasant: Rising expectations in the Third World. *The Futurist* 16:27–30.
   The author states that before the advent of the "communications revolution"

the average peasant was illiterate, and the range of conscious experience was limited to the life of his or her village and perhaps the neighboring market town. She suggests that modern communications have suddenly had a profound impact on the peasants' consciousness, jolting them out of traditional ruts and making them aware that their poverty and oppression need not be. The author warns that unless modernized countries take major steps to redistribute wealth in developing countries, these places may well turn into "infernos of the mass, mindless violence of millions of people who see no hope" for their futures.

Index

325